REBORN

THE PACERS AND THE RETURN OF
PRO BASKETBALL TO INDIANAPOLIS

Mark Montieth

HALFCOURT PRESS
Indianapolis, IN

Cover designed by Phil Velikan

The photographs contained herein are from my private collection
or were loaned to me for use in this book. No copyrights were
knowingly violated by the reproduction of the images within these
pages.

Packaged by Wish Publishing

Printed in the United States of America
10 9 8 7 6 5 4 3 2 1

Distributed in the United States by Cardinal Publishers Group.
www.cardinalpub.com

Table of Contents

Acknowledgements   v
Introduction   1
1: The Waiting Game   9
2: Back in the Game   18
3: Assembly Required   70
4: Off and Running (and Winning)   118
5: The Long-Shot Candidate's Moment   128
6: The Stars are Aligned   142
7: Reg-gie   165
8: Too Good to be True   216
9: Starting Over   233
10: No More Mr. Nice Guy   247
11: Tumult and Tragedy   269
12: A Heartless Profession   289
13: A Team is Born   324
14: Turning Point   350
15: Commitment   391
Epilogue   395

Acknowledgements

This book was decades in the making, an on-and-off-again project fit into the cracks of a career that spanned newspapers, radio and freelance writing. I talked with dozens of people and read a mountain of printed material during my research, especially if everything I read on the internet had been printed out.

My primary sources were from the microfilms of *The Indianapolis Star* and *The Indianapolis News,* printed out one at a time for 10 cents a page in the Marion County Public Library. Those eyeball-burning sessions were long, but not particularly grueling for a kid who had grown up in the city and enjoyed re-reading the sports sections of his youth.

Thanks to www.newspapers.com, I also combed through the Pacers coverage in the *Kokomo Tribune.* One of my great regrets is not meeting with Gene Conard to gather his recollections before he passed away in 2015. I'm told he was a pack rat, so he probably would have had reams of wrinkled paper to wade through in search of golden nuggets. I also found details in the *Madison Courier, Franklin Daily Journal* and *Tipton Daily Tribune* that appeared nowhere else. The website's inclusion of newspapers in Dallas, Detroit, Cincinnati, Louisville, Chicago, Minneapolis, Oakland, Los Angeles and Pittsburgh also was a major asset, one that added many more hours to my research but provided much more information and better perspective.

Special mention must go to Chuck DeVoe, who not only sat for an interview but passed along his brother John's files and oversized scrapbooks. They provided a treasure trove of inside information that had never been published.

Bill Halls of the *Detroit News* also deserves special thanks. He went well beyond the call of journalistic duty about 25 years ago by photocopying his newspaper's clip file on Reggie Harding and mailing it to me. He also passed along a classic anecdote on the tragic figure.

So many people were generous with their time and memory in granting me interviews, most of them numerous times. I began working on this book in the early Nineties, but real life kept getting in the way and delaying the project. Had I finished a couple of decades earlier, I would have had access to more people, including crucial figures such as Joe Bannon and Lyn Treece. But, I would not have had as much time to press others for details that never ceased to impress me, or have had access to the newspapers.com website.

I talked with every player on the original Pacers team of the 1967-68 season other than Harding, who died in 1972. What a fascinating conversation one could have had with him in his final months. I'll have to settle for his autograph, obtained at the Indianapolis airport when I was 12 years old. Unfortunately, the notes from my early 90s telephone conversation with Matthew Aitch were stored on a 3½-inch floppy disk and didn't withstand the test of time. Even more unfortunately, my conversations with Roger Brown before he passed in 1997 were either informal or geared toward more current events. I never did get the opportunity to grill him on his life or the early seasons of the franchise. I also talked with five members of the second team who hadn't played the previous season.

The following people were of great assistance by agreeing to be interviewed and being so generous with their time. Apologies and thanks to anyone I have mistakenly omitted from this list: Jerry Baker, Lisa Barnes, Rick Barry, John Beasley, Bob Bernath, Bill Bevan, Tom Bolyard, Ron Bonham, Larry Brown, Bob Collins, Carolyn (Brown) Jeffries, Steve Chubin, Louie Dampier, Cece Daniels, Mel Daniels, Oliver Darden, Jim Dawson, Chuck DeVoe, Jane (DeVoe) Nolan, Craig Dill, Terry Dischinger, Dick Ebershoff, Bobby Joe Edmonds, Wayne Fuson, Hilliard Gates, Joe Gregory, Bill Hampton, Jerry Harkness, Jim Holstein, Bob

Hooper, Tom Hoover, Larry Humes, Ron Kozlicki, Bob Leonard, Nancy Leonard, Freddie Lewis, Mike Lewis, Clyde Lovellette, Lyle Mannweiler, Bill Marvel, Jon McGlocklin, Bill McGowan, George Mikan, Dick Mittman, Jim Morris, Bob Netolicky, George Peeples, Ron Perry, Jim Rayl, Nancy Rayl, Gene Rhodes, Oscar Robertson, Will Robinson, Dick Russell, James Sommer, Dave Schellhase, Ted Sizemore, Joyce Staverman, Larry Staverman, Keith Stone, Mike Storen, Scott Tarter, Tom Thacker, Dick Tinkham, Gary Todd, Kip Treece, Tom Van Arsdale, Sandra Wheatley, Ted Wheeler, Fred Wiese, and Bill York.

And, not to be forgotten, thanks to my wife, Faith, for keeping the, uh, faith and putting up with all the hours, days, months, and years I spent completing this project — especially the late hours when I barely made it to bed before she had to get up to teach school. I couldn't have done it without her support and patience.

*"As of this moment, the Indianapolis club ceases to function.
It is not going to operate again."*

Introduction

Some beginnings require an ending. The Pacers couldn't have been born without one. Or three.

Before they could tip off a game in the American Basketball Association, three other professional basketball teams in Indianapolis had to fade into oblivion or die a painful death. Other teams that paid players had come and gone in the early decades of the 20th century, but three in particular combined to draw a (nearly) continuous line from 1932 to 1953, setting the stage for what was to come in 1967.

Their stories could fill a book of their own, and hopefully will someday, but for now a preface will have to summarize their histories to set the stage for what happened later.

The first professional team in Indianapolis that lasted a meaningful length of the time was the Kautskys. They were owned by Frank Kautsky, who owned a grocery store on South Madison Ave. He was a good guy by all accounts – emotional and generous by nature, not particularly knowledgeable about basketball, but committed to the game and the fun of hanging out with his players. They, also by all accounts, liked playing for him.

He got started with an amateur team. Pete Bailey, who had just graduated from Indiana Central College, talked him into sponsoring a group of players who went out and won the state championship. Flushed with enthusiasm for involvement in the growing game, Kautsky recruited Johnny Wooden to commit to playing for him on a professional team.

Wooden, who had just graduated from Purdue, ranked as one of the greatest guards in the sport's 40-year history. He had been a first-team All-American in all three of his varsity seasons and was his conference's all-time leading scorer. Before that, he had led his high school team, Martinsville, to three consecutive appearances in the final game of the state tournament and one championship.

Wooden had offers to play with barnstorming teams, but decided to make use of his degree and begin a teaching and coaching career. He took a job in Dayton, Ky. for a few years, and made the 110-mile drive to Indianapolis for $50 a game. That was more than many people were making per week in 1932, so it was worth the trouble. Most professional players made half that, and less. Later, after he moved to South Bend to teach and coach at Central High School, he drove about 150 miles to play in Indianapolis. He did that for another few seasons, until it became more trouble than it was worth and he retired from playing.

Kautsky continuously tapped into the talent flowing out of Indiana colleges to fill his roster, and always had competitive teams. Sometimes they were in a league, sometimes not, as leagues came and went in that formative era. They mostly played in armories and high school gymnasiums around the state, but they rented Butler University's fieldhouse to play the barnstorming teams that toured the Eastern and Midwestern states. The "Negro" teams, as they were called then, such as the New York Rens, Savoy Big Five and Harlem Globetrotters, sometimes drew crowds of 10,000 or more.

The Kautskys disbanded for three seasons during World War II, then came back stronger than ever. Kautsky lured Arnie Risen, an All-America center out of Ohio State during the 1945-46 season, providing the city's next star attraction. Risen, 6-foot-9 and hoping to get to 200 pounds eventually, was nicknamed "Slim" for a reason. But he could play. He had flunked out of college after the first semester his senior year because an injury and an illness had prevented him from going to class for stretches of time, so Kautsky out-bid a couple of other teams and got him for $75 per game.

Risen was paid $12,000 the following season, and led the Kautskys to a winning record and the championship of the World Professional

Basketball Tournament in 1947. The 14-team invitational sponsored by the *Chicago Herald-American* didn't include all the nation's elite teams, but most of them, including some of the units of black players. The Kautskys' 62-47 victory over the Toledo Jeeps in the championship game drew 14,413 fans to Chicago Stadium. The players received watches, and were thrilled. So was their growing fan base.

The following season was a disappointment, however. With the operation beginning to require more time and money than Kautsky had available, he sold 51 percent of the ownership to Paul Walk, a radio advertising executive who had helped manage the team. Suddenly, the atmosphere around the team changed. Kautsky had been a sportsman, while Walk was a bottom-line businessman. The players were upset Walk had not paid them bonuses owed from the previous season's playoffs. Their disenchantment affected their performance, which affected their won-loss record, which affected attendance, which affected gate receipts, which made Walk desperate.

Walk pulled the plug in January by selling Risen to Rochester for $25,000. He finalized the deal during a game at Butler's fieldhouse with Rochester's owner, Les Harrison. Risen, who scored 20 points in the game, found out about the life-altering transaction when Harrison approached him afterward and said, "You're with us now." Risen went to Walk for confirmation. Walk verified the deal, quickly excused himself to make a phone call. Risen went on to play in four NBA All-Star games and on two championship teams, one as the starting center for the Royals and the other as the backup center to Bill Russell with Boston.

Walk sold off a couple of other players as well that season to make ends meet, depleting the quality of the team's play and the quantity of fans who wanted to watch it play. The Kautskys joined a new league the following season, jumping from the latest version of the National Basketball League to the Basketball Association of America, but had to change their nickname because of a BAA rule that teams could not bear an individual's name. "Jets" was selected because of the jet engines that were manufactured at the Allison plant in Indianapolis.

The Jets, with no players with Indiana ties on the roster, won their season-opener over the St. Louis Bombers before 7,264 fans at Butler.

The first 3,000 through the doors received an orchid. That turned out to be the highlight of a season that ended with an 18-42 record. Their last game, a victory over Providence, the only team with a worse record than theirs, was declared a "sideshow" by *The Indianapolis News*, one that "typified the level the Jet management let its organization slip to this season."

Something big was about to happen, though. The BAA had absorbed four of the strongest teams from the National Basketball League that season, the Indianapolis franchise among them, and the NBL was wilting. Desperate for a lifeline, NBL executives extended an unprecedented offer to five University of Kentucky players to form their own professional team. Ralph Beard, Alex Groza, Cliff Barker, Wallace Jones and Joe Holland had led the Kentucky team that won the NCAA tournament in 1948 and '49 and formed the nucleus of the 1948 U.S. Olympic team that won a gold medal in London. They were a cohesive unit, nationally known and tested, and already were accustomed to profiting from basketball from their barnstorming games throughout the state of Kentucky.

They appointed the sports editor of the *Lexington Herald*, Babe Kimbrough, as their general manager. Barker, a Yorktown, Ind. native who had spent 16 months in a German prison camp in World War II, was designated the player-coach because he was older, although generally they would work things out as a group.

They were given the option of playing in any unoccupied city, and ultimately chose Indianapolis over Cincinnati and Louisville because of Butler's mammoth facility and the state's proven fan support. They were fronted a loan of $30,000 in working capital by the league, which they paid back within a few weeks by selling shares of stock at $1,000 each to 30 Indianapolis men.

Technically, Indianapolis had two teams at that point, because the Jets still had a lease on Butler Fieldhouse, but that was resolved in August when the BAA absorbed the stronger NBL teams and the bankrupt Jets were among those disbanded. The addition of the Olympians to the NBL had been a primary factor in the BAA's effort to consolidate the leagues and form a new 17-team enterprise to be called the National Basketball Association.

Suddenly, Indianapolis had a completely new team, the Olympians, in a completely new league, the NBA. It also had two of the most exciting players in the game to call its own. Beard, an athletic 5-10 guard who played with a desperate relentlessness, and Groza, a sturdy, skilled 6-7 center, had been voted All-Americans in all three of their varsity seasons in college.

The NBA teams were grouped by their previous league affiliation, which meant the Olympians – who had originally joined the NBL — were placed in the same division as the NBL survivors from Anderson, Ind.; Sheboygan, Wisc.; Waterloo, Iowa; Denver; and Tri-Cities, which was an amalgamation of Moline, Ill., Rock Island, Ill., and Davenport, Iowa.

The Olympians, who filled out their roster with players from a variety of colleges, won their division with a 39-25 record and advanced to the second round of the playoffs. They were eliminated by Anderson after Jones was elbowed in the eye and missed a game and Beard played with a flu bug, but they had captured the city's fancy with their ingrained chemistry and frenzied style of play. They finished second in the league in per-game scoring (85.8) and led the league in field goal percentage (.375). Groza, who averaged 23.4 points and led the league in field goal percentage (.478), was voted to the first All-NBA team. Beard averaged 12.9 points and was selected to the second team.

Most impressive of all was their bottom line. Even with a top ticket price of $2, the self-governed rookie operation drew so well it turned a profit in its first year. The players not only were paid their salaries, they owned a thriving business.

A harsher reality set in the following season, when the NBA shed most of the teams from smaller cities and shrank to 11 members. Faced with stiffer competition, the Olympians finished 31-37. Beard and Groza, however, continued to excel. Both earned first-team All-NBA honors and both started for the East in the league's first All-Star game in Boston. The West won, but Groza led the East with 17 points and 13 rebounds.

The Olympians remained a popular attraction that season, as fans flocked to see the game's greatest stars. A freshman member of Indiana University's basketball team, Bob Leonard, hitch-hiked from Bloomington to watch Beard go up against Boston's Bob Cousy. A junior high school student in Indianapolis, Oscar Robertson, went to a few games as well. He, like other kids, could get in for $1, but first had to walk 16 blocks to a community center, Flanner House, and then catch a bus.

The team was settling into the conscience of the city's sports fans, inspiring the kids and exciting the adults. And then it all came crashing down. On Oct. 20, 1951, after the Olympians had won three of their four exhibition games in preparation for the next season, Beard and Groza were nabbed by FBI officials in Chicago while attending a college all-star game. They were put in separate rooms, threatened without due process, and finally, in the wee hours of the morning, confessed to participating in a point-shaving scheme while at Kentucky. The stunning news ran on Page 1 of newspapers across the country the next day, including *The Indianapolis Star*, which jolted its morning readers with a bold black headline: "Bribes Rock Olympians."

At this point the story becomes too complex to even begin to adequately explain here. The bare facts are that Beard and Groza were suspended for life by NBA commissioner Maurice Podoloff, and the Olympians were thrown into disarray. They rallied against adversity to finish 34-32 that season, an impressive performance under the circumstances. But the following season, with all the members of the Kentucky group having moved on, they dropped to 28-43.

Their final game was played at Butler on March 23, 1953, in a first-round playoff matchup with the Minneapolis Lakers. Only 2,044 people could come up with a reason to attend, and even that modest turnout was a house divided. About 200 of the fans were pharmacy students from the University of Minnesota, guests of the Eli Lilly Co. and vocal boosters of the Lakers.

The Olympians put on a fourth-quarter rally, but fell short when rookie Gene Rhodes' hook shot bounced off the rim at the final buzzer and left them with an 81-79 defeat and two losses in the best-of-three series. The ghost of the team that had won the hearts of a rabid fan base three years earlier had exhaled its last collective sigh before the muffled groan of a small, stubborn gathering of fans. The team was $50,000 in debt, and the players hadn't received their final month's wages. Only coach Herm Schaeffer's good-faith promise to forfeit his share of the playoff pool to them swayed them to suit up for the playoffs.

A banner headline and story on the front page of the sports section of the *Star* on April 24 made official what had seemed inevitable. "As of this moment, the Indianapolis club ceases to function," league president Maurice Podoloff announced from Boston. "It is not going to operate again. The NBA is now a nine-team league."

The *News* twisted the knife a bit in its report, reminding readers of the state's rich basketball heritage: "The capital city of the state that is regarded as the original incubator of top-grade basketball has been dropped from the roll of the National Basketball Association."

For 21 years, aside from a break during World War II, the city had embraced stars from Wooden to Risen to Beard and Groza, and filled Butler Fieldhouse for the biggest games. It had proved itself a viable market for professional basketball, but customers need owners as much as owners need customers, and owners with the money, desire and talent to operate a professional basketball franchise would forever be in limited supply.

If not for the lifetime suspension of Beard and Groza, the Olympians would have continued, and probably would still be playing in Indianapolis today. Beard and Groza likely would be in the Naismith Hall of Fame, and one can only wonder what other star players would have passed through their roster.

But fate wasn't having it. Rhodes' missed hook shot ended a game, a season and a franchise. At that point, the future for professional basketball in Indianapolis was a dark chasm.

1

"Anyone who really wants into this league can get in.
But we've no room for dilettantes and shoe-string operators."

The Waiting Game

Upon the death of the Olympians, the only certainty was that Butler administrators were done with professional basketball. The scandal, the games at which gamblers had congregated in one lower section corner of the fieldhouse to openly conduct their "business," and the uncomfortable nature of rough-hewn pros mixing with fresh-faced college kids in a campus environment were stains they were eager to remove once and for all.

From that point forward, it seemed, any dalliances between the city and professional basketball would have to be carried out elsewhere, and the only other appropriate venue was the Fairgrounds Coliseum at the State Fairgrounds. Opened in 1939 as a Depression-era Works Progress Administration project, it had hosted plenty of hockey and basketball games over the years, including the finals of the state high school tournament from 1943-45 when Butler Fieldhouse was drafted for use as a World War II munitions depot.

The Olympians technically were still operating when a newspaper article in April of 1953 quoted Coliseum manager Dick Miller's interest in landing NBA games, as well as Globetrotters games. Less than a year later, on New Year's Eve, with the metaphorical dirt on the Olympians' grave still fresh, the NBA returned to Indianapolis as part of a doubleheader attraction. A capacity crowd of 13,616[1] turned out, but not so much to watch Fort Wayne

---

[1] Capacity apparently was larger at that time than when the ABA began. Perhaps renovation reduced the seating availability, or perhaps thousands of standing-room tickets were sold. Or, perhaps, the listed attendance was incorrect.

beat Philadelphia 83-56 in the preliminary as to see the follow-up game featuring the Globetrotters.

Angelo Angelopolous of the *News* wrote that the crowd "which seemed apathetic as the Warriors and the Pistons bruised themselves in a regular National Basketball Association game warmed quickly to the Globie shenanigans afterwards, and there probably wasn't a man or woman in the house who hadn't grinned at least once." It helped immensely that a local attraction, former Crispus Attucks High School star Willie Gardner, suited up for the Globetrotters and made nine field goals.

An All-NBA doubleheader later that winter, on March 10 of '54, was probably a better gauge of fan interest in the professional league. It drew 4,106 fans to the Coliseum, not all that bad considering the lingering sour taste from the Olympians' demise just a year earlier and the lack of a home team. Risen, the former Kautskys center, scored 18 points — 13 in the last quarter — to lead Rochester over Minnesota, 70-61, in the second game, despite the best efforts of its two centers, George Mikan and Terre Haute native Clyde Lovellette.

The first game, in which New York defeated Milwaukee, 72-65, wasn't as well-played but might have been more interesting. During a stoppage resulting from a clock malfunction, New York center Connie Simmons bummed a dime from a fan and purchased a soft drink from a vendor passing by the team bench. Milwaukee didn't play well, but the local sports writers were impressed it mounted any resistance at all, given its schedule.

Just the previous evening, it had engaged in a baseball-style doubleheader in Milwaukee — still the only one in NBA history — by playing two games against Baltimore. A game scheduled in Baltimore earlier in the season had been postponed because fog had prevented Milwaukee from flying in, so the teams agreed to make up the game in their next meeting. Bullets owner-coach Clair Bee, a future Hall of Famer whose college teams had won 95 percent of their games from 1931-51, had little reason to mind surrendering homecourt advantage. His team was headed toward a final 16-56 record and was on the verge of financial collapse.[2]

The Hawks – predecessor to future NBA teams in St. Louis and Atlanta – won both games of the doubleheader, 64-54 and 65-54. Bill Tosheff, a former Olympian, recalled walking past Baltimore's locker room between games and seeing a few of their players drinking beer. It made him feel optimistic about the outcome of the second game, to say the least.[3]

Players and coaches throughout the NBA were hoping Indianapolis would get another NBA team in the seasons immediately following the Olympians' demise. They, and for that matter the Kautskys, had been supported well when they had winning teams, and the NBA was desperate for good homes for its franchises, of which just nine remained after the Olympians folded. Problem was, the asking price was $50,000. In an article headlined "Hurry, If You Want NBA, Hoosiers Here," Angelopolous wrote that it was a good time to get back in because of the quality players about to graduate from Indiana and Notre Dame, some of whom could be acquired in the territorial draft. He even gave out commissioner Podoloff's office

---

[2] Bee sold to another owner after the season, but the Bullets folded early the following season, on Nov. 26, with a 3-11 record and about $50,000 in debts. They remain the most recent NBA team to fold during the season, although many have moved between seasons. Their players were dispersed to the other NBA teams. Minneapolis claimed guard Bob Leonard, who was serving a two-year military obligation after an All-America career at Indiana University. He began his career with the Lakers in 1956. Bee resigned his coaching position one week before the team folded to become athletic director at the New York Military Academy. He wrote more than 50 books, including the popular Chip Hilton series for young readers.

[3] Stranger yet, Milwaukee had played a game against Minnesota with 12-foot baskets the night previous to the doubleheader – an experiment by the NBA that counted in the standings. Minnesota won, 65-63, hitting 29 percent of its field goal attempts. Milwaukee shot 32 percent. The wire service story said the fan reaction ranged from "curiosity to amusement," but Milwaukee owner Ben Kerner called it the "worst travesty I ever saw in the game of basketball." Minneapolis' George Mikan, the dominant center of his era, hit just two of his 14 shots and declared afterward: "It stinks." Milwaukee also played a neutral-court home game in Omaha the night after its game in Indianapolis, meaning it played five games in four nights. It lost all but the doubleheader with the hapless Baltimore team.

telephone number in the Empire State Building at the end of his story for any prospective owners who might have interest.

Rumors persisted of an investment group headed by Nate Kaufman, a standout athlete, referee and insurance agent from Shelbyville, negotiating to bring a team to Indianapolis by purchasing the failing franchise in Milwaukee, but nothing came of it. Still, the city managed to host four NBA playoff games in 1955 by providing a temporary home for the Fort Wayne Pistons.

Memorial Coliseum in Fort Wayne was booked for the 52nd annual American Bowling Congress national tournament — a 72-day event that drew 30,000 participants and more than 100 media outlets, offered total prize money of $428,333 and ran for 15 hours on most days over 38 portable lanes. The Coliseum in Indianapolis was the best alternative, although Game 1 of the Pistons' semifinal series against the Minneapolis Lakers had to be played at Elkhart High School's new gymnasium. Game 2 was played two nights later, on a Tuesday, in Indianapolis. The Pistons won, 98-97, in an overtime game marred by a clock controversy at the end to take a 2-0 series lead. Attendance was 2,530, respectable given the unique circumstances.

The Pistons advanced to the NBA finals, where they met the Syracuse Nationals. After losing the first two games in Syracuse, they played the next three in Indianapolis. They won Game 3 on April 3, 96-89, before 3,200 fans. One of them – a man from Fort Wayne, it was later learned – threw a chair from behind the Syracuse bench at referee Mendy Rudolph because of a foul call he found objectionable.

Still, the Globetrotters ruled. They played two games against a national college all-star team that same day at Butler, one in the afternoon and one in the evening. The evening game drew 10,093. A rematch the following night, when the NBA teams were off, drew 15,069.

The Pistons won Game 4 at the Coliseum on April 5 to tie the series before just 2,611 fans, and came back to win Game 5 two nights later, 74-71, before an audience of 4,110. That one produced one of the more bizarre finishes in league history. According to Angelopolous' story, "several hundred badly behaving Ft. Wayne fans … went spilling onto the floor at the final buzzer and the champion child of them all grabbed Syracuse's (coach) Al Cervi, calling a name." Cervi, who had withstood taunts throughout the game, "clutched the child-man by the shirt and tie, ripping them as he held his tormentor at bay."

Although the Pistons led by two points when time expired, the game wasn't over. Fort Wayne guard Frankie Brian had been fouled at the buzzer, and the referees were insistent on meting out justice to the very end, although the outcome was determined. It took five minutes to get the Syracuse players off the court and restore order well enough to allow Brian to shoot the free throw, but it was impossible to get the jubilant Pistons fans off the floor. So, Brian took – and hit – the meaningless foul shot with about 150 Pistons fans gathered around him outside the foul lane.[4]

Podoloff attended all three games in Indianapolis, which provided Angelopolous another opportunity to report on the city's viability as a league member.

"Anyone who really wants into this league can get in," Podoloff said. "But we've no room for dilettantes and shoe-string operators."

The NBA's nine owners had worked hard and no doubt taken severe financial losses to keep the operation afloat, and the league itself had kept the Olympians going long enough to finish their final season. Podoloff said he was in no mood for "someone coming in who's just looking for the gravy."

No investors in Indianapolis, shoestring or otherwise, were coming forth, but the city did continue to attract a game here and there from nearby NBA teams — particularly Cincinnati, which was struggling to draw well.

---

[4] Syracuse won Games 6 and 7 on its home court to win the championship. Nationals guard George King, who would go on to become the head coach and athletic director at Purdue, hit the game-winning foul shot in Game 7. The series, however, remains tainted by fixing allegations. The Pistons led Syracuse 41-24 early in the second quarter, but lost the lead and eventually the game. "There were always unwholesome implications about that ball game," Pistons forward George Yardley told author Charlie Rosen many years later. Beyond that, the series convinced Pistons owner Fred Zollner to move the team out of Ft. Wayne. The lack of a home court when his team was playing for the championship was the final straw. Hilliard Gates, the Piston's radio announcer, recalled walking into the Pistons' locker room after the Game 7 loss in Syracuse and hearing Zollner say, "You can't win in this league when you don't have a home court." The Pistons moved to Detroit two years later.

The Royals came in for a game against Detroit on Nov. 19, 1959, and took a 110-93 loss. Corky Lamm, writing in the *News*, offered sympathy to the fans at the Coliseum who showed up "to see it and sit on their hands while it progressed agonizingly on Mel Ross' slick floor."

Ross must have been a transparent promoter, because Lamm had the bottom-line details. The game drew 3,323 fans, which brought in revenue of $7,111, which resulted in a loss of $1,900.

"It may be sacrilegious to say it, but in basket country it may be permitted: there was almost (not quite) more interest in the amateur preliminary ..." Lamm wrote.

The Royals came back the following season with a shiny new rookie: Oscar Robertson. He was merely the best high school player ever to come out of Indiana, having led Attucks to the state high school championship in 1955 and '56. The 1955 team lost just one game, by one point, and became the first from Indianapolis to win the state tournament that had begun in 1911 and the first all-black school to win an open state tournament. The '56 team went undefeated. Robertson set a state record with 39 points in the championship game.

He was a glaringly obvious choice for the Mr. Basketball award sponsored by the *Star*, and set another record in the annual all-star series with Kentucky by scoring 74 points combined in the two games, with 41 in the second one. "He's a pro playing with a bunch of high school kids," said Ted Hornback, assistant coach of the Kentucky team.

Robertson graduated to being a pro playing with college kids at the University of Cincinnati, where he was a three-time first-team All-American. He then dominated among the pros, too. As an NBA rookie, he averaged 30.5 points, 10.1 rebounds and 9.7 assists, was named Most Valuable Player of the All-Star game and earned first-team all-league honors.

Despite all that, his first appearance in Indianapolis as a professional, on Dec. 4, 1960, drew only 3,052 fans. The fact the game was played on Sunday at 8 p.m. didn't help. It also had to compete with the lighting of the Monument Circle Christmas "tree," which drew 2,000-3,000 people downtown. Robertson didn't disappoint, though. He scored 34 points in a one-point loss to Detroit, and already was outclassing his veteran teammates.

"The Big O not only dazzles the opposition with his cleverness, he fools some of his slower-witted teammates," Lamm wrote.

The Royals were back the following season, on Jan. 9, 1962, for a more interesting game. Robertson scored 33 points to lead them to a 113-106 victory over the Chicago Packers, but the Packers helped boost the gate to 4,815 despite minus-six degree weather. Their roster included two former Indiana University All-Americans, Walt Bellamy (1961) and Bob Leonard (1954).

Bellamy, a 6-11 center, finished with 33 points. Leonard, a 31-year-old guard, scored 21 and stole the ball from Robertson to set up a layup that gave the Packers a lead late in the game, but it didn't last.

It would go on like this for four more years, the Royals coming to Indianapolis and drawing as well as they did in Cincinnati, and Robertson doing his part to please his hometown fans. When they returned the following December he scored 30 points, grabbed 13 rebounds and passed out 19 assists before 5,478 fans in a 142-123 victory over Chicago, which was now nicknamed the Zephyrs. He found time to work the referees as well, "jawing about decisions most of the way," according to Lamm's story. Leonard did not play in that one, but was days away from being named the team's coach, replacing Jack McCloskey. Rookie Terry Dischinger, a former Purdue All-American, had 28 points for the Zephyrs.

Bellamy had another statistically impressive game with 22 points and 13 rebounds, but already was establishing a reputation for questionable effort and attitude. *Indianapolis Times* sportswriter Dick Mittman experienced it firsthand when he asked for a moment of Bellamy's time before the game. He related their conversation in the next day's newspaper.

"Am I going to get paid for this?" Bellamy asked.

"I represent the *Times* and I want to do a story on you for tomorrow's paper," Mittman responded. "Do you want to talk to me?"

Bellamy said nothing.

"Do you want to talk to me?" Mittman asked again.

Bellamy said nothing, ending the non-interview.

Chicago general manager Frank Lane, meanwhile, put in another plug for Indianapolis as an NBA market, saying it was "far ahead of any other that wants in."

Star sports editor Jep Cadou remembered that comment 15 days later, when the Zephyrs fired coach Jack McMahon and replaced him with Leonard. With the team struggling to draw fans through the turnstiles at the Chicago Coliseum, and with former state collegians Leonard, Bellamy and Dischinger on its roster, Cadou surmised it would draw well in Indianapolis. He probably was correct, but the Zephyrs moved to Baltimore after the season, with no mention of Indianapolis as a potential home.[5]

Robertson returned later in the season to score 34 points, grab 17 rebounds and pass out 12 assists in a two-point victory over Syracuse. An electronic malfunction provided "a hilarious finish in which the scoreboard clock, as if in protest to the evening's long entertainment, began to creep on the last 17 seconds despite it being shut down," according to the article in the *News*. The game finished under the authority of the shot clock.

Such inconveniences didn't seem to overly discourage Indianapolis fans. The popularity of the NBA game was growing, in and out of NBA cities. The Royals drew 6,590 fans to the Coliseum for a victory over Detroit the following season, in December of 1964. That was more than 2,000 beyond what they would average in Cincinnati that season, and even more impressive

---

[5]   The Zephyrs also considered Kansas City, Philadelphia and Cleveland as destinations. Owner Dave Trager said he had better offers than what he got in Baltimore, but was enticed by Baltimore's history as an NBA market and other perks. Baltimore had a new Civic Center that sat 14,000 and officials there offered favorable rental terms, a percentage of concession sales and a radio-TV package. That moment seems like a lost opportunity for Indianapolis leaders, who wouldn't have had to strain too hard to surpass that deal, but nobody stepped up. Trager moved his team to Baltimore despite what happened when the Zephyrs played a regular season game there late in the season as a trial run: a bomb threat was phoned in, delaying the game for 30 minutes late in the first half. The Zephyrs were stuck in an awkward position in Chicago, with a young team destined to lose for a while. They couldn't afford the rent at Chicago Stadium, the International Amphitheater did not have enough open dates to provide a permanent home, and their home, the Chicago Coliseum, only sat 7,000, making a profit difficult to achieve even if the team won. Management tried just about everything to entice fans through the turnstiles, such as running a promotion for Marshall Korshak Night early in the season to honor none other than a trustee of the Chicago sanitary district. At the Zephyrs last home game of the season, after it had been announced the team would move, a fan brought a trumpet and played "Taps" as the clock wound down.

because it came on the same night 5,300 fans were attending Butler's season opener across town and 6,929 were at Indiana University's opener in Bloomington.

Robertson rewarded the fans, who paid between $1.50 and $3 for tickets, with another display of grandeur: 25 points on 11-of-18 shooting and 19 assists, "several of them spectacular" according to the *Times'* account. Dischinger, who had been traded to Detroit by then, had 22 points for the Pistons, whose roster also included a promising 22-year-old, 7-foot center named Reggie Harding. The Detroit native had skipped college, but was showing exciting potential. He would average 12 points and 11.6 rebounds in his second NBA season, although he only scored four in this game.

Cincinnati was back for four more games at the Coliseum in the 1965-66 season.[6] The last one was the best attraction, bringing the Los Angeles Lakers with Jerry West and Elgin Baylor to the city. The Lakers won, 119-116, to clinch their Western Division championship before 6,310 fans. Robertson scored 39 points, West 31 and Baylor 27. For sheer talent and competitiveness, it was the best professional basketball game ever played in the city to that point.

The Royals' four games in Indianapolis that season drew an average of 5,873 fans. Their 31 games in Cincinnati drew an average of 6,020. It could fairly be considered a dead heat, because the team's management naturally saved most of the more appealing opponents for their own arena, aside from the game against the Lakers. It also provided reasonable evidence that Indianapolis was becoming a legitimate market for professional basketball. The quality of NBA play and administration was improving with each season, and national television was expanding its exposure. It sometimes was referenced with slight denigration in the Indianapolis newspapers, such as "play-for-pay" or "bump-and-bash," but appeared to have a steady fan base despite its role as a foster home for other teams.

The Royals had made a practice of playing several home games in other cities – 17 in the 1961-62 season alone, for example, to keep their fans from

---

[6] The Royals also played a game in Muncie that season, against San Francisco, drawing 5,601 fans.

becoming bored with the team and to maximize average attendance. They drastically cut back on the practice in the 1966-67 season, playing nearly all of their home-away-from-home games in Cleveland or as part of a doubleheader in other states. They played no games in Indianapolis that season, leaving the city bereft of professional basketball action that winter.

That would soon change.

2

*"There isn't any reason why big league basketball
shouldn't go in Indianapolis."*

Back in the Game

As the 1960s unfolded, Indianapolis was growing restless and hungry. The city's population had grown to nearly 750,000 residents and it had become the 13th largest television market in the country, yet it had no national sports identity beyond the Indianapolis 500. The high school basketball tournament's final rounds routinely sold out Butler Fieldhouse, but was a major event only within the state's borders. The Indians provided a stable minor league baseball franchise, but minor league football and hockey teams had come and gone. Baseball was as popular as ever, basketball was growing and football was booming. More and more, city leaders and residents felt a burning desire to fill in the barren gaps in the local sports calendar and become major league in *something*.

An initiative unprecedented in the city's history was undertaken in February of 1965 with the formation of the Greater Indianapolis Progress Committee, a privately supported, non-partisan, non-profit corporation which worked in concert with Mayor John Barton's office. The organization – known informally as "Gypsy" because of the phonetic pronunciation of its first letters – included more than 200 appointed members – most, if not all, of them men – who were making a wide-ranging, sincere and idealistic attempt to make the city a better place to live.

It consisted further of sub-committees addressing at least 11 areas, including downtown development, tax policy, urban renewal, traffic and transportation, arts and culture, industrial development and recreation and sports. It was an indication of the purity of their intentions that 25 members toured Pittsburgh and Philadelphia at their own expense in September of that year to review the results of renewal and development projects in those cities.

The Recreation and Sports Committee included its own subsidiary, a Sports Advisory Commission. It consisted of 50 members who were divided into seven sub-committees: executive, publicity, financing, facilities, promotion, amateur and professional. Those members included university athletic directors, notable ex-athletes and coaches, business leaders, and media members. Bob Collins, sports editor of the *Star*, was a member of the Financing Committee, while Wayne Fuson, sports editor of the *News*, was chairman of the Executive Committee.

Among the Commission's goals was to attract more state and national sporting events as well as a professional sports franchise. It also set out to study the feasibility of building appropriate facilities – perhaps in conjunction with the Convention Center already planned for downtown Indianapolis. That project was due to be completed early in 1971, and one plan called for a 13,000-seat basketball arena to be included. To analyze the viability of such projects, $13,000 was earmarked for a survey by Market Facts, Inc. of Chicago. According to minutes from a meeting on March 8, 1966, this was "a necessary step preliminary to getting a major league football or baseball franchise, and the construction of a stadium."

Indeed, obtaining a Major League Baseball or American Football League franchise was the group's primary objective – pending construction of a stadium, of course. An effort also was under consideration to obtain an American Hockey League franchise. Basketball appeared to be a lower priority, but was always on the mind of certain movers and shakers within the community.

Collins recalled in later years that he and civic and business leader Bob Welch had made a run at purchasing the Royals in 1959, realizing Robertson was going to be entering the NBA the following year and the Indianapolis franchise could claim him with a territorial draft pick. Collins called Royals vice-president Tom Grace with an offer, but Grace obviously knew Cincinnati also would have territorial rights to Robertson. No deal.

Collins and Advisory Commission member John DeVoe also had inquired about an NBA expansion franchise in March of '66, with DeVoe sending a letter to Grace to follow up on previous conversations about the issue. "We want a franchise for Indianapolis," the letter stated. DeVoe's letter said the group was aware an expansion franchise would cost about $1 million, and claimed it could meet that cost. He asked for a meeting with J. Walter Kennedy, the NBA commissioner. Kennedy sent ground rules for an application, which DeVoe acknowledged in a letter on April 1, but there is no record of steps taken after that.

At some point in the decade, Fuson and local real estate magnate Bud Tucker also had formed a group to try to secure a franchise. But, just as in the first few years following the death of the Olympians, it was apparent the desire to purchase a team for Indianapolis was far greater than the money available to do so.

The Royals might have provided another option at one point midway through the decade. Collins recalled Royals general manager Pepper Wilson once inquiring about playing a split schedule, with half of the team's home games in Indianapolis. Collins discouraged it, believing it would result in the team failing to draw well in two cities instead of just one.

As the decade entered its second half, the Indianapolis leaders were growing frustrated by their inability to land a major league team — in any sport. The cost of buying an existing team or an expansion team was beyond what anyone in the modest Midwestern city was able or willing to pay. Unknown to them, however, opportunity was on its way.

The success of the AFL had planted the idea of establishing another "major" professional basketball league in the minds of promoters and businessmen around the country. The AFL had begun play in 1960, and by '66 had achieved a merger with the NFL, one that would be enacted in stages until completion in 1970. Perhaps a new basketball league could survive long enough to force a merger with the NBA, too, allowing the daring league founders and franchise owners to cash in.

One attempt to do just that had already been attempted earlier in the decade. The American Basketball League began play in 1961, but lasted just 1½ seasons because of inadequate organization and finances. It was doomed from the start, really. Some owners controlled more than one franchise. The league's founder and commissioner, Abe Saperstein, owned a franchise in Chicago, and he was further distracted by the operation of his primary business venture, the Globetrotters. George Steinbrenner, 30-year-old owner of the Cleveland franchise, traded one of his players to the opposing teams at halftime of a game.

The league did manage some innovations, however. It introduced a three-point shot, a 30-second shot clock and a wider, trapezoidal foul lane. It managed to lure a few players from the NBA, giving the established league a taste of a bidding war, and broke a color barrier by employing two black men as head coaches, the first in any major American professional sport.

Innovative ideas can't overcome inadequate financing, though, and the ABL collapsed in a heap of debt and disorder on Dec. 31, 1962. Nearly four years later, however, fan interest in the NBA was growing as the quality of play improved and national television coverage expanded. Star players such as Robertson, Wilt Chamberlain, Bill Russell, Elgin Baylor and Jerry West were showcasing the game with more athleticism and substance than anyone before them. College and professional teams also were gradually admitting more black players, further improving the product, although quotas remained.

Despite its improving talent, the NBA was falling out of step with the Go-Go Sixties, so severely lacking in flair it barely even qualified as conservative. All its games should have been televised in black and white, so bland was the product. Giants who hunkered down near the foul lane tended to dominate the action, and guards rarely shot from beyond 20 feet. The AFL had provided evidence a colorful marketing approach and wide-open style of play, more in step with the increasing anti-establishment mood of the decade, could succeed. Perhaps a similar formula would work in basketball.

The most compelling argument for such a daring venture was the growing surplus of elite players coming out of colleges. Like soldiers returning from war, they needed jobs. The NBA still had but nine franchises in 1966, the same number as when the Olympians folded in 1953, so jobs were scarce. Even some All-America players were unable to muscle their way into rosters filled with veteran NBA players. Loyola's 1963 championship team included three players who received All-America recognition, but none of them were still playing in the league three years later. Of all the Most Valuable Players in the National Invitation Tournament since 1958, only two were playing in it by 1966.

The NBA was beginning to address the talent overflow by adding expansion teams. Chicago was to begin play in the 1966-67 season and Seattle and San Diego were to follow the next year. Still, the league had the feel of a stodgy country club, open only to well-heeled and buttoned-down businessmen. The timing was right for something new and different.

The first seeds for a new league were planted by a group of disconnected men with a shared vision. Californians Dennis Murphy and John McShane and New Yorker Constantine "Connie" Seredin eventually joined forces from opposite sides of the country, along with a few other dreamy pioneers, to try to spin loose straw into gold. That they would connect with the men in Indianapolis trying so diligently to attract a professional franchise seemed inevitable.

Seredin reached out to DeVoe, a prominent insurance agent and emerging city leader, via a letter dated Sept. 1, 1966, asking to meet and discuss the bold new venture. It came from New York under the letterhead of Professional Sports Management Company, Inc., and included a professionally prepared budget for a franchise as well as a letter of agreement in which interested parties committed to paying $5,000 for the opportunity to bid on a franchise at a meeting to be conducted in New York and then another $5,000 to complete the purchase.

The letter sent to DeVoe and other prospective owners around the country acknowledged the need to find new homes for the talent emerging from college campuses, stating, "Great players ... found and will continue to find their playing careers terminated because of a shortage of professional teams, to the greatest distress of the basketball-minded trade and public."

DeVoe, delayed by a family vacation in Canada, responded in a letter dated Sept. 9. Despite all the effort he and others had invested in landing an NBA franchise – or perhaps because of the knowledge gained from those efforts – he didn't view this as a suitable opportunity. His group was not "sufficiently prepared" to meet with the league reps, he wrote, because he didn't believe enough interest could be generated to consider a franchise in a new, unproven league. He added: "In Indianapolis, there would be a tendency to look upon this as a minor league project, and we have a poor record of supporting such endeavors."

He didn't close the door, however. He stated if Seredin and his associates built some momentum with their undertaking, he might be interested in meeting with them later. "That might seem a little unfair," DeVoe concluded in his letter, "but the problem of selling a new franchise in a new league, in a less than desirable arena at this time, is too great."

The would-be founders forged ahead, trying to find investors from major cities lacking an NBA franchise. Seredin and Murphy had independently contacted Mikan, by far the biggest name among retired NBA players, to be the commissioner. He had not agreed to anything, but his interest was sufficient to prompt them to use his name to add substance to their flimsy dream, to be called the American Basketball Association. They managed to bring together enough interested parties in November for an organizational meeting at the Beverly Wilshire Hotel in Los Angeles to move the concept forward. Indianapolis did not send a representative, but DeVoe kept the city's toe in the water by sending a telegram to Seredin on Nov. 18.

"Regarding ABA proposal, Indianapolis most interested in possible participation as league member pending outcome of professional sports feasibility study now being undertaken by city. Would appreciate being advised of your status as it might apply to possible Indianapolis franchise."

At some point along the way, probably shortly after that meeting in Los Angeles, Seredin and an associate flew to Indianapolis to meet at the Essex House hotel with two local representatives — Collins and Chuck Barnes, founder and president of Sports Headliners, a promotion firm for race drivers that was beginning to expand into other sports. Seredin, a glib promoter by nature, was joined by a man named Barry

Murff. Collins described Murff as a "gofer" whose job was to "nod his head every time Connie said something."

Seredin's original concept for the ABA was to have a league for players no taller than 6-foot-5, all of whom would sign contracts with the league rather than teams. He already had a nickname for it: "The Lively League." Collins became convinced Seredin also had in mind an all-white league. That idea obviously would have its limitations, and no appeal for any city wanting to become major league.

A second meeting was held shortly thereafter, with DeVoe and Dick Tinkham and perhaps others on hand, after which Collins decided the venture was serious enough to justify exposure to the public. The first mention of the possibility of professional basketball's revival in Indianapolis came on Nov. 24, 1966 in an article in the *Star* headlined "City May Get Pro Cage Club."

Along with reporting the discussions between representatives of the new league and city officials, the article stated an effort was being made to land an NBA expansion franchise. What wasn't mentioned was that Chicago had paid an entry fee of $1.2 million in 1966, and Seattle and San Diego were going to pay $1.75 million to join the league in the fall of 1967. Despite DeVoe's mailed declaration to NBA commissioner Kennedy earlier in the year, nobody in Indianapolis was flashing that kind of bankroll. An ABA franchise was going to be available for a fraction of that cost.

Still, uncertainty prevailed. The Sports Advisory Committee was awaiting the results of the Market Facts survey, along with evidence a suitable facility would be constructed.

"There isn't any reason why big league basketball shouldn't go in Indianapolis," DeVoe stated in the article. "However, we first have to make sure the city will begin constructing the new civic exhibition center."

On Jan. 18, the *Star* reported another meeting at the Beverly Wilshire in Los Angeles. By that time, wild rumors were flying about new franchises and their celebrity owners – such as a St. Louis team headed by baseball legend Stan Musial, an Anaheim team headed by singer/

actor Gene Autry and a Cleveland team headed by owner Art Modell of the NFL Browns.

Barnes, who was in California on business for his agency, attended the meeting at the Beverly Wilshire, and called in a report to Collins. "This is the funniest thing I've ever seen," Collins recalled him saying. "Every five minutes, somebody's running out to the telephone. They were all representing somebody else."

Barnes included.

Barnes, at least, could verify the authenticity of the effort to form a new league, and report back that legitimate investors were showing interest. The next step for the Indianapolis group was to find some of its own.

Collins was a native of Indianapolis who had worked for the *Star* since 1948. He was well-traveled and well-connected within Indiana, easily the state's most prominent sports journalist in a day when newspapers dominated the media marketplace. He was an unabashed drinker – some would say a functional alcoholic – who imbibed flasks of hard liquor in college football press boxes and wrote more than a few columns while under the influence. He fit the stereotype for a newspaper sports columnist of his era, but also was a socially progressive voice for an extremely conservative publication. He had championed the Attucks teams that Robertson led to state championships as well as Muhammad Ali's controversial career when and where it wasn't popular to do so.

He also involved himself in causes such as the sports-related projects of the Greater Indianapolis Progress Committee at a time when newspaper columnists could participate directly in community affairs without ethical concerns. Landing a major league franchise was a big deal for Collins, for both civic and personal reasons. He wanted one for the city, but also for his professional interests. He often had no choice but to write columns on national sporting events or personalities because the local landscape was barren beyond high school and college sports.

Shortly after Barnes returned from the meeting in Los Angeles, he and Collins drove together to Lafayette to attend a "wild game" dinner hosted by Lyn Treece at the Lafayette Country Club. It would prove to be a tipping point.

Over a dinner of exotic meats and no shortage of alcohol, they sat with Lafayette residents Treece, Joe Bannon and Dick Ebershoff and perhaps a sixth person and told them about the ongoing effort to create a new basketball league from thin air. They all laughed about the absurd elements of it all at first, but as the conversation continued it grew more serious.

Collins told them it would only require $6,000 to claim dibs on a franchise. As he remembered it, Bannon was the first to jump, shouting, "Let's go!" Ebershoff later remembered someone saying, "Why the hell don't we do it?" And with that the men from Lafayette, and perhaps Barnes as well, each pledged $1,000 for the cause. Others from Indianapolis would soon follow.

Bannon — president and chairman of the board of the Purdue National Bank — had already scheduled a business trip to New York that would coincide with the league meeting. Ebershoff remembered it being the next day. Barnes went, too. Collins, who did not invest money in the franchise but was a driving force throughout, recalled calling Barnes at 9 a.m. one morning and telling him he was on a 1:30 flight to New York that afternoon.

"What for?" Barnes asked.

"An organizational meeting for the ABA," Collins said.

"Who's paying for it?" Barnes asked.

"DeVoe," Collins said.

That was news to DeVoe, who reacted angrily the next time he talked with Collins.

"If you're going big-time, this is the way to do it," Collins said.

Thus, Bannon and Barnes attended the meeting in New York on Feb. 2 and laid claim to a professional basketball franchise. It was merely a down payment, but it was a start – and, after so many years of trying to land a franchise, qualified as a breakthrough.

Ebershoff recalled getting a call about 5 p.m. from an enthused Bannon, who said, "We've got a team!" *Great*, Ebershoff thought to

A franchise is born. Joe Bannon, Chuck Barnes (with ball), George Mikan and ABA co-founder Gary Davidson gather for a photo-op at the press conference announcing the formation of a new league.

himself, *we don't have a ball, we don't have shoes, we don't have players and we don't have a place to play.*

But they did have a franchise, or at least the whisper of one. Friends of the Lafayette owners thought they were crazy, but as someone had said at the wild game dinner, "Why the hell not?" It was that kind of time.

The next day's *Star* blared the news with a non-bylined lead story on the first sports page with a four-column, two-deck headline:

INDIANA BACK IN BIG LEAGUE
BASKETBALL; NEW PRO LOOP FORMED

Eleven men, including Collins, were listed as founding members of the Indianapolis franchise, which was to be joined by teams in New York, Pittsburgh, Minneapolis, New Orleans, Dallas, Houston, Kansas City, Oakland and Anaheim.

Bannon said the team would go by "Indiana" rather than "Indianapolis," as the Kautskys, Jets and Olympians had done. Basketball, he said, was a Hoosier game and belonged to the entire state. The team's home games would be played at the Fairgrounds Coliseum, but the owners hoped to play some of them in various locations throughout the state to honor the Hoosier heritage.

The article also said Mikan had been announced as the commissioner, reportedly signing a three-year contract that would make him the highest-paid commissioner in professional sports. Gary Davidson, identified as the league president and part-owner of the Denver franchise, estimated it would pay about $75,000 per year. Like so many of the early reports about the league, however, it wasn't true. Mikan only had reached a verbal agreement for a contract that would pay him $50,000 per year.

Still, Mikan attended the press conference and was emboldened. He threw down the gauntlet immediately, stating the new league would pursue the NBA's biggest stars. "We would like to have Wilt, Oscar Robertson and any players like that who are available," he said.

The *News*, forced to concede the break of the story to the *Star* because of Collins' involvement, followed that afternoon with a shorter article quoting DeVoe. He tried to suppress the notion of the ABA raiding the

NBA's talent, but added his group would be "foolish" not to pursue Robertson, who would be a free agent after the current season ended.

The rest of the new league's franchisees were less constrained. And more naïve. Johnny Murphy, brother of Oakland owner Dennis Murphy, attended the press conference in New York and said Chamberlain was a certainty to join the ABA. "We know he'll be in our league and we are assured other superstars will be in, also."

The bold leap of the big game franchise hunters made the Market Facts survey obsolete, but it was informative nonetheless. Revealed in the Recreation and Sports Committee's February report, its findings included estimations for the annual attendance for professional football, baseball, hockey and basketball franchises in Indianapolis. For basketball, it was 250,000, which broke down to an average of about 6,400 fans per game.

Whether that would be enough to turn a profit, however, was impossible to know.

The $6,000 down payment didn't guarantee a franchise for the ABA cities, it merely gave them the right to claim one publicly. It was going to take far more than that trifling investment to finance a new league, but for the moment it provided a starting point, and a reason for the franchise owners to begin publicizing their venture.

It certainly brought focus to the group in Indianapolis. They had spent money and they were announced members of a de facto league, so they went to work. On Feb. 10, Indiana Professional Sports, Inc. was formally incorporated and an organizational meeting was conducted. Bannon would be president and chairman of the board. DeVoe would be executive vice-president. Treece, identified as a "Lafayette businessman and sportsman," was secretary, and Indianapolis stockbroker Ron Woodard was treasurer.

Collins and Barnes became official board members, along with Ebershoff, who owned Lafayette Tent and Awning Corp. They were joined by the following: Robert Bowes II, President of Bowes Seal Fast Corporation; Chuck DeVoe, John's brother and an independent manufacturers' representative; Norb (Bud) Schaefer Jr., Vice President of Inland Container; and J. Fred Wiese Jr., Executive, Indiana National Bank.

Tinkham would be the legal counsel, and invest indirectly by performing services at reduced fees, or gratis. Later, another Lafayette businessman, Keith Stone, partnered with Treece to share the required investment. The DeVoes' parents also would purchase shares of stock.

It was a solid group. All of them were successful businessmen or bankers, not exceptionally wealthy but also holding little or no hope of becoming rich from their investment in professional basketball. Their motivation was largely altruistic, a simple desire to bring a professional franchise to Indianapolis. The only perk was the ego gratification of telling their friends they owned a team.

Bannon was the leader of the group, by title and otherwise. He had grown up outside Kansas City, but had lived in Indianapolis for 11 years before moving to Lafayette in 1949 to take over the Purdue National Bank. He was an ethical, disciplined and community-minded businessman.

"He put his money into things for the good of individual communities," said Bill Power, who worked for Bannon at the Lafayette bank. "He did a lot of things that people didn't know about.

"He was a wonderful person if you kept your nose clean. But he was tough as nails."

One of the first orders of business for the ownership group, even before they had officially secured their place in the league with a franchise fee or hired a general manager, was to pursue Robertson, by then a 28-year-old, seven-year NBA veteran. He would be a free agent at the end of the season for the second consecutive year. He had held out the previous season in search of a better contract, and then signed for one year and $96,000 with the Royals. That made him just short of the highest-paid player in the NBA. Chamberlain had signed for $100,000 per season in 1965, then Bill Russell took their classic rivalry to the negotiating table and one-upped him by convincing the Celtics to sign him for $100,001.

Robertson wouldn't have the freedom to sign with another NBA team after the 1966-67 season, but perhaps nothing could prevent him from jumping to another league. The Indianapolis group not only wanted him to play, they wanted him to coach the team. Folding a coach's salary into his contract would make it more feasible to construct an affordable player payroll.

Collins led the charge, having earned Robertson's trust while reporting extensively and favorably on his career at Attucks High School – a bold move in the mid-Fifties. Many people in Indiana had looked down upon the all-black school that had been banned from competing in the Indiana High School Athletic Association until 1943, but Collins – a reporter at the time – championed them, growing close enough to the coach, Ray Crowe, that he rode to some road games with the team. Collins made phone calls to Robertson to begin the recruiting process, and wasted no time goosing the public's interest in the team in his column just a few days after the Feb. 2 announcement of the franchise.

"The Indiana syndicate has only one man in mind for coach of the team," he wrote. "And it will talk to nobody else until he makes a decision.

"He has been contacted. And he is interested. But no direct offer has been made at this time.

"At this point, only one thing can be said. If he makes himself available, there will be nothing but smiles on the faces of Indiana basketball fans."

A few days later, Collins put Robertson's name in print, indicating he might be the target of Indianapolis' new franchise, but played coy as to his own involvement in the matter: "I still haven't paid off on bets I made with him 10 years ago," he wrote.

The interest was taken seriously in Cincinnati, where the wobbly Royals' franchise hinged on its "Big O." Perhaps to try to scare off his prized asset, Royals board chairman Ambrose Lindhorst weighed in with doubts about the viability of a franchise in Indianapolis.

"I just can't believe some of these towns will support pro basketball. Indianapolis, in my mind, is one of them," Lindhorst said. It seemed an unusual opinion, given the crowds that had turned out for the recent Royals' games in the city, but Lindhorst had an interest to protect.

Rumors of other NBA stars jumping to the ABA were flying by this time. One report had Robertson's Royals teammate, Jerry Lucas, being offered 20 to 30 percent of ownership by the franchise in Kansas City. The wildest of all was the one about Chamberlain being offered $230,000 to play in New York.

Chamberlain, the game's most dominant force and the reigning league MVP, was to become player-owner of a franchise, and supposedly had already hand-picked former Philadelphia 76ers coach Frank McGuire to lead the team. The truth was that Arthur Brown, the prospective owner of the New York franchise, had joined presumed coach and general manger Max Zaslofsky and business manager Mark Binstein in a meeting with Chamberlain in a hotel room in Pittsburgh, at Chamberlain's request. They offered him a salary of $50,000 per year, a $250,000 annuity and 20 percent ownership of the franchise.

Chamberlain, though, wasn't likely to seriously consider jumping to a new, unproven league. He was in the process of leading Philadelphia to a 68-13 record and the NBA championship. Chamberlain would average 24.1 points on 68 percent shooting, 24.2 rebounds and 7.8 assists that season, and, frankly, would have embarrassed most of the centers in a new league. He was using the meetings with ABA representatives as a negotiating ploy, as many other NBA players would do in the weeks ahead.[1] He leaked his conversations with the prospective New York owners to newspaper reporters in Philadelphia, Brown said later, to drive up his value to the 76ers. The New York offer was then withdrawn.

The pursuit of Robertson, though, was out in the open, for all to see. It blew up on Feb. 18, when the *Star* ran a story across the top of the first sports page with the headline "Oscar Says He Might Come 'Home.'" The subhead read, "Confirms rumor of player-coach job."

---

[1] After the ABA was officially formed, Lou Hudson, Clyde Lee, Erwin Mueller, Wayne Hightower, Jim Barnes and LeRoy Ellis signed ABA contracts, but went back to their NBA teams to avoid lawsuits. Some of them no doubt improved their salaries as a result.

Robertson, according to the article, had told the *New York World Journal Tribune* he had conducted "several talks" with members of the Indianapolis group, but said he would wait until the current season ended before having serious discussions.

"I wouldn't be acting very smart if I said I wouldn't consider any offer from anyone, anywhere," he added.

That comment was enough to inspire the article in the *Star*, in which John DeVoe offered a plug for the Indianapolis franchise: "Oscar is synonymous with basketball," he said. "At Cincinnati, the $100,000 he is getting is a lot of money, but he is a lot of player."

Public discussion of acquiring Robertson was great publicity for the infant franchise, but premature by any practical measure. The Indianapolis group didn't even have a franchise, officially, and nobody could guarantee the league would ever play a game. But it was working on that. DeVoe and Tinkham visited Mikan at his travel agency office in Minneapolis on Feb. 16. The would-be commissioner told them he hoped the ABA could achieve parity with the NBA in two years, that negotiations for a national television contract were underway and that he wasn't planning wholesale raids of NBA players – but also wasn't opposed to signing some whose contracts were expired.

The tipping point for the new venture would come in New Orleans, over the weekend of March 3-5, when representatives from each of the 10 franchises would gather to try to reach a final agreement with Mikan and establish enough ground rules to commence the league. The Indianapolis entry was represented by John DeVoe and James Sommer of the law firm Briggs, Berner, Sommer and Tinkham, who would record the meeting's minutes.

Mikan had agreed to accept a three-year contract at $50,000 per year, but the execution of it remained a sticking point. That would be the first order of business on Friday. He wanted a personal guarantee from one or more investors, but nobody was willing to sign off on that. He left the room so the matter could be discussed, and a lengthy and spirited debate ensued.

Recesses were taken for lunch and dinner, but the matter remained unresolved late into the evening. Mikan stayed in his hotel room, out of the conversation, while his attorney shuttled back and forth between the two sides to pass along offers, rejections and suggestions. Meanwhile, New York owner Arthur Brown began waffling whether to even have a team because of all the financial uncertainty he was witnessing. Finally, he said if each team could deposit $30,000 into a league treasury, to be forfeited if the franchise failed, he was in. The measure passed 9-2. One no vote came from Anaheim co-owner Art Kim, whose vote was in protest of the interminable debates. He had witnessed far worse frustrations as an owner of the Hawaii franchise in the ABL, but perhaps had little patience for them as a result. The other no came from Minnesota owner Larry Shields, who had arrived at the meeting at 12:07 a.m., five minutes before the vote was taken.

Mikan's attorney passed along that bit of news to Mikan, then returned to say Mikan would sign a contract if $30,000 could be taken out of the existing treasury of $50,000 and escrowed to assure payment of the commissioner's salary until a performance bond from all franchises could be obtained.[2]

Deal.

Finally, in the wee hours of Saturday morning, the new league had a commissioner. He was welcomed to the board room with a loud chorus of boos from his owners, although it wasn't mentioned in Sommer's notes if those boos were angry or sarcastic. Quickly, however, an atmosphere of relief settled over the room, followed by an eagerness to get down to pressing business matters the next day. Sommer offered an understanding viewpoint of Mikan's hesitation in his minutes, writing that Mikan understandably needed to be assured his good name and efforts would not be wasted on a "flimsy and questionable organization which might fold up before the first game is even played."

DeVoe and Sommer went to bed that morning believing the new league finally existed. It had 10 owners who had committed significant money, a verbal contract agreement with a name-brand commissioner

---

[2] Mikan unknowingly did NBA commissioner Walter Kennedy a favor. Kennedy got a raise from $50,000 to $60,000 per year in a five-year contract announced in June, a likely response to Mikan's salary.

BRIGGS, BERNER, SOMMER & TINKHAM

BIS MERCHANTS BANK BUILDING

JAMES A. BRIGGS
DWAYNE H. BERNER
JAMES K. SOMMER
RICHARD P. TINKHAM, JR.

INDIANAPOLIS, INDIANA 46204
639-2389

March 10, 1967

Mr. James H. Ackerman
625 Edison Building
100 Long Beach Boulevard
Long Beach, California 90802

Dear Mr. Ackerman:

We submit herewith the certified check of Indiana
Professional Sports, Inc., check #103, in the amount of
$30,000.00 and hereby designate you as our agent to
deposit such check in the account of the American Basketball Association subject to the following restriction:
the enclosed check is to be deposited only in the event
that certified checks in like amount from at least seven
other member clubs of the Association have been deposited
and/or are deposited simultaneously with the enclosed
check. In the event such restriction precludes you from
depositing the enclosed check on or before Friday,
March 17, 1967, then please immediately contact me for
further written instructions.

We hereby designate Mr. E. Joseph Bannon as Trustee
and the undersigned, John C. DeVoe, as Alternate Trustee.

Sincerely,

John C. DeVoe
Executive Vice President,
Indiana Professional Sports, Inc.

Briggs, Berner, Sommer & Tinkham

By _____
       Richard P. Tinkham, Jr.
       Assistant Secretary and
       General Counsel for Indiana
       Professional Sports, Inc.

The letter that launched a franchise. John DeVoe commits $30,000 to secure a place for Indianapolis in the American Basketball Association.

and reason to believe they were about to embark on something less flimsy and questionable.

Mikan had been the game's dominant player in the late Forties and early Fifties, playing in the National Basketball League, the Basketball Association of America and the NBA. A 6-10 center, he led five teams to championships and led his league in scoring five times. He was an obvious selection as a member of the inaugural class for the Naismith Basketball Hall of Fame in 1959, and was later voted the game's best player of the first half of the Twentieth Century. Fifty years after the NBA was formed, he was voted one of the league's top 50 players of all time.

Aside from that one game played in Milwaukee with 12-foot baskets, he ruled like no other player of his era, most prominently in his six seasons with the Minneapolis Lakers. He averaged more than 28 points over his first three seasons with the Lakers, who averaged about 85 as a team. The ultimate compliment for a player comes when a rule is changed to curtail his production, and that happened on Mikan's behalf when the NBA widened the foul lane from six feet to 12 for the 1951-52 season to force him a few feet farther from the basket. Known as the Mikan Rule, it met with some success, yet he still scored 61 of his team's 91 points in a double-overtime game against Rochester that season, matched up against Risen, the future Hall of Famer.

Mikan's legend was such that the drill his coach at DePaul University, Ray Meyer, used to develop his ambidextrous shooting skills around the basket became known as the Mikan Drill, and was a staple for beginning players throughout the country for decades to come.

He tried his hand at coaching after retiring from playing, but resigned with a 9-30 record during the 1957-58 season. He had been moderately successful in the outside world, practicing law and participating in business and real estate ventures. All in all, he seemed an appropriate choice to bring credibility and publicity to a new league.

With Mikan officially presiding, several other matters had to be resolved over the next two days. Saturday's sessions, running from 9 a.m. to noon and from 2 p.m. to 9 p.m., would lay the groundwork for the league.

Louisville had not been listed among the league's original teams, but had shown interest all along. It sent a representative to the meeting, and was voted in once DeVoe was assured none of its home games would be played in Indiana. That made for an odd number of teams, but Mikan reported he had been seeking a 12th franchise in Atlanta, Cleveland, Denver, Memphis, Milwaukee and Columbus, Ohio.

A 5-4-1 vote permitted Mikan to keep the league office in Minnesota so he could maintain his eponymous travel agency. Those who objected wanted it to be in New York City, where most of the major sports leagues had their headquarters, to provide a major league aura. The draft was scheduled for March 31 in Oakland, and a procedure for it determined.

The final order of business was to determine the fate of McShane and Seredin. They had been instrumental in giving birth to the ABA, but had nothing to show for it. Both were promoters by trade, appearing to some of the owners to lack substance, and had written $4,000 worth of bad checks after exhausting the league's account. They wanted a role in the new endeavor, however, and were given consideration.

McShane wanted to own a 12th franchise in Hawaii, while Seredin wanted to be granted the contract for the league's public relations and to represent it in merchandising and television rights, of which he would receive a 10 percent fee.

McShane was brought in first to present his argument, which consisted primarily of a prepared brochure. The issue was passed on to the five-member expansion committee – a bold initiative for a league that barely existed.

Seredin's presentation also consisted of a brochure, although he talked extensively. He also asked for $3,000 from each team as a reward for his previous efforts.

The final round of meetings resumed on Sunday at 9 a.m., and ran until 4 p.m. That was enough time for McShane to receive a unanimous "no" regarding his Hawaiian franchise, although he was told he could deposit a check for $6,000, as the other franchise owners had done, within 10 days to have the option of establishing a team in a more geographically suitable city. The ABL had provided a lesson in the scheduling and travel difficulties of having a team in Hawaii.

Seredin was refused as well, because his proposals overlapped with Mikan's plans and the owners wanted to maintain internal control of public relations.

The owners also agreed nobody in the new league would approach NBA players under contract to encourage them to jump to the ABA. And, most importantly, it was determined each franchise would wire or mail a certified check for $30,000 to guarantee a place in the new venture.

Sommer's summary at the end of his minutes laid out the cold reality to the hopeful Indianapolis owners:

"The moment of truth has come. There is a league with existing commitments. The businessmen and investors have picked up where the promoters left off, and if there is $300,000 in the league treasury by March 13, 1967, it will be pretty clear that everyone means business. For the Indiana franchise, this means that there is much to be done in a very short period of time. For example, schedule dates have to be submitted by March 15 and someone has to be prepared to know what he is doing at the draft scheduled for March 31. The name, colors and a logo need to be decided upon. A general manager must be employed. There remains the question of additional financing. The situation calls for prompt and effective action."

The next effective action for the Indianapolis group occurred on March 10, when DeVoe mailed a certified check to Anaheim co-owner James Ackerman, who was acting temporarily as league treasurer. DeVoe was cautious, though. He included a directive that the check be deposited only if at least seven other ABA franchises also sent payment. Ackerman apparently had to wait awhile to receive enough checks, because DeVoe sent a telegram to him on March 17 authorizing the deposit.

Finally, officially, after a 14-year drought, Indianapolis had a professional basketball franchise. What it did not have were players, a coach, a general manager, an office, equipment, uniforms, a nickname or anything else beyond an honorable group of owners with varying degrees of emotional and financial commitment.

Their immediate priority was to hire a general manager who would take on the challenge of building an organization from the ground up, so the owners could go back to focusing more on their day jobs. Collins in later years claimed he was offered the job by Bannon, but immediately turned it down. Given Collins' essential role in bringing the ownership group together and his connections in the basketball world, it's entirely possible. More certain is that the position was offered to Bob Young, a partner in the Ross and Young promotion company and the director of Starlite Musicals, a thriving outdoor theater on Butler University's campus.

Young, a close friend of Collins', was considered a good fit for the job because he had promoted many events at the Coliseum, including the Royals' games. Bannon interviewed him and was impressed with some of his ideas, such as selling signage in the Coliseum to promote products, a new concept at the time. Young was offered the job, and accepted. Briefly, anyway. The more he thought about it, the more he doubted his decision. Finally, he called Collins one morning at 1 a.m. to tell him he wanted to back out.

"The people at Starlite have treated me so well over the years, if I pick up and leave the whole thing would be chaos," he said, according to Collins. "I think that's where my loyalty is."

It was all for the best, in retrospect. Young was not well-versed in basketball, and the new franchise was going to need someone wise to the ways of the professional game – which quickly led to the second candidate, Mark "Mike" Storen, a longtime friend of Tinkham's.

Storen had grown up in Michigan City, Ind., where he played high school football, and went on to graduate from Notre Dame. He entered the Marine Corps in 1957, and was sent to Officers Candidate School in Quantico, Va. One week into training, Tinkham showed up. A DePauw University graduate, Tinkham's arrival was delayed by having taken the bar exam. He happened to arrive just as the Saturday morning inspection was beginning, with the drill sergeants in full scream mode. He looked like a preppy character out of central casting, dressed in a blue blazer, white button-down shirt, flannel pants and loafers – which, of course, made him an irresistible target of the sergeants.

"So you're a lawyer?" an amused drill sergeant inquired.

"Yes, sir," Tinkham said.

"That means you know the Constitution."

"Yes, sir."

"I'd like to hear the Constitution."

"Would you like to hear it frontwards or backwards?"

Standing at attention, Storen couldn't contain a smile. Up to that point, *he* had been a favorite target of the sergeants because of his loud and brash nature. Clearly, this new candidate was going to redirect a lot of their attention. The two seemed made for one another.

After completing tours of duty in California and Okinawa, Storen was assigned to Chicago, where he was placed in charge of the largest Marine unit in a 13-state area. He attended law school in the evenings, but was eager to get into the real world and apply his skills and determination. With his return to civilian life approaching in June of 1963, he decided to try to find a front office position in professional sports. He sent letters and resumes to hockey, baseball, football and basketball teams, and began accumulating rejection letters.

One morning he read in the *Chicago Tribune* that the local NBA team, the Zephyrs – who were winding down a season that would end with a 25-55 record – had fewer than 600 season ticket holders. He saw an opening. He called David Trager, the majority owner out of a group of seven investors, identified himself as "Capt. Mike Storen of the United States Marine Corps," and asked to see him on a personal matter. Utilizing all of his limited assets, he showed up in his formal "dress blues" and issued a promise: if a contract could be worked out, he would personally sell 600 new season tickets. It was a sales tactic, one he would refer to in later years as "the usual bullshit," but it got him in the door. Impressed with the young man's confidence, Trager offered him a job with his insurance firm instead. Storen declined, and was given a salaried position with the Zephyrs.

They had been called the Packers the previous season, their first in Chicago as an expansion franchise. Changing the nickname hadn't changed much, although they did improve from 18 wins to 25. They had two promising players in Bellamy, a center from Indiana University who was voted the NBA's Rookie of the Year in 1962, and Dischinger, who won the same honor in 1963. Their roster also included a reserve forward named Larry Staverman. Leonard had taken over as coach at mid-season.

His discharge date approaching, Storen's enthusiasm for his new opportunity grew with each passing day. He was eager to get out of uniform and into the real world. He had ambition, not to mention a wife and infant daughter to support. But on March 25, sitting in his apartment, he picked up the *Tribune* again and read that the team was moving to Baltimore to be named the Bullets.[3]

Storen called the front office to ask if he still had a job.

"Oh, we forgot about you," Trager replied.

Informed the plan was to staff the relocated front office with Baltimore residents, Storen panicked. He had mouths to feed. He asked for another meeting with Trager, and they were joined by Sid Hartman, a Minneapolis newspaper columnist who helped with the franchise's personnel decisions.

Digging even deeper into his bag of salesmanship, Storen reminded them that the Zephyrs were owned and run primarily by Jewish businessmen, had a roster full of black players, and were moving to a city where Catholicism was the predominant religion. "Look, you guys have got to get a good Catholic boy on your staff," Storen said, referring of course to himself. Storen also claimed his wife's family was from Baltimore, and had prominent connections there. The truth was that his wife's father had lived in Baltimore for one year during World War II, but not since – a detail Trager and Hartman didn't need to know.

Storen wound up moving with the team to Baltimore as the group sales director. He stayed two seasons, then took a job in July of 1965 with the Royals as the director of promotions and ticket sales.

He was just 31 years old and in his second season with the Royals when the ABA was formed, but was eager for the challenge of running a front office. The idea of being the boss and building something from

---

[3] The original Baltimore Bullets lasted from 1944-54. This version was starting over as an expansion team and would last until 1973, when it moved to Washington D.C.

scratch appealed to him. So did the prospect of reconnecting with Tinkham, with whom he had remained in touch. During his first season with the Royals, Storen had accompanied the team to Indianapolis for their games at the Coliseum and met with Tinkham. On one occasion, he arranged to have Robertson pose with Tinkham's kids for a photograph.

Even before Indianapolis committed its $6,000 to the ABA venture at the meeting in New York, the two had been talking about the new league. Tinkham's first call after the ownership group came together following that fateful dinner in Lafayette was to Storen, to ask advice on what questions should be asked of the league's founders. Telephone records showed a call went out to Storen in Cincinnati on Feb. 2, the day of the organizational meeting in New York, and again on Feb. 6. Storen clearly was in the loop from the start, but his immediate advice was not encouraging. "Forget it, you don't have enough time to get it done," he told Tinkham.

Storen's interest was piqued, however, as he observed the ownership group's diligent and professional approach to forming a franchise. Here was a new league with at least 10 openings for a general manager, Storen's dream job. He apparently asked Tinkham to provide names and addresses for representatives of all the ABA teams so he could apply to each one, because Tinkham sent a letter on Feb. 14 listing them. He saved the Indianapolis group for last and closed with a tongue-in-cheek suggestion: "I would strongly recommend that you affiliate with No. 10; it seems to be the most solid entry."

After Young backed out, Storen was a virtual shoo-in. He interviewed with Bannon and DeVoe on March 13 and was offered a one-year contract for $17,500, plus moving expenses. The next day, he signed a two-year deal for $20,000 per year and moving expenses. It qualified as one of the first in a series of fortunate breaks that had long-term ramifications for the franchise and the city.

Storen was introduced at a press conference at the Downtown Athletic Club on March 21. He was short, stocky and balding, with a commanding voice, energetic demeanor and upbeat nature. He had a way of joking with people while making a point to be taken seriously.

While bold and decisive by nature, he also was willing to exaggerate a bit when it served his purpose. He was a fan of Boston general manager Red Auerbach, and emulated him to a degree.

The article in the *News* described him as a "confident, tough former Marine." He was going to need to be, because he wouldn't have time to ease into the job. The ABA's first draft was barely more than a week away.

"We don't have any ballplayers, we don't have films on the top college prospects, we don't even have an office," Storen told reporters at the press conference. "But I wouldn't be here if I didn't think the ABA, and Indianapolis in particular, would be successful."

Meanwhile, the quest to land Robertson continued. Collins stayed in touch via telephone, and years later remembered driving to Cincinnati with Robertson's high school coach, Crowe, for a personal meeting around this time. DeVoe's notes indicate Robertson said he did not want to talk seriously about a contract until the Royals' season ended, but had been in touch with his lawyers regarding the possibility. Robertson also indicated he would have no problem working with Storen, who had not yet been hired in Indianapolis, and would prefer coaching a roster of players drafted out of college rather than NBA backups.

Where Collins had once been coy about his conversations with the superstar guard, he now shifted to the mode of making blatant pleas, such as in his March 15 column about the Robertson-led efforts of NBA players to gain improved benefits from their owners.

"If he never plays another game for the NBA (Oscar, baby, come home. We need you.) he has struck a blow for the freedom of the last of the indentured athletes in professional sports," Collins wrote. "When it comes to playing the game, there are none better than Oscar. Now it is obvious to one and all that the kid has talent he hasn't even used yet. And, just between you and me, I hope he uses the rest of it right here."

The Indianapolis owners drew hope from Robertson's role as president of the NBA Players Association. He had led a movement to strike the All-Star game in 1964 if the owners didn't recognize their union and agree to negotiate, a bid that was successful largely because the game was going to be nationally televised for the first time and cancellation would have been a serious blow to the league's image.

Still, progress was slow to come. The Players Association had submitted requests to the owners at the All-Star break in January of '67 regarding issues such as a pension plan, health and medical insurance, shares of national television contracts and the right to have attorneys review their contracts before signing. They threatened to strike on March 15 if their grievances were not heard.

A new league competing for the services of frustrated players could not have come at a better time – for the league or the players. NBA players weren't feeling much loyalty to their bosses, and many were willing to consider jumping for more money and respect. The ABA owners had agreed not to try to raid teams and deal with the inevitable lawsuits, but free agents were another issue entirely. And it so happened the NBA had some intriguing players with expired contracts, particularly for the Indianapolis owners.

Dischinger, for example.

The Terre Haute native and Purdue graduate had excelled in all ways during his playing career to this point. The 6-7 forward had started along with Robertson on the 1960 gold medal-winning Olympic team after his sophomore season at Purdue, then went on to become a two-time first-team All-American as a junior and senior while leading the Big Ten in scoring both seasons.

He then won the NBA's Rookie of the Year award in 1963 despite playing only on weekends and holidays until the end of December while completing his degree in Chemical Engineering. During the week, when not immersed in academics, he helped coach the freshman team and scrimmaged with the players. He was paid by the game during that portion of the NBA season, and then became a full-time team member. He appeared in 57 games as a rookie and averaged 25.5 points on 51 percent shooting.

He was an NBA All-Star his first three seasons, playing for the Zephyrs, then Baltimore (where the Zephyrs moved) and then Detroit (where he had been traded). He then served two years in the Army, the result of his ROTC commitment at Purdue. He had been stationed in Hawaii where he was an instructor in chemical, biological and radiological warfare and a player-coach on the All-Army team. He still had one year left on his contract with Detroit, but it was uncertain whether jumping to the ABA would be a violation because of his military service.

Tom and Dick Van Arsdale, meanwhile, were clearly free agents. The 6-5 identical twins had shared Mr. Basketball honors in 1961 after leading Indianapolis Manual High School to the final game of the state tournament, where it lost in overtime. They were towheaded All-American Boy types who shared the Trester Award for mental attitude at the state tournament and would go on to graduate first and third in their high school class. They were such hot recruiting commodities – a rare package deal of elite talent, two for the price of one – that their telephone was taken off the hook at night to silence the sales pitches.

They announced their college choice – Indiana – in late April, early for that era. IU coach Branch McCracken was ecstatic, telling a reporter, "They're not just good basketball players, they're good boys. It's simply wonderful."

They went on to earn first-team all-Big Ten honors at Indiana along with honorable mention All-America recognition. Two seasons in, their NBA careers were promising, too. Dick averaged 15.1 points for New York and Tom 12.2 for Detroit in the 1966-67 season.

Jon McGlocklin was prized as well. A Franklin, Ind. native, he had been a teammate, classmate and fraternity roommate of the Van Arsdales at IU. He was identical in size and similar in skills, and therefore became known as the "third twin." He had just finished his second season as a backup guard with the Royals, averaging 8.5 points.

Bringing Robertson, Dischinger, the Van Arsdales and McGlocklin together would have been a dream for the Indianapolis franchise, providing instant credibility and fan appeal. Whatever investment made to surpass their NBA salaries might well have been recouped in ticket sales, broadcast rights and souvenir sales. It wouldn't have made sense to try to fit them all into a starting lineup, though. Robertson was a 6-5 point guard, the Van Arsdales and McGlocklin were 6-5 guards who played off the ball and Dischinger was a 6-7 forward who played mostly on the perimeter.

But any one of them – or in the case of the Van Arsdales, two of them – would have been great acquisitions for a startup franchise.

Dischinger was the likeliest candidate. He and his attorney, John Alexander, met with DeVoe, Collins, Barnes and Storen at DeVoe's office at 10 a.m. on March 13, the same day Storen was negotiating his own deal. Years later, Dischinger would recall "very much" wanting to sign with the new team in his home state, a point confirmed by DeVoe's notes. He owned a lot in Lafayette and wanted to build a house there. His in-laws lived there as well. He was due to be released from the Army in August, and was anxious to return to professional basketball – ideally, in his home state.

Alexander asked for a five-year contract at $27,500 per season and wanted it personally guaranteed by the owners – a reasonable demand given the uncertainty surrounding the new league. The Indianapolis owners had budgeted a $20,000 salary for him, though, and rejected the guarantee – a reasonable response given their relatively modest financial status. There also was serious doubt whether he could escape his contract in Detroit without serious penalty or a lawsuit.

McGlocklin was claimed by San Diego in the expansion draft in 1967, but was a free agent. He had been paid $12,000 by the Royals the previous season. Storen, who had watched him personally that season, offered him $15,000 to jump leagues. He was offered $17,000 by San Diego, however, and readily accepted. He would go to Milwaukee after the following season in the 1968 expansion draft.[4]

As for the Van Arsdales, they might or might not have seriously considered signing on with the Indianapolis team. But they at least *showed* serious interest.

As early as February, before Indianapolis had a general manager or even an official franchise, Chuck Barnes told a Detroit newspaper columnist, Pete Waldmeir, at the Daytona 500 that his group was planning to make significant offers to both Van Arsdales. Talks progressed

---

[4] McGlocklin had serious conversations with Storen again in 1969, after finishing an All-Star season in Milwaukee. He was offered a three-year contract with a sizable increase in salary, but Storen was not able to guarantee it for each season. He finished his career in Milwaukee, where he was a starting guard with Robertson on the team that won the NBA championship in 1971, and remained as a broadcaster.

to the point that on April 1 the *Star* published a non-bylined story with the headline "Van Arsdale May Play Here." The reference was to Tom, who seemed the most interested in making the jump, but the twins were as identical as twins could be. They looked alike, acted alike and played alike.

Tom flew to Indianapolis via Delta Airlines on a Wednesday morning late in March. He was in town for four hours, during which time he met with team officials – including DeVoe and Storen – over breakfast at the airport Holiday Inn. Dick had a Friday lunch meeting with them a week or two later. The matter was settled on April 11, when each of the twins signed two-year contracts with their respective NBA teams after turning down offers that between salary and bonuses reportedly would have paid them $35,000 per season for two years to play in Indianapolis, according to the *News*.

Reportedly. Estimates of the offers varied. A wire service report said they had been offered three-year contracts for $30,000 per season. DeVoe's notes indicated the owners were willing to pay each of the twins $25,000 per season. The *Detroit Free Press* reported the contract Tom signed was thought to be for $20,000 per season. Somewhere amid all those numbers, the truth sat quietly and stubbornly, probably at about $25,000 per season.

Dick was visiting Tom in Detroit when *News* sportswriter Dick Denny spoke to them on the telephone.

"It took a lot of thought to make our decisions, and, in a way, we feel we let Indianapolis down," Dick said. "We know they were banking a great deal on us getting them started and we almost decided to go.

I thought Mike Storen and John DeVoe made a very fair presentation. They're great people and there wasn't any question of the integrity of the Indianapolis officials."

Dick said he and Tom had talked with one another on the telephone about eight times four days earlier, a Sunday, to reach a decision. Both had watched a playoff game between Philadelphia and Boston that afternoon, which reminded them of their desire to remain with a proven league featuring star players such as Chamberlain and Russell.

"It's a matter of pride," Tom told Denny. "We're only going to be playing three, maybe four, more years and we wanted to play the best basketball there is."[5]

"This decision might have been even tougher than my decision to get married," Dick added.

Years later, Tom would recall having talked with Storen, but said the offer "wasn't anything fantastic." Not nearly enough, anyway, to make him think about taking a chance on an unproven league of lesser quality. He and Dick no doubt had improved their bargaining power by talking with the Indianapolis group, but it would have taken a far greater offer than what their NBA teams paid them to convince them to take the plunge into the unknown waters of the ABA.

Clearly, the new league was failing to lure proven homegrown talent out of the NBA. Players were sticking with the security of an established league, and it was becoming increasingly obvious the Indianapolis franchise, like the others in the ABA, was going to have to settle for unproven players to fill its roster.

Toward that end, the ABA's first draft was conducted at the Edgewater Hotel in Oakland on April 2, two days after the originally scheduled date but a month before the NBA would conduct its draft. The delay was to clear up some vital business issues – such as how many teams would be in the league, and where they would play.

Once the first day's meeting was called to order at 9 a.m. on March 31, the Kansas City franchise was permitted to move to Denver. Then a second motion was approved to award a franchise to Louisville, after DeVoe again was promised it would not play any home games in Indiana. Owner Joe Gregory and his wife, Mamie, were on hand with a $30,000 check to make it official. Houston also submitted its $30,000 entry fee. It was two weeks later than the deadline established at the meeting in New Orleans, but a motion carried not to hold the franchise in default. A representative from Milwaukee was on hand to seek what would have

---

[5]   They wound up playing 10 more years, finishing together in Phoenix in the 1976-77 season.

been the 12ᵗʰ franchise, but was rejected after considerable discussion because the owners were not convinced of the financial stability of that group.[6]

It also was confirmed all franchises would have to submit a performance bond of $100,000 by May 1, completing their financial obligations and providing the capital necessary to operate the first year.

Budgetary issues dominated the second day of meetings, the primary resolution being that Mikan would be allowed a budget of $190,000 for office operations the first year.

The draft was conducted on the third day. Storen represented the Indianapolis franchise, with John DeVoe and Tinkham on hand as well. Predictably for a just-hatched league, the proceedings were a bit chaotic and comedic. Because of the lack of time for preparation – the Kentucky and Houston franchises, after all, had officially been in the league for less than two days – the owners had agreed to pool their research and share information on the draft-eligible players.

The ABA representatives decided not to divulge the rounds in which players were drafted, in order to discourage comparisons to the following month's NBA draft and avoid "offending" players who might be drafted higher in the other league. The ABA representatives were flying by the seat of a collective pair of pants, and realized mistakes would be made in their draft. If they selected a player in the fourth round who went in the first round of the NBA draft, their odds of signing that player were immediately reduced because the player would feel more valued by the other league. They simply listed players as drafted in either the top five or bottom seven rounds.

DeVoe's notes on his yellow legal pad, however, recorded the details.

A lottery was conducted to determine the order of selection. Minnesota won the first pick and selected Mel Daniels, a second-team All-America center from the University of New Mexico. New Orleans was second and took James Jones, a 6-4 guard from nearby Grambling

---

6   Herb Kohl, who later would own the NBA franchise in Milwaukee, wanted to have a franchise, but needed more time to put an investment group together. Mikan was against the idea of adding another franchise at that late date, believing it would make the league look "silly."

State University, who had gone largely unnoticed in other parts of the country. Indianapolis then drafted 6-foot-3 guard Jimmy Walker, a first-team All-American who had averaged 30.3 points his senior season at Providence.

Storen was succinct in his explanation.

"I saw Walker play last year and we drafted him on the basis of being the finest college player in the country," he said.

Indianapolis' second-round pick was Charles Beasley, a guard from Southern Methodist (listed as "Chuck Beesley" in DeVoe's notes). Bob Netolicky, a 6-8 center from Drake went in the third round, followed by Craig Dill, a center from Michigan; Jim Dawson, a guard from Illinois; Hubie Marshall, a guard from LaSalle; Gerry Jones, a guard from Iowa (listed as "Gary"); Ron Kozlicki, a center from Northwestern (listed as "Kozlicky"); Frank Gaidjunes, a center from Villanova; Gene Washington, a guard from Michigan State, Ed McKee, a forward from Rockhurst; and Bill Russell, a guard from Indiana.

Washington was a curious selection. He hadn't played basketball since high school and had already been selected eighth overall in the NFL draft after a standout football and track career at MSU. Storen dubbed him a "gamble."

Gaidjunes was equally puzzling. He had at least played college basketball, but just barely, having averaged 2.9 points as a senior at Villanova. He reportedly had showed promise as a junior, but fell out of the playing rotation his final season for some reason.

Filling 12 rounds worth of draft picks was a challenge, given the lack of time to prepare. Only four of the teams had coaches at the time, and scouting departments weren't even a consideration yet. New York dropped out of the final two rounds, but the other teams doggedly made picks to the bitter end, even if they had to stretch the boundaries of logic to do it.

New Orleans, led by future "shock talk" TV host Morton Downey Jr., drafted Bob Seagren, holder of the world indoor pole vaulting record, in the sixth round – likely as a joke as the draft wore on. Seagren later called the decision "hilarious," pointing out he hadn't touched a basketball in five years. The Louisville franchise drafted a 6-10 player with the last name Smith out of Kent State in the fifth round, but couldn't provide a first name. It turned out a Smith had not played for Kent State the previous season. Minnesota drafted a player named Clark out of Eastern Kentucky, but couldn't provide a first name. It turned out to be Richard Clark. [7]

Storen barely lost out on one notable player. He hoped to land Louie Dampier, an Indianapolis native and an All-America guard out of the University of Kentucky in the third round, when the ABA representatives had agreed to let teams select a player from their geographical area. Just how those territories were drawn up, if at all, remains vague, however. The Louisville group – which also claimed territorial rights to Dampier – took him with the third pick in the round, one spot ahead of Indianapolis, which settled for Netolicky instead.

Walker turned out to be as unobtainable for the franchise as the Indiana natives already in the NBA. He signed with Detroit on May 2, a day before the NBA draft was conducted, because the Pistons had long known he would be their choice with the No. 1 overall pick. His contract was reported to be for four years and $250,000, which likely would have exceeded the financial capabilities of the Indianapolis owners. He cited the NBA's status as a "more established league," for his decision, and his agent said the Indianapolis team had not made a "firm, positive" offer. [8]

Eight days after the draft it was announced Storen had traded Beasley to Dallas for Matthew Aitch, a 6-7 center out of Michigan State, although DeVoe's notes indicate it might have been agreed upon the day of the draft. The *Star's* headline was hopeful: "State ABA Team Makes Big Trade For Matt Aitch."

---

[7] Clark wound up playing 26 games for Minnesota in the first ABA season and 32 the following season for Houston.

[8] Walker went on to have a good NBA career, but not one befitting a No. 1 overall pick hailed as the next Oscar Robertson. He averaged 16.7 points over nine NBA seasons and was named to two All-Star teams. He died of lung cancer at the age of 63 in 2007, having never met the son whose best NBA seasons would come in Indianapolis: Jalen Rose, who by the way signed a contract for more than $90 million while playing there.

If nothing else, the swap made geographic sense. Beasley had attended Southern Methodist in Dallas, while Aitch had played in the Midwest and was familiar to Big Ten Conference fans. Aitch had been a team captain and second-team all-Big Ten selection his senior season at Michigan State. He was a good shooter who led the conference co-champion Spartans in scoring (16.3) and rebounding (9.2), and had scored 31 points against Purdue – a detail highlighted in the franchise's first press release, on Sports Headliners letterhead.

He lacked elite athleticism and would have to move to forward as a professional, but Storen was sufficiently impressed to award him a guaranteed contract. Thus, the first transaction in the history of the still-unnamed franchise became the first controversial transaction. Privately, anyway. Collins recalled being at The Masters golf tournament in Augusta, Ga. when he received a call from DeVoe to tell him the team had acquired Aitch.

"We have good news, we traded for Matthew Aitch," DeVoe told him. "Swell," Collins replied. "What have you been smoking? He couldn't play in the Big Ten."

That might have been an exaggerated recollection on Collins' part, given Aitch's successful senior season, but he wasn't alone in questioning Storen's enthusiasm. Storen admitted years later his familiarity with the Big Ten made him biased toward Aitch.

Jones was the franchise's first player to be signed to a contract, on May 9, a non-guaranteed deal for $15,000 with a $2,000 bonus. A 6-4 guard, he had been voted Iowa's Most Valuable Player the previous season. Bannon weighed in with a boilerplate quote, calling him "a boy who typifies the type of player we are looking for – one who will put out 100 percent. It is obvious from his record at Iowa that he will provide leadership and ability."

That sounded awfully optimistic for a seventh-round draft pick, but perhaps the team president could be forgiven some hyperbole in his excitement over the franchise's first signed player.

The newspapers extolled the virtues of most of the signed players, drafted and otherwise. The second to sign was McKee. To most fans in Indiana, he was an unknown player from an unknown college in Kansas

City. He signed a non-guaranteed contract for a mere $8,000, but so eager was the local media to begin reporting on this new team, the story in the *Star* ran for seven paragraphs and included a head shot. "We feel as though McKee will fit in with our plans of developing a well-rounded club and that he will be a productive ball player," Storen said, tempering his marketing instincts with a dose of common sense.[9]

If Jones and McKee lacked reputations to excite the infant fan base, the third player signed was sure to make people take notice.

Larry Humes, a 6-3 guard, had enough name recognition to merit a lengthy press release from the franchise. Voted Indiana's high school Mr. Basketball in 1962, he had gone on to team with backcourt partner Jerry Sloan and lead Evansville College to Division II national championships as a sophomore and junior. He also earned division All-America honors as a junior and senior. He finished his career as the school's all-time leading scorer, with a three-year average of 26.4 points and a high game of 48 against Ball State. He hadn't merely fattened his scoring average against small- or mid-sized programs, either. He had scored 39 points against Iowa and 37 against Notre Dame, with Evansville winning both games.

Still, Humes had been merely a fifth-round draft pick of Chicago in 1966, the 50th overall selection. He played forward on offense while defending as a guard at Evansville because he was most effective around the basket, where he made shots that would have gotten most players benched for even attempting: 15-foot hook shots, spinning one-handers, shots with his back to the basket, all sorts of off-balance flings that usually found their way through the basket. But while he had a variety of ways to score, he lacked a dependable perimeter shot. That convinced the Bulls to try him out at forward, where he was undersized.

He scored 33 points in a rookie intrasquad game in August and was one of 21 players invited to training camp in September, but was "taken off" the team according to local reports the day before the first exhibition

---

[9] McKee was released after the first wave of summer tryouts. He later became the Sports Information Director at Indiana State University, and worked there during Larry Bird's playing career.

game – meaning the team was retaining its rights to him but didn't have to pay him.

It had been a daunting challenge all along. The Bulls, as an expansion franchise, had plucked one or two players from every NBA roster that summer in the expansion draft and opened camp with 18 NBA veterans. While at first it might have seemed a blessing to go to an expansion team full of lesser talent, the reality was that the Bulls presented more competition for a roster position than any other league team. It would have been far better to be drafted by one of the more established teams that had lost a veteran or two to the expansion draft and had holes to fill. The fact the Bulls had drafted a similarly-sized player in Purdue All-American Dave Schellhase in the first round of the same draft added to Humes' obstacles.

Humes personified the control NBA teams had over players at that time. He had passed up opportunities to play in Italy or for the Globetrotters while waiting on the Bulls to finalize their roster. Cincinnati and St. Louis contacted him about trying out after his release, but Bulls general manager Dick Klein demanded compensation for him because the team still owned his rights. Bulls coach Johnny Kerr encouraged him to try out again the following season, and suggested he play for the local Jamoco Saints minor league team in the meantime.

With a wife and three-year-old son to support, Humes needed steady work, so he took a job teaching grade school physical education in Indianapolis. He couldn't afford to support his wife and son on his salary, so they stayed with his parents in his hometown of Madison and he drove down on weekends to be with them.

Suddenly, he had a new lease on a basketball life — in a new league, with less competition and in his home state. Storen's optimistic response to signing Humes made his place on the season-opening roster seem a foregone conclusion.

"Larry will certainly be an asset to the squad," Storen said in a press release. "He represents the type of players we hope to use in forming the team. He is an exciting player, has tremendous ability and this is what we are seeking."

The release went on to point out the difficulty rookies were having finding roster spots in the NBA, and cited Humes as an example of those who had enough talent but needed an opening to climb through.

The front office wasn't confident enough in Humes to offer a guaranteed contract, but was sufficiently convinced he would be on the team to schedule an exhibition and regular season game in Madison at the high school gymnasium where Humes had starred.

Humes in later years would remember being told by team officials, presumably Storen, he had a 95 percent chance of making the team. Thus emboldened, he moved his family to a house a short drive from the Coliseum. He signed a contract for a $10,000 salary, with a $2,000 bonus. He immediately took the bonus check to the bank, retrieved 100 $20 bills, went home and spread them out on his bed. Then he called for his wife to come admire the windfall.

"We were on Cloud Nine," he recalled years later.

Dill also was signed in May, for $20,000, with a bonus, and a lease on a Chevrolet Super Sport automobile. He had been chosen by San Diego in the fourth round of the NBA draft, and therefore had leverage. He planned to attend law school in the off-seasons and become an attorney, and Indiana University's law school in Indianapolis was an attraction for him.

Storen continued to sign players throughout May, but stopped announcing them because the Indianapolis sports pages were filling up with coverage of the Indianapolis 500 qualifications and race. He wanted maximum exposure by releasing them one at a time during the slow news period in June, and the newspapers gladly played along.

Marshall, a 6-foot guard out of LaSalle, was announced on June 6. He had averaged 26.9 points as a junior and finished as the school's all-time leading scorer, but as a 12th-round pick of Philadelphia in the NBA had no leverage and took a non-guaranteed contract.

The afternoon *News* was given the break two days later for the next signing, Billy "The Hill" McGill, a 6-9 center. He had been the nation's leading scorer five years earlier at Utah, when he averaged 38.8 points, but had careened between five NBA teams since then.

The undrafted Stan Washington – not Gene, but Stan – followed, signing a non-guaranteed deal for $11,000, with a $1,000 bonus. A 6-3 guard, he had finished his college career at Michigan State a year earlier as the second all-time leading scorer in school history, the team's leading rebounder as a junior and senior, and two-time team MVP. A fifth-round draft pick of the Lakers the previous year, he had failed to make it out of their rookie camp. He went on to play in the North American Basketball League, scoring 52 points in one game.

Kozlicki, the eighth-round draft pick, was next. A 6-7 center at Northwestern, he had been merely the third-leading scorer (14.4) on an 11-11 team, but was highly-regarded for his attitude and skill-level. He was a natural forward, but had to play center to fill in for an injured player. He had been a prized recruit out of high school in the Chicago area, good enough to attract an offer from legendary coach Adolph Rupp at Kentucky. Rupp considered him the missing piece in a recruiting class that included Dampier and Pat Riley, and Kozlicki always believed he could have made the difference when Kentucky lost to Texas Western in the 1966 NCAA championship game.

Despite being selected toward the bottom of the draft pile, Kozlicki had leverage. San Diego took him in the fourth round of the NBA draft, one spot ahead of Dill, and a team in Italy made a serious two-year contract offer to play there, for a handsome salary and free use of a car and apartment. He gave it serious consideration. He could play a season, save some money and come back to try out for the 1968 U.S. Olympic team, and then go play in the ABA or NBA. But, he was engaged to be married on Aug. 26 and didn't want to disrupt those plans.

Storen was convinced Kozlicki would be an effective player when moved to his more natural forward position. Tinkham recalled it as the first time he heard the expression someone had "played out of position." With two potential suitors to compete with, Storen signed him to a guaranteed contract for about $16,500.

What would turn out to be the premier signing to date, at least among those publicized, followed closely behind. It was announced on June 10, but probably had occurred well before that. Netolicky had been merely a second-team all-conference player in the Missouri Valley his senior year in college, and was drafted on potential more than accomplishment. The expansion San Diego Rockets of the NBA recognized it and made him their second-round draft pick, which granted him some status, not to mention negotiating leverage.

Netolicky did not seem a special acquisition, superficially, and didn't rate a guaranteed contract. How good could he be if he hadn't even been a first-team all-conference player in the Missouri Valley as a senior? He was, however, a late bloomer, one who hadn't hit his growth spurt until he was 16 and had played just one season of high school basketball. He averaged 17.6 points and 12 rebounds his final collegiate season, and while his attitude and effort had been sporadic, his athleticism and innate intelligence offered the hope of becoming a special player if he continued to mature.

The son of a surgeon in Cedar Rapids, his only experience with high school basketball had come as a junior at a Catholic school, where he was an average 6-foot-6 player. He was more motivated to have fun than to play basketball, so he didn't bother playing his senior year. He hung out for two years after graduating from high school, working through a self-described "misspent youth." He hung out in pool halls, sometimes from noon to midnight, and traveled to Florida, Las Vegas and California with friends. "I had a lot of experiences normal kids that age don't have," he recalled in later years.

As with anyone else, his upbringing had a major influence on his behavior. His father had grown up in a large, poor family and become a workaholic, often working from 5 a.m. to midnight, seven days a week through some stretches.

That didn't leave time to build much of a relationship with his children, which left Netolicky an unshackled kid in search of a good time. Basketball was just a past-time, something he could do well without great effort. His father barely paid attention.

"I could go two or three months without seeing my dad," Netolicky recalled. "He must have performed more surgery than anybody in the United States.

"There wasn't much to motivate me. I wish he had been there, because there were a lot of questions I would have liked to ask. Even when I tried to communicate with my father, he was too tired or too busy. I don't think he did it personally, he was just one of these guys whose life and love was medicine."

Netolicky's father had been a standout tennis player in college, and he inherited his father's athleticism. After high school, he found his way to AAU basketball during the winters in Cedar Rapids. He played for two AAU teams, Marion DX and Hall Clothiers, which competed against other AAU teams and college freshman teams in an era when freshmen weren't eligible to play varsity basketball. In that relaxed atmosphere, he improved rapidly as his body matured. He played his best games when challenged by players with reputations, such as when Marion DX played at Wisconsin against the freshman team. Warned beforehand by Wisconsin fans about the team's hotshot scorer, Netolicky, by his memory, dominated and his team won by a huge margin. With the game easily in hand, he and a teammate took to clowning, running off the court and sitting with the Wisconsin cheerleaders instead of playing defense, which infuriated the local fans.

"We almost didn't get out of town," he said. "There were a bunch of farmers waiting for us after the game and they weren't happy. If it had been a close game they probably would have shot us."

A breakthrough for Netolicky came in the state AAU tournament, where he had a standout performance against a junior college All-American and won a trophy for being voted the most promising player. That performance caught the eye of Drake coach Maury Johns, who made a home visit and offered a scholarship. He also got a house call from Bob King of New Mexico. Had he accepted that offer he would have wound up a teammate of another promising big man, Daniels, who went on to earn All-America recognition and become Minnesota's top draft pick.

Netolicky's unique combination of talent, athleticism, sporadic focus and adventuresome spirit was revealed often throughout his college career.

He scored 40 points in an early-season freshman game against a junior college team, but was suspended for a game in January after returning late from Christmas break. In his sophomore year, the *Des*

Moines Register ran a feature story on his habit of acquiring exotic pets. He adopted an ocelot named Socrates, but had to ship it off to Florida after a frightened elderly woman in the neighborhood objected. He drove to Fort Lauderdale to take it back during Spring Break, but decided instead to return with a six-foot boa constrictor, which he put in a sack and drove back to Des Moines in the back seat of his red Corvette. When he brought it into his fraternity house at Drake, the cook resigned and the housemother nearly did as well. Inspired by the movie "Born Free," he later paid $100 for a pet lion he named Julie. He had it declawed and defanged, but sold it to an animal compound in California a year later after it became too big to handle.

He antagonized his coach at times, too, alternating flashes of brilliance on the court with irresponsible behavior off it. As a junior, he scored 32 points and grabbed 18 rebounds in a road loss to fifth-ranked Minnesota in December. A month later he turned in a listless performance against Bradley and was taken out of the starting lineup for the rematch a week later. Later that month he missed a start against North Texas after being late to practice the day before the game, but came off the bench to lead the team with 18 points. He was declared academically ineligible shortly afterward, while Drake led the Missouri Valley Conference, and was lost for the rest of the season.

He was consistent in his fun, though. He rarely went to class, and did just enough to get by. Or, on occasion, not get by. His high IQ usually got him through. He majored in Biology, with an eye toward pre-med, but otherwise took the easiest classes possible.

"I wasted my brain power," he said upon reflection. "I could take an anatomy class and go to one lab a month and study before the class and get a C or D and that was enough. That was the sad part, because I didn't have any motivation. I just didn't care. I wish to heck I had gone, because I was capable of getting any grade I wanted."

Given the way his junior season had ended, he entered his final year with renewed focus and work ethic. He earned praise in the newspaper from Johns for his pre-season practice effort – a welcome contrast to the previous season, when Johns said he nearly dropped him from the team because of his lack of hustle.

"I feel badly that I let the team down last year by becoming ineligible and I think I owe the rest of the guys a good season," Netolicky told the *Register*.

The *Register* article told the story of a kid with a rich father who lived off-campus in a luxury apartment, drove yet another Corvette, this one a 1966 with a 427 cubic-inch engine, had earned a pilot's license, claimed an IQ of 135 and had adopted another exotic pet, a margay – a cat similar to an ocelot.

Netolicky's senior season went smoothly enough, although Drake finished just 9-16 with a young team. Earning second-team all-conference honors counted as improvement, and he went on to be named Most Valuable Player in a state-wide college all-star game in Cedar Rapids after scoring 21 points.

A *Register* article two days after that game spelled out the consensus on his odds of having a professional career.

"There is a general feeling that Netolicky has the tools to make it as a pro," it read. "Attitude. That's another area – and it will probably be the key item in his case."

Upon being drafted by the Indianapolis franchise, Netolicky flew himself to Indianapolis to meet with Tinkham and DeVoe – not in his own airplane, as legend would have it in later years, but in one borrowed from the flying club, a Cessna 172, a single-engine, four-seater. Tinkham tried to sell him on the fact he would become a household name in a basketball-crazed state if he signed with the new franchise, something that didn't make sense to Netolicky at the time. He also had dinner with Storen at a White Castle location, where he wolfed down, by his estimation, about a dozen of the cheapest hamburgers in town.

"They really wined and dined me," he joked years later.

The initial contract offer of about $12,000 wasn't much more impressive to him than the meal, so he went home to await the NBA draft. He had been receiving calls from teams making sure he wanted to play professionally, so he was confident of being selected. On the same day the expansion Rockets selected him in the second round, an anxious Tinkham called and told him not to sign anything without talking to the Indianapolis group again. San Diego coach Jack McMahon later called in a contract offer similar to what the group in Indianapolis had proposed, but Netolicky was barely awake at the time and the conversation hardly registered. If he had been more savvy about the pro game, he realized later, he would have at least gone out to San Diego to look around, throw a scare into the Indianapolis owners, and improve his negotiating stance. Still, just having another suitor provided some leverage. He and his father's attorney soon went back to Indianapolis for another meeting at the airport and signed a non-guaranteed contract for $16,000, with a $2,000 bonus.

Thanks to Storen's ignorance of the automotive world, Netolicky also wangled another Corvette out of the deal. He told Storen during the negotiations he would like a lease on a car as part of his contract.

"OK," Storen said. "What kind of car?"

"A Corvette," Netolicky said.

"What's a Corvette?" Storen asked.

"It's a Chevy," Netolicky said.

Figuring all Chevrolets were created equal, Storen agreed to include a one-year lease for one in the contract, not realizing it was the most exotic American-made car of its time. Netolicky's Corvette streak remained intact.

With the possibility of professional basketball in his future, Netolicky's motivation to crack the books and finish his senior year with a strong grade point average was at an all-time low.

He was already in trouble with the Dean of Students for a prank he had pulled on Skip Day, a longstanding Drake tradition. The dean was in crack-down mode about drinking on campus, so Netolicky set him up by organizing a major party at a city park with two large kegs with Budweiser stickers on them. When the dean moved in, accompanied by police cars, Netolicky nudged the youngest fraternity pledges toward the front to make the violation appear worse, and made a show of throwing blankets over the kegs. The dean then stepped forward and threw the blankets off the kegs. The smallest pledge ran off, in a pre-planned mock escape attempt. The police officer announced everyone was under arrest.

"Sir, what are we under arrest for?" Netolicky asked.

The officer asked what was in the kegs. Netolicky invited him to have a drink. The officer poured one – a strawberry Kool-Aid. He took a sip and then got on his radio to tell his superiors he had just busted a Kool-Aid party.

The dean's face turned as red as the Kool-Aid as the students began singing, "Bye, bye, Stevie; bye, bye Stevie; we hate to see you go!"

Netolicky also captured the dean's attention by violating campus rules after a dance. He took a freshman, the daughter of a senator, and then kept her overnight in his apartment rather than having her home by the 11 p.m. curfew. The dean was knocking on his door at 9 a.m., threatening to expel them both.

Called into the dean's office, with a signed contract under his belt and a signing bonus in the bank, Netolicky was in no mood to be threatened.

"Dean, do me a favor and kiss my ass!" Netolicky shouted. He then left and bought an airline ticket to Hawaii. While most college students use fake ID's to make them appear older so they can buy alcohol, the youthful-looking Netolicky had one that claimed he was 18, which allowed him to get a student rate on the flight. There among the South Pacific palm trees, he lazed away the days while awaiting his shot at pro basketball.

The signing of former Purdue star Bob Purkhiser followed that of Netolicky by a day. The 1965 graduate was the ultimate streak shooter. He had set a school record by hitting 18 consecutive field goals over the course of three games, but also missed his final 17 attempts in his final game as a senior. He had been teaching and coaching at Lebanon High School, about halfway between Indianapolis and the Purdue campus in West Lafayette. Two years removed from serious competition, he received a non-guaranteed contract as well.

Two days later, another "major" signing was announced. Dawson, a 6-foot guard, had been voted the Big Ten Conference's Most Valuable Player the previous season at Illinois after averaging 21.7 points, and was an Academic All-American. He was awarded a guaranteed contract for $14,000 and a $2,000 bonus, and was considered significant enough to receive a bylined story that ran at the top of one of the *Star's* sports pages.

Another two days later, the signing of Aitch – the trade acquisition – was announced. Having invested a top draft pick in a trade for him,

Storen wasn't going to let him get away. Detroit had not selected him until the 13th round of the NBA draft, so the competition wasn't particularly fierce.

The effort to land him was memorable, though. Storen visited Aitch in his dorm room in East Lansing. As they discussed a deal, Storen looked out the window and saw the Pistons' general manager making his way across the parking lot. Suddenly, an agreement became an urgent matter.

Aitch said he wanted a car. Storen said OK. Aitch asked what kind he would get. Storen – who hadn't realized a Corvette was anything special – didn't have a clue what to offer. He looked out the dorm room window again and saw his rented Chevrolet in the parking lot.

"See that yellow car?" Storen said. "That one."

When they finally agreed on a guaranteed contract for $14,000 with a $1,000 bonus, Aitch asked for the keys to the car.

"No, Matthew, not *that* car," Storen said.

Aitch then invited Storen to an off-campus party that evening to meet his fiancé, Karen. Storen agreed. When they arrived, several members of the university's football team were already there. They were coming off consecutive undefeated regular seasons, but had tied Notre Dame 10-10 in the final game of the previous season in an epic showdown between the first- and second-ranked teams in the country. They were still riding high, in more ways than one. Storen got his first whiff of marijuana at that party, although he had no clue what it was at the time.

No doubt, the times they were a-changin'.[10]

---

[10] Aitch would last just one season with the team, averaging 5.6 points. Storen recalled him playing well in the early stages of training camp when the offense was less structured, but struggling when sets were put in. Beasley, a 6-5 guard, went on to average 13.3 points the first ABA season and led the league in foul shooting (.872). He lasted four seasons before retiring. "We'd have been a helluva lot better off with Charles Beasley," Storen acknowledged in later years. Aitch, however, was wildly successful in his personal life after basketball. He went on to earn his Masters Degree in Education from Michigan State and work for the university as an assistant coach and administrator. He and his wife, Karen, had two daughters, one of whom became an All-American basketball player at Michigan State.

Despite all the newspaper coverage given to the signings of several players, including those with barely a chance of making the team, the acquisitions of the two most significant players were never announced.

Freddie Lewis, a 6-foot guard, had been the Royals' 10th-round pick, the 88th overall selection, in the 1966 draft. It was his understanding that even that negligible display of faith was a favor from then-Royals coach Jack McMahon to longtime friend Ned Wulk, Lewis' coach at Arizona State. Despite facing long odds, however, Lewis quickly established himself in intrasquad scrimmages, leading all scorers in the final two and earning a *Cincinnati Enquirer* headline that read "Lewis Looming As Star Rookie."

"He not only has scored well, he has passed well, defended well and demonstrated considerable court savvy," the story reported.

Lewis continued to perform well during the Royals' 14-game exhibition schedule, most of them against the Los Angeles Lakers in a barnstorming tour through remote outposts across the country. He scored 15 of his 18 points in the fourth quarter of a come-from-behind victory in Spokane, Wash., and followed with 26 points the next night in Boise, Idaho when he, Robertson and Jerry Lucas combined for all 35 of the team's points in the third quarter of a 114-105 victory over the Lakers.

He made the team, but Robertson and Smith dominated the backcourt minutes during the regular season. Lewis scored 22 points in a one-sided loss to Philadelphia in November, but was sent to the Battle Creek team in the North American Basketball League after 27 games to get playing time. He averaged 34 points in 10 games there, with a high of 48 – but actually had 50, according to newspaper reports, because one basket was incorrectly attributed to a teammate.

Lewis continued to play well after he was recalled by the Royals in March, scoring nine points in an 11-minute first-half appearance against the Lakers in his first game back, and 16 points against San Francisco in the final regular season game. Sportswriters invariably referred to him as "little Freddie Lewis," and one even took the liberty of assigning a nickname: "The Mouse." He wound up playing in 32 games for the Royals that season, and showed considerable promise. Each NBA team was going to have to leave three players unprotected in the upcoming expansion draft, however, and the new Seattle and San Diego franchises would choose from that group. Lewis was likely to wind up one of them.

The Royals' season ended on March 25 with a blowout loss to Philadelphia in the playoffs, which completed a three-game sweep for the 76ers. It was just four days after Storen had been introduced as the general manager in Indianapolis. He had not yet moved out of his house in Cincinnati, so he invited Lewis over on a Sunday afternoon to talk about a contract. Lewis recalled reaching agreement on an informal deal sketched out on a yellow legal pad.

The first season's salary was $13,000, with a $3,000 bonus. It would later be stated a used refrigerator was included in the deal, but one of the owner's wives arranged for him to get one when he moved into his apartment. It wasn't a lot for a player who had already shown promise in the NBA, but it was a healthy increase from his rookie contract with the Royals, which paid $9,000.[11]

Lewis had felt lucky to get even that. Royals general manager Pepper Wilson had originally offered him a one-year deal for $8,500.

"I don't care what you give me, I just want to be on the team," Lewis said.

"You know what, you're the first player I've ever negotiated a contract with who didn't try to bargain for more money," Wilson replied. "And you have a wife and children. I'm going to give you $9,000."

Lewis' lack of concern over his salary was sincere. As a low draft pick, he just wanted to get a foot into the NBA's door and prove himself. And it worked. He had played well enough to satisfy Storen, who had watched him closely throughout his lone NBA season and was aware of his success in the NABL.

---

[11] As low as the first-year salaries might seem today, they were attractive at a time when the median family income in the U.S. was $7,400. People who earned $15,000 or more were in the upper 10 percent of incomes across the country in 1967, and some families were getting by on less than $4,000. The average income for non-white families at the time was $4,623, and 30 percent of non-white people earned below the poverty level of $3,000. To balance the equation, however, one could purchase a new pair of loafers for $14.95, a winter coat for $22.95 and sirloin steak for .98 a pound.

The agreement with the new ABA team guaranteed that Lewis would be left unprotected by the Royals, and he was taken by San Diego in the May 1 expansion draft. It's unclear whether San Diego's management knew he had already signed with another team, but if so they might not have believed the new league would survive long enough to begin play.

The other unannounced player to sign with the Indianapolis franchise was 6-5 forward, Roger Brown. Although Lewis considered himself the first player to agree to a contract with the franchise, Brown became regarded as the first to put his signature on one. Robertson had seen Brown play a high school game at Madison Square Garden on an off night while the Royals were in New York to play the Knicks, and had played with and against him in the summers in Cincinnati and outlying areas after Brown settled in Dayton. When Collins called to try to recruit him to the new Indianapolis franchise, Robertson had an immediate suggestion: get Roger Brown.

Brown had been a schoolboy legend during his career at Wingate High School in Brooklyn, both for his play in scholastic competition and on the playgrounds around the city. His talent and status were matched only by that of Connie Hawkins of Boys High, with both forever ranking among the best to come out of the city. They were rivals and casual friends who played with one another on occasion in the summer, but most famously went head to head in the semifinals of the city tournament at Madison Square Garden in 1960. Brown outscored Hawkins 39-18 in their personal duel as Hawkins fouled out before the third quarter ended, but Hawkins' team won, 62-59, after a teammate contained Brown in the final quarter.

As the reigning kings of high school basketball in the nation's largest city, they were pursued constantly by street agents and college recruiters, most of whom were not above slipping them cash and the promise of further rewards – salaries for fake jobs, cars, girls – to lure them to a particular college.

Both became involved to some degree – and exactly what degree became very important in later years – with Jack Molinas, one of the most notorious figures in basketball history. Molinas had been an All-American at Columbia University and the fourth player taken in the

1953 NBA draft. He averaged 11.6 points as a rookie forward for the Fort Wayne Pistons, but was kicked out of the NBA after 32 games for betting on games. He went on to become an attorney and, essentially, a mobster, a central figure in a nationwide gambling operation that bribed college players to fix games.

He and his associates pursued talented but impoverished kids such as Brown and Hawkins, considering them easy marks. According to Hawkins' biography *Foul!* Brown often drove a car owned by Molinas, and both of them took cash from Molinas to play in summer tournaments and benefit games in the area. They also were asked to introduce Molinas to college players, although Hawkins said they were never told the purpose was to find someone willing to shave points, and there's no evidence they ever got around to following through on that request.

Hawkins and Brown took a recruiting trip together to Seattle University, and were promised a handsome payoff by a street agent to enroll there. Hawkins, however, enrolled at Iowa University and Brown at the University of Dayton in Ohio. It would be naïve to think neither received generous compensation for doing so, but that didn't distinguish them from many other elite recruits in that era. Both were declared ineligible after their freshman seasons when their loose association with Molinas was discovered. Neither had participated in fixing a game – after all, nobody bet on college freshman games – but their names had been brought up in testimony for being "intermediaries" in Molinas' gambling ring. Ultimately, they became unwitting victims of the latest attempt by political figures to sweep gambling out of college basketball, kids who took money and other favors from adults claiming to want to help them, without realizing Molinas' gambling involvement. They were blackballed from the NCAA, NAIA and NBA, just as Groza and Beard had been a decade earlier.

But, they couldn't have been barred from the ABL or ABA, which didn't exist at the time. Hawkins played one season for the Pittsburgh Rens of the ABL, for a salary of $6,500, then went on to play three seasons with the Globetrotters. Brown stayed in Dayton and took a job as a machine operator in a General Motors factory, working the night shift. It was a jarring comedown for someone accustomed to star treatment.

"A lot of people didn't like him 'cause he was pretty arrogant," Hawkins said of Brown in his biography, penned by David Wolf. "But I liked his playin' so much, I didn't mind his personality.

"I wasn't no cocksman like Roger," Hawkins added. "He was going steady with half the girls at Wingate."

The banishment from basketball humbled Brown, however. He had nothing to return to in New York, and probably was too embarrassed to want to go back anyway. He was taken in by a kindly couple in Dayton, then met and eventually married Carolyn Jeffries, a nurse. The former schoolboy star and "cocksman" had to hustle to get her, though, proposing three times before winning her hand. She said yes twice and took the required blood tests, but backed out each time before finally agreeing to commit to him in 1964. He was 22, and she was 21. Both worked night shifts and slept during the day. They were enjoying a simple, stable life together with no great desire to upset it when Storen showed up late one morning.

Storen claimed his first act after signing his contract with Bannon was to drive to Dayton to find Brown. Tinkham, who was on hand for the signing, said Storen immediately asked for a check for $500 to take with him as an enticement, although Storen didn't recall that detail.

Regardless of what gifts Storen came bearing, the Browns didn't jump at the opportunity offered by the stranger at their door. Roger, for one, was beyond wary of authority figures, having been wronged by so many in his past – the father who abandoned him, Molinas, and the participants in the system that allowed Hawkins and him to be used as pawns for politically ambitious prosecutors wishing to be perceived as tough on crime. Could he trust this man selling an opportunity in another city? He was about to turn 25 in May, an advanced age to begin a professional basketball career. And even if the opportunity was legitimate, what were the odds this uprooting venture would fare any better than the ABL had in its chaotic season-and-a-half?

Ultimately, he and Carolyn decided they had little to lose. The bosses at the GM plant promised he could return to his factory job if basketball didn't work out, and Storen provided an economic and psychological foundation by lining her up with a nursing position at Methodist Hospital in Indianapolis. That made it practically a no-brainer. He would have the chance to fulfill his childhood dream of playing professional basketball, and an opportunity to redeem himself with no loss of security.

Brown signed sometime in late March or early April for $15,000 and a $2,000 bonus – about what he and Carolyn were already earning with their combined incomes, according to her memory. He did not have a guaranteed contract, but he had competed successfully against NBA players in the offseason and had never lacked for confidence on the basketball court. All in all, it was as great a risk for the Indianapolis franchise as for Brown. Storen had never seen him play, and at the time couldn't have known the exact details of Brown's relationship with the fixers in New York. For all Storen knew, this factory worker whose only competition over the previous five years had been in AAU games and pickup games was another playground legend whose skills were exaggerated.

The Indianapolis group was image-conscious as well. Storen, the ex-Marine, wanted gung-ho men who comported themselves properly and contributed to the community off the court. Fairly or not, Brown represented a potential threat to the desired impression. Thus, no mention was made of the signing of the former schoolboy star whose reputation had been tainted by his association with a gambler.

It would be three months, in fact, before Brown's name appeared in an Indianapolis newspaper. Lewis' name, for whatever reason, would not be published for six months. But their time was coming.

"Guys were falling like flies."

Assembly Required

All these players signing contracts were eventually going to need a coach, and the team they were theoretically going to play for was going to need a nickname, and colors would have to be chosen for the uniforms that would bear that nickname. Those issues were finally resolved, publicly at least, at a press conference at the Marott Hotel on June 16.

The team would be called the "Pacers." None of the newspaper articles mentioned the originator of the unprecedented nickname for a sports team, and it was never clear who that might have been. Various people took or were given credit for it over the years, and some said it had been submitted by a fan. No requests for fans to send in nickname suggestions could be found in the newspapers, however, so it's difficult to determine how a fan would go about suggesting one to a team that had barely set up an office by the time the nickname was announced.

Storen claimed the unique moniker as "singularly mine," and he at the very least appeared to have final approval of it. (He joked in later years the second choice had been "Potholes" because of the treacherous condition of the city's roads.) "Pacers" referenced both the harness racing at the Fairgrounds dirt track across the street from the Coliseum, where the team would play, and the Indianapolis 500 auto race. In harness racing, a pacer is a horse that runs by moving its legs on the same side of its body together, as opposed to a trotter, which simultaneously moves its diagonally paired legs. "Pacer" is not a term associated with auto racing, but in the Indianapolis 500 a pace car leads the field to the start/

finish line to begin the race and returns to lead the pack under yellow light conditions after an accident or debris falls onto the track.

"This name was selected over many others that have been submitted, with the facts in mind that Indiana, as 'King of Basketball' sets the pace in the sport," Storen said at the press conference. "Indiana is known the world over for its 500-mile race where, each May, the pace in auto racing is set; (and) on the mile dirt track near our home, in the Indiana State Fairgrounds Coliseum, some of the world's finest pacer horses have established themselves ... It is with these many facts and the feeling that we, of the Indiana franchise, will set the pace in the ABA that we are taking the name Pacers."

A team logo also was unveiled: an upright, white left hand palming a gold ball inside a blue P. Nobody seemed to notice the seams were those of a tennis ball rather than a basketball. No mention in the newspaper articles was made of team colors, but the logo made it obvious they would be blue and gold. Those were the official state colors. They also just happened to be the colors for Notre Dame, of which Storen was a proud alum. It wasn't announced, but the team also would wear low-cut black shoes, just like the Boston Celtics and Notre Dame at the time.

The coach would be 30-year-old Larry Staverman. He was unknown to basketball fans in central Indiana, with the possible exception of some diehard Notre Dame followers. After playing at a small Catholic college, Villa Madonna, in his native Kentucky, he went on to play three seasons in the NBA with the Royals as a 6-foot-7 forward, beginning in the 1958-59 season. He wasn't a complete stranger to Indianapolis or the Coliseum, having appeared in the Royals' game there in December of 1960, when he scored 12 points off the bench. The Royals later traded him to Chicago for another forward, Dave Piontek.[1] After a season with Kansas City in the ABL, where he was among the league's better players,

---

[1] Piontek later became a television sports anchor in Indianapolis, and later married a woman he had met while working there. After dying of a stroke at age 69 in Scottsdale, Ariz., where he had retired, he was buried in Indianapolis because of his wife's connections there.

Staverman returned to the NBA to play a season for the Zephyrs in Chicago. He moved with the team – along with Leonard and Storen – to Baltimore, but was traded after six games to Detroit for Kevin Loughery. He was traded back to Cincinnati later that season, and retired in 1964.

Storen had met with Notre Dame coach Johnny Dee while in South Bend to check his interest in the job. Dee didn't have any, but recommended Staverman, one of his assistant coaches the previous two seasons. Leonard, who had coached Staverman in Chicago and Baltimore, also put in a positive word for him. Staverman had three games of professional coaching experience, as a temporary replacement. Dee was suspended for two games while coaching the Kansas City franchise in the ABL, so Staverman took over and went 1-1. Later, Leonard became ill while coaching the Zephyrs, and appointed Staverman his replacement for one game, "because you're the only guy who gets along with 'em," Staverman recalled him saying. The Zephyrs lost that game, a hardly unusual occurrence.

The introduction of Staverman was tacit acknowledgement of Robertson's lack of interest in coaching the team in Indianapolis. Robertson's name had been used freely to goose the interest of the local fan base, but an offer was made in May and a coaching hire put off because of that. When Robertson or his agent did not respond to the offer, Storen knew it was time to find a coach — and Staverman had not been the first choice.

Storen, with approval by the board, initially offered the job to Ed Jucker, who had been an assistant coach when Robertson played at the University of Cincinnati, and then won an NCAA championship in 1961 in his first season as head coach, after Robertson had graduated. Jucker's team won the championship again in '62, cementing his reputation as an elite coach, and then lost an overtime game to Loyola for the championship in '63. He stepped down from coaching after two more seasons in 1965, citing health concerns and burnout.

Jucker was animated and volatile, known to jump up and press the timer's button at the scorer's table to sound the buzzer and stop the game, rather than go through the formality of calling a timeout. But he also was sincere, idealistic and well-respected within the basketball community. He emphasized a stingy defense and disciplined halfcourt offense, so some questioned whether his style would be appropriate for professional basketball. He had no professional playing or coaching experience, but his reputation remained intact after his two-year sabbatical from coaching. And, not lost on the Indianapolis ownership group, he had a connection with Robertson from having coached him on the freshman team at Cincinnati.

The *Cincinnati Enquirer* reported the Pacers had offered Jucker a $100,000 life insurance policy to go with a multi-year contract totaling $28,000 in salary and bonuses. That was in the ballpark of the figures reported in the minutes from their April board meeting, which called for him to be offered a one-year deal for $24,000, with a $2,000 signing bonus, another $2,500 for winning the division and another $2,500 for winning the league championship.

He also was reported in the *Enquirer* to have received an offer from the Oakland franchise in the ABA. He ultimately chose stability and prestige over cash, signing a three-year deal with the Royals for $22,000 per season. Introduced at a press conference in Cincinnati on May 2, he had a simple explanation for turning down the best offer: "I wanted to remain in Cincinnati and I wanted to stay in the big leagues." He also said he was confident Robertson would not jump to the Indianapolis franchise. "He's not going to leave the big leagues," Jucker said.

Having lost out on Jucker, Storen turned his attention to another candidate with a connection to the University of Cincinnati. Jim Holstein had been a star player there, finishing his career in 1952 as the school's all-time leading scorer, and went on to play three seasons for the Minneapolis Lakers from 1952-55, two of which brought championships. He finished his professional career playing half a season for Fort Wayne before retiring in January of '56. He was in his sixth season as the head coach at St. Joseph's College in Rensselaer, Ind. when Storen came calling.

Storen talked of a one-year deal at $18,000. Holstein wasn't about to give up a stable job for that kind of risk, and asked for three years at $24,000. He knew the survival rate of pro coaches from his playing days in the NBA, and considered the job doubly perilous because of all the uncertainty surrounding the new league's survival.

Storen tried to assure him he would have sufficient talent to win enough to keep his job.

"You'll have all the horses," he said.

"But if a horse breaks his leg and can't run, I'll end up getting fired, and you know that," Holstein replied.

Their conversations never progressed to the point of a formal offer, and they parted amicably.

Storen was quickly learning that hiring an employed and established coach was going to be no easier than signing players with NBA contract offers. No proven coach was likely to give up a stable position to move and coach a new team in a new league that might not survive beyond its first season, if that. The memory of the failed ABL remained fresh in the minds of the basketball world, and it was impossible to know if the ABA would survive any longer.

Probably the most logical and qualified of the available candidates was Leonard, the Indiana native who had coached in Chicago and Baltimore. He was living just an hour's drive up the road in Kokomo, but he and the Pacers' leadership eyed one another warily. His reputation as a bit of a wild man off the court scared off the image-conscious owners, and he wasn't about to give up a secure position selling class rings and graduation supplies for such a shaky enterprise.

According to Collins, the idea of approaching Leonard was discussed at length, but ultimately rejected. Had he been approached, Leonard likely would have refused. He was curious enough to keep his toe in the ABA waters, however.

DeVoe's notes indicated Storen had been asked to contact Purdue coach George King about coaching the team. King seemed an ideal candidate, having played in the NBA for Syracuse in the Fifties, including the championship series at the Coliseum in 1955. Whether contact was made is unknown, but King likely would have rejected the notion without much thought. He and his staff had just recruited three consecutive Indiana Mr. Basketballs – Denny Brady, Billy Keller and Rick Mount – and his collegiate coaching future was promising.

Another candidate, John Givens, a Kentucky native who had played in the NBA in the early Fifties and coached Indiana high school teams in New Albany and Marion, initiated interest in the job by mailing a resume, but apparently was not interviewed.

Staverman likely was as close to an ideal candidate as Storen was going to get. He had played in the NBA. He had played in the ABL, where the three-point shot had been utilized. He was viewed as a promising coach by Dee and Leonard, and had the experience of two years as an assistant at Notre Dame. He was a congenial, clean-cut family man with five children (ages one through seven), *and* was willing to take the plunge into unknown waters for what was reported to be a one-year contract. His Notre Dame connection didn't hurt, either, from Storen's viewpoint.

He promised to take a firm approach to his new position.

"I'll be boss," Staverman said at his press conference. "If you lose control of your players, then you lose everything."

Unknown to Storen and everyone else involved with the newly-christened Pacers at the time, events had recently transpired in Cincinnati that would have a seismic impact on the franchise in future seasons.

A few hours after the press conference that introduced him as the Royals' coach on May 2, Jucker flew to New York to participate in the next day's NBA draft. He and Wilson stayed up past midnight cramming for the test of selecting the right player with the ninth overall pick. They settled on Daniels, a slender 6-9, 220-pound center from the University of New Mexico, whom they described as inconsistent but promising. They also drafted Sam Smith, a forward out of Kentucky Wesleyan, aware that he had already signed with Minnesota's ABA franchise, and drafted another forward, Tom Washington, unaware that he had signed an ABA contract.

The Royals seemed to be counting on the fact the ABA would not get off the ground, or at least would have to delay its debut a year, which would allow them to sign the likes of Smith and Washington. "If it does get off the ground," an *Enquirer* columnist wrote, "it appears no more than a carbon copy of the old American Basketball League, which didn't have a chance to begin with."

Regardless, the Royals were confident of keeping Robertson, who was described in the *Enquirer* in mid-May as still considering the offer from Indianapolis.

"Oscar ... is not acting like a guy ready to make a jump," columnist Jim Schottelkotte wrote. "He took time out, for instance, to help welcome Mel Daniels, the Royals' No. 1 draft choice, to Cincinnati. According to reports, Daniels was much impressed with the Big O."

Not as impressed as he was with Minnesota's money, however. Daniels signed with the Muskies on June 6, accepting a two-year contract that paid $27,500 the first year and a reported $10,000 bonus. (Daniels many years later would remember the bonus being $15,000.) The Royals' offer, Daniels would recall, was about $14,000, with a $6,000 bonus. His decision was as simple as elementary school arithmetic.

The Royals were operating in cost-saving mode, having turned a profit of just $4,473 the previous season, and figured they would need every dollar they could spare to re-sign Robertson. Upon losing Daniels, they quickly shifted to face-saving mode, as they were the only NBA team that year to fail to keep its first-round draft pick away from the ABA.

General manager Wilson said Daniels had rejected the advice of King, his coach at New Mexico, to sign with the unproven league, and that he had offered Daniels more money than any rookie in franchise history other than Robertson and Jerry Lucas. Daniels wasn't even likely to start for the team as a rookie, he added.

"To sign your No. 1 draft choice just to be signing him at an unreasonable figure is utterly ridiculous," Wilson told the *Enquirer*. "I don't want to be running Daniels down, but he was the ninth player picked and this was a poor year (for talent in the draft)."

"If it's a player we figure we really have to get, it's another thing."

Royals board chairman Ambrose Lindhorst totaled up and rounded off the Muskies' offer as he understood it and came to the conclusion his team had done the prudent thing. "From the standpoint we failed to sign our first draft choice, sure it's bad," he said. "But is it $58,000 bad?"

Jucker, who had participated in the decision to draft Daniels, and later met with him on his visit to Cincinnati, also rationalized the loss. "Maybe it's a blessing in disguise," Jucker said. "He never gave me the impression he had the confidence to make it in the NBA."

Daniels' signing represented a coup for the new league, but didn't merit mention in the Indianapolis newspapers. If only the city could have realized the long-range implications of his bold leap into the unknown.[2]

By mid-June, Storen had assembled a six-person staff, crammed into a small office on 38th St., just a few minutes from the Coliseum. The two members who would prove to be best-remembered over the long term were Bill Marvel, who had worked for Chuck Barnes at Sports Headliners and was brought on as the Pacers' media relations director, and Sandra Wheatley, the receptionist/secretary. She appeared as if straight out of Hollywood, a striking blonde who would have been described at the time – in polite circles – as voluptuous.

"We had the best waiting area in all of basketball," Storen would joke in later years. "Nobody minded sitting with Sandra."

---

[2] The Royals went on to become the NBA team most damaged by the upstart league, as four of their top five picks signed with ABA teams. Dampier was one of them. They also nearly lost forward Bob Love, who had averaged 6.7 points as a rookie, to the New Orleans franchise, but only temporarily. Love re-signed with the Royals in late August. The Royals didn't hold on to Love long enough, though, leaving him unprotected in the expansion draft in 1968. Milwaukee claimed him, then traded him to Chicago during the 1968-69 season. He went on to average 22.6 points over seven seasons with the Bulls and was selected to three All-Star teams. He had a severe stuttering problem. The *Enquirer*, in fact, quoted his stutter verbatim at least once, cruelly poking fun at it. He took a job busing tables and washing dishes after his playing career, but the restaurant owner later paid for him to work with a speech therapist, who helped him overcome his stutter. He later returned to Chicago as the Bulls' Community Relations Director.

Dedicated secretary Sandra Wheatley, posing with a game sponsor, was regarded as an instrumental front office asset in the Pacers' formative seasons.

"She was our secret weapon," Marvel would add. "Everybody loved to sit and talk with her. That was a good asset, really."

She wasn't a showpiece, however. She had plenty of work to do, and her personality and character were at odds with the image assigned to her in a male-dominated profession. Assumed to be flirty and glamorous, she in fact was conservative, not to mention grounded by some harsh realities. She had married young and had a child, but later separated from her husband and became a single parent. Shortly thereafter, her 5 ½-year-old son, David, died of encephalitis. She then shifted from the life of a wife and mother living in the country to a single woman living downtown in Riley Towers, two 30-story buildings and another 16-story structure that qualified as the city's most glamorous residence for apartment dwellers. She secured a stable job as a secretary for the director of metropolitan planning in the City-County Building, drove a green Volkswagen Beetle and worked nights as a waitress to supplement her income. She was in her mid-twenties but looked younger, and thus had to fend off approaches from males ranging from teenagers to those old enough to be her father. One time, a man ran into her car intentionally so he could meet her and ask her out.

Working for the Pacers represented another step toward a fresh start in life, just as it did for some of the players, but it took her two months to decide whether to accept Storen's offer of $125 per week. She had only agreed to interview for the posted position because a friend who worked for the employment agency had begged her to do it so he would get credit for it. She had no intention of taking the job at the time, but Storen was persistent and eventually won her over.

She fit in well with her boss' militaristic approach. She addressed him as Mr. Storen, dressed professionally and performed her job well.

The rest of the operation consisted of promotion director Chuck Finkbiner, ticket manager Mel Brown (a part-time employee) and trainer-business manager Bernie Lareau, who was hired from St. Joseph's College on Holstein's recommendation. Dr. F. Robert Brueckmann served as team physician as a sideline activity apart from his daily practice, and Bill York was brought in by Marvel to assemble and direct a stat crew. It would be inaccurate to say York had been hired, because he and his crew were not paid other than with tickets the first season.

Storen was proving to be an aggressive and adept leader. His no-nonsense work ethic set the tone in the front office, and he knew how to work the media outlets, most of whom were eager to be worked. He fed them raw information they could use as well as helpings of hype to keep things interesting.

"The board was amazed," Tinkham recalled. "He would play games with the press and the press loved it. He was always great copy. Something was always about to happen."

The franchise appeared to be on stable financial ground as well. The founding fathers had each received a letter dated April 10 requiring them to contribute $4,000 immediately and another $10,000 stock subscription by May 10. The plan was for each member to kick in $30,000 before the start of the season, and for the board of directors to be expanded to 12 from 10, for a total of $360,000 in the bank. That would be enough to finance the first season. They knew they were going to lose a great deal of money getting the franchise off and running, but hoped to reach break-even status by the second or third season. The grand plan, as with all ABA owners, was to force a merger with the NBA, at which point the value of the franchise would escalate astronomically.

Thanks to the hustle of Storen and professionalism of the owners, the franchise appeared to be maintaining a pace that was a step ahead of the rest of the ABA. That became publicly evident when it broke out basketballs in June for a one-week tryout camp. Leonard and another Terre Haute native who had played in the NBA, Clyde Lovellette, were hired to coach the players while Staverman and Storen observed.

The initial sessions would become part of the franchise's folklore, but are difficult to detail. According to the memory of some of the people involved, anyone interested in trying out for this new professional basketball team was welcome to put on a pair of gym shoes and take a shot at it. Estimates on the number of participants would vary wildly over the years, running as high as 600-plus in one article written in the Eighties. Leonard in later years would estimate 175. York, already signed on to keep stats, recalled 157. Netolicky, years later, guessed 130. Others simply said more than 100.

The *News*, in the article announcing the hiring of Staverman on June 17, reported the coach would begin work on June 19, a Monday, "screening between 40 and 50 players who will participate in a week-long training camp." That was a reference to the invited players, however. The *Star* ran a photo on Tuesday morning showing a photo of Staverman with Marshall and McGill from a team dinner the previous evening, each of them wearing a sport coat and tie and name tag. The caption reported they would begin practice the following morning at 10 a.m., with an evening scrimmage at 8.

While it's odd that an open tryout attracting more than 100 players out of nowhere didn't merit mention in the newspapers, it's also unlikely so many eyewitnesses would incorrectly remember something in such a consistent manner. The likeliest scenario is that an open practice session was conducted Monday morning, then the draft picks and other invited players reported Monday evening and began working out on Tuesday. In that case, the newspapers missed a great story.

The early workout was delayed, Staverman recalled, because nobody thought to bring basketballs. "Geez, was that my job?" he wondered. The players stretched, ran figure eights and did whatever else anyone could think of to loosen up for an hour or so before balls could be retrieved. Staverman also was surprised to see Leonard and Lovellette on hand to conduct the initial workouts. He hadn't been told of their participation in advance.

"Every guy who was a high school star thought he could play pro ball," Leonard recalled. One hopeful candidate stood out to Leonard most, a young man wearing cut-off bib overalls for a uniform.

"He was a good guy," Leonard recalled, laughing. "He could shoot it."

Leonard in later years claimed he thinned the herd by ordering layup lines, with the directive that anyone who missed one was cut. At the end of the session, he ordered everyone to the end of the court to run "baselines." They ran from the end line to the foul line and back, then to midcourt and back, then to the opposite foul line and back and then to the opposite end line and back. That was one. There would be 14 more, more than enough to induce vomiting throughout the Coliseum. He then ended the session with this proclamation: "If you think that was tough, we're going to double that tomorrow!" "Tomorrow," however, was Tuesday, when only invited players could participate.

Bill Hampton was among the masses who gave himself one last shot at glory, but only one. He had been a starter on the Crispus Attucks High School team that Robertson led to the state championship in 1955 and went on to have a solid playing career at Indiana Central College. He was 30 years old in 1967, but had nothing to lose by trying out – other than his breakfast, which plenty of participants wound up losing.

Years later, Hampton estimated that "at least 100" players tried out.

"It was a whole bunch of guys running around out there not knowing what they were doing – and I didn't either," he said.

"Everybody and his brother was there. It was like a bunch of bumblebees flying around."

Another unknown hopeful, Dick Russell, recalled the first practice lasting about three hours in a steamy Coliseum in which temperatures reached 100 degrees.

"Guys were falling like flies," he said.

Marvel put together a carefully typed, five-page list of 44 players for Tuesday's opening session, complete with hometowns, height and weight, age, marital status, names and ages of children if applicable, and career highlights if available. Hampton was on the list. He apparently had been invited back after Monday's workout, but didn't show. Other players with local connections were on the list as well. A few probably were holdovers from the open tryout.

Regardless of how many players reported for practice on Tuesday, it was a wide-ranging collection of talent. Ages ranged from 19 to 31, and qualifications ranged from first-team all-Big Ten selections to small college standouts to some who hadn't even played college ball.

Robertson was still in limbo, unsigned in Cincinnati but not showing much interest in the group in Indianapolis, either. His older brother Bailey was available, though, and among the players on hand. Bailey Robertson had been a small college star at Indiana Central, earning All-

America honors and setting the school's career scoring record. But he was 31 years old by this time.

Russell, a 6-1 guard, was another curiosity. He was "just" 25, but hadn't attended college beyond a freshman year at Butler. He had led the county in scoring as a senior at Ben Davis High School and received a scholarship to Butler, but left school to get married. His bio noted he had played industrial ball for eight years, during which he played on teams that won three city championships and one national championship, in 1966. From that steady diet of competition, his game was sharp.

Some of the players at the tryout were far more familiar to the public.

Bill Buntin had been voted the first-team all-Big Ten center as a junior and senior after leading the conference in rebounding both seasons. He was voted a second-team All-American as a senior and then became the second player selected in the 1965 draft, when the Detroit Pistons utilized their territorial pick on him. He played in 42 games his rookie season and averaged 15.1 points over an early seven-game stretch, which including a 25-point outing in his fifth game. His performance fell off as he struggled to control his weight, however, and he averaged just 7.7 points his rookie season. He held out for a better contract during training camp the following season, signed late, and was released after 12 preseason games in which he averaged 3.3 points.

McGill, a 6-9 center, had led the nation in scoring with a 38.8-point average his senior season at Utah in 1962, highlighted by a 60-point game against Brigham Young. He also averaged 15 rebounds, and earned consensus first-team All-America honors. His coach at Utah, Jack Gardner, called him "the greatest offensive center in the history of college basketball."

McGill was the first pick in the '62 NBA draft by the Zephyrs, but wound up bouncing between five teams over three seasons. Clearly, something was missing, but he had his moments. He averaged 15.1 points over a 68-game stretch with New York in his second season, one that included a 33-point game against Boston and Bill Russell, and a 41-point game against the Lakers.

He had a balky knee resulting from a high school injury, not to mention an unorthodox style of play. Most of his field goal attempts were sweeping hooks, even from 15 feet, and he shot high-arching underhand free throws. He was credited with inventing the jump hook, a shot he first tried in desperation in a pickup game when Chamberlain was guarding him. Waived out of the NBA, he had most recently played for Grand Rapids in the NABL, and was eager to try again with a "major" league, where the players were full-time employees.

The excellence of his offense, however, was matched by the ineptitude of his defense.

"I don't think he knew how to spell defense," Staverman said, referring to McGill's failure to stick with an NBA team, "but I understand he has been looking much better in a semi-pro league."

Both Buntin and McGill were nationally-known within the basketball world, players who had excelled in college and shown hints of success in the NBA. They ignited some excitement among the team's newborn fan base, and brought some credibility to the tryout camp. Surely players of their pedigree could help a fledging team scrambling.

The first scrimmage on Tuesday evening, free to the public, drew 2,200 fans to the Coliseum. They were given mimeographed sheets of rosters with numbers to identify the players, and a public-address announcer kept them informed of who was scoring. Leonard and Lovellette each coached a team – dubbed Leonard's Lillies and Lovellette's Lovelies – and 41 players participated, suggesting three who had been invited to Tuesday morning's session did not show up. Some had jerseys with their name on the back, but others had to borrow nameless jerseys from one another for their games.

Brown's name hit print in Indianapolis for the first time as he scored 10 points in the opening scrimmage. The bio on the information given to media members said nothing of his banishment from the NCAA and NBA, only that he had played freshman basketball at Dayton. The leading scorer, with 17 points, was a former local star, Bobby Joe Edmonds, who had led Crispus Attucks High School to the state championship in 1959.

Edmonds had found his way to the team practically by accident.

He had been a sixth-round draft pick out of Tennessee State by Baltimore in 1964, drafted by Leonard, but broke his wrist and went back to college to take graduate courses. He was in the Nashville, Tenn. airport one Friday morning, flying to Indianapolis to interview for a high school teaching job, when he crossed paths with Babe McCarthy, who had been hired to coach the New Orleans team. Edmonds was heading up and McCarthy down. As they passed one another, McCarthy said, "Hey, are you Bobby Joe Edmonds?" It turned out he was planning to locate Edmonds on his visit to talk about signing him to the Bucs' roster. They chatted briefly and agreed to talk the following Wednesday.

That weekend, Edmonds went to the Round Table, a lounge just a few miles east of the Coliseum, and ran into Tom and Dick Van Arsdale. Edmonds was telling them he had just run into McCarthy and talked about signing with the New Orleans team when he made eye contact with an Indianapolis sportswriter, Jimmy Angelopolous, who was talking with Storen.

"Hey, there's Bobby Joe Edmonds right now!" Angelopolous said. He and Storen had just been talking about Edmonds as a candidate for the Pacers, so the encounter seemed fateful. McCarthy later offered a contract for $9,500, but Storen came through with a better deal, what Edmonds recalled as a non-guaranteed contract for $12,000, with a $1,000 bonus if he made the team.

Wednesday's scrimmage included just 26 players after a cut was made following the morning workout. Brown and Edmonds stood out again, each scoring 19 points, and Russell emerged with 17 points on 8-of-14 shooting. Aitch had 13 rebounds

Another cut on Thursday sliced three more players. Surprisingly to those who hadn't been watching the scrimmages, Buntin and McGill were among them. Storen was blunt, without naming names.

"From the beginning of the Pacers' formation, we have stressed the point that our Indiana team will be formed by men who are willing to devote 100 percent of their interest and are willing to hustle 110 percent of the time."

Buntin's tryout got off to a bad start at his weigh-in. He told the Pacers he would report to camp at 235 pounds, and was listed as such on the initial roster. But he came in at 265 – far too many for his 6-foot-7 frame. Prone to putting on weight anyway, he didn't do himself any favors with his eating habits. The previous year, the Pistons had played the expansion Chicago Bulls in a series of exhibition games, and the two teams rode together on a bus to some of the games to save money. Schellhase, the former Purdue All-American, was a rookie on that Bulls team, having been drafted 10th overall, and noticed Buntin was carrying a briefcase. Having never seen a basketball player appear so business-like, Schellhase took a seat across the aisle from Buntin, eager to see the contents.

It didn't take long. It was full of candy bars.

McGill had no issues with his weight, but still failed to impress. Staverman was blunt. "McGill plays a great game of girls' basketball," he said. "He wants to be a star or nothing. We want hustling players who'll put out."

Most of the players were doing just that. Former Iowa center George Peeples, who could jump high and do it quickly, blocked a couple of Edmonds' shots during one of the practice scrimmages. Unable to win their battle in the air, Edmonds decided to fight a ground game. "Forget that, I'm going to take you out of the air," he told Peeples. And he did. Peeples fell hard, hitting his head on the court and requiring stitches.

Russell was hustling, too. He stood out again in Thursday's scrimmage with 24 points. Aitch did, too, with 22, hitting 11-of-16 shots. A reported crowd of 3,800 fans attended that one.

Humes led the scoring on Friday with 18 points, hitting eight-of-13 shots. He now was more confident than ever he would have a place on the final roster. He was playing guard, after having tried out as a forward in Chicago, and had been working on his greatest weakness, his perimeter shot.

"It seems things are working out right and everything is falling into place," he told Mittman in the *News*. "This time last year not a thing would fall in place. The people on this club are the opposite of those in Chicago."

Staverman, however, sounded a cautionary note to an Evansville reporter: "I'd say if Larry learns to hit the outside shot he'll definitely have a shot at making the club. I'd estimate his chances now at 50-50."

An estimated 3,000 fans watched Friday's scrimmage, inspiring impressive hyperbole from Denny in the Saturday afternoon *News*. With one scrimmage still to go, he declared the fan turnout for the new team "one of the most amazing weeks in sports history."

Kozlicki stepped forward with 22 points in the final scrimmage on Saturday at the Camp Atterbury National Guard training base in Edinburgh, 60 miles south of Indianapolis. Jim "Goose" Ligon, from Kokomo, added 17 points and 15 rebounds.

All in all, more than 12,000 fans attended the free scrimmages. While not quite "one of the most amazing weeks in sports history," it was still impressive. The Pacers' management team was ecstatic, sensing they had the nucleus for both a strong team and fan base.

Brown led the scoring in the final four scrimmages, after the initial cut had been made, with a 14.7-point average. Edmonds averaged 14.5. Humes was next at 13, and Russell, the guy from nowhere, averaged 12.7.

That presented a problem of sorts. The owners and Storen were looking for "names" who would attract fans, players with All-America or at least all-conference pedigrees, preferably from state high schools or colleges, who had proven themselves against elite competition. But here was an industrial league star standing out among them.

"That SOB is going to make us cut him," Storen said, half-jokingly, late in the week.

Russell felt he belonged. "I kind of mesmerized them with my conditioning and skills," he recalled years later. "They couldn't tell me nothing I couldn't do."

Ligon intrigued as well. The 6-7 forward was well-known in central Indiana as the center on Kokomo High School's state championship team of 1961, which defeated the Manual team led by the Van Arsdale twins in the final game. Ligon was a first-team Parade All-American in '62, but was later arrested for statutory rape and sent to prison for 3½ years. His stay was prolonged because nobody would offer a job to him when he was eligible for release. And, he claimed later, he was made to stay an extra six months to play for the prison basketball team.

Some people in Kokomo considered the allegation a trumped-up charge because he had dated a white woman, but his reputation was stained. In later years, he made school appearances in Kokomo and admitted to mistakes resulting from the swollen ego he had developed as a small-city celebrity, and admitted he had been passed through school without earning his grades because of his basketball ability. Regardless of what was true about his background, he presented a dilemma to the Pacers. He was talented and athletic, and he was local, too. But he had a troubled past, and image was important to Storen and the owners.

The Pacers cut him, but offered him (and six other players) to the Kentucky team in Louisville, by now dubbed the Colonels, which was conducting an open tryout the following week. He made that roster, and later claimed the Pacers cut him because of his reputation rather than performance.

"I'd have given anything to play for them and was quite angry about it," he told reporters there. "They didn't want me because of my (prison) record."

Storen and Staverman denied that charge, stating Ligon had been foul-prone and hadn't rebounded well enough. Leonard, however, backed Ligon's claim indirectly when he told the *Kokomo Tribune* he had stuck up for Ligon in conversations with Storen, Staverman and Lovellette. "Listen, you can't hold a guy's past against him," Leonard said. "Hell, all of us make mistakes at one time or another."[3]

The Pacers' draft picks and trade acquisition, were spotty in the scrimmages. Aitch barely averaged in double figures, as did Dawson

---

[3] The Pacers probably would have been wise to keep Ligon, although they never lacked for talent at forward in the early seasons. Ligon went on to play seven trouble-free years in the ABA, and was selected to one All-Star team. He struggled after his playing career ended, however, and was homeless later in life. Many people tried to help him financially, including the Van Arsdale twins, who had played on the Manual High School team that lost to Ligon's Kokomo team in the 1961 state championship game. None of the other players released by the Pacers made the Colonels' roster, although Richard "Boo" Ellis and Willie Merriweather survived the cutdown to 20.

and Kozlicki, but two of the other "top five" picks struggled. Netolicky averaged just seven points while Dill averaged 6.2.

According to newspaper accounts, 14 players were invited to remain with the team and continue working out in Indianapolis over the summer in scheduled sessions at the Jewish Community Center: Aitch, Brown, Dawson, Kozlicki, Russell, Humes, Marshall, Jones, Netolicky, Purkhiser, Edmonds and two others unmentioned in the newspapers before the camp began – Peeples, who had been a fourth-round pick of Baltimore a year earlier, and center Walt Sahm, an Indianapolis native two years removed from his playing career at Notre Dame, where he set a school record for rebounding average.

Actually, 15 players were kept. One name was inadvertently left off the original list given to the newspapers, and then was passed along inaccurately when updated: Jerry Harkness. Listed as "Larry" on the initial press releases, he had been a first-team All-America in 1963 after leading Loyola to the NCAA championship, and went on to earn Most Valuable Player honors in the East-West All-Star game. A 6-3 forward in college, he struggled with the transition to guard in a partial season with New York, and had been working as a salesman for Quaker Oats in Chicago when the ABA was formed.

That was no small thing in the mid-Sixties for a black man. Harkness' position with the company was stable, and he was being groomed for advancement. He also was being sent into the community to conduct youth sports clinics.

But he still longed to play basketball, and being released by his hometown Knicks had left an emotional itch he needed to scratch. He was moving on with his life, and had rejoined some of his Loyola teammates to play for Benton Harbor in the NABL for a per-game salary of about $150, but a wire service article in the *Chicago Tribune* on Feb. 2 caught his eye. A new professional league was being formed, and Indianapolis was going to have one of the franchises.

Harkness called one of his college teammates, Les Hunter, to talk about the opportunity. Hunter discouraged him, but Harkness decided to take the plunge. The article had not listed an owner for the Indianapolis franchise and none of the newly-announced franchises had general managers or offices yet, so Harkness wrote a letter to Collins at the *Star*. Collins passed it on to Storen, who invited Harkness to try out. The Pacers had nothing to lose, but Harkness did. His bosses at Quaker Oats, who had him on track toward a management position, weren't happy with his decision to leave and didn't promise him a job if he wanted to come back.

He worked out some with Hunter, who had decided to try out for the team in Minneapolis, but wasn't in basketball condition when he reported for the open tryout in Indianapolis. He was among the throng of vomiting players on the opening day of sprints, and struggled with his shot throughout the camp. But he still had some name recognition from his college career and Staverman in particular had seen something in him. When told by Storen and Staverman he had earned an invitation to training camp, he promised to get in shape.

Netolicky was barely hanging on as well. Deep down, he questioned whether he was good enough to play professional basketball, and given the meager salaries of the era and the wealth to which he had been exposed while growing up, his motivation for pursuing it was fragile. In the back of his mind, he figured he likely would return to college, clean up his academics, get his degree and go to medical school to become a doctor like his father. Beyond that, the vacation in Hawaii had left him woefully out of shape, and Leonard's conditioning drills had taken their toll.

"I thought I was going to die," he recalled. "I can remember going back to the room and laying there and thinking I was going to die."

He wasn't ready to give up, though. In a moment of genuine earnestness, he sat down and wrote a letter to Storen, claiming he could play much better than he had shown and was eager for another chance. Like Harkness, he was fortunate to get it.

Plenty of business had to be settled before a roster could be determined, much less a game tipped off. A league meeting was held in Anaheim on July 10, at which time some new-fangled rules were established. At Mikan's urging, team representatives agreed to adopt a three-point basket. It was initially and for a few more years described as a 25-foot shot before someone realized otherwise. The arc placed on each ABA court was 25 feet from the end line, but the basket was closer than that.

The shot had seemed a cheap gimmick when the short-lived ABL introduced it, but Mikan was anxious to revive it so smaller players would have a bigger role in the game. Guards in the NBA tended to shoot layups or mid-range jump shots in transition, or drive the lane for layups in the halfcourt. Mikan thought it would be more entertaining if they flung long shots for bonus points now and then.

He also considered placing an arc on the floor six feet from the basket and allowing just one point for shots taken within it, but didn't push hard for that idea – an ironic one for the game's first dominant center, who had made his living and legend close to the basket.

The ABL's 30-second shot clock also was adopted, six seconds longer than the NBA's clock, to allow teams more time to get off a good shot.

One old-fashioned concession to tradition was made by agreeing to use the 12-foot wide foul lane that had been established in deference to Mikan. The NBA had widened its lane to 16 feet three years earlier to curtail Chamberlain's dominance, but the ABA's decision to stay with the narrower lane was in practical recognition of the fact its teams would play on courts where NBA games had never been played, in arenas and gymnasiums often used for college and high school gymnasiums that used the narrower lane.

Also in July, the Pacers opened an office at 638 E. 38th St. It replaced a jewelry store, and had barely enough room for half a dozen employees to conduct their business. Storen, in fact, remembered working in the back of the store in his early days on the job before it moved out. It was just a couple of miles from the Coliseum, and accessible. Marvel included the office's opening in a press release, and invited media members to stop by and visit.

What the Pacers' front office members really wanted, though, was for people to stop by and purchase tickets. The next – and most crucial – order of business was a season ticket drive to begin on Aug. 1. The drive kicked off formally with a luncheon at the Marott Hotel, which Mikan attended. Marvel's press release to media members was creative: "Tip-off time is 12 noon. Warm-ups will be held in Suite #801. You will be able to get in shape for the game by bending your elbow at this time. Mr. Mikan will be there to participate in the warm-ups."

Suitably warmed up, Mikan gave the luncheon crowd an indication of just how colorful the ABA was going to be. The referees, he said, would be dressed in bright red shirts, with their names on the back in white letters, along with white pants and blue shoes. Even more dramatic, Rawlings would provide a ball with eight alternating panels of red, white, blue, white, red, white, blue and white.

"I'm really hot for this," he told reporters.

Mikan was 43 years old at the time and a decade removed from direct involvement with professional basketball, but he was bringing fresh ideas. He had witnessed plenty of Harlem Globetrotter games over the years, even playing against them on occasion, and was sold on the value of entertainment in basketball. The NBA in 1967 was as drab as its brown ball, and he knew a rival league would have to present something eye-catching to capture the public's attention. The country was undergoing a revolution in fashion and in music, and bogged down in an unpopular war in Vietnam. Anti-establishment viewpoints were becoming so prevalent as to practically qualify as the established position.

Basketballs had been various shades of brown, orange and beige over the years, and white balls were used briefly in the late Thirties, but a multi-colored ball was something entirely different. Mikan liked the idea of a ball that would be more visible to television viewers and fans sitting in the upper rows. Most of all, he thought it would appeal to women.

"All our endeavors were to get Mom to come to the game," he said years later. "If she came, she brought the family.

"The only mistake I made, I didn't copyright it."

Collins had talked with Mikan at the kick-off luncheon and reminisced about the center's appearances in Indianapolis as a player in the late 1940s and early 1950s. Mikan recalled one fan in particular who threw ice at him every time he walked from the floor to the locker room, and never seemed to miss.

Collins in turn declared Mikan the perfect man for the job, ending his column with a strong endorsement. "I have no idea whether or not it was their intent at the beginning, but the ABA owners have put a real tiger in the commissioner's office," he wrote. "And it can't do anything but help the league."

Mikan was equally impressed with the efforts of the Indianapolis franchise and the response of city officials and the fan base. He called it the "Green Bay of pro basketball," a reference to the NFL Packers' rabid small-market fan base.

Outwardly, everything seemed to be going splendidly for Mikan at the time. He told the *News* the only problem he was facing at that moment was "trouble" with the New York franchise. He didn't specify, but he was referring to a two-page letter he had received from Americans franchise representative Mark Binstein on ABC Freight Forwarding letterhead stationery detailing complaints about his performance. A copy had been sent to front offices around the league, including the Pacers.

"We do not feel that your time and interests have been or are pointed (toward making the ABA a second major league)," Binstein wrote.

Fans in Indianapolis knew nothing of the backstage rumblings, however. A buzz about the new professional team was growing, and now it was time to put money behind all those years of mouthed interest in having a major league franchise. More than 100 members of the Chamber of Commerce attended the luncheon at which Mikan appeared, and were divided into teams for an 18-day campaign during which they pledged to call on 1,000 businesses to buy sponsorships or season ticket packages.

Many members of the local business community were primed to pitch in. One example appeared within an advertisement for the L. Strauss men's clothing store in the first section of the *Star* on the opening date of the drive: *"Boost the Pacers! The Season Ticket Campaign starts today – get season or half-season tickets at a good savings."*

The schedule would include 32 home games at the Coliseum, with another five to be played around the state and one more in Dayton,

Ohio – a nod toward Brown's adopted home. Ticket prices for the games at the Coliseum would range from $1.50 to $4. Season ticket holders would receive a quantity discount, so the best seats in the house could be purchased for $116 – just $3.60 per game. Half-season plans were available as well, and could be purchased by credit card – a first for professional sports, according to the Pacers.

By the Pacers' early estimates, a sellout crowd would bring about $21,000 in revenue, assuming none of the tickets had been given away. Season ticket sales would be the lifeblood, bringing immediate upfront income crucial to the financing of day-to-day operations. They weren't going as well as hoped despite the concerted communal effort. Having been without a team for so long, fans weren't accustomed to the concept of buying tickets for so many games in advance. Nor could they be certain the new league would even last a full season, or that the product would be worth their entertainment dollar. A cautious approach was understandable.

By October 1, the team had sold season tickets to just 194 people, accounting for 598 seats, which brought in $49,275.50. Among the adventuresome buyers was Don Kautsky, son of the local basketball pioneer Frank Kautsky, who purchased two tickets through the family grocery store.

Most of the state newspapers continued to offer full-throated support, particularly those in Indianapolis and Kokomo.

"For too long our city has carried a bush league tag," Collins wrote in July. "Except for the 500-Mile Race, a big league sports venture never has succeeded here for any length of time."

The *News* ran a short editorial a couple of days before the ticket drive to encourage fans to take a chance on the new team.

"We believe that the time has arrived when Indianapolis can support major league basketball," it stated.

Up in Kokomo, Gene Conard of the *Tribune* declared Indiana sports fans "hungrier than a pack of refugees" for a successful professional sports franchise, given the failure of the Olympians and the minor league hockey and football teams. He was even willing to handle transactions personally, as the newspaper was carrying a limited supply of tickets.

"If I were you I'd get with the Pacers on tickets," he wrote. "Right now, you can buy admission to 32 home games for the price of $29. So, if you're interested – call me."

Actually, there was no $29 season ticket. The original order form for tickets in the *Star* incorrectly listed a $1 ticket. There would be a $1.50 seat, however, and the discounted 32-game package for that would cost $43.50.

Amid the community ticket drive, Storen wasn't opposed to giving away a few here and there, especially when connected with a promotion. Some of the Pacers played a two-inning softball exhibition game against members of the Indianapolis Indians minor league baseball team before its final game of the season, on Sept. 4. The first 500 children in attendance were given tickets to a regular season game – with the obvious understanding that the parents who took them to the game would have to buy tickets.

The owners also turned to the public for additional financing in September, offering 54,000 shares of common stock at $5 per share, with a minimum purchase of 50 shares. The ownership group's investment – $30,000 each in most cases – had deposited about $300,000 in the team's bank account, but it was going to need much more than that to keep the franchise afloat for a season. Every dollar that could be gained from the public was welcomed, and ticket sales certainly weren't going to be enough.[4]

The business of building a basketball team continued through the summer. The final cutdown of the week-long camp in June hadn't ended the search for talent, and three more players were signed in July — two of them with great local appeal.

Forward Oliver Darden, a member of Michigan's NCAA tournament runner-up in 1965 and an all-Big Ten selection in '65 and '66, had been a third-round draft pick of the Detroit Pistons in '66. Unimpressed with their offer of a contract for $10,000, he went to law school instead.

---

[4] Ultimately, the public stock offering netted just $22,000.

He had been the student body president at his Detroit high school, Western, and an academic All-American his final two seasons at Michigan. He didn't consider himself exceptionally intelligent, just disciplined enough to do the work that needed to be done when it needed to be done. His father, a factory worker at a Ford plant, had set a positive example with a quiet work ethic that provided him with a stable childhood, and he knew he would have to apply himself in school if he didn't want to work in a factory. His ambition at the time was to become an attorney and, eventually, mayor of Detroit.

Law school quickly lost its appeal, however, and his coach at Michigan, Indianapolis native Dave Strack, helped arrange a meeting with Storen. Darden, his wife and Storen sat together in the stands while watching the June tryouts and reached an agreement on a non-guaranteed contract that paid $15,000. It was announced on July 10.

Next came Ron Bonham, Indiana's Mr. Basketball in 1960, on July 30. Nicknamed the "Blond Bomber" because of his shooting ability and handsome features, he had set a single-game scoring record in the afternoon game of the state finals his senior season with 40 points, surpassing Robertson's record of 39. He scored 29 before fouling out with three minutes left in the championship game, when his Muncie Central team was upset for its only loss of the season.

He was a natural. He hadn't picked up basketball until he was in the eighth grade, but adapted quickly. He had an easy-going, star quality, too. He had been a tap dancer as a kid, good enough to appear on national television, and was a member of a singing group, The Originales, which released a 45-rpm record in 1959 with the songs "That Bandstand Sound" and "Lend Me Your Ear."

Perhaps the greatest indication of his popularity was the controversy created by his college recruitment — controversy of his own doing, mostly. He wavered between Purdue and Cincinnati after his high school career ended, finally announcing late in July he would attend Cincinnati, from where Robertson had just graduated. That wasn't an unusual time to make such an announcement in that more relaxed era of college basketball, but on Aug. 29 he took the unusual step of announcing he had changed his mind and would attend Purdue.

That set off a celebration in West Lafayette, where the *Journal and Courier* ran a story headlined "Ron Bonham Will Enroll at Purdue!" Exclamation mark included. Purdue coach Ray Eddy declared himself "elated" and called Bonham "a fine boy, an excellent student and one of the best basketball prospects anywhere."

The news inspired absolute outrage in Cincinnati. *Enquirer* sports writer Dick Forbes charged Purdue with stealing Bonham unethically, and encouraged UC officials to filed a complaint with the NCAA — but added it would be wrong to try to win back "a young man whose word means nothing."

Bonham's mother told reporters her son didn't want to live in a city as big as Cincinnati, and would feel too much pressure playing for Cincinnati's freshman team, which played a competitive schedule against amateur teams and other university freshmen groups. Purdue's freshmen at that time merely played intrasquad games. She also admitted she wanted him to attend an Indiana college rather than go out of state.

Bonham enrolled at Purdue, paid his fees for the semester ($140) and moved into his dorm room. His girlfriend, Lana Lowery, enrolled as well and had her own dorm room assignment. But on Sept. 13, the day before classes were to begin, he and Lana gathered their belongings and returned to Muncie. Reached by reporters, Bonham said he was leaving the decision to Lana.

The *Muncie Star* reported Bonham felt too many restrictions at Purdue – mainly that he wasn't allowed to have his car (a new white convertible) on campus and that he would have to enroll in the ROTC program, like all the other male students. He called Cincinnati coach Jucker and asked if he still could enroll there. He could. Eddy drove to Muncie to have breakfast with Bonham's parents, but was unable to win back their son.

Suddenly, Bonham was a hero again in Cincinnati.

"It takes courage to do what he's doing," Jucker said.

Finances might have been a factor, too. Cincinnati offered full athletic scholarships. Purdue did so only for students from lower-income families, and Bonham didn't qualify.

Bonham's two head fakes spilled a lot of ink in the newspapers in Cincinnati, West Lafayette and Muncie. One letter on the editorial page of the *Muncie Star* said he was "tragic evidence on how the wonderful sport of basketball has been so overemphasized in our schools that it robs the young players of the very strength of character that the educators say it is supposed to develop." Another in the *Cincinnati Enquirer* stated: "What a perverted sense of power the Ron Bonhams of this day and age must have to know that they have two large universities such as UC and Purdue wrapped around their little pinkies."

As a sophomore, in his first season of varsity competition, Bonham started on Cincinnati's 1962 NCAA tournament championship team. He was a first-team All-American in 1963, when he scored 22 points in Cincinnati's double-overtime loss to Harkness' Loyola team in the championship game, and was voted a second-team All-American as a senior in '64. The Celtics drafted him in the second round, with the 16th overall pick, and he was a backup on their championship teams in '65 and '66. The trajectory of his fortunate career met resistance when he was claimed in the '66 expansion draft by Chicago, where he was to compete with the likes of Humes and Schellhase for a roster spot. He and Lana were going through a divorce, however, and he left camp to sort out his personal life.

He spent the 1966-67 season playing for a semi-pro team in Columbus, Ohio and serving a six-month tour of duty at an Army base in San Antonio. The Pacers' arrival seemed fortuitous, offering him the opportunity to live near his hometown of Muncie, an hour north of Indianapolis, play professional basketball again and perhaps have a bigger playing role than in Boston.

The most highly-publicized signing of the summer came on Aug. 7. Jimmy Rayl was an Indiana high school basketball legend out of Kokomo High School, one of the greatest scorers to come out of the state and possessed of one of the most unique personas. He was listed at 6-foot-2 and 145 pounds throughout his high school and college careers, and some thought both figures were inflated a bit.

Regardless of his exact measurements, he was certifiably skinny, and virtually every newspaper story written about him – and there were many – referenced that. Sportswriters dubbed him the "Splendid Splinter," a nickname stolen from baseball great Ted Williams. He also was called "Slim" Jim Rayl in the newspapers, or whatever other nicknames sportswriters could think of to indicate his slight build. One Associated Press reporter wrote that he looked like the "before" picture in a muscle-building advertisement.

Regardless of his dimensions and nickname, two things about Rayl were unanimously recognized: his shooting ability and passion for the game. He was one of the greatest marksmen to come out of the state, a legacy that would last decades past his playing career. He laid claim to once hitting 532 consecutive free throws in a church gymnasium in Kokomo, shooting 10 at a time with friends, but he was best-known as a long-range bomber unopposed to letting fly from beyond 30 feet.

Despite his fragile frame, he played with a passion that bordered on reckless abandon – at least on offense. He had unexpectedly lost his father, Durward "Dude" Rayl, to a heart attack, as a 13-year-old boy, a burden that no doubt weighed on his emotional nature. His four-year-old sister also had died in his youth. But he found solace in basketball, which became practically an obsession for him.

He was a first-team all-state selection as a junior and senior, and became one of the most written-about and highly-regarded players in the state's basketball history during his final season at Kokomo, when he led a team that filled the high school's 7,500-seat gymnasium for every game. He averaged nearly 30 points that season and surpassed 40 five times, including some games that became etched in the state's collective basketball memory.

There was the one, for example, against top-ranked Muncie Central, Bonham's team, when he scored 45 points in a 79-77 victory. He played that one with a 101-degree fever, and at one point chased after a loose ball and collided with the scorer's table, suffering a knot on his forehead and opening a gash over his eye that required four stitches to close.

Collins, before he became sports editor at the *Star*, covered the game and couldn't control his admiration, writing: "With the fabulous Jimmy Rayl scoring an equally fabulous 45 points, the Wildcats shot Muncie Central off the top of Indiana's high school totem pole ..."

Rayl hit 18-of-30 field goal attempts in the game, scoring from "inside, outside, topside and sometimes nearly upside down," Collins wrote.

Corky Lamm, who covered the game for the *News*, waxed poetic: "Sickly, spindly Jimmy Rayl, caught a Bearcat by the tail; wouldn't let him out alive, shot him dead with 45."

Rayl also played a lead role in what became known as the Church Street Shootout, the final game played in the Church Street Gymnasium at New Castle High School. Rayl scored 49 points, but New Castle guard Ray Pavy scored 51 to lead his team's victory.

Rayl set a North Central Conference scoring record by the end of his final regular season, although Bonham would break it a year later. He went on to score 40 points in a state tournament game in Fort Wayne, hitting 18-of-19 free throws. The United Press International account of that one began, "Slim Jimmy Rayl, a nervy fire horse, rammed in a one-hander at the final gun to give Kokomo a spine-tingling 92-90 victory over defending state champion Fort Wayne South Saturday."

Rayl led Kokomo to the final game of the state tournament, where it lost by 38 points to an Attucks team led by Edmonds. Rayl scored 26 of his team's 54 points, and rang up 114 points over the final four games of the tournament, breaking a record once co-owned by Robertson. He also received the Trester Award, a prestigious honor within the state's basketball community, for sportsmanship and academic achievement. Rayl joked in later years about his lack of qualification for the award, but he was a unanimous selection in the voting — perhaps as a tribute to his popularity and consolation for not winning the championship.

Asked on the court after the final game how it felt to receive such a prestigious honor, he was inconsolable. "Aw, it's all right," he muttered, "but to get beat like that …"

He was voted the state's Mr. Basketball in 1959, an honor that went to Bonham, the Van Arsdales and Humes in subsequent years, and then enrolled at Indiana University. After playing sparingly as a sophomore on the varsity, he went on to earn first-team all-Big Ten and third-team All-America recognition as a junior and senior. He set the Big Ten single-game scoring record of 56 points, and did it twice — first as a junior in an overtime win over Minnesota and again as a senior in a victory over Michigan State. He averaged 29.8 points as a junior and 25.3 as a senior, the drop-off resulting from the improved talent around him, namely the addition of the Van Arsdale twins and McGlocklin to the varsity team as sophomores.

The NBA scouts were skeptical of Rayl's slight build. Still, he was a third-round draft pick of the Royals in 1963 and participated in their rookie camp in September. Coach McMahon praised him in the newspaper as one of the standouts of the first day of practice, and he later was invited by general manager Wilson to return for training camp with the guarantee of being kept through all the exhibition games. McMahon, however, told him he only had "an outside chance" of making the team, so Rayl decided not to bother.

He returned to IU to continue working on his degree, then joined the Army Reserves, then went to work for the Goodyear tire company in Akron, Ohio. His position was in management training, but his real purpose was to play for the company's powerhouse AAU team, the Wingfoots. He traveled the country, playing more than 30 games a year against junior college and other amateur teams, and even made overseas trips. A highlight of one was kissing the Pope's ring at the Vatican.

Like the two other former Mr. Basketballs under contract, Humes and Bonham, Rayl seemed an obvious target for the Pacers. The ABA's three-point line made him a natural for the new league, and his name recognition had value as well. He wanted a guaranteed contract to make it worth his while to give up his comfortable job and playing opportunity in Akron, but Storen balked. Finally, he signed a non-guaranteed deal in August, partially at the urging of Leonard, who publicly declared him the outside shooter the Pacers needed. He moved back to Kokomo with his wife, Nancy, his high school sweetheart, and their four-month old son.

While most of the recent Pacers signings had generated little fanfare, or in some cases no mentions at all in the newspaper, Rayl still had enough of a reputation to justify a press conference. He was four years beyond his college career, but unlike Bonham had stayed in the state to play collegiately and enhanced his reputation among fans. His high school coach, Joe Platt, attended the media gathering and was pictured with Rayl in the *Star* while Rayl signed his contract.

"I play a more rounded game, and I play defense for a change," he said, half-jokingly, at his press conference.

It was true that Rayl's body had matured over the four years since college, and so had his game while playing for the Wingfoots. That boded well for his professional opportunity, but without a guaranteed contract his future remained in doubt.

The final league meeting of the pre-season was conducted in Denver on Aug. 18 and 19. Storen represented the Pacers, and, contrary to Collins' glowing tribute to Mikan at the kickoff luncheon earlier in the month, came home unimpressed with the commissioner's performance behind closed doors.

"Overall, I was very disappointed with the conduct of the meeting and with the lack of action on the part of the commissioner's office," Storen wrote in a memo to the owners, citing the lack of an agenda for the meeting as an example.

Some decisions were made, however.

Oakland, which had signed Rick Barry away from the San Francisco of the NBA, was being threatened with a lawsuit. Barry had been paid $48,000 and a $20,000 signing bonus by Golden State the previous season, a bargain for a player who averaged 35.6 points and 9.2 rebounds in his second NBA season. Barry had jumped across the Bay at Oakland's offer of $75,000 per year and a bonus based on ticket sales, plus an option to buy 15 percent of the team – rejecting the Warriors' offer of a $10,000 raise. Oakland's representative at the meeting asked that the other ABA teams share equally any financial damages resulting from a potential judgment, arguing Barry would benefit all the teams and therefore all the teams should support the Oaks.

"After many hours of heated discussion," Storen wrote, "it was determined that the league would share in one-third of the Oakland legal fees and two-thirds of any damages."

United Airlines was adopted as the official airline for the league, which meant nothing to the Pacers as it didn't serve the Indianapolis airport at the time. The U.S. Rubber Co. signed on as a sponsor and provided shoes for the players – Pro Keds, which were a distant second to Converse All-Stars in popularity at the time, but a similar product. Mikan also said he was negotiating with CBS for a national television contract, something he had been all but promising since that March meeting in New Orleans, but had nothing firm to report.

Most relevant to fans, the league officially adopted use of a red, white and blue ball. Mikan had pushed for it from the start amid great skepticism from the owners because he thought it would appeal to women and be visible from the cheaper seats. Regardless of his purported lack of leadership and organizational skills, it stood as one of his triumphs. Mocked at first, it would become the ABA's signature.

Storen, the NBA veteran, had been among those opposed to it, but was won over upon further review. He described it in his memo as "very colorful and better than it sounds."

Storen had kept the Pacers-in-waiting busy throughout the summer. Staverman supervised workouts two nights a week at the Jewish Community Center through August and part of September, although some were excused to attend summer school. Storen also found jobs for those from out of town so they could stay and participate. Aitch and Harkness worked at the Indianapolis Urban League, Darden worked in public relations at Eli Lilly, a pharmaceutical company, and Dill and Netolicky worked at the Indianapolis Motor Speedway.

Their job wasn't too terribly demanding. Hired as "security," they sat in the bleachers most days and napped, or watched testing — one car at a time taking laps around the track, usually. During lunch break, they walked down to the pit area and had lunch with the drivers and their crews. Netolicky was photographed crammed into a race car while Dill looked on.

The players also put on clinics – 56 in all – at schools, playgrounds, parks, community centers and Boys Clubs, and Storen established a speakers' bureau to send players into the community. Rayl and Darden, for example, spoke to 450 boys at the Indiana Boys' School reformatory on its 100th anniversary.

George Peeples and Bobby Joe Edmonds discuss finer points of the game with kids from the Jewish Community Center.

The inaugural training camp would be conducted at St. Joseph's College in Rensselaer, about a two-hour drive north of Indianapolis. Lareau, who had worked for the Chicago Bears when they trained at St. Joseph's, had the connections to arrange the hookup. It would be a full-fledged camp, isolated from the distractions of Indianapolis, and further evidence that the Pacers were ahead of most if not all the other ABA teams in their preparations.

Sixteen players would try out. Purkhiser, who survived the June cut, had since joined the Army and thus was released by the team the first week of September. That left, in alphabetical order, Aitch, Bonham, Brown, Darden, Dawson, Dill, Edmonds, Harkness, Humes, Kozlicki, Lewis, Marshall, Netolicky, Peeples, Rayl and Russell, the unlikely playground veteran.

The agate list of candidates that ran in the *Star* on Sunday, Sept. 10, the day before the beginning of the 12-day camp, marked the first mention of Lewis in the local newspapers. He had been exempted from the summer tryout sessions and no press release went out to announce his signing, so from the perspective of the general public he had been dropped from the sky, a mysterious apparition of unknown origin and quality.

Storen and Staverman ran a serious training camp. The players were housed in a college dormitory, with no televisions to help pass time. Not that they had much time to pass away from the school's tiny gymnasium. They were awakened at 7:15 a.m., had breakfast at 7:45, weighed in, and then practiced from 9:30 to 11:30. After dinner at 5, they returned to scrimmage in the evening from 7:30 to 9:30. Monday's schedule included an afternoon media session, an opportunity for whatever newspaper reporters were willing to make the trek to Rensselaer to talk with players and get photographs.

Staverman got down to business quickly. Denny reported in the *News* that the coach "ran his 16 candidates until their sneakers nearly melted on the refurbished St. Joseph College floor" the first day. Most of the players were in decent shape, thanks to the summer program and disciplined tone established by Storen. Some of the players, in fact, had made significant strides since the June camp, utilizing the group workouts and their own initiative to improve their conditioning. Aitch was reported to have trimmed 22 pounds from his June weight, and Harkness – Jerry, not Larry – had worked himself into near-peak condition by swimming at the downtown YMCA on Senate Ave.[5]

Not all the players were feeling fit, however. Darden and Rayl reported five to eight pounds overweight, according to Lareau, and

[5]   The Senate Avenue YMCA was informally known as the "Colored Y." It had opened in 1913 exclusively for black residents and became a focal point of their community. The Rens had stayed there when playing the Kautskys in the Thirties, as did other traveling teams. It was integrated in 1950. Its membership remained almost exclusively black for a couple of more decades, but whites were welcome. The Van Arsdale twins went there in the summers between their high school and college seasons in the early Sixties in search of quality pickup games. "Dick and I would be the only two white guys there, and we had no problems at all," Tom said.

Darden suffered a sprained knee in one of the first practices. He missed most of training camp, and the first exhibition game. Bonham had aggravated an injury to the heel of his right foot in the summer workouts and lost some of his quickness because of a calcium deposit. He was moved from guard to forward as a result.

Early impressions were premature, but nevertheless reported and intriguing. Bonham, according to Overpeck's story in the *Star*, led the scoring in the two scrimmage games on the second day. Humes impressed with his defensive effort and shooting. Brown looked like "a carbon copy of Oscar Robertson," and "continued to look like the new league's first possible super star with his all-around play." And yet, Staverman said he was impressed with Marshall more than anyone else.

Staverman also began trying to establish a team culture. "If a guy scores 45 points and he's happy even though we lose, I'll fire him," he told his players at one practice. "If you score 30 and we win, then be happy. If you score two and we win, be happy. But if you're unhappy about anything I'm saying, then quit."

As the camp wore on, talent gradually emerged. Conard attended eight practices over five days, and wrote optimistically in the *Kokomo Tribune* of Staverman's coaching and some of the player performances. In one Friday night scrimmage at the end of his visit, Edmonds led all scorers with 32 points, hitting 15-of-23 shots. Brown, Netolicky and Dawson had 23 each. Humes had 17. Rayl hit just 2-of-8 shots, but had a team-high six assists and "hustled more than I've ever seen him," according to Staverman. Perhaps pandering to Conard's audience, or perhaps not, Staverman added Rayl would have received his MVP vote for the game if asked.

There likely were political overtones to Staverman's compliment. Not long before that, perhaps the previous day, Rayl had left camp briefly after arguing with the coach. His shooting and his popularity were valuable attributes, though, and Storen and the owners no doubt wanted him to succeed well enough to justify keeping him, because his name recognition would sell tickets.

With the first exhibition game and roster cut looming, the scrimmages became more intense. Dawson and Lewis squared off and nearly came to blows in one, and Dill and Netolicky in another. It was a stressful time for the players, most of whom did not have guaranteed contracts and did not have desirable jobs waiting for them if they failed. "Being away from your family and not knowing what the future was going to hold, it was difficult," Darden said.

Conard, meanwhile, continued to double as a volunteer ticket salesman, this time for the opening exhibition game the following Tuesday at St. Joseph. "It's an hour's drive, and if you're interested call me here. I have 50 tickets right now," he wrote at the close of his column.

The first time a Pacers team took the court against an actual opponent came on Sept. 28, at the Alumni Gym in Rensselaer. The story in the *News* claimed 2,100 fans turned out, while the *Star's* story claimed 1,100 fans attended. It was unreported whether they had been charged to attend, but they probably paid $1 or $2.

Those who showed up saw the Pacers defeat Minnesota, 100-92. Brown scored the first two points in franchise history, if exhibition games count. Lewis, the mysterious guard who had gone unmentioned in the newspapers, led the scoring with 18 points and was "fast becoming the team's floor leader," according to Denny's story in the *News*. Netolicky, starting at center, scored just one point, but his backup, Peeples, scored 15 and grabbed a team-high eight rebounds.

Daniels, the rookie who had rejected Cincinnati's offer to play in the NBA, led the Muskies with 22 points and 15 rebounds despite fouling out with more than six minutes remaining. He told Denny he had struggled with second thoughts over the summer about his decision to sign with the new league, but was increasingly confident it would survive.

Russell, the summer sensation, never got the opportunity to play a professional game, even an exhibition in a small college gymnasium. He had been released the previous day. No mention of it was made in the newspapers despite the compelling story of his attempt to jump from an industrial league team to a professional team eight years after graduating from high school.

He took the news in stride, at least in the long run. He had done all he could do to make the team, supplementing his summer workouts with the other players by running, swimming, jumping rope and abstaining from alcohol.

"So when they cut me, I couldn't say I should have done more," he recalled. "I was thankful to the Lord, He blessed me with talent. I had some fun. It was who you know and not how good you were. I understood. They wanted somebody to be a draw. That's just business. I accepted it."

Storen was honest about the reason for the dismissal in a press release the Indianapolis newspapers didn't use.

"Russell is certainly a leader when it comes to displaying the 110 percent that we are asking of all our players," he said. "The decision to make this cut was made by the lack of Russell's background in basketball."

In other words, he lacked name recognition. He also lacked the refinement of players with four years of college experience, and the combination of those two factors was lethal.

Russell went home, re-entered the real world, and worked 38 years for the Ford manufacturing plant in Indianapolis. He went back to playing in the industrial leagues, and occasionally played in preliminary games before Pacer games at the Coliseum.

The Pacers lost to the Muskies in their second exhibition, played at New Castle High School. The following day, the ax swung again. Humes and Marshall were released. It was an abrupt ending for both, given their solid play in practices and scrimmages, but the lack of playing time in the games dropped a hint. Both had played less than two minutes in the first game. They played more in the second, long enough for Marshall to score 11 points on 4-of-6 shooting and Humes five points, but Staverman and Storen had made their decision.

The release of Humes required explanation, given his respected name within the state and the optimism that had surrounded his signing.

"We were very disappointed Humes was unable to make the ball club," Storen told Denny in the *News*. "We hope Larry will get picked up by another team because we think he deserves a place in this league.

He has a lot of ability and desire, but he didn't fit into the overall program with our other guards."[6]

The cut ran deep for Humes. What about the 95 percent odds management had placed on him making the team? Why had two games been scheduled at his former high school? Why had they given him that $2,000 bonus? The harsh truth was that signing Humes had seemed a big deal in the intoxicating early weeks of the franchise, but that was before Dawson signed a guaranteed contract, before Harkness wrote his letter to Collins to request a tryout, before Bonham and Rayl were signed as free agents, and before Lewis stepped out of the shadows.

Years later, Humes remained puzzled by the proceedings. "It was a strange situation," he said. "It was a done deal and then overnight some things changed."

None of the players without guaranteed contracts felt secure before the final cut, including the in-state products Rayl and Edmonds. They were roommates in training camp, and tried to boost one another's spirits by reminding one another of the homecourt advantage they each possessed. It turned out not to help Humes, but surely the front office would favor local flavor in most cases.

That advantage was evident away from the basketball court occasionally. Edmonds recalled riding with Rayl to get a beer one night during camp. Rensselaer was a dry town, so they had to travel to a nearby community. On the way back, Rayl was driving his Shelby Cobra nearly 100 miles an hour down a two-lane highway, leaving Edmonds in a mild panic when they saw lights from a police car flashing behind them.

Rayl pulled over, hopped out of the car and shouted, "Hey, boys!" The officers recognized him immediately. One of them, in fact, had been at practice that day. Asked who was in the car with him, Rayl said, "You remember Bobby Joe Edmonds, don't you?" "Yeah, come on out here, Bobby!" one of the officers said.

---

[6] Storen kept his word and arranged a tryout for Humes with the Kentucky Colonels, but the twice-burned guard's heart was no longer in it and he was soon released.

They all chatted awhile. One of the officers asked for tickets to the opening game. Edmonds gladly offered his. As Rayl and Edmonds returned to their car, an officer said, "Now, Jimmy, just cool it from here."

Rayl peeled out and headed back to camp.

The roster still was at 13, one over the limit, after the release of Humes and Marshall, but that detail was resolved a couple of days later when Dill – the Pacers' tallest player at 6-11 but also the skinniest at 210 pounds – was traded to Pittsburgh. The Indianapolis papers reported the Pacers received cash and a draft pick. The *Pittsburgh Post-Gazette* reported it as an "if" deal, meaning the Pipers would only have to compensate the Pacers if they decided to keep Dill.[7]

And that was that. The 12-man roster for the first season was set. The final decision had been whether to keep Harkness, Humes or Marshall for the final guard spot. Marshall was at a disadvantage, lacking Humes' connection to the state and Harkness' maturity and pedigree. Harkness edged out Humes because ... well, by the flip of a coin, practically. They were similar players in many respects, but Staverman and Storen were impressed with the initiative Harkness had shown by giving up a good job to try out for the team, the effort he had invested

---

[7] The Pipers kept Dill, and were happy to do so. His career there began with promise as he became a starter and scored in double figures 14 times in an early 18-game stretch, with eight points in two of the others. Injuries took their toll, however. He developed ankle and knee issues, and missed games with the flu as well. He later suffered a concussion when Oakland's Jim Hadnot threw an elbow to his head, causing a hard fall that left him in the hospital for five days with a concussion. He played sparingly at the end of the season, then collected his playoff share as a member of the Pipers' championship team and returned to Michigan to attend law school and begin practicing. He had a long, successful career in his hometown of Saginaw. His lasting memory of his season in the ABA was getting to play with and watch Hawkins. "Best player I ever saw," he said. "It was 'show time' every night. And he was a class guy." Storen, by the way, didn't recall receiving compensation for Dill.

in getting into shape for training camp, where he was the best-conditioned player, and his general maturity.

Harkness had felt a lot of pressure during camp, having sacrificed so much in his effort to make the team. He had a wife back in Chicago, and no job to fall back on if he failed. Conscientious by nature, he didn't play well in the early scrimmages, but settled in just in time.

"I thought for sure I was gone; I really did," he said years later.

Like Humes, he wasn't a shooter, practically shot-putting the ball from the perimeter. He was an able and willing defender, though, better than anyone else in camp. Staverman, frustrated with Rayl's effort during one training camp scrimmage, had pulled Harkness aside and told him to hound Rayl relentlessly to bring more out of him.

Harkness scored 13 points in the second exhibition game and hit all three shots, including a three-pointer. That game rebutted his greatest weakness, and might have given him the edge. The respect he already was earning from his teammates couldn't have hurt, either. Some of Harkness' teammates compared him to a pastor because of his maturity and gentle demeanor. He had a certain chemistry with Brown and Lewis, too, which couldn't have hurt. Harkness and Lewis had met the previous year when they played against one another in NABL games in Michigan. Harkness and Brown had known one another in high school in New York, having competed against one another in basketball and track.

Harkness, in fact, recalled an episode that spoke not only to their relationship, but their personalities. After Harkness won the 1,000-yard run in the city track meet, he stood doubled over while trying to catch his breath. Brown, a high jumper, sidled over and said, "Why do you do yourself that way? All I gotta do is jump over that bar, and I get the same medal you do."

Thrilled as he was to make the team, Harkness never lost empathy for Humes.

"It must have been really, really hard to make that final decision," he recalled. "(Humes) scared me to death. I was really worried about him. He was such a hard-worker, he was aggressive, he did well under the boards and we were similar in a lot of ways. I thought he shot a little better than me. I didn't know which way it was going to go."

Most likely, it went the way it was supposed to go, as the passing years would indicate. Humes returned to a teaching and coaching career in Indianapolis high schools and at Indiana Central College. Upon retirement, he worked part-time as an usher at Pacers games. He didn't become wealthy and his fame faded with time, but he lived a stable, contented life. He and his wife stayed together and raised successful children. Who knows? The lifestyle of a professional athlete might have brought many distractions of the type that disrupt the lives of many players, and his career might have been brief, anyway.

Still, coming so close and not making the team was a crushing blow for Humes. As for Harkness, destiny awaited.

More exhibition games followed in rapid succession, as the Pacers worked to justify the "Indiana" in their name.

They played at Lebanon High School, 20 miles northwest of Indianapolis, where they easily defeated Hawkins and Pittsburgh, then lost in overtime to the Pipers the following night in Nappanee, another northern Indiana town. [8] Harkness, his confidence boosted by surviving the final cut, scored 12 and 17 points off the bench in those games.

After a night off, the two teams met again at the high school in Scottsburg in southern Indiana. The Pacers lost that one by 12 points, but Rayl had his first big game with 20 points and hit two three-pointers. The final exhibition was played farther south in Madison, in what was supposed to be a homecoming for Humes. Without him, the game drew less than 1,000 people, and many of those left at halftime according to sports editor Graham Taylor's account in the *Madison Courier* the following day.

Taylor stayed for the entire affair, but left with an unfavorable opinion.

"Yesterday's folly was filled with errors and mistakes," he wrote, adding, "the crowd of viewers left the gymnasium wondering what Rick

---

[8]   Fun fact to know and tell: Nappanee is the longest name in the U.S. that contains each of its letters twice.

Barry or Oscar Robertson would do against the type of competition floored by Indiana and Pittsburgh."

He added that Bonham was balding and slower than in high school and that Rayl had a "pot belly" and was yanked for poor defense in the second quarter. Noting the Pacers were returning in February for a regular season game, he concluded they would "have to prove their worth to local fans before that time, or the empty feeling will continue to prevail..."

Only three players earned a passing mark from Taylor: Dawson, Lewis and Edmonds. Dawson was the game's leading scorer with 18 points, and hit a game-winning three-pointer at the buzzer over Hawkins' outstretched hand for a three-point victory that left the Pacers with a 3-3 exhibition record.

It was a harsh review, but hardly void of truth. Storen wasn't seeking truth, however. He was trying to drum up interest in a new team. He clipped the article and passed it on to Marvel, jotting a note in red ink that read, "Bill: Please work on the knowledgeable Mr. Taylor. Thx – Mike."

Brown led the scoring in exhibition play with a 17.2 average on 62 percent shooting. Lewis was second (12.2), but shot just 34 percent. The other double-figure scorers were Peeples (10.7), Harkness (10.5) and Dawson (10.2). Netolicky, the highest draft pick on the team, averaged just 7.5 points. Kozlicki, who had merited a guaranteed contract, averaged just two. They, however, likely suffered from lack of shooting opportunities on a team in which guards trying to make a favorable impression dominated the ball. Six of the seven players who scored more than Netolicky took more shots than he did, but he hit half of what he got and led the team in rebounding.

The opening game was six days away. Just where the Pacers were among the other ABA teams was impossible to measure. But, contrary to the prediction of many within the basketball world, the league was going to begin play. For the moment, that was victory enough.

The roster was set, and the lineups established. Lewis and Dawson would start at guard, Darden and Brown and forward and Netolicky at center. Darden, having been injured throughout much of training camp, had feared being cut, and was surprised to wind up in the starting lineup. The bench would consist of Rayl, Harkness, Bonham, Aitch, Peeples, Edmonds and Kozlicki.

There were plenty of connections.

Of the 12 players on the first roster, three were from Indiana – Rayl and Edmonds had graduated from high school in 1959, and Bonham in 1960. Rayl had played against Edmonds in the championship game of the state tournament as a senior, and against Bonham in hotly contested conference games. Five of them had played against one another in the Big Ten Conference – Darden (Michigan), Rayl (Indiana), Aitch (Michigan State), Peeples (Iowa) and Kozlicki (Northwestern). Harkness and Bonham had played against one another in the NCAA championship game in 1963. Bonham, in fact, had defended Harkness well enough on the final possession of the overtime period to force Harkness to pass off for what turned out to be a game-winning tip-in at the buzzer. Harkness and Rayl had played against one another as juniors and seniors in regular season games, both won by Loyola. Peeples and Darden had taken a recruiting trip together to the University of Louisville, but decided not to help the southern institution break its color barrier.

Relevant to the time, seven of the 12 were black. That amounted to a bold statement in 1967. Most NBA teams were adhering to an unspoken color barrier that kept rosters half-white at the bare minimum. Even the New York Knicks and Los Angeles Lakers, representing the nation's largest and most cosmopolitan cities, conformed. Black players, however, were making gradual inroads. Joe Falls, columnist for the *Detroit Free Press* at the time, wrote that the U.S. population in 1966 was 90 percent white, but 47 of the NBA's 99 players were black. Thirty-one of those 47 were starters, and 14 of the 20 players in the 1965 All-Star game also were black.

The ABA teams, all bent on survival, were playing it similarly safe, particularly those in the south. The Kentucky Colonels, New Orleans Bucs and Dallas Chaparrals would carry no more than four black players at any time during the regular season. Although the NBA had first employed black players in 1950, the Olympians had none in their four seasons. Now the Pacers were pushing the envelope by becoming the only professional basketball team made up mostly of black players – seven of the 12.

The Civil Rights movement was in full roar in 1967, and Indianapolis by its conservative nature was slow to keep up with societal changes. Local newspaper headlines still referred to black people as "Negroes," and it had been only a couple of years since articles made a point of identifying blacks as such, whether it was relevant to the story or not. Black professional athletes were about to settle into the city for the first time, and they were more educated and worldly than the average citizen. All but Brown had attended college for four years, all had traveled extensively throughout the country and all were well-paid by the standards of the era, earning roughly double the average income at the time.

Housing, though, was a challenge for some of the black Pacers. Lewis bought a house just east of the Coliseum. Edmonds kept it simple and moved in with his parents just a few miles west of the Coliseum. Others dared to attempt to rent apartments in buildings intended for whites. Aitch's wife, who was white, rented an apartment in a new complex in the Meadows area a few miles east of the Coliseum because the managers were unaware her husband was black. Harkness came by shortly after that, but was told all the units were filled.

It wasn't a new experience for him. After being transferred from New York to Chicago by Quaker Oats, he had tried to rent an apartment for his family near the Loyola campus. He was told, "Jerry, we're just not ready for this yet." He rented a place on the south side instead. Now, however, he had political connections to intervene on his behalf. His wife had been raised a Catholic, and through church connections in Chicago was directed to Bill McGowan, a young Indianapolis native and Notre Dame graduate who was becoming part of the city's power structure. McGowan, who was white, started by calling an apartment complex at 61st and Keystone Ave. and telling them he was looking for housing for a Pacer.

"We already have one!" came the immediate and loud response.

One, meaning a black player. That was Darden, who already had been granted an apartment.

"I was really embarrassed," McGowan recalled years later. "I didn't think it would be that hard. I didn't realize how bad it was."

McGowan then called civic leader Bob Welch, a residential and commercial real estate developer who owned the Gaslight Square apartment complex, a three-year-old development at 38th and Post Rd. that was reasonably close to the Coliseum. Welch saw that the Harknesses were admitted.

Darden had become the "one" to get his apartment only by threatening to sue. He and his wife visited a few complexes and were told nothing was available. Around the fourth or fifth attempt, they knew something was amiss. Storen was putting heat on them, wondering why they hadn't moved out of the Holiday Inn where the Pacers were footing the bill. Darden explained, and when Finkbiner went with them to look for a place, the truth became apparent. Darden finally was granted an apartment on Keystone Ave. at a newly-constructed complex after his threatened lawsuit.

"Indianapolis was in a time warp," Darden said. "I was surprised.

"But once we got in, it was fine. The neighborhood kids kept bugging me for autographs. I thought, Hell, I had to threaten them to get in here, and now that I'm in here I'm the neighborhood celebrity."

The Pacers' preseason ticket drive got a final boost, from Barry of all people, on Oct. 9, five days before the season opener against Kentucky. Barry, who had been ruled ineligible to play the first season for anyone but Golden State by a California court, came to town to talk with media members. He was on Oakland's payroll, and would earn his salary as a goodwill ambassador for the league and analyst for the team's radio broadcasts, but the Pacers paid $668.90 for his appearance, some of that no doubt for travel expenses. He performed his duties well, explaining his reason for bailing on the NBA (simple economics) and praising the quality of many of the ABA players who had been squeezed out of the NBA's exclusive club.

Shortly after Barry left town, Robertson's status became official. He ended his holdout on Oct. 13, one day before the Pacers' opener and three days before the Royals' opener, (20) by signing a contract to stay in Cincinnati. The *Enquirer* reported it as a three-year deal for an estimated $115,000 to $125,000 per season with "a number of unusual clauses" that could bring added bonuses, and use of a car. It kept his salary comfortably within the upper echelon of NBA superstars.[9]

The news came as no surprise to Storen or members of the ownership group, who had long given up hope of landing the hometown superstar. Storen had told newspaper reporters during the second week of training camp the Pacers' offer was still open for Robertson to play with the team, but knew it would take some sort of miracle – such as the Royals completely botching the negotiations – for Robertson to sign anywhere but Cincinnati. In fact, Storen said years later he never considered landing the Big O a possibility in the first place. He had become acquainted with Robertson while working for the Royals, and didn't view him as the type of person to give up his security and status in the NBA for a new and lesser league.

Collins always believed Robertson might have been persuadable early on. He recalled driving to Cincinnati with Robertson's high school coach at Attucks, Crowe, shortly after the franchise was formed to present an offer of $150,000 annually, which would have made him the highest-paid player in basketball. "Is that a firm offer?" Robertson asked, according to Collins. Assured it was, Robertson asked for something in writing. Collins passed on the request to Storen, who came back with an offer of $116,000.

"What the hell are you doing?" Collins asked.

"Well, you've got to leave yourself room to negotiate," Storen said.

"You idiot, Oscar doesn't negotiate," Collins said.

Collins believed Robertson's primary motivation was to get an offer to force the Royals to improve their offer. Whatever the Pacers ultimately offered, their heavily-reported interest at least accomplished that.

"If (the Royals) wouldn't have countered with something close, I'm positive he would have come here," Collins said year later.

Storen didn't remember it that way and didn't agree. Robertson in later years shrugged off the Pacers' interest as "pie in the sky." Regardless

---

[9] The holdout didn't seem to affect Robertson much. Despite just a couple of practices with the Royals, he scored 23 points in their opener at Detroit, then had 41 with eight assists the next night back in Cincinnati against San Francisco.

of the amount of the offer, the Pacers at least had made a sincere attempt to pull off the coup of landing one of the game's all-time greats. A plan for a contract offer had been drawn up in March by Michael Quinn of Peat, Marwick, Mitchell and Co., a downtown accounting firm. Using Robertson's salary for the 1966-67 season of $96,000 as a guideline, their offer called for him to be paid a salary of $71,000, with $25,000 deferred annually for 10 years. It would be guaranteed against injury.

On April 25, a board meeting had been conducted at the Holiday Inn Northwest that included all board members, along with Collins and Storen. The second order of business that evening, after discussing the Coliseum's steep rental demands, was Robertson's contract. It was resolved to offer $100,000 in cash and $25,000 worth of common stock. Tinkham was to write a letter formalizing the offer. DeVoe's notes from that month listed other possible enticements, including a $200,000 life insurance policy, financial interest in Burger Chef franchises owned by Treece, a ghost-written syndicated column, a new car each year, a rented home for his mother and new suits.

It's unknown whether those perks were offered or merely ideas. Either way, the Pacers had failed in their longshot fling to land the local legend. The Van Arsdales, Dischinger and McGlocklin all stayed in the NBA. So, too, did Schellhase, who, having played his rookie season in Chicago, met Storen at the Indianapolis airport over the summer to talk about signing with the Pacers, but decided to return to the Bulls.

The Pacers also had not signed their first-round draft choice, Walker. Clearly, they were going to have to try to make a go of it with a realistic roster for a first-year team in a first-year league — one dotted with a few promising players but void of established talent.

There would be no shortcuts to success. Not yet, anyway.

"I'm sure glad someone thought of this league."

Off and Running (and Winning)

And so it began, 14 years after the death of the Olympians and about nine months after the frenetic process of birthing a franchise had begun. Finally, on Saturday, Oct. 14, the Pacers were going to play a real game against a real opponent, the Kentucky Colonels. The fuse had been lit for months, even years, creeping closer and closer to this big bang moment of truth.

The response from the community had been impressive from the first of those summer scrimmages in June, but neither the owners nor front office members knew quite what they were getting into. Would this new team in this new league with these crazy ideas really take off? Would it even survive one season? They were about to find out.

The support had been beyond reasonable expectations. Government and community leaders had jumped to its cause from the start. Collins, although not an investor, qualified as a founder and made sure the *Star's* sports department provided coverage that was generous in both quantity and tone. It published a 20-page tabloid insert — perhaps the first of its kind for the newspaper's sports section — on Thursday, two days before the game.

The afternoon *News* was on board as well. Its beat reporter, Denny, reported on every development with enthusiasm, and it ran a rare front-page color photo in its Friday edition featuring Wheatley, Brown and Bonham posing with the ABA ball. Wheatley, wearing a gold sweater, was allowed away from the grind behind her front desk in the 38th St.

office long enough to pose for the photo. Brown and Bonham wore Pacer warmup jackets – "outside jackets," the photo caption called them – and put on their friendliest smiles.

The next day, on the afternoon of the game, the *News* ran a gung-ho editorial. It was headlined "Good Luck, Pacers," and finished with a hearty endorsement: "Indianapolis can show that it is strictly big league by giving the Pacers whole-hearted support. The Hoosier capital must stand behind the team if it is to succeed and the community is to attract more professional sports."

The *Star* plastered its Saturday game preview across the top of its first sports page with a banner headline and oversized head shots of Staverman and all five starters: Lewis, Dawson, Brown, Darden and Netolicky. The *News'* preview, meanwhile, described it as "the long-awaited, and hopefully successful, debut ..." The *Courier-Journal*, by contrast, published a 10-paragraph story under a one-column headline to advance the game, with no photos.

Objectivity clearly was secondary to the cause of upgrading the city's sports landscape. The newspaper reporters and editors wanted the franchise to succeed as badly as anyone, for their own business and pleasure.

Mikan returned to Indianapolis for the game, one night after the ABA debuted with a game between Oakland and Anaheim in Oakland. The Pacers' ownership group hosted a dinner for him at the Woodstock Country Club the evening of the game. They didn't have to rush, because the game wouldn't begin until 8:30 p.m.[1] Mikan helped himself to two large steaks.

The trip from Woodstock at 1301 W. 38th St. to the front gate of the State Fairgrounds where the Coliseum sat at 1202 E. 38th St. was just 2.7 miles. The Pacers office at 638 E. 38th St. was more than halfway along the way, on the left side of the road heading east. As the members of the founding group made their way to the game in separate cars, they

---

[1] For the public, the Pacers held a tipoff banquet at the Elks Club on Thursday, two nights before the game. Tickets were $5 per person, and the newspaper advertisement specifically mentioned "ladies invited."

The only known photo of the Pacers' original team, taken after practice.
Front row: Ron Bonham, Bob Netolicky, Matthew Aitch, Jimmy Dawson, Bobby Joe
Edmonds, Oliver Darden, Jerry Harkness.
Back row: Coach Larry Staverman, Ron Kozlicki, George Peeples, Roger Brown, Freddie
Lewis, Jimmy Rayl, trainer Bernie Lareau.

ran into a traffic jam. It didn't dawn on some of them that the game was the reason for it. Chuck DeVoe assumed there had been an accident.

Collins was traveling the same road from his house near 38th and Kessler, near Woodstock. He was more attuned to the passions of the fan base in the city, and had experienced his share of vehicular issues getting to a game. "This is the first time I've ever enjoyed being in a traffic jam," he told his wife on the way to the game.

But Tinkham, driving the car in which Mikan was riding, was doing a slow burn. The Pacers already had a strained relationship with the State Fair Board, which operated the Coliseum, and Tinkham assumed it must have scheduled another event on the fairgrounds that same evening – perhaps a cattle show. What if he didn't get the commissioner to the game on time?

Tinkham was haunted by another worry, too.

"What happens if we don't make a basket?" he asked Mikan.

"What?!" Mikan asked, incredulously.

"What if we just don't make a basket?"

It had been a long, arduous process to nurse the franchise to its season-opener. Hints of paranoia could be forgiven, but a shutout was highly unlikely. The public response to that point had been enthusiastic, and Storen was determined to introduce the team with a splash, no matter what it took.

Merchants within the Eagledale Shopping Plaza on the city's west side sponsored the game, and had been given 3,000 tickets to distribute. They also hosted the players on Friday evening, the night before the game, from 6:30 to 7:30, when they would give away most of their allotment. A shooting exhibition was scheduled, but rain forced everyone inside one of the stores, where the players signed autographs and tickets were passed out. Tickets also were available for sale at all 22 Tuchman Cleaners locations in the city, and another 150 tickets had been sold at the front desk of the *Kokomo Tribune.*

Storen further "papered the house" by giving away tickets to various civic groups, youth organizations, police and fire units and military personnel. He had no way of knowing how many of the free tickets would be used, though, or what kind of walk-up sale to expect.

Chuck DeVoe in later years praised Storen for assuring the sellout, even if it meant passing out too many free tickets.

"I'm not sure how much he papered that night, but he was very good at that," DeVoe said. "That was one of our better smoke and mirror deals."

Storen had honed the strategy in Cincinnati by sending coupons for $1 tickets to schools throughout the area and letting the kids in the back door by the bus-load. One dollar wasn't much income, but it was more than nothing. He always distributed the free or discounted tickets discreetly, so the fans who paid full price wouldn't be offended. He also made it a point not to provide free tickets to his owners, believing it was important for them to set an example, but told them their friends could call the office and receive tickets. Stat crew members, newspaper employees and others connected to the franchise were able to pick up tickets for the lesser games and pass them out. One stat crew member, Bob Bernath, learned in later years people tended not to show up when given free tickets, so he charged them $1 and gave the money to the Tabernacle athletic program.

The local newspapers predicted a crowd of 7,000 to 8,000 in the Coliseum, which had a seating capacity of 9,135. Down in Louisville, the *Courier-Journal* reported about 5,000 fans were anticipated. As it turned out, the passion and hunger of the local fans exceeded the most optimistic hopes, as did Storen's marketing talents.

Years later, Storen would recall being told on the afternoon of the game a sellout was anticipated. And when Denny dropped off the afternoon *News* to him at his office at about 4 p.m., it all sank in.

"(Ticket manager) Mel Brown came in and said we were clean," Storen said. "And I remember getting the afternoon paper and we had this unbelievable coverage. I was sitting in my office alone and I started crying. All this time and all this effort and all this work. There wasn't anything else you could ask for. It was really emotional."

Whether Storen could have known in advance the game would sell out is debatable. After all, it was impossible to guess whether all those free tickets that had been passed out would be used. Regardless, he had every reason to be emotional over the birth of this baby. From that initial meeting in Lafayette, where the seeds for a franchise had been planted, the gestation period had included blood spilled by the players in the open tryouts and training camp, sweat from hustling front office members and tears of both joy and sorrow, from players kept and players cut.

A reported crowd of 10,835 fans squeezed into the building, 1,700 of whom had to stand for the privilege of watching history unfold. Another 2,000 or so were turned away according to the *Star's* account. Adding to the confusion, Collins stood at a side door and let in friends for free. Other team officials probably did the same. With tickets priced at $4, $3, $2 and $1.50 (and $1 for standing room), and so many of them given away, the proceeds from the game were severely compromised.

This game, however, was more about exposure than profit, and Storen went all out to exploit the public relations potential of the occasion. A pep band of unknown origin played before the game and during breaks in the action. One of its selections was "Mame," a Broadway hit from the previous year, in recognition of Mamie Gregory, the wife of Kentucky Colonels owner Joe, who would turn 25 the next day. Storen brought over a group of young gymnasts from Hamilton, Ohio – billed as the "Flip Twisters" – to entertain at halftime, having utilized them while with the Royals.

Various local and state politicians were on hand. Team president Bannon, the linchpin of the ownership group, was introduced. So was Mikan. So was Mayor John Barton, who tossed up a ceremonial jump ball at mid-court. Collins remembered being introduced, too, with Storen proclaiming, "This is the man who did it!"

The Coliseum was darkened for pregame introductions, with players from each team brought onto the court via a spotlight. The Pacers players ran through a paper-covered hoop set at the end of the court to the foul line, where they greeted their teammates. Rayl, introduced ninth, got the loudest cheer according to the *Kokomo Morning Times*. Even Ligon, the other Kokomo native who had caught on with the Colonels after being cast off by the Pacers, received a warm welcome, and not just from the estimated 500-600 fans from Kokomo who attended the game.

The game lived up to the hype, for Pacers fans at least. All the preparations Storen and his staff had put into this moment – the tryouts in June, the informal workouts in July and August, the demanding training camp in September and the six exhibition games – paid off on the Coliseum's court that night. Buoyed by the cheers of the raucous sellout crowd and the sheer joy and anticipation of becoming professional basketball players, the Pacers defeated the Colonels 117-95.

Details of the game are sparse. None of the known newspaper accounts recorded who scored the first basket in franchise history, which didn't seem a big deal at the time. The *Star's* article, however, mentioned Rayl scored the 100th point on a driving layup with 3:57 left and Aitch scored the game's final points on a 15-footer with two seconds left. The *Kokomo Tribune* mentioned the Colonels jumped to a 14-8 lead, but the Pacers came back to lead 28-25 at the end of the first quarter behind "fabulous Roger Brown, husky Ollie Darden, spunky Freddie Lewis and hustling Jim Dawson."

According to the *Courier-Journal*, the Pacers "gave the Colonels a few lessons in showmanship, shooting, savvy and sound defense."

Kentucky made efficient use of the three-point shot, hitting 7-of-9 attempts while the Pacers missed all three of their flings, but the Colonels hit just 29-of-105 field goal attempts overall. The Pacers hit 49 of their 105 attempts.

The red, white and blue ball and three-point shot went over well with the fans, although the three-point shot caused some confusion for those who hadn't been following along closely in the newspapers. Mike Richardson, reporting for the *Franklin Daily Journal*, wrote that one woman asked her husband why one of the Colonels' shots had counted three points. "This is *professional* basketball, Martha. They can do anything they want," he replied.

The Pacers made up for Kentucky's three-point shooting by running, and broke open the game in the second half with their fastbreak scoring. The Colonels' management contributed to that issue, however, by managing to put their players at a scheduling disadvantage in the very first game. Kentucky had played its fifth exhibition game in six nights on Thursday, and had just one day to rest and prepare for the regular season debut. The Pacers had been off for six days.

Pacers fans didn't know that, and wouldn't have cared anyway. They gave the players a standing ovation as they left the court. Nobody could possibly have imagined what was in store for the franchise, and nobody grasped the historic merits of the evening. If they had, someone would have recorded the radio broadcast, documented the evening on film, and recorded every possible detail in writing. The prevailing mood at the time was mere survival. One day at a time. And the first day had gone better than anyone could have expected.

"It was absolute bedlam," Tinkham recalled years later. "It was a happening. Everybody had done something to make it happen, and it just exploded."

The headline across the top of the *Star's* first sports page the next morning declared "Pacers Soar and Over 10,000 Roar." The article noted the official attendance had been 9,135, with another 500-plus standing room customers, but added "that's to keep the fire marshal happy. Actually, there were about 10,500 on hand and another 2,000 were turned away at the gate."

All those in attendance surely were impressed.

"There was no way they could come out and see that game and not like it," Storen told reporters afterward.

Collins, in a follow-up column that ran on Monday, two days after the game, recalled rushing up to Mikan afterward, "all fired up with prideful provincialism," looking him "square in the belt buckle," and saying, "Let's see you top this, George – any place in the league!"

"Robert," Mikan replied, "we can't even tie it."

Brown was the show's headliner. Finishing with 24 points, eight rebounds and four assists, he "brought down the house with his dazzling drives down the lane and his knack for getting shots against bigger men underneath," according to the *News*. According to Collins, he "showed all the makings of a genuine superstar."

Four years removed from his banishment from the NBA and NCAA, and six months removed from working the night shift in a factory in Dayton, the ABA had opened a new life for him. At this moment, he felt nothing but gratitude.

"I'm sure glad someone thought of this league," he said in the locker room. "The guys who never had a chance with the NBA have the chance here."

Conard, in the *Kokomo Tribune*, was less restrained, writing: "And man, that Roger Brown … can he do it! Rog' fluttered, twisted and squirmed for 24 points … and when he fakes, half the other team leaves."

Dawson was the second-most impressive performer, finishing with 17 points and playing "with an abandon that had to remind old pro fans of Ralph Beard," according to Collins.

Darden scored 16 points, and Netolicky 13.

"Sure, I was nervous," Netolicky said afterward. "I was scared to death."

Givens, who had applied for the Pacers' coaching job and wound up with the Colonels, didn't take the loss gracefully. Shaking hands with

Staverman amid the postgame celebration, he said, "Man, I really got homered tonight."[2]

It wasn't what Staverman wanted to hear at such a joyous moment. "What the hell are you talking about?!" he screamed. "I didn't have anything to do with the goddam officials! What are you talking about?!"

Staverman didn't stay angry for long. Talking with reporters later, he referred to a sign in the locker room, white with red letters, that read "110 percent effort, 100 percent of the time."

"That's our motto," he said.

It had originated with Storen, and applied to the entire organization. Marvel, the media relations director, had ordered pins that read "110%" and distributed them to players, media, front office personnel and stat crew members, paid for out of his own pocket. Such was the spirit of the day.[3]

The Pacers were officially launched. An unknown but intriguing future awaited.

---

[2] This was according to Staverman's memory years later. Staverman, by the way, took home the game ball, perhaps the most historic memento in franchise history. His family still has it. It's not for sale.

[3] Marvel lived the motto. He worked so hard he had to go to a hospital to be examined because of chest pains the first week of December. Overpeck wrote that Marvel "has spent a lifetime trying to prove that sleep is greatly overrated." Marvel said he worked 86 consecutive days and stayed in the hospital for a week undergoing tests.

5

"It was like it had eyes ... We're standing there like, 'Damn!'"

The Long-Shot Candidate's Moment

The second game in franchise history, the following Wednesday, was certain to be less magical. Still, it brought a 106-103 victory over Anaheim before 5,923 fans. Lewis, who led the Pacers with 23 points, said afterward they had taken the Amigos lightly, meaning it took just two games in franchise history for the players to experience a letdown.

Edmonds was revved up enough, however, to throw the ball at referee Dick Sheldon's head in protest of a call. He was charged with a technical foul, and later fined $25. He might have had a legitimate complaint, though. Sheldon was fired within the first month of the season. He was probably typical of some of the referees in the early years of the ABA, which had to somehow come up with referees qualified to work professional games on relatively short notice. Some came from working Globetrotters games, or had been part-timers in various minor leagues, and many of them apparently were not up to the task. One, Pat Denoy, was described by *Star* sports writer Max Stultz, as "a roly-poly showboat who looks like a crew-cut glob of silly putty. And referees like one."

A few of the Amigos had a costlier evening than Edmonds. Someone broke into their locker room during the first half and stole valuables belonging to some of the players. One newspaper account reported cash and a topcoat were stolen from the locker room. A letter from the Amigos director of player personnel, Lauren Proctor, to Storen said some of the stolen items were found in another part of the Coliseum, but three players remained victims. Harry Dinnel lost a class ring valued at $75, Bill Garner a gold lighter at $35 and Steve Chubin a wallet and cash at

$25. The letter, forwarded to John DeVoe, asked if the Pacers had insurance to cover the losses. DeVoe replied they did not, and suggested the players try to collect under their individual policies.[1]

The Pacers won their next three games as well, all coming on the road in less than 72 hours. They defeated well-rested Kentucky on Friday night in its home opener before 10,427 fans in Louisville, caught a bumpy early-morning flight to New Orleans and defeated the Bucs on Saturday afternoon before 1,020 fans, then took another flight to Dallas for a Sunday afternoon game, which they won 121-101 before an announced crowd of 2,000 fans – obviously a rounded-up number.

Those informal summer practices and the two-week training camp in Rensselaer were paying off. The Pacers probably were the most organized franchise in the ABA, and the players likely were in better condition and more cohesive than the other teams as a result.

They went on to endure a second three-game-in-three-nights set a month into the season, playing a home game on Nov. 12, flying to Denver for a game the following night (a rare loss that dropped their record to 11-3) and then back to Dallas for a game the following night, a Tuesday.

That one turned out to be historic.

Grueling schedule aside, Harkness wasn't too fatigued to heave a shot the length of the court at the final buzzer for a three-pointer that defeated the Chaparrals, 119-118. It originally was declared a 92-foot shot, but was later amended to 88 feet. As with the three-point shot, it would be months, perhaps years, before anyone remembered the basket does not hang directly over the end line.[2]

---

[1] Dinnel, a 6-4 guard, played just 11 games for the Amigos, scoring 19 points. He later took over as coach after Al Brightman was fired. Garner, a 6-10 center, lasted 53 games, scoring 81 points. Chubin was the team's best player, and would become well-known to Pacers fans the following season.

[2] Harkness' shot stood as the longest in the history of professional basketball until 2001, when Charlotte's Baron Davis hit a shot measured at 89 feet at the end of the third quarter. Davis' shot was televised and can be viewed on YouTube. Even if it was a foot longer, Harkness can claim superior drama. His was a game-winner, a point he cheerfully pointed out when the two met after Davis retired.

The game was not televised, so Harkness' shot was seen only by the personal witnesses in Memorial Auditorium in Dallas — and there weren't many of those. The announced crowd was 2,115, but the actual number of observers was no doubt less. Probably closer to 1,000 according to some eyewitnesses.

Darden had hit a layup with 31 seconds left to tie the game. The ABA rule at the time required the clock to stop after every made field goal in the final two minutes. This time, however, it didn't restart immediately when Dallas inbounded the ball, according to Staverman's memory years later, so he was near mid-court screaming at the timekeeper as Dallas brought the ball upcourt.

Staverman turned his attention back to the game after the clock restarted. When John Beasley let go of a mid-range jumper to the right of the foul line, Staverman screamed "Check out! Check out!" as was his habit. Netolicky contested the shot with his hand up, but the ball fell through the basket cleanly with one second remaining. Staverman was angrier than ever now, believing the shot wouldn't have counted if the clock had started on time after Darden's basket. That's questionable, however, since the Chaps ran down the clock before Beasley let go of his shot. They could have shot sooner if necessary.

His anger over the defeat amplified by the clock issue, Staverman was walking off the court toward the locker room while the Chaparrals celebrated Beasley's apparent game-winner. But the ABA's clock rule – and perhaps another slow reaction from the timer – allowed Harkness time to take Darden's inbound toss just a few feet inside the baseline, bounce the ball once, and heave a high-arcing, left-handed hook toward the opposite basket.

The ball sailed through the air as if in slow motion amid the echoes of the final buzzer and the shouts of the Dallas players and fans celebrating Beasley's shot. It smacked the backboard with such force that it "jolted the very floor" according to the account in the *Dallas Morning News,* and fell through the basket.

Throughout the barren arena, pockets of bedlam and stunned silence followed. Some of the Dallas players who had been heading off the court, celebrating what they thought was a victory, stopped in their tracks, unsure what had just happened. Referees Joe Belmont and Gene Moyers huddled to decide whether it should count, while Harkness rushed to the scorer's table to plead his case. "Please! Please!" he begged while a few of his teammates mobbed him. Netolicky and some of the other Pacers rushed to the bench, ready for more action. "All right, we're going to kick their ass in overtime!" he recalled shouting.

A month into the season, they had grown accustomed to the three-point shot. But this was something else entirely – a lucky heave from the other end of the court rather than a long jump shot from just behind the line. But it counted three points, too.

Decades later, the memory remained fresh for many of them.

"Boys, that's a three-pointer!" Rayl he shouted to the Dallas players. "You are beat!"

"Hell, that's a three-pointer, get off the floor!" Staverman screamed at his players.

Belmont, who was standing near Harkness, was certain it should have counted and told Moyers, who signaled the call to the statistician. "The ball was definitely in the air when the buzzer sounded," Belmont told reporters afterward. "I don't know what the clock said. It's not the officials' job to watch the clock. I was listening for the buzzer and it had not sounded when he put the ball in the air."

Darden, whose inbound pass set up Harkness' brush with history, had watched it unfold before him.

"It was like it had eyes," he said years later. "It was kind of a hook shot. It curved and it went in the basket. We're standing there like, 'Damn!'

"Your first inclination is that the game is tied. But the referee signaled that the game was over. It was eerie, because nobody knew what to do. They were ahead by two, suddenly, and this shot goes in and everybody's standing around like, 'No, this can't be true.'"

The Chaps couldn't believe it either. Most of them wondered how Harkness could have gotten off the shot before the buzzer sounded. But player-coach Cliff Hagan, who scored 30 points, blamed his players for not defending better.

"I remember him saying we should have guarded (Harkness)," Beasley recalled. "He said if we had put our hands up, it wouldn't have happened. I was thinking, Yeah, well, what are the odds of that one?

"It was amazing. I can still see him do it. It was so freakish."

The same could have been said for the entire beginning of the Pacers' season. The win in Dallas nudged their record to 12-3. They were riding atop the Eastern Division and had just won a game in a most incredible fashion. They celebrated madly in the locker room. Harkness, unfailingly polite and humble, took a lot of kidding from teammates under ordinary circumstances, particularly from his schoolboy friend Brown, and this extraordinary circumstance provided even more reason to pile on. Rayl, for one, joked that the worst shooter in all of basketball had just hit the longest shot in the history of the game.

Harkness took in all in stride.

"I've been practicing that shot all day," he jokingly told reporters.

"Really, I didn't dream it would go in. I didn't aim it or anything. I knew I could get one shot off, though, so I let it fly."

The two-column, two-line headline in the *Dallas Morning News* read "Bomb at Buzzer Sinks Chaparrals." The *Star* ran a banner headline across the top of the sports page that read "Pacers Win On 92-Foot Hook Shot," with the subhead "Harkness Pops Just At Buzzer."

Both Indianapolis papers ran non-bylined stories, although Overpeck was on hand for the *Star*. Quotes from Harkness, Staverman and Belmont in the game story were dead giveaways that it wasn't a standard wire service story. The Pacers had offered the *Star* a free seat on their team plane early that season to gain as much exposure as possible, and Collins approved. It would be regarded as a severe ethical violation in later years, but the looser journalistic mores of the time and the newspaper's dedication to the Pacers' survival allowed it to happen.

News of Harkness' shot spread throughout the nation, his name appearing in headlines over wire service stories in major cities and small towns everywhere. The written accounts were all the evidence the world would have of Harkness' feat aside from the memories of the eyewitnesses, and some of them no doubt were busy celebrating Beasley's shot rather than watching Harkness' desperate prayer slam through the hoop. The

Above: Conquering hero Jerry Harkness returns home after hitting a game-winning 88-foot shot at Dallas. From left: Freddie Lewis, Oliver Darden, Harkness, Ron Kozlicki, Bob Netolicky and Bobby Joe Edmonds.

Right: A member of the Marine Corps color guard attaches a sharpshooter's pin to Harkness' jersey in a pre-game ceremony before the Pacers' home game with Oakland on Nov. 15, 1967, two nights after his historic shot in Dallas.

two Dallas newspapers had reporters at the game, but ran no photographs related to the closing rocket launch.

That frustrated Storen, who never wanted to miss out on a marketing opportunity. He caught up as best he could with a pre-game ceremony when the Pacers played Oakland at the Coliseum two nights later. He arranged for a member of the United States Marine Corps color guard to attach a sharpshooter's pin to Harkness' jersey. Sid Tuchman, owner of the Tuchman Cleaners stores that were among the Pacers' sponsors, then presented Harkness with $110 in the form of 11 ten-dollar bills – a reference to the team's "110 percent" motto. Harkness took the public-address microphone and announced he was going to share the windfall with his teammates, because basketball is a team game.

"And while they all whooped it up, Jerry did just that," the *Tipton Daily Tribune* reported.[3]

The Pacers defeated Oakland that night, running their record to 13-3. It was viewed by the smallest crowd of the first six home games, 5,885, but most of the ABA teams would have been jealous of a crowd that "small." A few fans unfurled a banner after the victory that blared "Bring on the Celtics!" The team was rolling beyond anyone's wildest dreams, both on court and in the box office, propelled by front office preparation, surprising talent and one magical moment.

Harkness' shot wasn't quickly forgotten. Storen put an X on the Coliseum court to mark the spot from where Harkness had his date with destiny. Harkness remembered someone with the Chaparrals painting a black square on their court from where he launched his shot as well. In April, the shot was among the items mentioned in the popular weekly "Ripley's Believe It Or Not" cartoon feature that ran in newspapers across the country. The ball, meanwhile, was mailed to the Naismith Basketball Hall of Fame for display, with a letter of authenticity from Marvel. It eventually was returned to Harkness, who sold it many years later for $10,000.

---

[3] Harkness does not remember receiving $110 before the game, but Marvel and a few players do. Memories are cloudier on whether he distributed $10 to each his teammates, but it seems unusual the Tipton writer would have made it up.

"He ought to send me some of that, since I didn't guard him," Beasley joked when he heard of the sale.

Harkness later regretted selling the ball, but the memory was the important thing. His shot served as the exclamation point to a dramatic and courageous personal story, a red, white and blue comet across the nighttime sky that brought an eternal glow to his life.

Harkness had experienced a difficult childhood in Harlem. His father, a window washer, had left the household, leaving his mother to raise him and his sister. They lived in public housing and in poverty. He had nothing more to eat than bread and syrup some days, and put cardboard in his shoes to cover holes in the soles. When it rained, the water soaked through anyway, dampening his spirits even more. Increasingly frustrated with what seemed his life's dismal fate, he dabbled in occasional mischief, such as stealing a piece of fruit off a vendor's cart, or hopping over a turnstile to catch a free ride on the subway.

He wasn't applying himself academically at DeWitt Clinton High School, but he was athletic. He ran cross country and was a distance runner for the track team, but couldn't work up the nerve to go out for the varsity basketball team. He still liked to play, though, and as a junior led his intramural team to the school's championship. He wanted nothing more than to play for the varsity, but the players on that team were from another part of town, and Harkness' confidence was so fragile he could only assume that meant they were better than him. No way was he going to risk trying out for the team, getting cut, and bringing another disappointment into his life.

Then came nothing less than his life's turning point.

One day, during the summer of 1958, before his senior year in high school, he was shooting around in the gymnasium at the Harlem YMCA, just killing time. He didn't do that often, because it cost a quarter to use the facility and quarters weren't exactly spilling out of jars at home. On this day, however, Jackie Robinson passed through the gymnasium on his way to visit a friend who managed the Y. Robinson, who at the time was two years retired from his historic Major League Baseball career, took notice of the kid putting up left-handed shots and threw out an off-hand compliment as he passed by.

"Hey, kid, you're not bad!"

Or something like that. The comment was so brief and so casual that Harkness didn't remember every word in passing years. Robinson might also have thrown out something about getting a scholarship if he worked at it, but Harkness wasn't sure. What he remembered was the uplifting nature of the words and the fact Jackie Robinson of all people had spoken them. To him, Jerry Harkness.

"Just for him to give me those words of encouragement …" Harkness recalled years later. "I had so many disappointments in my life. He was the one who pushed it over the top."

Emboldened by his hero's compliment, Harkness went out for the varsity team at Clinton. And made it. And moved into the starting lineup early in the season. And led it to the city championship, playing a starring role in the title game at Madison Square Garden.

He could have gone to St. John's on a track scholarship, but his grades weren't sufficient. NYU later offered a basketball scholarship, but he failed the entrance exam. He had to take a summer school class to become eligible for college and sat out the following school year. Meanwhile he kept playing, first at Rucker Park against the likes of Roger Brown, Larry Brown, and another local prep star, Donnie Walsh, and then in winter tournaments during the evenings at public school gymnasiums.

It turned out to be for the best. He kept improving during the year off from school, and Walter November, a local AAU coach and mentor for players in the area, lined up a basketball scholarship for him at Texas Southern. The dormitory in which he was to live burned to the ground, however, canceling that opportunity.

November then convinced Loyola of Chicago coach George Ireland to give Harkness a chance. Ireland was about to revolutionize college basketball by ignoring the cultural norms of the day and recruiting black players. It was the only way for a small Jesuit school to compete with the major powers. By the time Harkness was a senior at Loyola, four black players were in the starting lineup, a major breakthrough in an era when most colleges adhered to the unwritten rule of starting no more than two.

Loyola won the NCAA title that year, in 1963, with an overtime win over Cincinnati, which had won the two previous championships. It had to clear some of society's hurdles along the way, and knocked them down for future teams in the process. Southern teams in the early 1960s were heavily segregated, and southern cities were inhospitable to blacks. Loyola's black players heard taunts from fans in Houston in the form of a revised version of a popular cheer – *"Our team is red hot! Your team is all black!"* — and were not allowed to eat at the same restaurant as the whites after the game. They had to stay with local families in black neighborhoods rather than at a downtown hotel with the rest of the team in New Orleans, but that turned out to be a blessing because they were received as conquering heroes.

Ranked second in the country behind Cincinnati entering the tournament, Loyola was to meet sixth-ranked Mississippi State in the second round — which presented a problem. Mississippi State was so mired in segregation it had never played against teams with black players. It had passed on competing in the tournament in 1959, '61 and '62 for that reason, despite having been eligible after winning the SEC title. This time, university president Dean Colvard could no longer ignore the pleas of the team's players and a sizable faction of the student body. He declared the school would participate.

That didn't go over well with Mississippi governor Ross Barnett, who had campaigned as a segregationist. Barnett filed an injunction to prohibit the team from leaving the state, but Mississippi State's coach, Babe McCarthy, left the area to avoid being served a summons and Colvard helped organize a plan in which the players were driven across the state line into Tennessee and flown out of Nashville under the cover of darkness to escape authorities.

State's participation at the game at Michigan State's fieldhouse made for such a historic moment that when its captain, Joe Dan Gold, shook hands with Harkness at center court before the opening tip, the sound of popping flash bulbs from the cameras of newspaper photographers echoed throughout the fieldhouse. Loyola's players at that time weren't aware of all that State's team had gone through to get to the game, but

Jerry Harkness risked a stable career to chase his dream of playing professional basketball, and caught it.

neither was the significance of the moment lost on them. "Deep down, we knew this was something special," Harkness said.

Harkness scored 20 points in Loyola's 61-51 victory, and it wasn't that close. It went on to beat Big Ten champion Illinois by 15 points, with Harkness scoring 33, and then Duke by 19, setting up the championship game with Cincinnati.

Cincinnati, led by Bonham and another All-American, Tom Thacker, led by 15 points with 14 minutes to go, but Loyola's desperate fullcourt press began taking its toll. Harkness hit a 12-footer to force overtime, and then scored on a layup off the opening tip of the extra session to give Loyola its first lead of the game. Harkness had a chance to win the game for Loyola in overtime, but Bonham got his hand on the ball as he went up for a shot on the left baseline. Harkness quickly passed off to his right to Les Hunter, whose missed shot from the foul line was tipped in by Vic Rouse at the buzzer. It wasn't as dramatic as an 88-footer, but it made Loyola one of the most historic national champions of all time. It also helped make Harkness a first-team All-American, along with Bonham and Thacker.

His year off after high school turned out to be doubly beneficial because it put him in better alignment with the other starters, allowing him to play with them for two seasons before graduating. Had he entered Loyola immediately after high school, he would have played with them for one season, probably not enough time for the combination to develop into a championship team.

Harkness lived in a radiant glow after the tournament. He was voted the Most Valuable Player of the East-West All-Star game in Kansas City as a member of the West team, which was coached by Wooden, who by then was coaching at UCLA. Then, on April 30, his hometown Knicks selected him with the 10th overall pick – the first one of the second round – in the NBA draft. Harkness balked at signing, holding out briefly for a guaranteed contract, but it wasn't his nature to go to war and he didn't have leverage. He signed a one-year deal for $12,000 in June.

It seemed a perfect fit. Harkness would be going home, playing in Madison Square Garden where he had led his high school team to the city championship five years earlier, and the Knicks would benefit from adding a local kid who had achieved national fame. But it didn't work out. Harkness, 6-foot-3, had played small forward in college, and struggled to make the transition to guard in the NBA. He played in just five games, scoring 29 points, before he was released. The transition to a new position and knees that already were beginning to ache from all those miles covered as a high school distance runner and on the asphalt playgrounds, were too much to overcome.

He had better options than most discarded players, though. He had a college degree, some celebrity, and a solid reputation as a model citizen and leader. He landed a sales job with Quaker Oats in New York, then was transferred back to Chicago, where his name had the most value. Part of his corporate duties included running youth clinics that emphasized physical fitness. As the company's first black salesperson, he was breaking through another barrier, and was seemingly fast-tracked toward a management position, an exceedingly rare opportunity for a black man of that era. Meanwhile, he played semi-professional ball for a North American League championship team in Benton Harbor, Mich. on weekends, scratching his playing itch and learning to play guard. Just in case something came up.

It did, three years later, when he read a short item in the *Chicago Tribune* about the formation of the ABA. Indianapolis was one of the cities mentioned as a charter member. Harkness, 27, still believed he had more to offer than he had shown with the Knicks. Not knowing who to contact – the Pacers had no general manager or mailing address yet – he wrote a letter to Collins at the *Star*, asking for a tryout.

"I'll never be satisfied until I prove to myself once and for all that I can't play pro basketball," he wrote. "I don't ask for a contract or anything else. All I want is a chance to try out. I'm willing to quit my job if you'll give me that chance."

Collins passed the letter on to Storen, who invited Harkness to participate in the open tryout in June. Like all the others, however, he was unprepared for the Leonard and Lovellette boot camp. He finished poorly in the sprints, and vomited. And, being four years beyond his glory days at Loyola, his name value was declining. In fact, his name wasn't even recognized by some. The Pacers listed him as "Larry" Harkness on the tryout camp roster, and it appeared in the newspapers that way after he scored 10 points in an early public scrimmage. And, unlike the players who had been signed to guaranteed contracts, his name wasn't printed on the back of his practice jersey. He was a bad combination of anonymous and misidentified.

Worst of all, he was a poor shooter. He had used a two-handed set shot for his free throws in college, and was having difficulty adjusting to shooting long-range shots as a professional. "Jerry looks like a girl catapulting the ball to her boyfriend when he releases a shot from any distance at all," Denny wrote in the *News*.

Staverman, though, saw enough in him to invite him back for the next phase of pre-season preparations in July and August and training camp in September. The front office arranged a summer job for him with the Indianapolis Urban League, which allowed him to stay in the city and participate in scheduled workouts with other Pacer hopefuls at the Jewish Community Center and work out on his own at the Senate Avenue YMCA. He ran, he swam, he played pickup games, and when training camp opened at St. Joseph's College he was winning sprints and playing much better because of his superior conditioning.

He wound up the team's fourth-leading scorer in six exhibition games, averaging 10.5 points, and brought needed maturity to the roster. Still, he had barely made the team, barely made his huge risk pay off. Had he failed, who knows what he would have had to do to earn a living for his family?

When told he had survived the final cut, he walked into a bathroom at the St. Joseph's gym, closed the door and "cried like a baby." It became comical in the retelling in later years, with teammates banging on the door to get in, and him blubbering that he would be out shortly. He just needed a minute to get over the realization of a lifelong dream.

The long-shot candidate had made it.

6

"We figured, though, that if anyone could do the job,
the Indiana gang could."

The Stars are Aligned

The Pacers were fast out of the gates largely because of Storen's hustle and organization. Those summer workouts at the Jewish Community Center had laid the foundation of a professional approach that let the players know they were part of a serious endeavor. Even Brown looked back on them with appreciation.

"I thought it was wrong, but it's really paid off," he said.

The training camp was more rigorous and detailed than most if not all the other ABA teams, and six exhibition games had helped, too. The players were in shape and reasonably familiar with one another when the season opened, while most of the other teams were operating on the fly.

Gradually, reality set in. The 12-3 start was followed by two homecourt losses, the first of which, a 116-90 loss to Pittsburgh, was partially the result of playing their fifth game in six days, not to mention Pittsburgh's talent. They won five of the next seven, however, the last of which was a 110-99 Thursday night victory over Denver before the smallest crowd at the Coliseum to date, 3,601. Those who bothered saw Lewis score 41 points and grab 12 rebounds in 48 minutes without committing a turnover.

At that point the Pacers were 18-7 and percentage points behind Minnesota (17-6) for the Eastern Division lead.

Also at that point, the bottom fell out.

They lost the next game, 110-101, at home, to New Orleans, which had brought the league's best record (18-6) into the game. It was

Jerry Harkness, Bob Netolicky, Ron Bonham and Oliver Darden.

memorable for its mishaps. Lewis was given credit for hitting a shot just inside the three-point line that clearly had come after the buzzer to end the first quarter. The clock didn't start to open the second period and the timer sounded the buzzer twice to stop play. The league rule was that play couldn't be stopped by a buzzer, so a basket by Edmonds counted although the clock hadn't yet started.

All of that helped brew up enough irritation in New Orleans guard Larry Brown to receive two technical fouls and earn an ejection with 5:06 left in the game. Brown, angry a couple of fouls had not been called on his drives to the basket, didn't go quietly. He took a seat on the bench at first. Told he had to leave the court, he sat in the front row of the west end seats. Told again to move on, he sat in the third row. Finally, the cantankerous point guard headed for the locker room.

He didn't shower, though. The second-floor visitor's locker room at the Coliseum had just one shower head according to Denny's account in the *News* – maybe two or three according to the memory of others in later years. The Bucs, like many visiting teams, dressed at their hotel. Denny conducted a postgame interview with Brown while standing outside the Coliseum on a street corner while waiting for a cab, dressed in his uniform and overcoat.

"I deserved it," he said of the ejection. "It was worth $50 just to sit in the stands and watch us win one."

They wouldn't be Brown's last technical fouls in Indianapolis.

That defeat was the first pebble of a seven-game losing streak for the Pacers. Along the way, they lost to Pittsburgh at the Coliseum 122-117, a game in which Pipers forward Art Heyman finished with 36 points, 16 rebounds and 12 assists, and blew kisses to hecklers near the end of the game. Heyman was that type. At Duke, he had initiated a brawl against arch-rival North Carolina that involved Larry Brown and his backcourt mate, Donnie Walsh. By the time he got to the ABA, Heyman had already played for New York, Cincinnati, Philadelphia and Boston in the NBA as well as in the Eastern League. He was a flashy, egotistical and insecure athlete who lived across the street from New York Jets quarterback Joe Namath in New York City, and had a knack for inspiring fan reaction.

At the end of the landslide, a 129-128 loss to the Oakland Oaks before all of 986 fans at the Auditorium in Richmond, Calif., Lewis broke his own franchise scoring record with 43 points. He hit a layup with five seconds left to get the Pacers within a point, but the timer let the clock run out rather than stopping it as ABA rules stipulated. So that was that.

The Pacers, once proud owners of a league-best 12-3 record, were now 18-14 and in third place in their division. The league was catching up to them. They ended their losing streak the next night in Anaheim, their third game in three nights on the road trip, pulling out a 144-142 victory. Netolicky led that one with 36 points on 17-of-23 shooting and 16 rebounds. He also sparked a comeback from an 81-68 halftime deficit – in the locker room.

"Everybody was sitting around ready to die," he recalled years later. "I started looking at Roger, and he started looking at me, and I started

Freddie Lewis appears to be in disagreement with snazzily-dressed referee Ron Rakel in the Dec. 13 loss to Minnesota, the fourth in a seven-game losing streak.

laughing. I just couldn't stop laughing. I almost fell off the bench. Staverman got mad and wanted to know what we were laughing at. Pretty soon, everybody was laughing. And we went out and killed them."

Tension broken, the Pacers indeed dominated the second half. Oakland owner Art Kim wasn't pleased by the officiating and followed referees Pat Denoy and Doug Harvey into their dressing room afterward to seek an explanation for their ruling on an intentional foul call in the final 15 seconds. When Denoy failed to provide what Kim considered an adequate answer and turned away to undress, Kim flew into a rage, threatening to apply his karate skills to Denoy. Harvey intercepted him and forcibly removed him from the locker room. Kim kicked and pounded on the door, trying to get back in, and then screamed at a building official and demanded to be let back in.

He wasn't successful. Overpeck's account suggested Mikan was likely to slap Kim with a hefty fine – perhaps even $1,000.

That comeback victory didn't create momentum, however. The Pacers lost their next game, to Minnesota, back at the Coliseum, 104-101, but were praised in the newspapers for their hustle. Rayl led a comeback that nearly pulled off the upset and finished with 21 points, although he hit just 8-of-28 shots.

Their next game at the Coliseum was the feature event of a doubleheader. New Orleans was playing its home games at the Loyola University Field House, but moved some of them to Memphis when that facility wasn't available. The games in Memphis didn't draw well, however, so the Bucs spread the games that couldn't be played in New Orleans to other venues. One with Anaheim wound up as the preliminary game for the Pacers-New Jersey matchup on Dec. 26. With Lewis out with the flu, Harkness started for the first time, played 46 minutes of the 48 minutes, and finished with 21 points and eight assists in a 117-107 victory. Rayl started with him in the backcourt and added 11 points and 10 rebounds.

That led to a homecourt overtime loss to Dallas in which the Pacers blew a 14-point second-half lead. Staverman, normally, low-key after games, including losses, "screamed and hollered" after that one, mostly about the fact his team was outrebounded 91-61. That led to a one-game revival, as the Pacers defeated Kentucky, 124-80. The game drew 7,111 because the Southport Jaycees bought up a large block of tickets in honor of hometown hero Louie Dampier, who made his first appearance at the Coliseum. He scored just five points, hitting 1-of-13 shots.

Rayl had a worse night. Years later, he recalled a point roughly midway through the game when Netolicky didn't switch off on a screen and allowed Darel Carrier – Rayl's assignment – an uncontested layup. Rayl struggled enough on defense as it was, and was having a difficult time with Carrier, who was on his way to 25 points. He didn't appreciate his assignment scoring points he didn't consider his responsibility.

A timeout was called, and Rayl began screaming at Netolicky.

"Is there any chance you might get off your lazy ass and switch off?!"

Staverman substituted for Rayl during the timeout, which only enraged him more. "Here's Neto not switching and I'm the guy coming out," he recalled years later.

Rayl didn't play the rest of the game. Coming off the floor, a jolly Netolicky, who had played an exceptional game with 30 points while hitting 12-of-13 shots and 12 rebounds in just 30 minutes of action, threw an arm around him to console him.

"Get the hell away from me!" Rayl shouted.

Rayl, who finished with nine points and seven rebounds, threw off his uniform in the locker room and rushed into the shower, planning a quick getaway. Storen, thrilled with the one-sided victory and large turnout, stuck his head in the shower and shouted, "Nice game, Jimbo!"

Rayl wasn't having it. "Bullshit!" he shouted, and threw a bar of soap against the wall. Some of the soap fragments and water splattered on Storen, who laughed, dusted himself off, and said, "I think Jim's mad."

Rayl walked out of the shower into the celebrating locker room, heard more ribbing from his teammates, told them all to go to hell, got dressed and hurried home.

"That's how I'd get sometimes," he recalled calmly years later.

The Pacers lost their next four games, all on the road. Rayl scored just four points in the first one, at Pittsburgh, but bounced back with 12, 15 and 21 points in the next three games. The Pacers then returned home and pulled out a victory over Houston. Brown played guard, and Staverman declared the move permanent. Aitch took his place at forward and contributed 15 points and 11 rebounds. Rayl played off the bench, a move that didn't agree with him very well as he hit just 2-of-10 shots and scored six points.

Playing at Minnesota the following night, the Pacers trailed by 17 points with less than five minutes to play but got within a point with 40 seconds left. They wound up losing 109-106 despite a 42-point fourth quarter. Staverman used just seven players. Rayl wasn't one of them.

While the team floundered, the Pacers' front office barely had time to notice. It was gearing up for the ABA's first shot at grabbing national attention in a positive manner.

Some of the Pacers' owners had bravely volunteered to host an All-Star game at the final pre-season league meeting the weekend of Oct. 6-7 in Dallas. They promised to handle all expenses in return for keeping all revenue except television rights, and promised a first-class event. They talked of giving color television sets to the players, perhaps even a car to the MVP, and trumpeted Storen's experience promoting and organizing such a game. They also said they would attempt to secure use of Hinkle Fieldhouse on Butler University's campus for the game. A motion was made by Oakland co-owner Ken Davidson, seconded by Houston coach and general manager Slater Martin, and passed unanimously.

It was a bold initiative for a new team in a new league that was laboring to get off the ground. No first-year league in professional sports had ever attempted to put on an All-Star game. The ABL didn't have one in its first – and only – full season. The American Football League didn't have one until its second season. None of the other professional basketball leagues had ever bothered with one until the NBA did in 1951, as a reaction to the negative publicity generated by the college point shaving scandals that were beginning to fill the newspapers.

Storen was unfazed. The previous year he had played an instrumental role in organizing the NBA All-Star game that drew 13,653 fans to the Cincinnati Gardens and was regarded as one of the best events in league history. Adrian Smith, a Royals player who was added to the East team by coach Red Auerbach as a late replacement, won MVP honors by scoring 24 points. For the first time in the history of the NBA game, the

MVP was awarded a car, and Smith later claimed a blue Ford Galaxie convertible – a car he still owned 50 years later.

A letter sent to ABA media members on Nov. 22 stated the game would be played at the Coliseum, but Pacers officials continued to work behind the scenes to secure Butler's fieldhouse. It was a larger and more suitable facility, and the Pacers didn't trust the State Fair Board.

The relationship between the two parties had turned sour even before the season began. Storen recalled one pre-season meeting with the Fair Board in which he said, "It's really difficult to negotiate with you guys, because I get the feeling you don't care if we play here or not."

"That's right," came the reply.

Fact was, the Fair Board considered its only major responsibility to be putting on the State Fair each year. Dealing with a basketball team was more a nuisance than an opportunity, although it paid well.

The Pacers were paying an annual rental fee of $70,000, among the highest in pro basketball, for use of the Coliseum. They received no percentage of concessions and had to hire their own ushers and parking attendants. The building was rarely available to them for practice, and promises weren't being kept. Storen, according to internal memos, had been told the court would be available to the team the morning of the season-opener with Kentucky, but then was notified the day before the game it would be open to the public for ice skating until early that afternoon. Workers had to scramble to prepare the floor for the game. He also had been promised a new scoreboard to replace the antique model that had been used since the building was erected in 1939. It didn't arrive in time, and a temporary one had to be secured. The Board had even failed to attach new nets to the rims, as promised, to replace the worn ones.

Fairground signage graphically demonstrated the Fair Board's malaise regarding the Pacers. Four days after the dramatic season-opener, when they were to play Anaheim, the sign outside the north entrance promoted public ice skating in the Coliseum, while the sign on the east end was still plugging the season-opener with the Colonels. When it was updated later in the day, an incorrect start time was posted.

The locker room facilities were worse than in most Indiana high schools. There had been security issues, such as the break-in of the Anaheim locker room in the second home game, and maintenance issues as well. When Anaheim came back on Dec. 2, the roof began leaking in the fourth quarter, drizzling water at midcourt and at the west end of the court. The referees considered stopping the game with more than seven minutes still to play, but decided to carry on. The players simply avoided the wet spots as best they could and the court was dried during dead balls.

Everything about the facility was spartan — for fans, players and media members. The work room for reporters was a converted public restroom, about 15 feet by 15 feet. It included one work table for reporters writing after the game and another smaller table for a mimeograph machine. An enclosed stall with a stool was left in, as a convenience.

Even the three-point lines had been insufficient. The original ones were put down with white water base paint, but soon became scuffed and faded. Finally, after Overpeck complained in a story in the *Star*, they were replaced with red enamel lines early in January.

Whatever "luxuries" existed in the building tended to be donated. Marvel leaned on a friend from the telephone company to rig up a communications system so the stat crew members could talk back and forth on headsets during games. Radio play-by-play announcer Jerry Baker once complained on the air of having cold feet because of the skating rink beneath his courtside seat, so a local carpet dealer provided him with samples to help insulate him from the ice.[1]

All in all, it was no place to put on a game that would go out to a national audience when you're trying to make a favorable first impression.

Hinkle Fieldhouse was older, having been built in 1928, but held nearly 15,000 fans for basketball, about six thousand more than the

---

[1] Donated services were in play, too. The 11-member stat crew, headed by York, worked as volunteers, although each member was given complimentary tickets – anything to fill seats. A few years later, each worker would be paid $5, and York, being the boss, $7. Because they weren't being paid, and because of their excitement over the team, the crew members often heckled the referees, sometimes viciously. Overpeck joined in as well, occasionally.

Coliseum. It also was maintained better and was more suitable for televising a game because of its sight lines. Only problem was, Butler officials were holding firm to their post-Olympians ban of professional basketball. The passing of 14 years had not eased the sting.

Tinkham fired off a letter to local attorney Harry T. Ice, chairman of the Board of Trustees at Butler, on Oct. 12 to request rental of the fieldhouse for one night. Ice, whose stern countenance seemed a perfect fit for his last name, promptly refused, citing the university's unfortunate experience with the Olympians as well as with other professional events such as roller derby, bike races and midget automobile races. He claimed to represent the wishes of the entire university administration.

"The protests in those days from students, faculty and residents became a mighty chorus," he wrote to Tinkham. Ice also pointed out the precedent of refusing other requests for sporting events and expressed concern that allowing the game might impact the fieldhouse's tax-exempt status.

Tinkham, aiming to be as gently persuasive as possible, responded with a four-page letter. He stated he could easily understand the reasons behind Butler's rejection "were it not for one fact and one fact alone." Indiana and Indianapolis, he wrote, had "ONE final opportunity to prevent the door of professional sports opportunities from closing forever." He mentioned the positive long-term economic impact the Pacers could have on the city if they survived and the considerable financial risk the ownership group had taken to host the game. He also recalled Mikan's promise to obtain a national telecast for the game.

"We are thus placed in the position of having accepted the responsibility of making the league's first All-Star game a success," Tinkham wrote. "When you stop and think about what is at stake for the league and particularly what is at stake for the state of Indiana, I hope you are led, as we are, to the conclusion that we cannot fail."

Star publisher Eugene Pulliam put his considerable weight behind the effort as did Butler's legendary coach, Tony Hinkle, after Storen and Tinkham paid him a personal visit. Still, on Nov. 15, another rejection from Ice arrived in the mailboxes of Storen and Tinkham, stating the matter had been discussed at length but "it was felt the university could not live with a situation that might be based on an exception here or an exception there."

Storen immediately fired back a letter thanking Ice and the Board for considering the request and called the decision "very understandable." But he and Tinkham weren't giving up. Tinkham then enlisted the support of Otto Frenzel, chairman of the board of Merchants National Bank and a trustee at Butler. As Tinkham recalled years later, the conversation went about as follows:

"There must be some way we can work this out."

"No, there really isn't."

"What if we pay you $2,500 in rent?"

"Well, if you're talking about money, let me get back to you."

Ultimately, the Pacers offered Butler $7,000 for use of the fieldhouse. Tinkham wrote a two-page letter to Frenzel on Dec. 6 with a formal offer for that amount, or 10 percent of the total gate, if that turned out to be higher. Tinkham's letter estimated the expense of putting on the game at $25,000, along with another $2,000 for reprinting tickets and other materials that listed the Coliseum as the game site. He added that the rental offer was "several hundred percentage points above what any basketball arena in this country rents for on a one-night basis." As a bonus, he wrote, that amount would discourage 99 percent of all other potential applicants from asking to use the fieldhouse.

The university agreed, and on Dec. 13 an announcement was made to a public blissfully oblivious to all that had gone on behind the scenes: the game would be played at Butler on Jan. 9.

The challenge for Storen, Marvel and the rest of the Pacers' staff was daunting: put on a first-class game on an economy-class budget, and do it on the fly. The opportunity, however, was tremendous: boost the image of the ABA, the Pacers and the city.

"The nation's attention is going to be focused on Indiana, Indianapolis and the ABA, and the people are going to make a judgment," Storen told the *News*. "If the fans walk out of Hinkle Fieldhouse smiling and if the millions who watch the game on TV and hear it on the radio say it's a fantastic show, it's just another feather in the ABA's cap.

"And if we fill Hinkle Fieldhouse, there's no way the NBA can have a better overall show for its All-Star game in Madison Square Garden."

That was debatable, as the NBA's game in New York later drew more than 18,000 fans. But Storen was a bold promoter, always willing to drift into the realm of hype to promote his cause. He had no idea of the obstacles, foreseen and otherwise, that awaited him, however.

It helped that 44 media voters from around the country put two Pacers – Brown and Lewis – in the starting lineup for the East team, which appealed to Pacers fans. They were joined by Minnesota's Daniels, who was the top vote-getter, Minnesota guard Donnie Freeman and Pittsburgh star Connie Hawkins. Minnesota coach Jim Pollard, who would coach the East team because the Muskies had the best record at the cutoff date, selected Netolicky among the reserves.[2]

Three all-stars weren't enough to prevent the Pacers' slide toward mediocrity, however. They had lost their seventh consecutive game on the same day the East starters were named, and later lost four in a row, all on the road. They were 22-21, having lost 14 of their previous 18 games, on Jan. 9, and were 6 ½ games back of Minnesota and Pittsburgh. The All-Star game would at least provide a break from their troubles.

Only a brief one, though. There was no All-Star break, per se, just one day off. Six of the ABA teams played on Jan. 8 and eight would play again on Jan. 10. But Jan. 9 was reserved for the showcase event. Marvel claimed he distributed credentials to 97 reporters and 40 photographers from around the country, including non-ABA cities such as Detroit and Cincinnati. That might technically have been true, but that didn't mean all credentials would be used. The actual turnout would be much smaller than that. The afternoon *Minneapolis Star* didn't bother covering the game despite the Muskies having a coach and two players in the game, and the Minneapolis-based Mikan in attendance as well.

---

[2] Netolicky was maintaining the adventurous lifestyle he had established in college. He lived with an ocelot the first season. He also had a menagerie of roommates for as long as he lived at his north side apartment. Dill was his first roommate, then Dawson, followed by Lareau. Others would follow.

Storen followed through on the promises made at the owners' meeting in Dallas. He arranged for the MVP to receive a red Chevrolet Malibu convertible, valued at $3,600, which was put on display at the Coliseum for all to see during the two weeks leading up to the game. A local Chevrolet dealer, Bill Kuhn, provided the vehicle in return for promotional considerations as a game sponsor. Each player and coach would receive a gold star-sapphire ring, valued at $200, and a nine-inch General Electric portable color television set, valued at $285. Gift bags were waiting in the rooms at the Marott Hotel for the players, owners and other league personnel, an uncommon gesture at the time.

The local Jaycees were drafted to form a transportation committee to pick up players at the airport and chauffeur them as needed. Storen had learned a valuable lesson the previous year in Cincinnati, when he provided rental cars for the visiting players. They scattered vehicles all over the city before leaving town, sometimes taking the keys with them.

A cocktail party was conducted for the early-arriving league officials and media members on Monday evening at the Marott, followed by a noon luncheon on Tuesday, game day, at the Murat Temple. It was open to the public for $5 per ticket, and drew more than 700 guests. It would prove to be nearly as memorable as the game itself.

Mikan, for one, spiced things up with a couple of gaffes. After being presented with a key to the city by newly-elected Mayor Richard Lugar, he blasted the media for daring to offer negative criticism of the new league.

"I wish the press would get off our backs," he said. "I know I've made mistakes and so has the league. But I'm tired of the press constantly making fun of us."[3]

---

[3] Mikan had a knack for gaffes during speeches. Later, while appearing as commissioner in Oakland, he would open his remarks by saying, "It's nice to be here in Oklahoma." This habit became a common complaint among the ABA management and ownership groups, often mentioned in meeting minutes and private correspondence. He also had come under fire from franchise representatives within a few months of his hire. Tinkham, for example, sent Mikan a three-page, single-spaced letter in August of '67 detailing complaints over his handling of a vote taken at a league meeting regarding Barry's contract.

The ABA had indeed been mocked in some NBA cities, particularly New York and Los Angeles, and in some national publications as well, but hardly at all in the ABA cities – and certainly not in Indianapolis, where Overpeck admitted in his column the local media had "bent over backwards to help the ABA."

Those remarks brought quick apologies to media members from league officials, but there wasn't anything they could do to take back Mikan's lame swipe at a joke. It was something along the lines of, "You know why they call my undershorts 'Burger King?' Because they're the home of the Whopper!" It drew hesitant, uncomfortable laughter from the mixed audience.

Bob Richards, the luncheon's featured speaker, surely didn't approve of such salty humor. He was the Olympic pole vaulting gold medalist in 1952 and '56, and had been gracing the cover of Wheaties boxes since 1958. An ordained Protestant minister, he was nationally regarded as a paragon of virtue, clean living and physical fitness. "The pole-vaulting parson," he was sometimes called.

He put a fright into organizers when he hadn't arrived by the banquet's noon starting time. Two minutes later, however, the 41-year-old sports icon sauntered into the room, looking fit enough to grab a pole and vault over a couple of Mikans. He had already been in town for two days, he said, working out. He spoke for nearly an hour, keeping the crowd of more than 700 "spellbound," according to one newspaper account, and was rewarded with a standing ovation. He provided a solid return on the investment of bringing him in: $1,166.50, including travel expenses.

For those who saw it, however, the highlight of the banquet might have been Netolicky's lounge act in the back of the ballroom. He had seen a hypnotist perform while at Drake, and was amazed by the process. As a lark, he imitated the procedure and successfully hypnotized Marvel. He had the diminutive public relations director lay his feet on one chair and his head on another, told him he was stiff as a board, and stood on him. He then told him he was freezing, and Marvel began shivering. Then he told him he was hot, and Marvel began sweating.

All in an afternoon's fun in the ABA.

Time and budget didn't permit hiring national entertainers for the game, so the Pacers kept it regional in nature. Tipton High School, about an hour's drive to the north of Indianapolis, sent its Devilettes, a dance team, to perform before the game. They were followed by the Persian Murat Temple Patrol drill team and the Marian College Drum and Bugle Corps.

Butler even pitched in by allowing its pep band and "Halftime Honeys" to participate. The Honeys, a group of 21 female students, lined up around the perimeter of the court and held up an American flag that covered the entire floor for the national anthem. They had to hold their position for several minutes, however, while commercials played before the television broadcast could resume and include the anthem. "Their arms were drooping," the *Star* reported.

The "Flip Twisters" from Hamilton, Ohio, who had performed on opening night, returned to perform a halftime show. Marvel and a few ballboys tossed about 150 rubber regulation-sized red, white and blue balls, valued at $5 each, into the stands at the end of the halftime break.[4]

The game's most important feature, however, was the network television broadcast. KTTV, an independent station in Los Angeles,

---

[4] Marvel's hustle led to an internal conflict. Barnes, probably believing the Pacers had turned a profit on the game, asked Storen to pay Marvel a $1,500 bonus for all the hours he devoted to the All-Star game. Storen, while offering high praise for Marvel's job performance, disagreed, saying the All-Star duties were part of Marvel's day-to-day responsibilities. Barnes responded with a request to cancel the two-year contract between Sports Headliners and the Pacers. The Board agreed to do so at their meeting on Feb. 13, thus freeing Marvel to return to working full-time for Barnes in the racing world. He was forever remembered fondly for his work ethic by Storen and media members. His routine after home games was to type up a press release with updated stats, run off copies on the Coliseum mimeograph machine, and drop them off at the local radio and television stations and the *Star* and *News* building. He then drove to the airport to mail them overnight to the league office and other teams. "It was like a newspaper route that he ran after every game," Storen said. "He knew how to get in the back door of every radio station in the city and hand a stat sheet to the disc jockey to read on the air." Marvel said Overpeck often rode along to get a free breakfast out of the deal. Marvel later put together a nine-page typed outline detailing the administration of an All-Star game for future ABA media relations directors.

agreed to broadcast the game to a cobbled together network that included New York and Los Angeles and seven of the 10 ABA cities. All of Indiana was blacked out, as were Louisville and Dallas. In some cities, the game was aired on a delayed basis. The league likely received no rights fee; the exposure would be payment enough. Barry, fulfilling his role as league ambassador while waiting to become eligible to play, served as color commentator while KTTV's Tom Kelly handled play-by-play.

The national exposure would be vital to the league's future. To that point the ABA was little more than a rumor, even in some of the cities where its teams played. The Pacers were leading the league in attendance at the break, averaging 5,945 fans, well ahead of second-place Denver at 3,836. Four franchises – New Jersey, New Orleans, Houston and Anaheim – were averaging between 1,000 and 2,000 fans, and probably inflated those numbers. Beasley, Dallas' all-star forward, recalled playing at Houston earlier that season and counting 35 fans in the stands shortly before tip-off. The touted break-even figure for most teams was an average of 4,000.

National exposure, then, was like plugging into life support. The league was hanging on for dear life, gasping for air and grasping for whatever dollars and slivers of attention it could manage. It was under-financed and embarrassingly amateurish at times in both its play and presentation, but it was colorful, daring and earnest. The luncheon had reflected that, and the game needed to do the same.

Tip-off was 8:30 p.m., a typical starting time for that era, but also one that would accommodate the West Coast television audience. Tickets were priced at $6, $5 and $3, and all Pacers season ticket holders were given a free $6 ticket for each season ticket held. Storen declared that was a way of saying thanks to their loyal customers, but it also helped boost the turnout.

A story went out on the wires that more than 12,000 tickets had been sold in advance, which was far from the truth. The *News* reported that more than 10,000 fans were expected, and a capacity crowd of 14,521 was possible. Those were wildly hopeful projections, however, and complicated by the weather. The forecast for Tuesday called for an inch or two of snow as well as freezing rain and sleet. As it turned out, four inches of snow fell on the city, sending street-cleaning crews into action, but by evening the weather had cleared.

The game also had serious competition for the local basketball fan's attention. Indiana University was playing a televised game at Illinois beginning at 9 p.m., and Purdue's home game with Wisconsin at 7:30 was available on the radio.

As the game approached, it became clear to Storen he was going to have to "paper the house," as he had done for the season-opener. Once again, the police and fire departments, government offices, youth organizations and just about any group willing to venture into the cold winter's evening was offered tickets.

The Indianapolis newspapers, meanwhile, pitched in with advance coverage that amounted to unvarnished promotion. Multiple stories were published, and the *News* even produced an eight-page All-Star tabloid insert four days before the game.

Just as in the Pacers' sold-out debut three months earlier, the game lived up to the hype. Or, at least it didn't disappoint. The players approached it with genuine enthusiasm for an all-star gathering, fully aware of the league's desperate need to make a favorable impression on the nation. They had selfish interests, too. Most of them had never played in such a widely-broadcast game, and television coverage for regular season ABA games was local and minimal. Their excitement for the game was genuine.

The only player reported to be blasé in his approach was the war-torn veteran Hawkins, who had visited too many of basketball's dark sides to find joy in an unessential game amid an injury-laden season. He wore tape on fingers of both hands, a heavy shin guard on one leg, a bandage under an eye and multiples bruises. No doubt preferring a night off, the league's best player scored just three field goals, all on dunks, and banged another breakaway dunk off the back of the rim.

The quality of play was spotty, understandable because most of the participants had played the previous night and arrived the afternoon of the game. Hagan, the 36-year-old player-coach from Dallas, didn't reach

Indianapolis until 6 p.m. because of travel complications. The players generally treated the game with respect, however. Three-point attempts were kept to a minimum – each side made only two — and the play around the basket was physical. All things considered, the show went off as well as anyone could have hoped.

The East won, 126-120, after Daniels led a comeback by scoring eight points in the final 3:38. He finished with a game-high 22 points and 15 rebounds in 29 minutes, which would have made him a lock for MVP honors and the new car but for one thing: the ballots were collected with six minutes remaining, when the West led 108-104, to enable the announcement to be made immediately following the game.

Larry Brown won it instead. He had been a last-minute addition to the game (just as Smith had been in the NBA's game in Cincinnati the previous year before winning MVP honors) and was a controversial selection at that. The gentleman's agreement within the league was that no team could have more than three players in the game. But as with most of the league's gentleman's agreements, it proved to be flexible. McCarthy, the New Orleans' coach who was directing the West team, insisted on adding Brown after Dallas rookie Bob Verga had to pull out because of Army reserve duty, despite the fact three of McCarthy's players already had been selected to the team.

Brown came off the bench to score 17 points, hitting two three-pointers with two-handed set shots, and added five assists in 22 minutes. He had nine points and two assists during the fourth-quarter run that built the West's four-point lead, just in time for the voting tabulation.

He won MVP honors with 11 votes. Most newspaper reports had Daniels with 10, but at least one, the *Courier-Journal* in Louisville, had Dampier (who finished with 18 points) with 10 votes and Daniels with nine. Regardless, the consensus was that Daniels had been robbed. The fans booed as Mikan presented the four-foot tall trophy to Brown, with Barry standing alongside for the photo op.

Mikan was embarrassed by the early vote tabulation.

"The game was too close for anyone to make up his mind on the MVP at that point," he said later. "We'll wait until the game is over from now on."

Larry Brown, with ABA commissioner George Mikan and TV commentator Rick Barry, accepting the MVP trophy he knew he didn't deserve.

Brown was embarrassed, too, and apologized to Daniels upon entering the locker room the two teams shared. McCarthy jokingly threw an arm around Brown's shoulder and said, "Good things come to those who least expect it."

Brown sold the car to a friend in Indianapolis to avoid having to transport it, but, naturally, wished years later he had kept it.[5] He was grateful, though, that his offer to New Orleans teammates James Jones and Doug Moe had been rejected. Brown had suggested before the game they all agree that if one of them was voted MVP, the winner would sell the car and split the proceeds among the three of them. Jones and Moe didn't bite, believing their odds of winning had to be much better than those of the 5-foot-9 point guard who wasn't much of a scorer and had only been tacked onto the roster at the last minute. Brown got to keep the money.[6]

---

[5] Beasley was voted MVP at the following year's All-Star game in Louisville by scoring 19 points and grabbing 14 rebounds, but received a lesser prize: $500 according to a newspaper account, or $600 according to his memory. It was significant in an era when that would have qualified as a monthly income for many people, but, having seen Brown receive a car the previous year he felt shortchanged.

[6] Brown was a fiery and cocky competitor on the court, but soft-spoken and well-mannered away from it. He later wrote a letter to the Pacers to thank them for the car and to congratulate them for putting on a quality event. The final example of the franchise's professional effort came 10 days after the game, when Marvel mailed letters to all the media members who attended the game on special All-Star stationery, thanking them for their coverage – partly as an attempt to soften the impact of Mikan's complaint at the luncheon.

Daniels could have used the car. After he signed his contract with the Muskies out of college, he took the unusual step of trading in his 1959 Chevrolet for an even-older model, a blue and white 1955 Buick station wagon. He made a small profit on the Chevy and paid just $850 for the Buick, which had fewer miles.

Daniels was disappointed in the voting result, but offered no public complaints that night and would laugh about it in later years.[7] New car or not, it had been a special evening for him. Largely unknown except to fans of the teams for whom he had played, he had aced his first test on a national stage.

One of the few out-of-state reporters on hand for the game was *Cincinnati Enquirer* reporter Barry McDermott, who took advantage of Daniels' performance to revisit his negotiation with the Royals the previous year. Jucker's first team was struggling along at a .500 pace, and by now he was claiming to have wanted Daniels all along. "I'll tell you, we could have used him," he said. Daniels said he wasn't opposed to signing with the Royals later, if the money was right. "This is professional basketball," he said. "It's a means of making a living. You have to go with the best offer."

Pollard – who along with Mikan had played in the first NBA All-Star game in 1951 — offered Daniels some consolation in the form of hearty praise. On this night, that was going to have to be enough.

"I think Mel is the best player in the ABA and I think he could make it in the NBA if he got the chance," Pollard said after the game. "That's the good thing about the ABA."

The Pacers were a good thing, too, having made a major financial and man-hour sacrifice for the good of the league.

---

[7] Less than three months later, on March 31, another player would be cheated by a premature MVP vote at Hinkle Fieldhouse. Purdue sophomore Rick Mount led a comeback toward victory in the final minutes of the East-West College All-Star game, but lost the MVP award by one vote to Pete Maravich because the ballots were collected with five minutes remaining.

★★★★★★★★★★
1ST (ABA) **annual ALL-STAR GAME**
★★★★★★★★★★

January 9, 1968
Hinkle Fieldhouse
Indianapolis, Ind.

January 19, 1968

Dear Members of the News Media:

On behalf of the Indiana Pacers, hosts of the recent ABA
All-Star Game, I wish to take this opportunity to say
'THANK YOU '.

There are many facets to such an extensive promotion
as the All-Star Game, and the one and only way for such
a promotion to be successful is to have the vehicle of
'NEWS coverage,' with which to reach the public.

It is quite evident from the success that the ABA, the
Pacers, and All-Star promotion enjoyed, that the News
Coverage was very extensive.

The constant in depth coverage that you have given the
Pacers, the ABA, and the fine All-Star coverage has
been tremendous.

The success of the All-Star game was certainly a team
effort and please accept our sincerest thanks for all
you contributed to its success.

If I or any member of the Pacer staff can be of assistance at any time, please feel free to contact us.

Sincerest best regards,

Bill Marvel

Bill Marvel
Publicity Director

BM/bs

YOUR HOST: **INDIANA PACERS** ⎸ 638 E. 38th St.   Indianapolis, Ind. 46205   Mike Storen, Gen. Mgr.

*To help soothe hard feelings over George Mikan's unfortunate remarks at the All-Star
banquet, a gushing letter went out to the media members who covered the game.*

The official attendance given to the media was 10,872, a figure the *News* pointed out was more than the NBA had drawn in its first three All-Star games in the 1950s. Storen told reporters more than 5,000 fans had purchased tickets the day of the game. None of that was true, however. The Pacers' internal gate receipt report at the end of the season listed the total attendance at 7,529. That, at least, was enough to make the lower levels appear full after people spread out on the fieldhouse bleachers. But the *paid* attendance was just 2,540. Most of those 5,000 game-day walkups had walked in with free tickets. With an average sold ticket price of $4.48, total revenue to the Pacers was $11,393.

The game had been billed in the newspapers as Storen's "$40,000 gamble," the amount of money he said the Pacers risked on it. Immediately after the game, Storen told reporters the Pacers would "probably be in the black," but months later their internal documents were bleeding red. They lost $27,536.82. The lack of television revenue, the weather, the competition from the college games and the necessity of giving away so many tickets all conspired to ruin hopes of turning a profit.

Still, the event had made a favorable impression on the local fans and, more importantly, the television audience. The Pacers later would claim three million fans had watched on television. That figure probably was exaggerated as well, but regardless of the actual eyeballs directed toward the the game the league had achieved a new level of exposure and respect. Financially, it was a bloodbath for the Pacers, but nobody had to know that. The attendance figure of 10,872 ran in virtually every newspaper in the country, and was assumed to be true.

Cold, hard facts aside, the Pacers and the ABA benefited from the game, especially locally. A headline in the *Kokomo Tribune* read, "Pity The City That Has To Put On Next Year's All-Star Game." Another in the *Tribune* read, "Pacers Go All Out, All-Star Game Proves ABA To Stay."

Thurlo McCrady, the assistant ABA commissioner who had helped get the AFL started, was impressed, too.

"The AFL had nothing as organized or attractive as this in its first All-Star game," he said.

Hagan, a 10-year veteran of the NBA's St. Louis Hawks, for whom he had been a five-time All-Star, said he had seen the Hawks general manager in the crowd and guessed other NBA officials had attended as well. "I imagine they're getting pretty curious about this new league," he said.

The day also wound up in the win column for the commissioner, despite his luncheon blunder. No matter how many people had purchased tickets, the ABA had never looked better.

"This will be hard to follow," Mikan told reporters after the game. "We figured, though, that if anyone could do the job, the Indiana gang could. And, after all, it seems only fitting and proper that the game should be played in Indiana, the hub of basketball."

7

"He had charisma before we knew what the hell charisma was.
And he could play. Boy, he could play."

Reg-gie

As tends to happen with big parties, a hangover followed.

The Pacers met Minnesota at the Coliseum the night after the All-Star game, in an affair that bore no resemblance to the previous night's extravaganza — for quality or atmosphere. The Pacers had lost all five previous games to the Muskies, but won this one 105-79 after outscoring them 29-10 in the first quarter.

Daniels, still stuck with that '55 Buick station wagon, was not in MVP form, scoring five points on 2-of-12 shooting. Darden was given credit for good defense, but Daniels' performance was at least partially the result of playing for the fourth consecutive night. He had scored 22 points and hit two game-clinching free throws in the Muskies' win over the Pacers in Minneapolis on Jan. 7, then scored 25 points in a loss to Kentucky in Louisville on Jan. 8. After leading the East's All-Star victory on Jan. 9, he stayed overnight in Indianapolis and faced another game on the 10th.

He wasn't alone in his fatigue. Freeman, Minnesota's other all-star playing four games in four nights, hit just 4-of-17 shots. The Muskies combined to hit 27-of-108 attempts – 25 percent – and had to heat up to manage that. They made just 3-of-25 shots in the first period.

Netolicky, who had contributed 12 points and 11 rebounds in the All-Star game, was still perky, scoring 28 points and grabbing 21 rebounds (10 offensive) against the Muskies. Brown, starting in the backcourt with Lewis for the second straight game instead of at forward, added 27 points. Staverman declared it a permanent move.

Herff Jones salesman Bob Leonard kept a close eye on the Pacers from the beginning. Here he watches the Jan. 10 victory over Minnesota with Mike and Hannah Storen.

Only 3,021 fans braved the foul weather, the smallest crowd of the season, but it could have been worse. Over at Hinkle Fieldhouse, Butler drew an announced crowd of 500 for its loss to St. Joseph's. The weather delayed referee Jim Smith's arrival until halftime, so Boynton Robson, the athletic supervisor at the Jewish Community Center and a local high school referee, worked the first 24 minutes. But regardless of the flimsy crowd, Daniels' compromised condition and the substitute referee, the Pacers welcomed their victory.

"We've got our confidence back and we're going after Pittsburgh," Lewis declared. "We think we're the best club in the league and we're going to prove it."

Neither the All-Star "break" nor the victory soothed the issues between Rayl and Staverman, however. Rayl had attended the game at Butler and ran into his coach in the parking lot, where he angrily asked him why he hadn't played against the Muskies in Minneapolis.

"I thought you needed the rest," Staverman said.

"The attitude you got me in now, I don't care if I never play for you again," Rayl said.

"That's fine, you won't," Staverman said.

"That's fine with me," Rayl said. "A damn church league coach would tell you why you're not playing. At least you could have told me."

Rayl didn't play in the post-break game against the Muskies, either. Staverman asked him to report with a couple of minutes left in the blowout victory, but Rayl refused.

The Pacers split their next two games, a home-and-home series with the Pipers. Rayl scored nine points off the bench in the first one, but didn't play in the second, a 113-99 victory at the Coliseum on Jan. 13. Netolicky starred again, with 29 points and 15 rebounds, and Brown once again looked comfortable at guard with 27 points, nine rebounds and nine assists. Aitch, starting again at forward, had 17 points and 10 rebounds. Kozlicki had an effective game off the bench with 13 points and five rebounds.

They were now 24-22, six games back of East-leading Pittsburgh and 5½ back of Minnesota. Their slide toward a .500 record had been blocked by three wins (all on their home court) in their previous five games and Staverman appeared to have found the right starting lineup. Brown had settled in at guard, Aitch was making solid contributions in his place at forward and Netolicky was excelling, averaging 22.7 points over the previous 11 games.

A sense of optimism was returning.

Briefly.

The day after the uplifting victory over Pittsburgh, the Pacers flew to Houston to play the lowly Mavericks. Netolicky began feeling ill on the flight. Upon arriving at the hotel, he looked in the mirror and recoiled at what was staring back at him. His face was swelling and red spots were breaking out. Lareau took him to a doctor, who gave a shocking diagnosis: mumps.

Netolicky returned to his room at the hotel, walked over to his roommate, Bonham, leaned in to show off his condition and said, "Well, babe, I've got the mumps." A couple of weeks later, Bonham would get them as well, essentially ending his professional career. Harkness soon came down with a less severe case, and missed seven games.

Netolicky might have been the least expendable of the Pacers, given the lack of an adequate replacement at center. His primary backup, Peeples, was athletic and aggressive, but undersized and less of a scoring threat.

The Pacers lost at Houston as Netolicky and Lewis, who had the flu, sat out. They lost again the next night in New Orleans after blowing a fourth-quarter lead for the second consecutive night. The only positive to come out of the game was the revival of Rayl. After barely playing at Houston, he led the scoring with 21 points while hitting 7-of-11 field goal attempts and all seven foul shots.

The loss to the Bucs dropped the Pacers to 24-24, their first non-winning record of the season.

With a road-heavy schedule and illness conspiring against them, doubts were creeping in. The thrill of that opening-night victory over Kentucky was a distant memory now, and the season's motto just a tease.

"Since Dec. 10, I don't think we've been giving 110 percent effort 100 percent of the time," Staverman told the *News*.

"Really, the blame belongs to everyone, myself included. I'm learning right along with the players."

His headaches were only going to get worse.

A 36-point loss to Pittsburgh on Jan. 17 in the only home appearance of a seven-game stretch brought something new to the Coliseum: boos. Only 3,128 fans showed up, which perhaps was a good thing under the circumstances, but still disappointing given the presence of the league's most entertaining player, Hawkins. He treated them to 28 points, 16 rebounds and 18 assists in what Overpeck described as an "effortless" performance. The Pacers helped make it that way for him, defending poorly and hitting just 38-of-118 shots. Aitch, who had generally played well while starting in Brown's former spot at forward, hit just 3-of-21 shots.

In three months, the Pacers had fallen from the glory of their victorious debut in front of a capacity crowd to the embarrassment of being booed by an audience one-third of capacity. They now had a losing record and a shorthanded roster. It was beginning to feel like a crisis, and Storen wasn't the type to sit back and hope things worked themselves out. He went looking for a center, and before long a good one was flying to Indianapolis. But he would arrive with plenty of baggage.

Reggie Harding's life story could fill a book. Shakespeare would have written it as a tragedy. Decades later, the mere mention of his name would bring laughter from people who knew him, but tears would have been the most appropriate commentary on his wasted life.

Harding grew up on the East side of Detroit. His only natural asset was his height, and that would turn out to be an obstacle at times. His birth mother was 17 when he was born. His father had no interest in helping raise him or financially supporting her, so she gave him up for adoption to a kindly couple who lived in a better neighborhood. He never met his father, although he was told in later years he might have been standing next to him in a craps game one night. He met his biological mother as an adult and grew close to her, but never would resolve the conflicts of his upbringing.

Harding fell under the negative influence of older boys in the area while growing up, and lacked motivation in school. He was sent to the Moore School for Boys, a reform school for incorrigibles, for a few years, but attended a public high school. He grew to 6-10 by his freshman year, and was blessed with size, strength, agility and soft hands. While he could score, shot-blocking was his forte, and he loved to pass as well. That season an opposing coach, Floyd Groves, called him "the finest ninth-grader I've seen in my 33 years as a coach." He went on to become a three-time all-city selection, a two-time first-team all-state pick and one of 30 players chosen to the *Scholastic Magazine* All-America team as a senior in 1961, when he averaged 29.1 points and 23 rebounds.

The best indication of his ability had come in the city championship game as a sophomore and junior, when he went up against 6-10 Bill Chmielewski, who was a year older. Harding's team won the title both

Reggie Harding, the one and only.

years. Harding was outscored by Chmielewski as a sophomore, 18-14, but won the individual matchup the following season, 27-17. Those performances were meaningful, because Chmielewski went on to lead the University of Dayton to the NIT championship and earn tournament Most Valuable Player honors as a sophomore in 1962, before marrying and dropping out of college.

"Reggie is going to be one of the really great players of all time," Bob Samaras, his coach at Eastern High School (later renamed after

Martin Luther King) told Detroit reporters. "There isn't much he can't do with a basketball now, and he'll get better."

Harding was a beloved team member. He had no siblings, so his teammates were family members to him. He kept their spirits high. He often referred to them as "little brother," as in "Don't worry, little brother, we'll get these guys. No ulcers." He didn't care much for practice because he could excel in the games without it, but improved in that regard toward the end of his high school career.

Samaras wasn't sure what to do with him at first, having never coached a seven-footer, but gradually gained his trust. He had developed a pressing, fastbreaking style of play that he branded "Blitz Basketball," which he explained in a book published in 1963. He won over Harding by playing him at guard in practice to develop his ballhandling and passing skills. Harding rebelled at first – *"That's too much work, Coach!"* – but as soon as he stole the ball in a game while playing the back line in Samaras' fullcourt pressure defense, drove downcourt for a dunk and sent the fans into hysterics, he was sold.

Samaras never knew what to expect from his young center. In a rebounding drill one day, Harding was outdone by a couple of 6-3 players. Frustrated, he stormed out of practice and declared, "You guys just lost your city championship!" He came back a week later, saying, "Where's those two boys? We've got a score to settle!"

Harding was a challenge off the court, too. One time he decided to get a haircut shortly before the team bus was to depart for a game, assuming it wouldn't dare leave without him. When it did, Harding bolted out of the shop with the barber's collar still tied around his neck, running down the street to catch up.

Harding was such a local attraction that the 1961 city championship game, his senior season, drew 9,200 fans at the University of Detroit. Scalpers were getting $3 for 70-cent tickets and $4 for $1.25 tickets before police officers shut them down. Harding led Eastern's victory with 19 points and 21 rebounds.

Naturally, he attracted passionate interest from college recruiters all over the country. There was a sticking point, though: he hadn't earned his high school diploma. He was smart enough to do the work, but hadn't applied himself. Some considered him illiterate, and claimed he had been passed from grade to grade to stay eligible for basketball. He was shipped off to a private school in Tennessee, Nashville Christian High, for a year to get a diploma, with the plan of enrolling at Tennessee State, a college for black students in Nashville.

Harding's dominance was even greater at Nashville Christian. A story in the *Detroit News* reported he was averaging 35 points and 41 rebounds at semester break. He went on to receive his diploma – "receive" likely being a more accurate description than "earn" – but the plan to enroll in college was quickly rejected as superfluous when the Detroit Pistons made him their fourth-round selection in the 1962 NBA draft.

The NBA's rule at the time was that no player could be drafted until he had been out of high school for at least one year, but Harding's status was uncertain. Had his time at the private school in Nashville counted as a year away from high school, or was that his final year of high school because he hadn't earned his diploma at Eastern? NBA commissioner Podoloff and the Boston Celtics objected to the selection, sending the matter to the league's Board of Governors. The Pistons argued his year in Nashville had been post-graduate work, but the NBA disagreed and ruled Harding would have to sit out a season. That was hardly a bad circumstance for him, though. He appeared at banquets and clinics on the team's behalf while on its payroll, and played for a North American Basketball League team in Holland, Mich. on weekends.

He immediately became a fan favorite in Detroit. He was the local, promising and mysterious 7-footer waiting in the wings to bring better days to a beleaguered franchise, and was a natural for public relations. He had a calm, gentle demeanor, and a knack for connecting with people, at least when he desired. At one clinic, a six-year-old white girl latched onto him throughout the afternoon, following him everywhere and literally clinging to his legs when it was time for him to leave. She told him she was going to go home and tell her father she wanted to marry him.

"Honey, would I like to be there to see his face," Harding said, laughing.

With naivety to match his talent, he had no doubts of becoming a star with the Pistons. Most people who had seen him play agreed. Asked near the end of his high school career if he thought he would play in the NBA, he smiled and said, "Is the sun gonna shine?"

The black community in Detroit was especially eager for him to succeed. The Pistons, like all the other NBA teams in the early Sixties, only carried a few black players on their roster. The possibility of someone from the city's streets making the team, and perhaps becoming a star, was inspiring.

The Pistons had to draft Harding again in 1963, in the sixth round this time, and he began playing for them the following season. Legal issues delayed his debut until Jan. 20, 1964, but he made an immediate splash. Coming off the bench in the second quarter, he scored nine points and grabbed five rebounds in the period, a solid contribution toward a 118-107 upset of the Lakers in Los Angeles.

He averaged 11 points and 10.5 rebounds in 39 games that season, and had some memorable outings against star players. He scored 18 points on Feb. 11 against the San Francisco Warriors, a performance dwarfed by Chamberlain's 59 points. He scored 18 against Baltimore's All-Star center, Bellamy, on Feb. 15. He scored 23 against Boston on Feb. 24, two more than Bill Russell, who had won the three previous league MVP awards. He had a season-high 27 against Baltimore on March 5, two less than Bellamy, in a game played in Indiana at Marion High School.

All in all, it was an impressive and promising debut for a 21-year-old rookie who should have been a junior in college.

The Pistons owned the second selection in the 1964 draft, excluding territorial picks, but passed on the likes of Willis Reed because they believed they already had their center of the future. They took forward Joe Caldwell instead. Harding backed up that strategy in his second season (1964-65) by averaging 12 points and 11.6 rebounds over 34.6 minutes through 78 games. One national magazine rated him the fifth-best center in the NBA.

He had 14 games of 20 or more points, including a 29-point effort against the Lakers in Pittsburgh in January. He hit 14-of-18 shots in that game, and blocked a high-floating layup attempt by Jerry West. "If (Harding) is not overpowering, he gave the wrong impression to everybody else at the Arena last night," the story in the *Pittsburgh Press* reported.

He had a 24-point and 28-rebound game against Russell and the Celtics in February and later that month finished with 25 points and 15 rebounds (and a technical foul) in leading a comeback from a 19-point deficit to beat Chamberlain and Philadelphia. Chamberlain finished with 32 points and 21 rebounds, but it still counted as an impressive and promising showing for the young center.

Harding was humble, though. "Aw, sometimes Wilt has a tendency to give up," he said.

Harding was living his dream. His salary was $15,000, he was driving a Ford Thunderbird, and he was in every way a big man in Detroit, seemingly headed for fame and fortune.

That wasn't a good thing. Unprepared for such a sudden lifestyle change, his off-court troubles began mounting in lockstep with his drug and alcohol abuse. He was suspended indefinitely and fined $2,000 after a confrontation with a police officer on Aug. 6, 1965. The day after the Pistons levied that fine, thought to be the largest in NBA history, he was arrested for visiting a "blind pig," an after-hours, illegal drinking establishment. The Pistons suspended him for the season, which only gave him more free time to be sucked into the influences of the streets. He came back to play 74 games for the Pistons in the 1966-67 season, but averaged just 5.5 points and 6.1 rebounds over 18.5 minutes per game.

The Pistons had run out of patience, but there's always a market for talented 7-footers, no matter how troubled. Chicago traded a future draft pick and cash for Harding in September, just before training camp began for the 1967-68 season.

It didn't work out. He averaged 4.6 points and 6.7 rebounds in 21.8 minutes in 14 games with the Bulls and was released on Nov. 25.

He was just 25 years old, and already had accumulated a few lifetimes' worth of mistakes. The unabridged version of his police record at that point was astounding, both for its sheer volume and for the lack of consequences that resulted. Mitigating circumstances always seemed to cloud the issue of his guilt, and someone always seemed willing to forgive him.

For example:

- His first brush with the law came in the summer of 1959, when he was arrested for stealing a car in Pontiac, Mich. He had been sent there by his foster parents to take a job picking cherries and escape the negative elements on Detroit's east side. Harding, though, was the only black kid on the job and was teased mercilessly for his size and color. He wanted to return home. But when he asked the farmer for the money owed him, he was refused. So, one night Harding stole the farmer's truck and drove to the nearest town before giving himself up the next day. It got him out of picking cherries, at least. He was returned to Detroit and put on probation.

- On May 26, 1960, Harding was arrested at his high school track meet for statutory rape, based on an accusation from a 15-year-old girl. On Aug. 8, after a one-day trial, the judge ruled there was "reasonable doubt" Harding had committed a crime and declared him innocent. The girl had been unable to specify the location of the assault and admitted she also had relations with two other men, one 26 years old and one 50.

  (What went unreported for nearly 50 years was the accusation by Florence Ballard that Harding had raped her while in high school. Ballard, who went on to become a member of the Supremes singing group, never filed charges but gave her account to *Detroit Free Press* reporter Peter Benjaminson in 1975, a year before she died of heart disease. He published her description of the incident in 2008 in his book, *The Lost Supreme: The Life of Dreamgirl Florence Ballard.)*

- Once eligible to play for the Pistons, Harding stayed in their good graces for exactly one day. He failed to attend the second day of their summer training session in July of '63, missing a morning practice session and then an afternoon clinic for kids. The Pistons suspended him from the rest of the camp and threatened to drop him outright. It could have been worse, though. The Pistons' other 7-footer, Walter Dukes, didn't show at all.

- Later that month, Harding was accused of felonious assault for displaying a pistol during a confrontation with a bouncer at the Twenty Grand Bar in Detroit. The bouncer, McKinley Johnson, told police Harding had drawn a gun on him before leaving. Harding was later arrested at his home. He was cleared of that charge the following month when his attorney convinced the judge the pistol had actually been a cigarette lighter, and displayed what he claimed was the lighter in question. Harding told the judge he was "just bluffing."

  Although Harding had been cleared legally, the NBA refused to approve Harding's contract with the Pistons, telling them they could re-submit it when he was "more responsible." Pistons executive Fran Smith told the *Detroit News* he wasn't sure of Harding's whereabouts, but thought he was playing with former Harlem Globetrotter Goose Tatum's traveling team on the West Coast. Smith said Harding had called him collect twice, but he had refused the charges. The NBA later accepted Harding's contract, apparently believing he had become "more responsible," and he began playing with the Pistons in January of '64.

- In December of '64, midway through Harding's second season with the Pistons – his best in the NBA – he missed a flight to Philadelphia. He claimed he went to the wrong airport. The Pistons let him off with a warning, but instituted a club policy of $100 fines for missed flights. Four days later, Harding became the first player subjected to that fine after he missed a flight to New York. He told team officials he had been caught in traffic. A few days later, he showed up late for a home game in Detroit on Dec. 18, claiming he had fallen asleep. Fed-up Pistons owner Fred Zollner told player-coach Dave Debusschere to suspend, fine or release Harding outright, whatever he preferred. Debusschere chose to fine him $500 for the third offense, but incorporated the previous $100 fine into that amount, and tacked on another $33.20 for the cost of the airline ticket Harding had not used. It was the largest fine in the Pistons' two-decade history, dating back to their beginnings in Fort Wayne, and surely remains the only $533.20 fine in NBA history.

- Although Harding told the Pistons he was late for the home game because he had fallen asleep at home, his wife, Nadine, later told a reporter he had been with her. She had moved out with her two children, Reggie Jr. and Rachael, while Harding had been away on a road trip because, she said, he had become physically abusive toward her. When he returned to Detroit he tracked her down and refused to leave until she promised to get back together. By the time she said she would, just to get rid of him, it was too late for him to make it to the game on time. He arrived five minutes before tip-off. She filed for divorce later that month.

- On Feb. 7, 1965, Harding pleaded guilty to a reckless driving charge and paid a $50 fine to avoid going to jail. He had run a stop sign. The police officer who wrote up the report said it took 10 men to restrain him. Harding told *Detroit News* columnist Pete Waldmeir one of the officers had suggested he had stolen the car, asking sarcastically where he had gotten such a "greeeaaaat biiiiiiiig car." When he couldn't produce his registration, he said, some officers grabbed him roughly to take him to jail. He fought back, tearing the sleeves of his sport coat. He was told he needed a $50 bond to get out of jail. His wife came at 3 a.m. with $200, but they told her he was sleeping and to come back at 6 a.m. Waldmeir was sympathetic, ending his column by suggesting Harding had been treated unfairly. "How many times have you been stopped for a traffic violation and had to spend the night in jail because you couldn't produce your registration?" he asked readers.

• Harding had explanations for the incidents that caused his suspension for the 1965-66 season, too. The confrontation with the police officer in August of '65 began when Harding stopped in a no-parking zone for 15 minutes at 7:45 a.m. while a friend went inside a tavern to look for other friends. When the officer, James Coffin, asked for his license and registration and returned to the squad car, Harding walked back to plead for mercy. The officer told him to move because he was blocking traffic by standing in the middle of the street. With about 30 bystanders gathering around them and egging him on, Harding said, "Make me get out." Harding said the officer then slammed down his clipboard and burst out of the car, approaching him aggressively. Harding then slapped the officer and knocked off his cap, but did not injure him. Coffin tried to arrest Harding on the spot, but the assembled crowd moved in and blocked him. Six squad cars soon arrived, and Harding was arrested without incident. In court a month later, Harding claimed Coffin had called him "boy" – witnesses supported him on that claim – and said he had inadvertently struck Coffin when he raised his arms in self-defense. Harding was given a suspended sentence.

• The day after his court appearance and the resulting $2,000 fine from the Pistons, Harding was arrested in the "blind pig" incident at 4:30 a.m. His explanation was that he was simply attending a friend's birthday party, and knew nothing of illegal alcohol sales. He was one of 27 people arrested, but claimed vengeful police officers had followed him all evening, waiting for an opportunity to arrest him for *something*. He apologized at every opportunity that week, and the judge dismissed the charges on a technicality. The Pistons, however, did not relent. He remained suspended for the season. "This is the first step in trying to clean up my record so I can resume basketball playing," Harding said in court. "As things stand now, man, I'm washed up at the age of 23."

- Harding was in the news again on Dec. 9 of '65, during his winter in exile, for falling $4,040 behind in his child support payments of $40 per week. He had made only one payment.
- He received more sympathetic media coverage a week later, however, in a column by Joe Falls of the *Detroit Free Press,* titled "A Helping Hand For Reggie." Falls visited Harding at a tuxedo rental store, Broadway Clothes, where Harding was working. Store owner Richard Jarrett had taken him in and was trying to teach him how to hold down a job and save money. In a good week, Harding was earning $125 with commissions, and Jarrett was putting $12 of it into a savings account. Harding told Falls he had been a victim of circumstances and had only been hit with one conviction, which had been suspended. Jarrett praised Harding's work in the store, which including cleaning the floors and windows, and said he had displayed a professional manner with customers. He also said Harding was going to spend one night a week at a police precinct, mentoring underprivileged boys. "Reggie got in with the wrong crowd," Jarrett told Falls, entering the competition for understatement of the decade.
- A few days later, on Dec. 21, Harding appeared four hours late in traffic court to plead guilty for driving without a license. He also had six previous violations totaling $185 in fines. Asked for an explanation by the judge, he said, "I can't give you any reason."

Realizing that the fountain of sympathy was running dry, Harding put on a public relations campaign heading into the 1966-67 season, when he returned to the Pistons after his suspension. With his attorney in tow, he flew to New York to beg the NBA's new commissioner, Walter Kennedy, to reinstate him. He took his case to the media as well. Late in September, Waldmeir wrote another favorable column in the *News.* He reported Harding was wearing a neatly tailored sport coat, cuff-less trousers, new shoes and had shaved his mustache. He also mentioned Harding had spent a few days in jail, lost his home and Thunderbird, and had no money in his wallet. He added Harding had "been before more judges than Perry Mason," and "had more chances than Matsumuri

(Chicken) Yamamoto, the famous Japanese Kamikaze pilot who flew 76 missions," and had "more guys go to bat for him than the Los Angeles Dodgers."

Debusschere was one of those. He still needed a center, and was willing to give him yet another chance. Harding seemed eager to make it work this time, Waldmeier wrote.

Years after the fact, it became known why Harding's final season with the Pistons didn't go well: he had become hooked on heroin while sitting out under the suspension the previous year. Nadine, his estranged wife, later said he had been taking methadone pills during the season to try to overcome his addiction, but probably was still using heroin, too. His stats reflected the inevitable decline.

There was no evidence of a heroin habit during Harding's time with the Bulls, but his other habits caught up with him. The highlight of his final shot in the NBA came in San Francisco on Oct. 29, when he scored 17 points against future Hall of Fame center Nate Thurmond. But he left the team before its next game in Seattle on Oct. 31 to attend the funeral for his adoptive mother, Fannie Harding, the woman who had taken him in and done her best to raise him against all odds. He then disappeared into the city's east side streets, missing the Bulls' first win of the season after nine losses on Nov. 2, in Chicago. He missed another home game on Nov. 7 and then rejoined the team in Chicago for the Bulls' game against Boston on Nov. 9. Dubbed the "vanishing American" by the *Chicago Tribune's* Bob Logan, he had been fined for his absence, and was reinstated shortly before the game.

Harding accompanied the Bulls on another Western road trip, which began with two games in Los Angeles. They had a chance to get their second win of the season in the first of those, leading by a point with just a few seconds to go. The Lakers had an inbound pass underneath their own basket in the final seconds and threw the ball away, but Harding, Bulls coach Red Kerr would recall in later years, "decked" Mel Counts away from the ball for an unknown reason and Counts hit the game-winning foul shots. (The *Los Angeles Times* reported Harding "shoved" Counts.)

Harding, who grabbed 16 rebounds in that game, scored 10 points in the next game against the Lakers three days later, but Kerr was running out of patience. He used Harding only sporadically in games over the next 10 days, sometimes not at all. Finally, a few days after a scoreless appearance against Philadelphia on Nov. 25, 1967, Harding was released.

Schellhase, the former Purdue All-American playing for the Bulls, wasn't surprised, given what he had witnessed earlier that season when the Bulls played at Detroit. Harding had disappeared as soon as the Bulls arrived the day before the game. When he rejoined the team at the arena the night of the game, he fell asleep while the trainer taped his ankles.

"He's been smoking dope all day," teammate Keith Erickson said.

The Pacers were aware of Harding's history — some of it, anyway – but either didn't know of or chose to ignore the extent of it. Had they dug into the clip files of the Detroit newspapers, they would have learned plenty. They didn't have time for that, however. Netolicky had the mumps, Peeples had the flu, they were facing a stretch of four games in four nights and no warehouses were stocking capable centers.

"If you get up in the morning and you see your team is without a center, you ask who's available and who they are," Storen explained years later. "He was available."

Storen telephoned Harding, who was playing for a New Jersey team in the Eastern League after his release from the Bulls, and flew him to Indianapolis. He and Tinkham met Harding at the airport at about 6 a.m. on Jan. 19. Harding was the only passenger on the flight, Storen recalled. He walked off the plane and through the door leading into the gate area wearing a black trench coat several sizes too small with a pair of basketball shoes flung over his shoulder, tied together by the laces.

"Suppose that's him?" Tinkham said in his best deadpan voice.

Harding's handshake was so strong, Tinkham recalled, it brought tears to his eyes. The three men went to the airport coffee shop, found a booth and began to talk. Storen slipped into his sales pitch, telling him how much he would like Indianapolis and how good the team could be with him playing center. Harding wasn't interested in that, and what little conversation he did offer was laced with profanities. He said he could bring the Pacers a championship, but had just one guiding interest: money.

The problem was determining fair value for a player whose talent and potential were equaled only by the immense trouble he created.

Memories of the exact negotiations are slightly conflicting. Storen remembers offering $10,000 for the rest of the season. Tinkham says it was $12,000, maybe $13,000. Either way, Harding wasn't impressed.

"If you were planning to go buy a Cadillac, would you take just enough money for a Chevrolet?" Harding asked.

Finally, Tinkham handed Harding a napkin and told him to write down how much he wanted, adding he would try to give it to him on his own conditions.

"Are you serious, man?" Harding asked.

Tinkham assured him he was.

Harding wrote down $15,000. Then Tinkham responded with the conditions.

"There's 29 games left in the season," he told Harding. "If we're going to win the championship, that's three rounds of seven games, for 21 games. That's 50, total. We'll give you what you want and divide it by 50, and we'll pay you on a per-game basis."

In other words, $300 per game – which happened to be more per game than any of the other Pacers were making over the course of their 78-game schedule.

Harding eyed him suspiciously.

"Does that add up?"

Tinkham assured him it did.

"OK, man," Harding said with a smile.

Harding had missed a couple of key points. For one, the first round of the playoffs was a best-of-five series, so there could only be 48 remaining games at most. It's possible Tinkham wasn't aware of that, and nearly certain Harding wasn't, but also not that big of a deal. More importantly, what were the odds the Pacers would play every potential playoff game? Harding hadn't bothered to consider that likelihood.

Harding's education was limited, but not as much as his options. He needed a job, and basketball was his only proven skill. The Pacers, meanwhile, had no proven starting center, and Harding was the best they could find. It was a match made in desperation.

The Pacers had a strict dress code for travel and hair length, but there wasn't time to get a custom-made suit for their new 7-footer, or for him to trim his bushy Afro, as the team was leaving soon to play a game that evening in New Jersey. He boarded the plane, with little more than the clothes on his back, but didn't play that night. The article in the following morning's *Star* reported "the ex-bad boy of the NBA" had joined the team, but hadn't met two of the three conditions Storen had laid out for him (probably pertaining to dress code issues). Most likely, he also didn't have a uniform yet. The Pacers lost to New Jersey, 122-110.

Harding had a quiet debut in the rematch the following night, scoring three points on 1-of-5 shooting and grabbing four rebounds in a 10-point loss. He made more noise the next night at Minnesota, scoring 19 points and grabbing nine rebounds against the Muskies. Daniels scored 25 and grabbed 18 rebounds, though, and the Pacers lost their sixth straight game, 103-88.

That loss was forgivable. Having flown into Minnesota early in the morning from New Jersey, they were expecting to play a 7:30 p.m. game. Upon reaching their hotel, however, they learned they would be playing at 1:30. The starting time had been changed to accommodate a hockey game that evening, but nobody had bothered to tell the Pacers in advance. Rushing to the Metropolitan Sports Arena on short notice, they hit just 4-of-21 shots in the first quarter and fell behind 35-15. They outscored the Muskies the rest of the way and got within six in the third quarter, thanks largely to Harding's performance off the bench, but fell short.

Harding started for the first time the next night in Louisville and scored 17 points against Kentucky. The Pacers lost again, their seventh in a row, but it was understandable as well. They had played their fourth game in four nights, all on the road, and were breaking in a new center.[1]

And a promising one, at that. Even in the previous two losses, Harding had shown enough flashes of production to bring optimism to a fading team. He had provided low-post scoring, deterred opponents from driving to the basket and drawn defensive attention away from his frontline teammates. Darden was the early beneficiary, scoring a season-high 24 points at Minnesota and a team-high 19 at Kentucky.

Harding also was displaying his contradictory personality. He had played poorly in the fourth quarter of the loss to the Colonels, and apologized afterward to Staverman. "I'm sorry, Coach, I let you down tonight. I just didn't have it out there," he said.

"Nobody else has ever come up to me and told me that," Staverman told Overpeck after relating Harding's message.

The Pacers wouldn't play again for five nights after the loss at Kentucky, providing a needed opportunity for the team to catch its collective breath and get back on the practice court to assimilate the new center. It also gave Harding a day to go back to Detroit and gather whatever belongings he had left there.

That only meant trouble.

He was due back for practice Wednesday evening, Jan. 24, two days after the loss in Louisville. He didn't make it. He missed Thursday's practice as well, and failed to call Storen to explain his absence until late that afternoon. Just six days into yet another "second chance," he had managed to mess up badly enough to be disciplined.

"We're not going to compromise our organization for anything or anyone," Storen told the *News*. "That's been Reggie's problem. People have always been doing things for him. He definitely can help our program, but he has to show he wants to be a part of it. He has to sacrifice, too."

---

[1] Schedules were bizarre for all the ABA teams that first season, as they scrambled to secure arena dates at the last minute. Anaheim, for example, played 23 of its first 29 games on the road.

Storen's use of the word "program" wasn't accidental. Because of his military background, he ran the Pacers in a rigid, conservative fashion. Decorum counted. Hair and sideburns were to be kept trimmed, shorter than the popular styles of the day. Suits and ties were to be worn on airplanes, and fines were issued for tardiness. Harding, though, was accustomed to running a program all his own.

He was fined and dropped from the starting lineup for his home debut against Minnesota, but scored 12 points and grabbed 16 rebounds to help the Pacers to a come-from-behind overtime victory, 115-108. The win not only ended the seven-game losing streak, it came over one of the league's best teams in a well-played game. Denny called it "easily the finest contest of the season." A crowd of 5,287 turned out on a Saturday night despite the losing streak to check out the new 7-footer.

Lewis and Brown, still excelling together in the backcourt, combined for 50 points, and Brown had a game-high nine assists. The most encouraging aspect of the victory, however, was that Harding and Netolicky – who had practiced for the first time the previous day after his bout with the mumps – played together for 21 ½ prosperous minutes off the bench. Darden played a third-straight strong game with 24 points. The Pacers also outrebounded the Muskies for the first time in their eight meetings, 59-57, neutralizing Daniels and Skip Thoren.

It was just one victory, and it followed a seven-game losing streak. But it felt like the season had just reversed course.

"We can be the best one-two punch in the league – if the guards give up the ball!" Harding said in the locker room, loudly enough for all to hear, as he slipped into a French-cuffed shirt.

He was kidding. He already had established enough rapport with his teammates to make jokes, and the feeling was becoming mutual.

"Reggie's going to help us a lot," said Netolicky, who scored six of his 12 points in the overtime, including a crucial hook shot over Daniels. "With him in the lineup, I'll be able to work against the smaller men."

Brown, rarely one to enthuse about anything, was impressed as well.

"Harding is a real good pivotman to work with," he said. "He waits for the cutters and he can shoot good when close to the basket. There's no doubt he's going to help us."

Harding was coolly optimistic, too.

"It's a new opportunity and I'm happy to be in Indiana," he said. "The enthusiasm of the fans is something.

"This game is my living and I love it, and whenever I go in I'll give my best. But I can't do it by myself. It has to be a joint effort. Bob Netolicky is a good ballplayer. We'll have to get our signals straight, but I think everything's going to work out."

The renewed optimism ramped up another level after the next game, when the Pacers defeated the Eastern Division's other power, Pittsburgh, 119-113, at Shelbyville High School, a game sponsored by the Shelbyville Lions Club. The two teams rode to and from the game on the same bus out of Indianapolis to save expenses, then faced off before a sellout crowd of 5,875. "Most of them were doubtlessly drawn by the presence of 7-foot Reggie Harding in the Pacer lineup," Overpeck wrote in the *Star*.

If so, Harding didn't disappoint, finishing with 18 points and 22 rebounds. Neither did Netolicky, who started with him for the first time and had 22 points and 20 rebounds. Lewis led the Pacers with 31 points, Brown had 13 points and a team-record 10 assists and Darden added 17 points and nine rebounds.

Suddenly, the Pacers had a starting lineup loaded with size, talent and chemistry. They were 26-29, still 10 ½ games back of the lead, but had just defeated the two teams ahead of them in the Eastern Division. They had more momentum and optimism than at any time over the past month, and more legitimate hope to compete in the playoffs because of Harding.

Denny's story in the *News* the next day opened with two questions that provided one roundabout answer: "How good are the Pacers with Reggie Harding at center? How high is the moon?"

Denny's hyperbole was justified on this occasion, given the comments coming out of the locker room.

"The big man makes the difference," Brown said. "We're going to win a lot of games from now on. Pittsburgh won 15 straight and so can we. We might even go 24-0 the rest of the way."

Brown chuckled at the thought, but Lewis, sitting nearby, chimed in.

"I'm serious about that," Lewis said. "I think we can go 24-0."

Harding, meanwhile, said he was two weeks away from achieving top physical condition and regaining his timing and touch. But as a per-game employee, he had his own motivation for going deep into the playoffs.

"I can't see any reason why we can't be right at the top at the end of the season," he told Denny. "It would be kinda nice to be a champion and get a little of that playoff money."[2]

He gave a similar quote to the *Pittsburgh Press*: "I don't care where I play, as long as I play for money."

The Pacers were getting a bargain for this kind of impact. Overpeck pointed out the risk factors in a Sunday column titled, "Reggie And Pacers Are Both On Spot," but also the potential rewards.

"If he will direct his obvious touch for buffoonery to enliven the club's dressing rooms, he can be a big help to the Pacers," Overpeck wrote.

"Harding may be turning a corner in his life," he added later. "For his sake and the Pacers', let's hope so. If he is, Reggie can do a lot for both himself and the club."

---

[2] The Pipers later filed a protest to the league office over the fact the game was played on an 84-foot high school court rather than a standard 94-foot professional floor. Pipers' general manager Gabe Rubin said the ABA rules required all games to be played on 94-foot courts. Staverman claimed the ABA rule book stated the 94-foot length was the "optimum length," adding, "The Pipers apparently don't know the meaning of 'optimum.'" Pittsburgh coach Vince Cazzetta claimed the shorter floor limited the fastbreak opportunities for his undersized team. Staverman fired back that Cazzetta had not said anything about the court length before or after the game when the teams shared the bus ride. Storen weighed in, too, on Rubin's comment that playing in a high school gym was not "major league." "I say you judge something major league by how many people come out to watch your product," he said. "Maybe we won't want to play anymore in Pittsburgh, because they don't draw enough people." Vaughn, who hit 1-of-9 three-pointers in the game, claimed the hastily-placed three-point lines were too far out, adding, "You can ask Freddie Lewis." The protest was later denied by the league office. Another memory from that game: York, head of the stat crew, was asked to get off the bus and go back to the locker room to retrieve Harding's duffel bag afterward. When he looked inside, it contained nothing but three copies of a book by Malcolm X, the Muslim minister and civil rights activist.

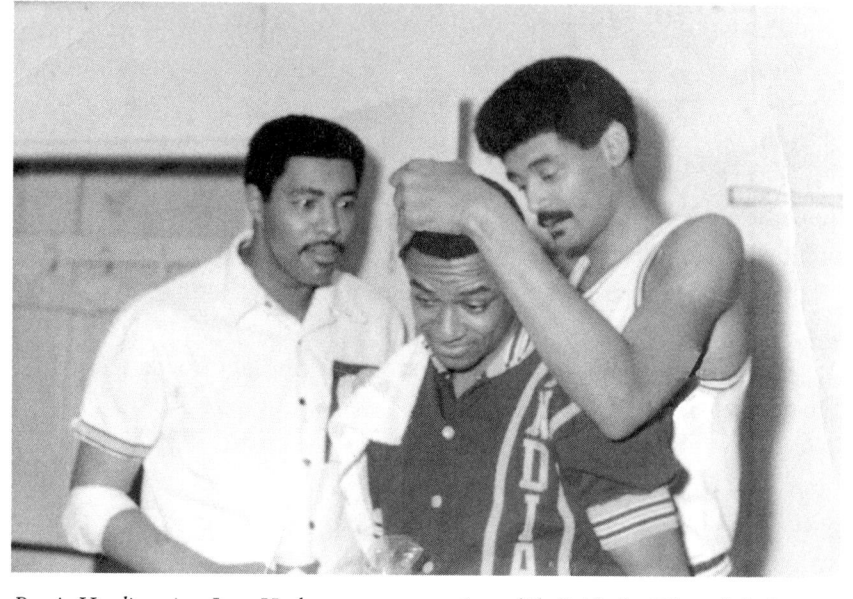

Reggie Harding gives Jerry Harkness a pregame trim, while Bobby Joe Edmonds looks on.

The Pacers won their next game as well, in New Jersey, breaking a 12-game road losing streak and winning a third straight game for the first time since Dec. 7. Harding and Netolicky were mediocre this time, but Lewis and Brown continued to thrive together in the backcourt. Lewis finished with 31 points and 11 rebounds, while Brown had 26 points and six assists.

Not everyone was happy, though. Rayl scored 14 of the Pacers' 16 points in a 5 ½ minute stretch to close the second quarter, leading a comeback from a nine-point deficit to a two-point halftime lead. But he didn't play a second in the second half.

He confronted Staverman in the locker room afterward. Staverman replied Lewis and Brown had been playing too well to take out, and the game was still close.

"What kind of game do you think I was having?!" Rayl fumed. "I was only scoring at a rate of about 200 points a game!"

That blip aside, the Pacers continued to roll. They won at Pittsburgh four days later, 113-100. Hawkins, on his way to being voted the league's MVP at the end of the season, missed the game because of a blood clot in his left calf, the result of a bruise suffered in the game in Shelbyville. His absence dulled some of the shine of the Pacers' win, but their continuing improvement was undeniable. Lewis led with 26 points. Netolicky followed with 22, Darden 20, Harding 15 and Rayl 11. Netolicky also had 20 rebounds, and Harding 16. Brown had just nine points, but had 10 rebounds and six assists.

Dill, traded by the Pacers to Pittsburgh just before the start of the season, had 18 points and 13 rebounds for the Pipers.

The Pacers won again the next night back at the Coliseum, over New Jersey by one point, running their win streak to five and their record to 29-29. It shouldn't have been that close against a weak team such as the Nets and Staverman wasn't pleased, but it counted just the same.

"We're trying to be the nice guys in the white hats," Staverman said. "I just wish we'd be the bad guys in the black hats for once."

If anyone could change a team's personality, it was Harding, who was bringing an inner-city demeanor to the team. He grabbed 27 rebounds against the Nets, a franchise record and one short of the ABA record shared by two other Detroit natives: Daniels and Pittsburgh center Ira Harge. Harding also scored 18 points. He hit two free throws with 1:32 left to give the Pacers a four-point lead, and fed Darden for a layup on the next possession to open a six-point advantage.

Netolicky led all scorers with 30 points and added 15 rebounds, reinforcing the potential of his partnership with Harding. Brown had 22 points, eight rebounds and seven assists, reinforcing the reality of his all-around skill-set.

Harding promised Staverman he would break the rebounding record the following night at Kokomo High School, where the Pacers would play Denver. It would be their third game in three nights, but they were riding the momentum of a five-game winning streak, made even more dramatic because it followed a seven-game losing streak. The aura of defeat and despair had evaporated.

Harding was hyped in the advance story in the *Kokomo Tribune* as the Pacers' "new 7-foot cure" and "7-feet of medicine." Tickets were available throughout town at sporting goods stores, barber shops, a bowling alley and a dry cleaning store, at $3 and$2, and $1 for children 12 and under. Rayl, the hometown hero, was the primary attraction, but Harding also was inspiring ticket-buyers.

"Many people apparently consider the Pacers on the scrap heap," Conard wrote in the *Tribune* four days before the game. "Maybe they ought to look a little closer. That monster you see hovering over everything else is Reggie Harding ... the guy that could put the Pacers atop the ABA heap."

The game was a disappointment. Denver won, 98-91, as the Pacers – "lifeless and uninspired" in Denny's estimation in the *News* – fell back below .500. The crowd (3,771) was disappointing, too, but the game wasn't without excitement.

Harding finished with 16 points and 18 rebounds, but was outplayed by Denver's 6-9 rookie center Byron Beck, who finished with 29 points. Beck outscored Harding 14-1 in the first quarter and was having his way in the second, too, holding and pushing Harding to try to negate his height advantage. Finally, midway through the second period, Harding fired an elbow at Beck's mouth and knocked him down. Beck jumped up with fire in his eyes and went after Harding, who, according to Marvel and York, ran out the gym's south doors and into the lobby to avoid confrontation. Beck was eventually corralled by Staverman and some of the other Pacers, and nobody was ejected.

Asked afterward about the "scuffle," Harding replied, "What scuffle? There wasn't any scuffle. He just got caught doing something he shouldn't have been doing."

Shortly after the game resumed, play stopped for a free throw in front of Denver's bench. Rayl, who had started the game – partly because of his local status and partly because Brown had a sore back – turned to Denver forward Tom Hoover, who at 6-9 and 230 pounds was one of the ABA's most intimidating players and a former sparring partner of Muhammad Ali.

"Hey, Tom, if anything else breaks out, it's you and me!" Rayl shouted. "I want you!"

The joking intent was obvious. The Denver players erupted in laughter.

That loss aside, Harding was looking more and more like a savvy acquisition by Storen and Tinkham. Perhaps even a savior. Playing as well as any center in the ABA, he had restored order and confidence to the starting lineup. The Pacers had outrebounded every opponent during their five-game winning streak because of him. His unselfishness and passing ability in the low post produced easy baskets for teammates, and his outlet passes off defensive rebounds led to fastbreaks that had been nearly nonexistent before his arrival.

He was as enjoyable to watch as he was to play with. His raw height, accentuated by a healthy Afro only slightly trimmed down to meet Storen's specifications, made for an intimidating presence, and his enthusiasm was infectious. He nearly always played hard and with emotion. After scoring, he ran back on defense with a fist raised high in the air. It was his version of the "black power" salute that was in vogue at the time, but in this context the conservative element of the Pacers fan base didn't seem to mind at all.

"He was always striving to do his best," Harkness recalled in later years. "He really wanted to win."

Overpeck, writing in the Sunday *Star* three days after the game in Kokomo, revisited the acquisition with unabashed optimism, stating, "There can be little doubt now that the Indiana Pacers' gamble on Reggie Harding has paid off."

His second paragraph, however, would prove foreboding.

"It has paid off even if Harding does an about-face and returns to his old ways of temper and trouble."

The loss in Kokomo was followed by a loss in New Jersey, which was followed by a loss in Kentucky. The losing streak ended with a win over Oakland at the Coliseum, 120-109, in which Brown scored a pro career high of 37 points, along with 13 rebounds and five assists.

Afterward, Brown acknowledged he needed glasses, but had never been able to afford them. Dayton's program was going to provide them after his freshman season, but his suspension prevented that from happening. He hadn't brought it up when he signed with the Pacers because he didn't want to hurt his chance of making the team, and by now had grown accustomed to squinting his way through games.

"I'm blind out there," he told Denny in the *News*. "Everything's a blur. Most guys shoot at the rim, I guess. I shoot at color. If they ever changed from orange to something else and didn't tell me, I'd be in trouble."

The rims were orange in Minneapolis, where the Pacers played the next night. Brown, however, hit just 7-of-23 shots and the Pacers squandered an eight-point lead in the third quarter in a 99-96 loss. The two teams met again the next night in Dayton, where Storen had scheduled a game for Brown's benefit. Brown played well this time, finishing with 28 points, seven rebounds and eight assists, but the 122-101 loss was otherwise a dismal performance. The Pacers committed nine turnovers and hit just 6-of-17 shots in the second quarter, and were so poor defensively Minnesota scored 27 points despite committing eight turnovers of its own in the period.

Harding scored just seven points off the bench, but might not have been in a good frame of mind for the game. The players, having flown overnight from Minneapolis, were tired by the time they got to their hotel in Dayton. Some of them, however, passed on sleeping to play craps in one of the rooms during the afternoon. Harding's dice were cold, and as his losses mounted the razzing from his teammates grew, to the point he accused them of ganging up on him.

Later that evening in the locker room before the game, Harding was still angry at Rayl, one of his primary tormentors.

"There goes Tweety Bird now," he scoffed as Rayl walked past him. "He thinks he's slick. You put his brain in a bird, it'd fly backwards."

Amid some laughter from teammates, Rayl kept walking but fired back with an over-the-shoulder shot: "Yeah, Reggie, but at least it would fly."

That brought louder laughs, which only angered Harding more.

Storen wasn't laughing on the way home that night. Just a week earlier, his team had won a fifth straight game and was talking of winning its final 24 of the season. Now it had dropped five of its previous six games and fallen to just two games ahead of last place. Venting his frustration on the drive home to Denny, who was riding with him, he planted some seeds for Denny's story the next afternoon. Chief among them was his belief that the players were becoming spoiled by the trappings of their success. That was Storen's manner. He didn't ask for favors from the beat writers, but he suggested themes for their stories.

Denny bit, inserting Storen's thoughts in the 10th paragraph of his story: "Indiana ... seems to be a team that drives fancy cars, wears expensive suits and plays bad basketball." Later in the article he quoted Storen calling the performance "abominable," and added, "Maybe we've been too good to the players. I don't think we're getting near what we should be getting in return for the what we've given."

Denny received some blowback from the players, particularly Lewis, after the article appeared and was guilt-ridden for having been manipulated. But his compliance exemplified the spirit of the favorable newspaper coverage at the time. Collins had refused stock in the team to avoid a major ethical violation, but boosted it from his powerful position at the *Star*. Just as importantly, Storen thought in later years, Fuson didn't assume a contrary position with the *News* to try to drum up interest from readers. He was a supporter as well. In another decade, such a supportive journalistic approach would not have been acceptable, but in this time and in this place, it was indulged.

Journalistic mores aside, Storen considered the newspapers' enthusiastic coverage essential to the franchise's early survival, and appreciated the open microphone he was provided to market the team and send messages to the players.

"In those days, you could tell the press anything and they would believe it," he said years later.

Storen's blunt message to his players made a difference. They bounced back two nights later with an energetic 115-99 victory over a Houston team careening toward the ABA's third-worst record, 29-49.

Denny, aiming for a makeup call, lathered on the praise. His lead paragraph read, "The Indiana Pacers answered their critics, this writer one of the harshest among them, the best possible way Saturday night: with a strong, aggressive all-for-one-one-for-all performance …"

He described the game as "beautiful to watch," claimed the Pacers were "sharp in almost every phase" and possessed "a go-get-'em attitude." Netolicky, whose nature was to respond to criticism, scored 26 points and Harding added 15 points, 14 rebounds and a new nickname.

"Diamond Reg sparkled in the stretch," Denny wrote.

The next game came on Feb. 19 against Kentucky at Madison High School, two hours south of Indianapolis. Like the preseason game, it had been scheduled several months earlier, when it seemed safe to assume Madison alum Humes would be on the roster. As it turned out, the local fans were likely more offended than excited by the arrival of the team that had cut their hometown hero. The official attendance was 2,121, which had the ring of a made-up attendance figure and probably was exaggerated. Regardless, it was the smallest crowd of the season, and some of those who did attend were Kentucky fans who made the drive across the Ohio River bridges. They, at least, were pleased with the Colonels' 134-129 victory.

Rayl made it interesting, scoring 30 points off the bench, 15 in the third quarter, to lead a comeback to which two other reserves, Aitch and Harkness, also contributed. Rayl started the next game in Indianapolis, against Denver, filling the opening created by Harding, who was benched for arriving just 20 minutes before tip-off. The Pacers won, 123-110, as Rayl played his best game of the season. He finished with 33 points, although he needed 29 shots to do it, and added 14 rebounds and seven assists. He played 46 of the game's 48 minutes, as Brown moved back to forward and Netolicky to center. Harding watched from the bench.

"Maybe I ought to miss more often," Harding said after the victory. "I just overslept."

Harding was given the choice of paying a fine and not dressing for the game, or paying a stiffer fine and dressing, with no likelihood of playing. He took the latter option, saying he owed it to the team to be available if needed, and was praised for the decision by Overpeck.

He didn't play, but wasn't needed. Netolicky's 26 points and 17 rebounds took up the slack on the front line. The evening belonged to Rayl, though, who admitted to Denny he had been angry over lack of playing time and struggled with his temperament.

That victory started a four-game win streak, all at home.[3] The third of those victories came over Oakland, in two overtimes, 122-116. Rayl scored seven points in the second overtime to lead the victory, and Harding locked up Oaks center Jim Hadnot. Netolicky had allowed Hadnot nine points in the first quarter, but Harding gave up just nine on 3-of-17 shooting in the 26 ½ minutes he defended Hadnot.

By now, the pattern with Harding was obvious. If you could get him to the game on time, he probably was going to help you win. He was becoming a favorite of fans and media alike for his enthusiastic play and calm demeanor off the court. Denny referred to him as the "genial giant" and praised his defense and experience, further noting Harding always asked for his rebound total rather than scoring total after games.

After a fourth straight victory over Anaheim, the Pacers played New Orleans in Fort Wayne for their seventh and final "home game" of the season away from Indianapolis. Harding asked permission to go back to Detroit the day before the game, claiming he needed to visit a sick relative. Predictably, he didn't get back to Fort Wayne until five minutes after tip-off, and Staverman refused to allow him to dress. The Pacers lost, 128-118.

They lost the next two games as well, at New Jersey and Houston, with Harding coming off the bench. Staverman, however, was so

---

[3] The second of those wins came over Kentucky, and brought an unexpected revelation. The three-point line at the Coliseum was about a foot too far from the basket. Dampier told coach Gene Rhodes, who had replaced John Givens earlier in the season, it didn't look right during pregame warmups. Rhodes took the complaint to Storen, who initially scoffed at the idea, thinking it was just another bit of gamesmanship from the rival opponent. The line was measured, however, and the Colonels were correct; it was 13 inches too far from the basket. Storen offered to have the lines moved then and there. The Colonels were willing to wait, but enjoyed having the last word. "Indiana has been smoking and steaming about being the best organization in the league, and then something like that happens," Rhodes said afterward. "It seems a bit ridiculous."

unhappy with Netolicky's play in the three losses that he returned Harding to the starting lineup for the game against New Jersey at the Coliseum on March 9, and was rewarded with a 120-99 victory. Harding responded with 14 points and 18 rebounds. Brown had 36 points on 15-of-19 shooting, along with 13 rebounds and five assists. Rayl scored 24 while hitting four three-pointers, and had seven rebounds and six assists. Lewis scored 22 points. Regardless of who started with him, Harding seemed to make everyone and everything better.

The Pacers were learning what the players, coaches and administrators in Detroit and Chicago already knew: Harding was a strange brew of talent, charisma and confounding irresponsibility. They enjoyed his affable nature and sense of humor, but generally kept their distance from him off the court, figuring he would only bring them trouble. Besides, most of the players were married and none of them shared the experiences of Harding's upbringing. He was mostly left alone in Indianapolis.

Some of them had no choice but to be involved, though. He didn't own a car, so he needed rides everywhere. He was living at the Marott Hotel, a five-minute drive from the Coliseum, so picking him up wasn't much of an inconvenience. Cooperating with Harding on anything, however, was destined to bring frustrations. Edmonds recalled stopping by one morning to pick up Harding for practice but having to wait because he wasn't ready. They both wound up late, and both wound up getting fined.

Darden, the fellow Detroit native, was assigned the primary task of transporting and mentoring Harding. He was the perfect choice. A college graduate who had a goal of becoming the mayor of Detroit, Darden was one of the most mature members of the organization, front office included. He had played against Harding in high school, and they had mutual acquaintances back home. He knew all about Harding's personal background and badly wanted for him to rise above it and build a successful life.

He did what he could. He invited Harding over to his home for dinner, loaned him money, and offered advice.

"This is Indianapolis, it's a basketball town, you can make it here," Darden told him. "It's not that far from Detroit, so you can go back home occasionally. You're running out of chances, though. You can't keep messing up. You've got to be a better person than this."

Harding would listen, and say he would try. But his good intentions never translated to positive behavior for long.

The real adventures involving Harding came on the road, where his teammates were forced to spend time with him. Edmonds recalled one revealing moment during a trip to New Jersey when they went into Harlem for haircuts, and then for lunch at Sylvia's, a renowned soul food restaurant on Lenox Ave., between 126th and 127th Streets. Afterward, they walked to catch transportation back to their hotel.

Standing at an intersection near the restaurant, waiting for the light to change, Harding stepped off the curb onto the street and said, "This is right where I need to be, Bobby Joe. Right in the gutter."

"Surely you don't mean that," a stunned Edmonds said.

Harding didn't answer.

The most infamous incident involving Harding during his time with the Pacers occurred on March 10, in New Orleans. In those days of lax security, a man could pack a gun in his duffel bag and carry it on an airplane, and Harding did just that. Where he came from, carrying a gun was normal, even necessary. On this early-morning trip, just hours after the 21-point homecourt victory over New Jersey, the Pacers checked into their French Quarter hotel and headed for their rooms to get a few hours of sleep before an afternoon game against the Western Division-leading Bucs at Loyola Field House.

Rayl turned out the lights and settled into bed. Moments later, he heard the cock of a gun hammer. He turned on the light and saw a smiling Harding sitting on the edge of the bed next to him, pointing the gun at him.

"Reggie, I'm afraid of guns, don't point that at me," Rayl said calmly.

Harding laughed and began twirling it around.

"Tweety Bird's afraid of guns!" he said gleefully.

"Yeah, I am. Let me see it," Rayl said.

After convincing Harding to hand it over, Rayl emptied the shells into his left hand and returned the gun to Harding.

"I'll give them back to you when I wake up," Rayl said, as he lay back down.

Moments later, Harding turned on the light again.

"Tweety Bird, you think you're slick, don't you?" Harding said. He reached into his shaving kit, pulled out another box of shells, reloaded his gun and slammed the cylinder shut.

"Well, I think I'll go down and get something to eat," Rayl said.

"You think you're slick, you're going to get a beer, aren't you?" Harding asked.

"Yeah, whatever," Rayl said.

Rayl's plan was to get another room and some sleep, but the hotel was sold out. He sat on a couch in the lobby for an hour or so, and then returned to the room, figuring Harding would be asleep by then. Harding was, laying on his back with soul music blaring out of the radio. His gun was tucked between the mattress and box spring, with the handle sticking out.

The day was only beginning. The team left for Loyola Field House, the university facility where the Bucs played, at about 11 a.m. Someone got a finger caught in a door at some point, Rayl later recalled, with Harding somehow involved in the mishap. The game turned out well, though. With temperatures inside the building with no heating or air conditioning approaching 100 degrees on that hot, muggy day, the Pacers won, 113-105.

Roomies Rayl and Harding played a crucial role. Rayl scored six points in the final minute, starting the closing run with a 20-footer to give the Pacers a 107-102 lead. Netolicky then rebounded a New Orleans miss and fired an outlet pass to Rayl, who fed Darden for a layup and a seven-point lead. Leland Mitchell hit a three-pointer for New Orleans to make it a four-point game, then fouled Rayl in the backcourt to stop the clock. Rayl hit both free throws, and added a layup with six seconds left after the victory was secure.

Brown, continuing his stretch of superlative play, led the Pacers with 32 points on 12-of-19 shooting and 10 rebounds. Harding had 15 points

New Orleans forward Jesse Branson converts an easy field goal while Reggie Harding, Freddie Lewis and Roger Brown watch. Earlier in the day, Harding pulled a gun on Jimmy Rayl.

on 7-of-11 shooting and nine rebounds. The sleep-deprived Rayl hit just 5-of-19 shots but managed 18 points. Netolicky, still playing off the bench, grabbed eight of his nine rebounds in the final period.

The story from the hotel room became legend, but also twisted. In the book *Loose Balls,* Storen claimed he called Rayl into his office after the team returned to Indianapolis to scold him for a 1-of-14 shooting performance. The box score and game story easily refute that statistical detail. Rayl also said he was never in Storen's office during his career with the Pacers. And, he fiercely denied Storen's claim of what Harding said when he pulled the gun on Rayl in the hotel room: "Tweety Bird, I hear you hate niggers."

Rayl didn't believe his poor shooting performance in the game was the result of the early morning turmoil; more likely it was due to lack of sleep and the hot, humid conditions inside the building.

Even the final buzzer failed to contain the day's excitement. Rayl and Netolicky grabbed a few beers out of the galvanized container in the locker room afterward and planted them in their pockets for the ride to the airport. The flight was delayed, so they sat and drank a few with referee Joe Belmont. Rayl got himself worked up over a call he thought Belmont had missed during the game, pounded a glass table and shattered it.

"I felt like an idiot," he recalled.

Still wound up from the victory and the beer, he and Netolicky were "cutting up" on the flight home. Before long, a stewardess approached Staverman, who was seated a couple of rows ahead of them, and said one of his players was going to have to be removed from the plane. Rayl and Netolicky grew quiet, thinking it was one of them.

It turned out to be Harding, who had flashed his gun to Darden in the back of the plane. A stewardess saw it and loudly scolded him. He fired back with profanities and told her she had red clay between her toes – something he often said to or about white people from the south if he thought they were displaying racist behavior. She rushed to the cockpit to notify the pilot. They wanted Harding off the plane. Immediately.

At this point, versions of the story diverge. Staverman said he convinced them to let the team fly on to Indianapolis after taking the gun from Harding and turning it over to the pilot. A couple of players agreed Harding flew home with the team, but Darden and Peeples remembered Harding being dismissed when the plane made a scheduled stop on the way back, probably in Memphis, and having to find his own way to Indianapolis.

Either way, just another day in the life of Reggie Harding.

The Pacers needed one more victory to clinch a playoff berth, and had three games left to do it. They got it on the first try when Minnesota, the second-best team in the ABA behind Pittsburgh, and winner of eight of 10 games against the Pacers that season, came to Indianapolis three days after the win in New Orleans. The 116-106 victory on March 13 was their third straight and 10th in a row at the Coliseum, and leveled their record at 38-38.

Harding must have been invigorated by all the excitement on the flight home, because he played his best game yet, reiterating why teams kept giving him chances to redeem himself. He scored 30 points on 15-of-21 shooting. Five of his field goals came off offensive rebounds and two came about 20 feet from the basket. He also grabbed 22 rebounds, and while blocked shots were not yet an official statistic, both Indianapolis newspaper accounts credited him with "at least" 10. The *Minneapolis Tribune* story, meanwhile, reported he hit 15-of-20 shots and blocked eight shots.

It was an impressive performance, particularly coming against Daniels. The should-have-been All-Star MVP was "feeling a trifle under the weather" according to Overpeck's account in the *Star*, and finished with 20 points and 11 rebounds.

Rayl also excelled. He scored 30 points, his third 30-plus game of the previous 11, a stretch in which he averaged 20.9 points. He hit 10-of-20 field goal attempts and matched his franchise record with five three-pointers in 10 attempts. He also had a game-high eight assists.

The other three starters, Brown (15), Darden (14) and Lewis (11), all scored in double figures as well. Once again, with Harding playing well at center, the pieces seemed in place, whether Netolicky or Rayl completed the starting lineup. Denny returned to nicknaming mode, dusting off "Diamond Reg" in his story and adding another one: "Reg The Sledge." Contrary to that colorful imagery, however, Harding was a voice of reason in the locker room in his comments with reporters.

"Sure, it's great to be in my first playoff," he said. "But let's wait to celebrate. We haven't done anything yet. But we can win about anything if we play together like we did tonight."

Rayl, inspired in part by the presence of his college coach, Branch McCracken, was as excited as he had been frustrated just a few weeks earlier.

"We hit the open man, popped the ball out on the fast break and had a great team effort," he said. "We should have been doing this earlier, but I think we're all pulling together now."

They lost their next game at the Coliseum, to Kentucky, 108-96. One of the largest crowds of the season, 7,881, voiced their disapproval of the officiating by showering debris onto the court. They cheered Harding, though, for scoring 23 points, grabbing 25 rebounds and passing out five assists.

Staverman criticized his players for relaxing after locking up the playoff spot, and questioned the referees for calling a three-second violation on Harding while he was in the act of making a hook shot with 4:58 left that would have put the Pacers ahead. Staverman, though, was questioned in the newspapers for pulling Harding and the rest of the starters for the final 9 ½ minutes of the first half, seemingly treating the game as an exhibition.

The ABA schedule that season was nothing if not quirky. The Pacers had played three games in three nights on 10 occasions, and four in succession once. They had gone through one stretch of nine games in which eight were played on the road, and another 11-game stretch with eight road games. They had played eight straight games at home, too, although three of them had been farmed out to Dayton, Madison and Fort Wayne.

Now they were going to have to wait seven days to play their final regular season game, a rematch against the Colonels in Louisville. That could only mean one thing: Harding, riding high from two standout performances in which he had totaled 53 points and 47 rebounds, had nothing better to do than head to Detroit for an extended visit.

Staverman gave the team Saturday and Sunday off after the loss to Kentucky, but scheduled a practice for Monday morning at the Jewish Community Center. Harding called the Pacers office that morning and said he couldn't get out of Detroit because of fog, and promised to be at practice the next day. He didn't show then, either – or Wednesday or Thursday for that matter. He finally arrived back in Indianapolis Thursday evening.

Storen suspended him indefinitely, but told him to accompany the team to Louisville. He refused to get on the team bus Friday morning unless he would be allowed to play, but lost a heated argument with Storen and boarded. It was an ugly ride all the way around, as a freak late-March storm dumped six inches of snow across Indianapolis and southern Indiana, delaying the Pacers' arrival and the start of the game by an hour.

The Pacers would have been better off to skip it entirely. Netolicky, who had not been playing well off the bench, was back in the starting lineup in place of Harding. Bonham, who had not played since Jan. 31 because of the mumps he contracted from Netolicky, also returned. Most of the players were virtual no-shows, however, as the Colonels won 119-106 in a game televised back to Indianapolis. Dampier scored a league-record 54 points while hitting 23-of-43 shots, despite being held scoreless by Harkness for seven minutes in the second quarter and six minutes in the fourth.[4]

Most of the Pacers weren't around to see Dampier break the record. Rayl was ejected after picking up a second technical foul in the fourth period. Moments later, Lewis, who already had one, was hit with another

---

[4] He broke the record held by Denver's Larry Jones, but needed some manipulation to get it. He hit a 10-footer with 11 seconds left after rebounding and scoring off his own miss to tie the record. The Colonels then fouled Aitch to stop the clock. Aitch hit both foul shots, and one of the Kentucky players fired a baseball pass to Dampier, who was waiting at the other end for a layup. That was the *Star's* account, anyway. The *Courier-Journal* in Louisville reported that the floor-length pass to Dampier came after a missed shot.

and ejected with 4:26 remaining. Staverman was so incensed he ordered the remaining players on the bench to the locker room as well, leaving the five players on the court to finish the game.

The game was officiated by Moyers and a substitute referee from the area, Hubert Louden – a replacement for Dick Starczyk, who couldn't make it to Louisville because of the inclement weather. As if a replacement ref wasn't bad enough, Moyers was regarded as one of the worst of the regular officials. He had come to the ABA from refereeing Harlem Globetrotter games, and brought his showmanship antics with him. He'd blow the whistle and hop up and down on one foot and point while calling a foul, making a scene that embarrassed the offending player. He had been hung in effigy in the Coliseum at one game with a bloated dummy bearing his name, a stunt initiated by the stat crew. He was overweight, and therefore unable to keep up with the pace of play much of the time. He also refereed roller derby on the side, leading many to suggest that was his true calling.

Staverman had already engaged in a "belly-bumping contest" with Moyers during the first half, according to the Louisville *Courier-Journal,* so he wasn't in an understanding mood by the fourth quarter.

"They put Frank and Jesse James in jail for less, and they made them use a gun to steal," Staverman said afterward.

Rayl recalled telling Lewis before the game they would have to be careful with their emotions with a high school referee working the game, but they weren't able to follow up on that plan. Rayl's first technical came in the first half for questioning a foul call on Lewis, and Lewis got one of his own later. Rayl's ejection came after he had switched off to defend Randy Mahaffey, Kentucky's 6-foot-7 forward. Mahaffey elbowed him hard in the chest, so on the Pacers' next possession Rayl threw a punch that knocked down Mahaffey. Moyers called a technical foul from midcourt, and Rayl wound up and threw the ball at him, hitting him in the back of the head, according to his memory years later.

Taking his early shower, Rayl heard several teammates enter the locker room, talking and laughing loudly. "Hey, what was the final score?" he asked. It turned out the game was still ongoing. Rayl had merely heard the players Staverman told to leave the bench.

The Pacers finished the season 38-40, but were in the playoffs. They would play the league's best team, Pittsburgh, in the opening-round series, but had proven they could compete with anyone when at their best. They had defeated each of the league's three best teams – Pittsburgh, Minnesota and New Orleans – in their most recent meetings with them, and were confident they could compete with them in the postseason.

But only if Harding played. Which posed a major issue. Should they play him and sacrifice the standards Storen had established? Or sit him and sacrifice winning?

Storen and Tinkham had shouting matches over the dilemma. Tinkham wanted Harding to play. His bottom line was winning and the desperately-needed gate receipts an extended playoff run would bring. Storen wanted Harding to sit. His bottom line was establishing a code of behavior and culture for the franchise. Storen, being the general manager, won. Harding was suspended for the first three games of the series with the Pipers, but the possibility was left open he would play after that if the series went longer.

"His reason for missing practice all last week was invalid and that is why we are willing to lose three playoff games, if necessary without him," Storen told the *News*. "We had to show some strength, that our franchise means more than just Reggie Harding's appearance in a Pacer uniform."

The first three games were played on successive nights. The Pacers rented a Purdue University plane as a charter to avoid airport hassles while flying back and forth, but that luxury didn't help. Without Harding, they were no match for the team that would go on to win the league's first championship.[5]

The subplot of the series was the rematch between Brown and Hawkins, the New York City schoolboy legends. Before the first game in Pittsburgh, during warmups, Hawkins shouted across the midcourt line at Brown, "We gonna kill you!" Hawkins then went out and scored

---

[5]   The Pacers received $4,800 for their trouble in the playoff series, to be divided among the players and Lareau, the trainer. Pittsburgh went on to win the championship and had $39,800 to divvy afterward.

38 points, grabbed 19 rebounds and passed out eight assists in a 146-127 victory. Brown – who had received a trophy for being voted the team's Most Valuable Player before the final regular season home game – did his part, finishing with 32 points and 12 rebounds.

Pittsburgh won the second game back in Indianapolis, 121-108. Hawkins managed just 10 shots while his teammates took over the offense and settled for 21 points and 10 rebounds, but he blew kisses to the crowd of 3,684 at the Coliseum. Rayl, who started throughout the playoffs, was presented a trophy from Tuchman Cleaners before the game for winning the fan vote as the team's Most Popular Player. Rayl then scored five quick points to get the Pacers off to a 5-0 lead, but rarely saw the ball after that as Brown and Lewis each forced shots, according to both newspaper accounts.

Down 2-0 and facing a sweep, Staverman tried a desperate lineup change in Game 3 back in Pittsburgh, starting Peeples in place of Darden. It worked for a while as Peeples grabbed 16 rebounds in the first two quarters and helped the Pacers to a one-point halftime lead, but Pittsburgh scored 48 points in the third quarter to win easily, 133-114. Brown bounced back from a poor performance in Game 2 to contribute 17 points, 11 rebounds and 10 assists — the first playoff triple-double in franchise history, although such statistical feats weren't noted then.

Netolicky, starting at center in place of Harding, at least provided a bright spot by reasserting himself and averaging 22.3 points in the series.

A season that had begun with so much enthusiasm, promise and support ended quietly, amid discord and defeat. Storen, in *Loose Balls* and other interviews, claimed Harding met the Pacers at the airport after their Game 3 loss and granted a television interview in which he said, "It's a crime I wasn't allowed to play, and if I had a gun I'd shoot Mr. Storen."

More likely, that interview took place before or during the series. It's unlikely Harding went to the trouble to greet his teammates at the airport after they were eliminated. He likely wouldn't have known the arrival time of a charter flight, and he hadn't even bothered to attend Game 2 at the Coliseum. Overpeck's column in the *Star* reported Harding had appeared on television interviews earlier in the week in which he said the Pacers had made a mistake by not letting him play, but didn't mention a threat. It wouldn't have been out of character for Harding, though, and Storen was consistent in his telling of the story.

Harding's status remained in limbo when the season ended. His body of work had been alternately thrilling, intriguing and infuriating, offering equal arguments for bringing him back and trying to rehabilitate him or for cutting him loose and eliminating the distractions. He had averaged 13.4 points and 13.4 rebounds in 25 games. He had been suspended for three games, and missed several practices, too. He almost always played hard when he played and at his peak had been the ABA's best center, but he couldn't even be counted on to show up for every game.

The upside for the Pacers was that all the missed games and fines reduced their financial obligation to him. He appeared in 25 games, not 50, and didn't even earn $300 for the games he did play because of all the fines taken out of his check for missed practices. All in all, he probably earned about $7,000. He had been a throbbing headache to the franchise, but at least hadn't been an expensive one.

Ultimately, as always, he had been an enigma. Storen and Tinkham knew they were taking a risk by signing him, but didn't expect to have to deal with guns on airplanes and so many missed practices and games. Harding had usually played well, though, when he played, and if he had a drug problem at the time it wasn't noticeable to the other players.

Years later, Storen could laugh about it.

"We were totally naïve," he said. "We were concerned with things like bell bottom trousers and guys having sideburns below the lobe of the ear."

Staverman shared the same set of problems all of Harding's coaches had experienced. What does a coach do with an irresponsible player who's talented enough to mean the difference between winning and losing? How long do you trust a guy fully capable of lying?

"He would come in late and say he had been put in jail for non-support," Staverman recalled years later. "You'd call up there and find out it wasn't true. He told me a lie once and I suspended him again and

Storen got mad about that. I called the jail and the guy knew him. He said, 'Oh, we haven't seen Reg in a long time.'"

Storen, however, claimed to have been the disciplinarian. One night, he said, he was in his kitchen listening to the pregame show on the radio when Staverman called from the arena at a road game and said, "What am I going to do? Reggie didn't get here on time."

"Don't play the SOB," Storen recalled saying. "Don't let him dress."

Staverman then called back and said Harding had dressed anyway and demanded to play.

Storen also recalled Harding coming into his office one day after missing practice with tears in his eyes, claiming his daughter had died back in Detroit. Storen made calls to send flowers, but discovered it wasn't true.

And yet, Harding remained likeable. Denny recalled driving down 38th St. one night with his wife, perhaps after a game, and seeing Harding walking by himself, sober and well-dressed. They offered a ride and took Harding to his apartment, engaging in pleasant conversation along the way.

Baker, the team's radio broadcaster, recalled the March 13 victory over Minnesota, when Harding had scored 30 points. The game was an Easter Seals benefit, with some of the proceeds from ticket sales going to the charity, so Baker asked Harding to record a public service announcement for the charity in the locker room before the game. His teammates were joking with him as he tried to read Baker's script, trying to make him laugh or break his concentration. Harding quietly but forcefully told them all to leave. And they did.

"One of the strangest, most likable people I've ever met," Baker said.

"He had charisma before we knew what the hell charisma was. And he could play. Boy, he could play. He had the potential to be one of the greatest ever."

The most popular anecdote about Harding's life after leaving the Pacers, told in slightly varying versions, was of the time he robbed a liquor store in Detroit with a stocking over his head to try to conceal his identity – an obviously futile exercise for a 7-footer well-known in the neighborhood.

"Ah, come on, Reg, I know it's you," the man behind the cash register said.

"This isn't Reggie!" Harding supposedly replied.

It's uncertain if the story is true. There's no known source of it, and it was never referenced in the Detroit newspapers, which chronicled his legal issues in extensive detail. It certainly was within the realm of possibility, however.

Regardless, Harding's troubles continued after he returned to Detroit. A few months later, in June, he was shot in both legs. As with most events in his life, different versions of the story emerged, but the most dependable account was written by Tom Ricke in the *Detroit Free Press*.

Harding, Ricke wrote, had taken to robbing drug dealers because he was too well-known to hold up retail establishments. Perhaps the legendary story of his futile holdup attempt of the liquor store, if true, inspired that strategic shift. When he learned the dealers were looking for him, seeking revenge, he found them instead and tried to settle the difference. One day he ran into a dealer he had robbed the previous week. The dealer, Marvin Williams, said not to worry, he understood Harding's problem, and invited him over to his house for free heroin. When Harding arrived, however, Williams fired two shots through the door. The bullets passed through his right thigh and lodged in his left leg. Other newspaper accounts reported Williams shot at Harding through the door in self-defense, and then ran outside and shot Harding as Harding ran to his car. Regardless, stray bullets wounded a bystander, Ella Lyons, as well. Harding was hospitalized, but recovered.

Another series of robberies and weapons charges followed as Harding tried to finance his drug addiction, until finally, on Oct. 18, 1969, he was sentenced to 2 ½ years in prison for violating his four-year probation.

"You have exhausted the resources and the patience of this court and of all the friends who have tried for several years to straighten out your life," Judge Joseph A. Gills told him. "This is the end of the line.

You have let us all down and there is no choice now except to put you in prison."

Harding was released on June 4, 1971. Five days later, he visited Falls at the *Free Press,* to announce a comeback attempt. He had already visited the Pistons to try to get the addresses of all the NBA and ABA teams so he could write letters and ask for another chance. He said he had taken courses in math, psychology and speed reading while in prison, worked as a trustee in the facility's Recreation Department, and for the Highway Department as part of a job training program. He had paid his debt to society, he told Falls, and wanted a fresh start. He claimed to still have his basketball skills, but realized he would have to prove that to a skeptical public. He also wanted an opportunity to counsel kids to stay away from drugs.

"I know this," he said. "I can't go any lower than I've been in the past two years. I can only go higher. But I've got to get out there and do it. Talking isn't enough."

Harding had indeed, by all accounts, kicked his drug habit in prison, and was sincere about starting a new life. He wrote letters to ministers and drug centers to offer his services. He also wrote a letter to the *Michigan Chronicle*, Detroit's African-American newspaper.

"Being in prison has opened my eyes to a lot of things," he said. "Maybe that's why I can recognize when a man gets so big he feels that he can coast, give up, stop trying. What he doesn't realize, however, is that during the process, he loses his pride."

Harding hadn't lost his pride. He was 29 – still young enough, he thought, to help a team. Watching New York defeat the Lakers in the 1970 NBA Finals had convinced him he had something to offer.

"After seeing L.A.'s fiasco, I know that I still have what a pro team can use: the will to win," he wrote.

When no tryout offers came, he tried to find a job. His story was well-known throughout Detroit, though, and nobody was willing to assume the risk of hiring him. He moved back in with Nadine, but their relationship frayed again and he left a few months later.

Finally, he gave up. He returned to the familiarity of his old east side neighborhood, the only place he felt like part of a family. He was still admired there, and he had a knack for making everyone feel important. He made friends easily, and, just as in high school, he referred to them as brothers and sisters. They called him, and he called himself, "Big Fellah." Eventually, though, he returned to drugs, and then inevitably returned to a life of crime to support his habit. He still talked of going straight and helping kids again, but was struggling to make it happen. He went back on methadone to try to kick his heroin habit and began visiting his wife more often, but also kept up a relationship with a woman who had written him throughout his prison stay and talked of marrying her.

In mid-August of '72, his biological mother, Lillie Thomas, 47, died from an accidental gunshot wound. Thomas was 17 and unmarried when Harding was born, and had made a responsible decision by giving him up for adoption. She was known in her neighborhood as a good-hearted woman who struggled with alcohol abuse. Harding, who had established a relationship with her during his career with the Pistons, attended the funeral, and while there gave the director details of how he wanted his own funeral service to be conducted.

If he had a premonition about his death, however, he wasn't preparing for it.

Despite his drug issues, he was going to church twice a week, according to Ricke's account. He also was getting up at 6 a.m. each day to work out with a friend – his barber, Bill Ervin – in case the call for a tryout came. He was organizing pickup basketball games in the neighborhood. And, he had finally been hired for a factory job, his first since going to prison. He was due to start work on Monday, Sept. 4.

All his hopes and dreams ended three days before that, however, late in the afternoon.

Again, it would become difficult to separate fact from urban legend when sifting through the details. What's known is that one of Harding's best friends, 26-year-old Carl Scott, shot and killed him. How they arrived at that fateful moment is hazy.

Ricke, whose two-part opus in the *Free Press* Sunday magazine was published within a few weeks of Harding's death, wrote that Harding had befriended Scott in the Jackson prison, and they had spent considerable time together after their release. Harding had taken him to church the previous week and was trying to convince him to go to the methadone clinic to kick his drug habit.

On the last day of Harding's life, Scott and a few other friends were standing on a street corner talking with a girl when Scott, for reasons nobody understood, suddenly slapped Harding in the face.

"Are you for real?" Harding asked.

"Yeah, I'm for real, nigger!" Scott shouted, and slapped Harding again.

Harding then slapped Scott and held him up in the air in front of the others, but said the "Big Fellah" didn't want to hurt his friend. Scott ran away as soon as Harding put him down. Harding then walked over to the porch in front of a nearby house, sat down and began crying. He asked his friends if he had done the right thing, and they assured him he had. He then walked toward a friend's house, stopping to talk to a couple of girls along the way. Suddenly, a car stopped around the corner. Scott emerged with a gun, and walked toward Harding.

Harding didn't take him seriously. After all, they were friends.

"If you shoot me," Harding said, smiling, "shoot me in the head. I don't want to feel no pain."

Scott obliged him.

Another version of the story had Harding running away from Scott as he was shot, and still another had Harding sitting on the porch when he was shot. All accounts, however, had Scott firing two bullets into Harding's skull. Harding died the next afternoon in Detroit General Hospital. The motive remained unclear, although Samaras heard Scott was angry that Harding had embarrassed him by picking him up and dangling him in the air in front of the girl.

Scott entered an innocent plea the following April, but no record could be found in the newspapers of the verdict. Some police officers believed Scott had been hired by other drug dealers to kill him in retaliation for unpaid debts. Regardless, it seemed an appropriately tragic and confusing ending to Harding's life.

Services for Harding were conducted on Sept. 9, a Saturday, at a church just down the street from his old high school, which by then was vacated and literally a shell of its former self. It was a hot, sunny day, prompting some of the newspaper guys at the service to recall Harding's prediction in high school about playing in the NBA: *"Is the sun gonna shine?"* It was shining, all right, but not on Harding.

Per his request at his mother's funeral a couple of weeks earlier, two floral arrangements decorated his service: black and white roses in the shape of a Cadillac, and red and yellow roses in the shape of a basketball backboard. The Cadillac represented the car he had dreamed of owning, but never obtained. The backboard represented the dream he had obtained, but fumbled away.

Hundreds of people attended the service, including a few front office members of the Pistons. The casket was nine feet long, but after it was marched a mile to the cemetery, it turned out to be too long for the cement vault. The funeral director asked everyone to leave, promising to take care of the matter. Harding's wife became hysterical and insisted the body be returned to the funeral home. Even in death, he had inspired chaos. Ultimately, Harding was buried with the coffin in a slanted position.

Harding's death brought endless reflections of a promising life gone wrong. He had known so many people in Detroit, including newspaper reporters and columnists who made him further known to the public. He had inspired affection, sympathy and frustration in equal doses. His charisma was such that people always wanted to help him. His reality was such that he couldn't be helped for long.

"He was an immensely talented boy in a man's body," Storen recalled. "He never, ever got it together."

Will Robinson, on his way to becoming a legendary coach at nearby Pershing High School while Harding played at Eastern, had been hired as a personal mentor during Harding's time with the Pistons. He regarded Harding as simply too nice for his own good. Harding's adoptive parents, Robinson said, exacerbated the situation by being passive and lenient. They meant well, but weren't emotionally equipped to deal with a child as problematic as Harding, who associated mostly with older kids because he was so much taller than his classmates.

"His own good nature was his undoing," Robinson said. "(The other kids) took him down the wrong road."

Added Darden: "I didn't know anybody in Detroit who didn't like Reggie and want to help him."

Harding left behind an endless trail of stories, most of them sad, but many of them funny.

Bill Halls, of the *Detroit News*, recalled working in the newsroom one night when Harding telephoned from a bar.

"Hey, Bill, tell this guy I'm 7-foot!" Harding said.

"Reggie, he's standing right next to you, tell him yourself."

"He won't believe me!"

"Well, put him on then."

Harding handed the phone to the man.

"It's true," Halls said. "He's 7-foot."

"No shit?!" the man said.

The constant retellings of the stories often wore away the edges of the truth, but they painted a consistent portrait of the man. Kareem Abdul-Jabbar wrote in a book that Harding, while with the Pistons, had fired a gun at the feet of his Pistons teammate, Dischinger, and ordered him to dance. Dischinger adamantly denied that, claiming, "I can't dance, anyway." Chico Vaughn, a teammate of Harding's with the Pistons during the 1966-67 season before catching on with the Pittsburgh Pipers, claimed in *Foul!* that Sonny Dove had been the target. Dove and Harding, however, were never teammates with the Pistons. The most accurate account likely came from Debusschere, who told Ricke that Harding had pulled the gun on the Pistons' trainer.

The week before Harding was killed, he had visited Ervin, his barber. "If anything happens to me, and Buster (Harding's nickname for his son, Reggie Jr.) comes to you, I want you to treat him just like you treated me," Harding told Ervin. "That's something I could never understand about you, Billy. You could make a lot more money, you could do a lot better, but here you are in this one-chair barber shop. I know you love your family and that's something I wanted more than anything."

Reggie Harding Jr., a.k.a. Buster, longed for a family, too. He had only sporadic contact with his father while growing up in the ghetto, and then lost him for good at the age of 8. The streets eventually inhaled him as well, and in 1983 he and another man were found guilty of assault and robbery after they beat a man, shot him and dumped him in a sewer.

The man survived, and Harding and his accomplice were sent to jail. When the victim died in 1988 of a heart attack related to the injuries suffered in the assault, the case was retried. Harding Jr., already in jail, was charged with felony murder and returned with a life sentence. Yet another casualty of the ghetto.

Given the tragic arc of Harding's life, his two-month residency with the Pacers was just a brief aside, and by his standards a relatively pleasant one at that. But it was full of what-ifs for him and the Pacers.

What if their crazy, patched-together schedule hadn't included a week-long break before the last regular season game, which allowed Harding time to go back to Detroit and all its negative influences? If he had finished the season with the Pacers and not been suspended, he probably would have performed well in the playoffs. If he had done so, he might very well have signed a guaranteed contract for the following season and started a new life in Indianapolis. That might have led to several productive seasons as an All-Star center, capturing the affection of a basketball-crazed city, and living happily ever after, a changed man and a positive force in the community.

That likely was too much a fairy tale ending for someone engulfed by inferior genetics and a treacherous environment that posed all kinds of obstacles. Harding's life seemed destined to reach an unhappy ending practically from the day he was born. So many people cared about him and tried to help him, but he ultimately proved helpless. Like he had told Edmonds, he believed he belonged in the gutter. Nobody could convince him otherwise.

The Pacers would have to move on without him. And it just so happened fate was about to smile on them once again. Another product out of Detroit – a smaller model, but far more dependable – was about to become available.

8

"He had a winning spirit.
He tried all the time, after he found out the swing of things."

Too Good to be True

The failed experiment with Harding at least accomplished one thing. It proved how much better the Pacers could be with a true center, and Netolicky playing forward. They had convincingly defeated the ABA's three best teams with that lineup, and excelled even when they started Harding with a smaller unit and brought Netolicky off the bench.

Problem was, a warehouse stocked with capable centers to replace Harding did not exist. They had always been, and always would be, the rarest commodities in basketball. Harding had averaged 13.4 points and 13.4 rebounds in the 25 games in which he had managed to participate. He also had defended well around the basket, created space for teammates to operate and brought positive intangibles to the locker room –when he managed to get there. Replacing that sort of production would be difficult. Netolicky had averaged 16.3 points and 11.5 rebounds and made the All-Star team, but his best and preferred position was forward.

The ABA conducted a "secret" draft in Louisville in March, before the season ended, as a means of getting a head start on the NBA in the race for collegiate talent. The NBA responded by conducting the first round of its draft on April 3 and the later rounds on May 8 and 10. It was taking off the gloves to contend with the new league, going all out to sign premier players such as Elvin Hayes and Wes Unseld for unprecedented rookie salaries reportedly exceeding $100,000 per season. Mikan called it an "unholy war."

It was later learned the Pacers had taken four players in the private portion of the draft. Don May out of Dayton was the first, but he quickly made it known he would play in the NBA. Mike Lewis, a 6-7 center out of Duke was second. He had averaged 21.7 points and 14.4 rebounds and earned third-team All-America honors. He was introduced to the Indianapolis media at the Pacers office on April 10, two weeks after their season ended, having signed a two-year contract publicly announced as totaling $75,000. If that had been true, he would have been the highest-paid player on the team. It actually was about $35,000 over two years, guaranteed.[1]

Lewis quickly learned the harsh realities of negotiation for a professional athlete in that era.

"Storen was the master at making you feel like a piece of crap," he said. "He'd say, 'I don't even know why we drafted you.' I'd say, 'That's fine, I'll go someplace else.' And he'd say, 'No, you can't.'"

Lewis was undersized to play center, but physical and hard-working. Once signed, he was trumpeted as the likely starting center the following season. Little did anyone know, he was about to get trumped by a more proven player.

Minnesota's first season in the ABA had been an artistic success and a commercial flop. It finished 50-28, second-best in the league behind only Pittsburgh. That wasn't enough to impress the hockey-loving locals, though. Reports of their average attendance ranged from 1,200 to 2,800, with the lesser figure likely the more accurate one, given the face-saving knack ABA teams had showed for inflating attendance figures.

Although the league's best draw, the Pacers were known to exaggerate on occasion as well. According to York, Storen would drop by his seat among the stat crew during home games and give him the evening's

---

[1] While the ABA's first draft had been divided into tiers of five and seven players, the second was slightly more specific. Some teams announced their first-round pick, some their first two. Most released the next three together in alphabetical order, then another group of five, then another group of five, totaling 15 rounds in most cases. A couple of teams drafted one or two players beyond that. The Pacers drafted May in the first round, then Lewis. Don Dee, Bob Quick and Phil Wagner were selected with the next three picks in unknown order.

The Pacers failed to sign first-round draft pick Don May in 1968, but wooed second-rounder Mike Lewis, shown at right with coach Larry Staverman at the Pacers' office.

attendance figure. Occasionally, they would exchange knowing smiles in the process. For most games, free tickets were easy to come by if you had the right connections. The stat crew, in fact, was paid off in tickets that first season.

The Muskies claimed to have lost $400,000 their first season. Early in May, team president and majority stockholder Larry Shields announced a public stock offering of 300,000 shares at $1 per share. Advertisements ran in the newspapers, but the response was as underwhelming as attendance had been. The Muskies' financial plight left blood in the ABA waters, and Storen and Tinkham were eager to pounce.

Shields, a Californian businessman, asked Tinkham and Storen at the league meetings, which began on May 5, to support his appeal to have the performance bond reduced from $100,000 to $50,000. The Pacer executives asked for a player in return for giving their support. Shields, according to *Loose Balls*, offered forward Sam Smith,[2] who had averaged 9.8 points with the Muskies. Tinkham and Storen said no, they wanted Daniels. Shields balked. They talked some more. Both sides were desperate, so nobody walked. Shields put a $300,000 price tag on Daniels. Storen laughingly countered with an offer of $1, and negotiations began. They eventually split the difference, with Tinkham offering $150,000. The written part of the negotiations took place on a lounge napkin.

Shields wasn't in a strong bargaining position. He urgently needed the money, and had little to lose. He was moving the team to Miami regardless, so it didn't matter what Minneapolis' minuscule fan base thought of selling Daniels off so cheaply. Presumably, people in Miami would be happy just to be getting a team and wouldn't care much about the details of the roster. In fact, many of the would-be fans in that remote outpost for basketball likely had never heard of a player named Mel Daniels.

---

[2] Smith was sold to the Kentucky Colonels instead. Although he only played that one season with Daniels in Minnesota, he still felt a strong enough connection that he rode up from Kentucky with his daughter to attend Daniels' funeral service in 2015.

Shields wanted players in return, so Storen offered Dawson and Kozlicki. A first-round draft pick also was said to be included, but draft picks were such vague and flexible commodities in this new league fighting for survival that they were nearly meaningless. If a team could sign a premier college player, it simply went out and did it, regardless of what draft picks it happened to possess.

It amounted to grand larceny. Dawson and Kozlicki had each been among the select players who received guaranteed contracts the previous summer, but neither wound up playing much, and neither would play again as professionals. Daniels, on the other hand, had been voted the ABA's Rookie of the Year after leading the league in rebounds (15.6) and finishing sixth in scoring (22.2). He was a first-team all-league selection and would have been the MVP of the All-Star game if not for the premature tabulation.

Just one problem remained: The Pacers were barely more solvent than the Muskies. Their balance sheet of June 30 would show an operating debt of $336,351.72 and the owners were reluctant to throw good money after what would turn out to be bad if the league didn't survive. According to minutes of the board meeting in early May, "considerable discussion" led to the conclusion that $150,000 was too much to spend for a player, even the Rookie of the Year.

But the matter was not closed.

The minutes also stated: "It was decided, however, that certain of the directors might be inclined to underwrite the acquisition of Daniels if the acquisition price was somewhat under $150,000, and Chairman Bannon appointed a directors' committee consisting of Treece, Wiese and Chuck DeVoe to determine whether or not in the several days following this meeting a figure could be arrived at with Minnesota respecting the acquisition of the contract rights to Daniels, which could then be underwritten for the corporation by the guarantees of directors of the corporation."

It also was determined that if a group could come up with sufficient funds to acquire Daniels, those directors would accept stock options or shares of stock as compensation.

The newspapers reported the sales price to be $100,000, and that remained the most commonly cited figure. The Pacers also were to assume Daniel's three-year contract, which had paid $22,500 the first year. According to Collins and Ebersoff, Treece signed a promissory note for all or most of the money. He was perhaps the wealthiest of the group, being a real estate investor and owner or co-owner of 41 Burger Chef fast food franchises.

Chuck DeVoe recalled his brother, John, calling him one night and telling him they needed to come up with $100,000 for Daniels, adding, "We need to know by tomorrow." Chuck's initial reaction was, "Wait a minute, $100,000 for one ballplayer?" He later remembered two other owners being involved, likely Treece and Wiese.

Whoever put forth the money to land Daniels, they unknowingly made the greatest assist in franchise history.

As time passed, a tale emerged that Kentucky's owners were on their way to the meeting with $200,000 to purchase Daniels' contract as the Pacers completed the transaction with the Muskies, only to fall a couple of hours short of the franchise-shifting opportunity. There's no evidence of that, however. The *Courier-Journal* never reported it, and neither Storen nor Gregory, the Colonels' primary owner at the time, had any memory of that. Gregory had attended the league meeting as well. One would think Shields, once he had acquiesced to trading Daniels, would have shopped him for the best offer.

The trade wasn't announced for about two weeks. Shields needed time to prepare the move to Miami, and wanted to announce the trade simultaneously. *Minneapolis Tribune* columnist Sid Hartman wrote of Shields' trip to Miami to secure owners on May 18, and the newspaper broke the story of the move on May 22. "The people in Minnesota just don't want to back the team," Shields said from his office in Anaheim. The *Tribune* also reported a rumor of Daniels being traded to the Pacers in the story, but Storen said he had no knowledge of such a thing and Shields flatly denied it. "There is no way I would trade Daniels," he said.

A day later, the trade became official.

Shields conducted a press conference in Miami on May 23 to announce a five-man group there had agreed to purchase half ownership of the team. The next day's edition of the *Star* spread the news throughout Indiana with a banner headline on the front sports page: "Pacers Land Muskies' Mel Daniels."

It no doubt caused a lot of double-takes among Pacers fans. It wasn't April Fool's Day. It wasn't Christmas. How could such a thing happen? But while fans in Indiana were ecstatic over landing one of the ABA's best players, Daniels was disappointed after receiving the phone call at his off-season residence in Albuquerque, N.M. Loyal and sentimental by nature, he was hurt by the Muskies' willingness to let him go, although he was soothed somewhat after learning of the financial crisis facing the franchise. His wife, Cece, reminded him he was the Muskies' best asset, and should view the trade as a compliment.

Daniels was flown to Indianapolis on the 24th, met at the same airport at which Harding had arrived to join the Pacers barely more than four months earlier, and whisked off to a 3 p.m. news conference at the Indianapolis Motor Speedway. It was a practical location because most of the local media members already were gathered there on that Friday, a day ahead of the opening of the second weekend of qualifying for the Indianapolis 500. Daniels, wearing a suit and tie, talked with reporters and posed for photographs with 500 polesitter Joe Leonard and Bannon while holding aloft an ABA ball with an STP oil treatment sticker attached.

Daniels' disappointment was further eased by the enthusiastic reception he received from the media and fans at the track, as well as his memory of the fan support in Indianapolis as a visiting player. He also could see how perfectly he might fit with Lewis, Brown, Netolicky and a fifth starter. A forward most of his season with the Muskies, he said he didn't care if he played center or forward. "I'll play any place I think I can do the job to help the team," he said.

The media members who covered the Pacers were amazed by the incredibly one-sided nature of the deal. Overpeck, writing in the *Star*, joked "there are reports that Pacer General Manager Mike Storen is going to take over as chief U.S. Negotiator in the Paris peace talks next week, too."

Daniels' future teammates with the Pacers were happiest of all. For them, this was simply too good to be true. Brown drove to the Marott Hotel where Daniels was staying to greet him. Lewis, the team captain, recalled thinking, *Oh, my goodness, how did this happen?* after learning of the deal.

"He was exactly what we needed," Lewis recalled of his reaction years later.

Storen initially said Staverman planned to use Daniels and Netolicky at forwards with Mike Lewis playing center, a reasonable assumption given the way Daniels had been used in Minnesota. Storen also gave a roster update, announcing that Harding had been placed on waivers at the completion of the season, contrary to his statements at that time.

"Harding does not figure into our plans for the summer, for the fall, or for the winter," Storen told Overpeck, probably with a hearty laugh.

A week later, Daniels was riding in a convertible in the downtown 500 Festival Parade, still wondering what had hit him. Kozlicki and Dawson, meanwhile, were wondering the same thing, but from the opposite end of the spectrum. They had experienced difficult rookie seasons, and now were throw-ins on a trade to a team that didn't particularly want them.

Dawson's best game as a pro would forever stand as his first. He played in just 21 games because of his National Guard obligation, and averaged 5.6 points. Storen was under no obligation to pay him following the trade, but kept him on the Pacers' payroll through the end of August. Although officially a member of the Floridians, Dawson sold season tickets for the Pacers and helped put on youth clinics with Brown and Bonham.

"As strange as it sounds, it wasn't strange then," he said years later.

Equally strange, he also donned riot gear and tried to help keep peace at the Democratic National Convention as a member of the National Guard.

Kozlicki had averaged 2.9 points in 39 games. His best game had come in New Orleans, when Netolicky was out with the mumps and he scored 14 points. A month earlier, he had gotten a glimpse of opportunity when Staverman played him nearly three quarters in a blowout loss in Denver and he scored 10 points. With Brown slowed by a sprained ankle, he started the following night in Oakland and scored six points in a one-point loss. He was back on the bench the following night in Anaheim. He never started again and rarely played. He scored his last points of the season on Jan. 22, with 25 more regular season games to play.

Looking back, he thought he had gotten off on the wrong foot with Staverman by not staying in Indianapolis and participating in the summer workouts at the Jewish Community Center, but he was committed to taking one more summer course to complete his degree requirements and following through on his plan to marry on Aug. 26. He wound up being nearly as much an assistant coach as player. Staverman, who didn't have a paid assistant, praised him for the advice he offered during games.

"He's helped me a lot on the bench by suggesting things that might have slipped my mind in the heat of a game," Staverman told Denny.

Kozlicki had been somewhat of a misfit on the team, a straight-laced man in an often-hedonistic profession. At Northwestern, he had been one of 10 students – and one of just two athletes – selected to a senior honorary society, Deru, which recognized students for their overall contributions to the university. That sort of thing and his conservative nature made him an easy target for teasing among his teammates. Netolicky, for one, took advantage on a road trip, penning a fake postcard to Kozlicki while Rayl watched gleefully. Netolicky wrote something along the lines of, "Sorry I kept you out all night. I hope it didn't bother your play. I'm really looking forward to seeing you the next time you're in town."

He signed it, "Love, Sherry."

Kozlicki's 20-year-old wife, Renee, was livid when it arrived at their apartment, and marched into Storen's office to protest. He promised to address it, and a team meeting was called before a game in Minneapolis. With players straining to keep straight faces, Kozlicki said he thought he knew who wrote the offending note, and if he found out for sure there was going to be trouble.

Brown then got up and said, "Hey, is there anybody in this room who wouldn't —— a girl if they had a chance to do it?" Kozlicki said he wouldn't, he was happily married and would never consider cheating on his wife. But with the attention diverted from the postcard, the meeting dissolved.

Kozlicki was listed on the Floridians' training camp roster the next fall, but he wasn't able to come to contract terms with the new and underfunded franchise. Acknowledging to them he had not gone to college to become a professional basketball player, he plunged into the real world, starting with an insurance firm in Miami.[3]

Dawson reported to Miami's training camp, but was caught in a glut of guards that included former Muskies Freeman and Perry. He played in one exhibition game, then was released. He moved back to Chicago and took a job with Merrill-Lynch, having already made contacts in the Indianapolis office with former Olympian Lefty Walther and Sahm, the Cathedral High School and Notre Dame graduate who had tried out for the Pacers before the inaugural season. He eventually found his way to New York City, where he became a successful stockbroker and institutional broker before retiring in 2009.

In Daniels, the Pacer got a player at the opposite end of the human spectrum from Harding. Both grew up in Detroit, both were talented centers, and both were amiable off the court. The similarities abruptly ended there, however.

Harding had been given up for adoption by an alcoholic mother, never met his father, and was raised by caring adoptive parents who weren't able to harness him. He was an outcast from early childhood because of his height, and fell in with an older crowd that led him astray. He lacked education, and had seen little of the world outside Detroit before he joined the Pistons.

Daniels had strong, caring parents. His father, Maceo, worked in an auto parts factory, earning enough to provide all the necessities, and

---

[3] Kozlicki later took a managerial position with the American Hospital Corp. and moved to Atlanta, where he retired after a successful career. He and Renee celebrated their 50th wedding anniversary in August of 2017.

instilled discipline and fear into his son. "I brought you into this world and I can take you out," he told Mel on more than one occasion. Mel's mother, Bernice, who was three-quarters Cherokee, was the nurturer who read poetry to him and his sister and instilled a love of horses. He had attended college for four years, he was married, he was humble and he respected authority. Ultimately, as a basketball player and friend, he was as dependable as a sunrise.

He wasn't a natural like Harding, though. He was slender and awkward, and had arrived late to basketball. It wasn't until he was 17 years old, his junior year at Detroit Pershing High School, that he was introduced to the game — forced into it, really.

Pershing's coach, the same Will Robinson who had tried to help Harding from afar, recalled noticing a student on the roll for one of his physical education classes by the name of Mel Daniels who had not shown up for it. After a few days went by, he went looking for the truant and finally caught him as he rounded a corner in the hallway. He ordered him to show up the next day for class. Two days later, the scrawny kid still hadn't shown. Robinson went looking for him again, backed him up against the wall and got his point across.

Daniels remembered it somewhat differently. He was in Robinson's physical education class, but had no interest in playing on the basketball team. Robinson, Daniels said, stopped him in the hallway one day and ordered him to report to practice.

"Chief, I want you in the gym today," Daniels recalled Robinson saying. "If you're not in the gym, I'm going to come get you and beat your ass."

Either way, Daniels wound up on the basketball team. Somehow, despite his childhood in the streets of Detroit and the fact the city had an NBA team, he had never touched a basketball or even watched a game. He was tall and lanky, though, so Robinson gave him a pair of black high-top Chuck Taylor Converse shoes that were a size-and-a-half too long and put him on the junior varsity team.

"Not that he belonged there, just to keep tabs on him," Robinson would say years later.

He also gave Daniels a clear and fundamental definition of his role, which Daniels gleefully retold in later years:

"This end is called offense. There's a block here and a block here, and there's a basket in between. If your teammates shoot it, you try to rebound it and put it back in the basket. On the other end, it's called defense. The idea is to stop the other person from scoring. If you get the rebound, wait for someone to come and retrieve the ball from you. Once they retrieve the ball from you, you may proceed down the floor to the offensive end. That's your responsibility."

Daniels required long hours of hard labor to develop skills, and he was given no choice in the matter. Robinson put his players through a demanding pre-season conditioning program before they even touched a basketball, one that included rope-climbing, push-ups, sit-ups and long runs around the indoor track that circled the gymnasium from above, one that made shooting from one of the corners of the court impossible.

"Jesus Christ, he would always be a bad last," Robinson recalled. "Not just last, but a *bad* last. The guys would lap him."

Daniels recalled fainting in one early practice, and trying to quit the team. Robinson wasn't having it. Daniels barely played at first, getting in for the final few minutes of the JV games, clomping up and down the floor in his oversized shoes while trying to figure out a sport that was a foreign language to him. His father was too busy working or sleeping and had no interest in the silly game anyway, but his mother faithfully attended every game and cheered him on.

Despite his late start and lack of natural agility, he had valuable assets. He was tall, he was strong, he was stubborn and, thanks to his father and Robinson, he had a strong work ethic and respect for authority. Maceo Daniels might not have paid attention to his son's new endeavor, but Robinson gave Mel enough guidance for two men. He required his players to participate in three summer leagues, which kept them occupied nearly every night in the off-season. By his junior year, although still rail-thin, Daniels had grown to nearly 6-8 and was showing promise.[4]

---

[4] Daniels needed an extra semester to graduate from high school, so he played half of the 1962-63 season before his high school eligibility ran out.

"He had a winning spirit," Robinson said. "He tried all the time after he found out the swing of things."

Daniels also had a human spirit. Pershing High was a bona-fide melting pot, filled mostly with the children of factory workers. He grew up in a neighborhood that was primarily Polish. Sixty percent of the students at Pershing were white, but 60 percent of the starters on the basketball team were black, as was Robinson. One of the two white starters was Ted Sizemore, who went on to a 12-year Major League Baseball career as an infielder and was voted the National League Rookie of the Year in 1969, one year after Daniels won the honor in the ABA.

The team members were close, on the court and off. Daniels always kept the memory of hanging out at Sizemore's house with other teammates and eating Sloppy Joes on Saturdays. One of Sizemore's lasting memories, meanwhile, was the effort Daniels put into the game.

"Will worked him," Sizemore said. "One thing Mel never did was give up. He kept coming back and Will made him work, work, work. He just kept developing and developing. He just did a lot of work. A lot of drills, footwork, handling the ball … he just got coordinated all of a sudden."

Whatever amount of discipline Maceo Daniels didn't instill in Mel, Robinson did. Daniels recalled getting a flat tire late one night while out with teammates Sizemore, Ted Wheeler and John "J.T." Sharp in his beat-up Dodge, which they had dubbed the Gray Ghost. Filled with mischief and peer pressure, they stole one off a car in the school parking lot – a car that turned out to belong to the school principal. Daniels had been found out by the time he got home.

Robinson came down on him hard. He gave him 100 lashes with his lanyard, the long cord to which he attached his whistle – 50 for being a thief and 50 for being stupid, according to Wheeler in later years. Robinson then stood Daniels up in front of his teammates and said, "Here's a thief. This is what a thief looks like." Daniels had to stand and watch his teammates practice that day. Every now and then Robinson would say, "Thief, turn your back," and refuse to let him watch.

"He just dogged me," Daniels recalled. "Just dogged me."

That was the last time Daniels took something that didn't belong to him, a fundamental lesson Harding never learned. Still, Harding contributed to Daniels' game, and Daniels had respect for him. The two knew of one another within the circles of high school basketball in Detroit and had competed against one another at least once as high jumpers in a track meet in 1961. Harding was two years older, bigger and far more advanced while Daniels was learning basketball in high school, so Robinson – who seemed to coach the entire inner city either in or out of the school year – had Harding mentor his young prospect.

"He'd come over and help me out," Daniels told Mittman in the *News*. "He taught me about blocking off and going and getting the ball. He taught me to watch where the man shoots from … you can almost tell the angle the ball will come off the boards."

Daniels originally enrolled at West Texas State along with Wheeler, who was on a dual scholarship for football and basketball. A package deal arranged by Robinson, they arrived on campus in June, after an adventurous Greyhound bus ride from Detroit. When the bus stopped in St. Louis for lunch, they walked in the diner and were immediately ordered "to the back." Directed to the kitchen, they were pointed toward a small white table, where a lone black man was eating. They decided to leave without eating.[5]

It was the first encounter with blatant racism for the two kids from Detroit's inner city.

"We cried all the way to Texas," Wheeler recalled.

More adventures awaited them in Canyon, a Texas panhandle town 18 miles south of Amarillo. They were set up in living quarters in the university fieldhouse and provided with food, a television and a car to drive. Daniels taught Wheeler how to shoot a rifle and drive a stick shift. Together, they watched a cougar climb a tree, a calf being born and shot rabbits. Best of all, they rode horses for hours at a time at a ranch where just-graduated West Texas State football star Dory Funk Jr. and his younger brother, Terry, lived — and were about to begin professional wrestling careers. At night, they turned on the fieldhouse lights, opened the doors to the public and played basketball into the wee morning hours.

---

[5] Wheeler went on to play three seasons in the NFL for the St. Louis Cardinals and Chicago Bears, then finished his career in the Canadian Football League and World Football League.

Because of their athletic stature, they were mostly loving life there. It wasn't as pleasant for other minority citizens, though. Wheeler recalled a sign prominently placed in town that read, "Don't let the sun set on your black ass." After 2½ months, they returned to Detroit before heading back to Texas for the start of fall classes. There, Daniels said he received a warning in the mail: "Nigger, do not return in the fall."

Even if he wanted to go back to Texas, he couldn't have at that point. He had failed to achieve the required ACT score over the summer. He enrolled instead at Burlington Junior College in Iowa, another school to which Robinson had established a pipeline for Detroit players. Daniels played one season there – Netolicky attended one game, having no idea he was watching a future teammate – and then was eligible to attend a four-year college.

He had several offers, but Robinson made it easy for him. One night the University of New Mexico's coach, Bob King, arrived in Detroit and took Robinson and Daniels to dinner. Robinson had already sent players to King, including some from other area high schools, so they had established a rapport. They talked for a while after dinner, and then Robinson made an announcement.

"Chief, we are going to New Mexico," he said.

"We" meaning Mel. And that was that.

Daniels excelled in his three seasons at New Mexico, and fell in love with the open spaces of Albuquerque. His mother had instilled a love for the cowboy lifestyle, and he felt at home there. He kept getting better at basketball, too, making up for his late start, and earned second-team All-America honors as a senior. It wasn't until then that he even considered the possibility of playing professional basketball. All along, he had assumed he would return to Detroit and find a blue-collar job similar to his father's.

That was hardly his preference, however. His father had lined up a job for him in a Ford factory one summer, unloading box cars and trucks. He had to get up at 4:30 a.m. to report to work, was still obligated to help around the house and was still under orders to be home by midnight on weekends. Finally, late in July, he decided to head back to Albuquerque and begin preparing for the fall semester.

"Mom, I really can't take it anymore," he said. "He's trying to kill me."

Choosing the Muskies' contract offer over Cincinnati's following the ABA and NBA drafts in 1967 had been easy, given the drastic difference between the two. His decision to turn down the security of the NBA, though, had a long-range impact on more than those two franchises. Had he signed with Cincinnati, he obviously wouldn't have been available to the Pacers a year later.

It's not that he couldn't have gotten by on the Royals' lesser salary. Having grown up in a blue-collar household with no frills, he was a man of simple tastes – by necessity, but also by his nature. He had proved that by trading in his 1959 gold Chevy Bel Air – a square, winged vehicle he called his "Batmobile" – for the even-older '55 Buick station wagon after collecting his bonus money from the Muskies.[6]

He sent most of his bonus money to his parents. Maceo was astounded when Mel told him what he would be paid for playing basketball as a rookie. To a factory laborer and former field hand, it didn't make sense for someone to be rewarded so handsomely for playing a game.

"They pay you *what* to do *what*?" he said when Mel told him his salary and bonus.[7]

The financial windfall didn't affect Daniels' competitive spirit, though. It was part of his DNA, his upbringing and his basketball training to play hard and to play physically. He wasted no time making that point as a professional. In his first regular season game with the Muskies, against visiting Kentucky, Colonels benchwarmer Kendall Rhine shoved

---

[6] Daniels' nature was to keep things of sentimental value. When he cashed his first paycheck from the Muskies, he was given a few hundred dollar bills and a twenty at the bank. He never let go of the twenty. He also kept the too-large pair of black Converse shoes that Robinson gave him all those years ago, but they were lost in a barn fire on his property.

[7] One of Daniels' favorite anecdotes in later years reflected his father's character, and the respect he had for his father. His parents once attended a game at the Coliseum. Daniels was his typical emotional self in the first half, reacting angrily to referees' calls and spitting out curse words loud enough for those sitting near the court to hear. When he walked off the court at halftime, his father was waiting for him. Maceo poked a finger in his son's chest and said, "Young man, don't let me *ever* hear you talk that way in front of your mother again!" Daniels just lowered his head and said, "Yes sir."

him hard from behind and threw an elbow to his head. Daniels turned and threw a punch, the benches cleared, and both players were ejected. In future decades, such an act would have branded him a thug. In the Sixties, it qualified him as a warrior.[8]

One game into his career, he had sent a message. It wasn't his nature to start trouble, but he certainly wasn't opposed to finishing it. It wouldn't be long before he realized some players were willing to fight and some were not. He didn't hold grudges against those less inclined to fight, but he believed circumstances occasionally called for a man to stand up for his team.

"There's a lot of nice guys like that," he said of the peacemakers. "You want them around, you want them to marry your sister, you want to buy them ice cream, but when a fight starts, it's 'Where are you going?'"

Harding was the type to run, as he did that night in Kokomo. And when he left, no one knew when or if he would return. Daniels was the type to stand and fight for his team when necessary.

Lewis had said it best: he was exactly what the Pacers needed.

---

[8] Daniels in *Loose Balls* claimed Bobby Rascoe was the offending player. The Minneapolis and Louisville newspapers, however, reported it to be Rhine – a far more logical choice since he was tall enough to be guarding Daniels. The double ejection was a good trade-off for the Colonels, who went on to win their first game after two losses to the Pacers. Daniels had 19 points at the time and Rhine three. Daniels apologized afterward for letting his emotion get the best of him, but it wouldn't be the last time.

9

"There will be more discipline this season ... There'll be waves this year if I feel someone isn't 100 percent with the program in every way on and off the court."

Starting Over

Stealing Daniels from Minnesota wiped the slate clean. He was just one player, but, as John DeVoe had said about Oscar Robertson, he was "a lot of player." It was widely assumed Daniels would make a drastic difference for the Pacers, and his acquisition shifted the focus from the fizzled season in the rear-view mirror to the promising campaign ahead.

Storen's hustling front office operation did all it could throughout the summer to continue the momentum of the "trade." As part of the city's "Upswing '68" program, instituted by Mayor Lugar, Pacers players conducted more than 60 two-hour clinics over three afternoons and three evenings each week. The players arrived at various locations in the city, as many as six at a time, with two trucks containing portable baskets and all the equipment necessary to block off a street and set up a makeshift court.

For the white-collar community, a film of the previous season's All-Star game was available to groups of 25 or more, a valuable tool to re-introduce Daniels to potential ticket-buyers. Players also were available to speak to groups of 25 or more.

It was a time for aggressive marketing. Improvement seemed a given, optimism was easily justified and dreaming of a championship was understandable.

Training camp was less chaotic the second time around. There would be no open tryout to inhale wanna-be players from the streets, and all workouts were kept in Indianapolis. The morning sessions were conducted at Park Tudor, a private prep school on the north side, and the evening scrimmages at Indiana Central, a college on the south side.

Staverman made his cuts quickly to get down to the serious business of preparing for the season, as only a couple of roster positions were open. One of the early casualties of rookie camp managed to make a lasting impression, however. Dave Benedict was a guard out of Central Washington State who had averaged 15.2 points and earned first-team NAIA all-district honors. He had been drafted either third, fourth or fifth the previous Spring, and was described in the Pacers' release as "a hardnosed player who never stops hustling."

He was kind of crazy, too. He had grown up in a farm labor camp, and was about as poor and uncivilized as a person could be in the latter half of the 20th century. He spent four years in the Navy before enrolling in college, so he was 26 by the time he finished college and arrived on the Pacers' doorstep. Most of his acquaintances called him Coyote because of his wild nature. The publicists and fans at Central Washington often referred to him as Mr. Excitement. But he had another nickname for himself: Mr. Wonderful.

Naturally, Benedict wound up living with Netolicky for awhile, adding to the revolving menagerie of creatures and characters in Netolicky's north side apartment. He arrived early, and settled in. Mike Lewis was living there as well, creating a mix of established, hopeful and hopeless professionals. Benedict, for one, always seemed to have a hungry look in his eye, literally and figuratively.

"He looked like he hadn't eaten for about eight years," Netolicky recalled. "One time I grilled a steak and was eating it in front of the TV. Coyote was looking at it like he was going to attack it. I cut off a corner and gave it to him and he said, 'God bless you, partner.'"

Given his self-assigned nickname, Benedict obviously didn't lack for confidence. When Netolicky tried to offer Mike Lewis and him advice on what to expect in the camp practices, Benedict cut him off. "Hey, I've played more basketball than you guys put together," he said. "I played in the Indian League." He also told Netolicky, in all earnestness, that he was the greatest athlete who had ever lived, capable of throwing a rock farther than anybody in the United States could throw a baseball.

Netolicky couldn't resist poking fun at him, sometimes in a manner that went over Benedict's head.

"I'd tell Neto, 'He's going to kill you in your sleep if you don't stop that,'" Mike Lewis recalled.

Benedict didn't make it past the first day or two of rookie camp. When Staverman cut the first swath of players, he tried to soften the blow by encouraging them to keep their hopes up and look for other opportunities if they still wanted to play professional basketball. "You never know, we might have made some mistakes," he said. Benedict fired back with, "You sure did, you just cut the world's best ballplayer!"

Lewis didn't quite agree. He considered Benedict "the fastest human being I've ever seen getting from one end of the floor to the other," but added, "he couldn't play a lick."[1]

The Pacers settled for keeping a pair of other drafted guards, Phil Wagner and Bobby Hooper, to complete their backcourt, and – surprisingly – sold last season's starting forward, Darden, to New York for an undisclosed sum to reach the 11-man roster limit.

Denny predicted in the *News* the Pacers would win the Eastern Division, finishing ahead of the defending champion Pittsburgh team that had moved to Minneapolis to replace the Muskies. The ABA coaches still predicted the transplanted Pipers would win the East, but the Pacers were being taken seriously. None of the league's media members had them worse than second.

"This year, the Pacers very easily could get off to just as fast a start as they did a year ago," Overpeck wrote in the *Star*. "And the chances of another collapse seem reassuringly remote at this point."

Staverman agreed, proclaiming his team had "a good shot at the championship … if everybody wants to play as a unit for 48 minutes."

He issued a warning, too.

---

[1] Benedict eventually returned to Yakima, Wash., and became a high school health teacher – a beloved one, judging by his obituary after he died of cancer at age 74 in 2016. He was praised for his "electric and magnetic personality," as well as his youthful athleticism. His son claimed he wrote "Coyote was here" on a piece of paper, table top or napkin in every bar he visited.

October 18, 1968

Mr. L. Charles DeVoe
3637 East 71st Street
Indianapolis, Indiana 46220

Dear Chuck:

I hate to do this, friend, but because of
the fact that we have approximately $30,000
tied up in season ticket accounts receivable
and the fact that we have cleaned up the
vast majority of our unpaid bills from last
year, our cash position is not very favorable. As a result, your $5,000 would be of
great benefit to the cause.

Since last May, $124,500 in additional
capital has been paid into this venture
out of a subscribed total of $154,500.

Sincerely,

J. Frederic Wiese, Jr.
Treasurer

This internal memo from treasurer Fred Wiese to Chuck DeVoe reveals the constant financial pressures on the team.

"There will be more discipline this season," he said. "I was a rookie, too, last season and I tried to turn my back and not create any waves. There'll be waves this year if I feel someone isn't 100 percent with the program in every way on and off the court."

The public's first glimpse of the Pacers with Daniels in uniform (although not the regular season uniform) came in an exhibition game against the Spanish Olympic team at Indiana Central College on Sept. 21. The Pacers won, 102-82, with an unimpressive performance. Only 1,121 fans attended on a college football Saturday. Netolicky led with 19 points.

The second viewing came in the opening exhibition game against Kentucky, a 115-104 loss before 2,831 fans at Southport High School. Rayl, a starter nearly by default with Brown's move back to forward, led the scoring with 17 points, hitting two three-pointers. The game's insignificance was so extreme the Colonels let Ed Kallay, a 51-year-old sports director for a Louisville television station, put on a uniform and play briefly to accommodate a 30-minute special to be televised later.[2]

Daniels made his Coliseum debut on Oct. 3, in what turned out to be one of the more notable evenings in franchise history – a time capsule of a unique era in sports.

The Oakland Oaks, who had finished with a league-worst 22-56 record the previous season, were completely revamped. Barry was eligible now, freed from his season-long sabbatical as a league spokesman. Larry Brown and Moe had been acquired from New Orleans. Warren Armstrong, a promising rookie, had been drafted out of Wichita State.

Although just an exhibition, it would mark Barry's ABA debut, and not a minute too soon to boost the league's national profile. Two years earlier, playing for the Golden State Warriors, he had led the NBA in scoring (35.6)

---

[2] That was nothing. On Nov. 27 that year, Gregory, the Colonels' owner, insisted that a horse racing jockey, Penny Ann Early, play in a regular season game against the Los Angeles Stars. Wearing a miniskirt and a turtleneck sweater, she warmed up with the players and sat on the bench with the team. She checked into the game in the first quarter during a timeout, and inbounded the ball to Rascoe, who quickly called a timeout. She then exited the game to a standing ovation.

as a second-year pro. He was just 22 at that time and one of the most glamorous athletes in the country, a handsome, well-spoken 6-8 forward made for television. He had jumped leagues for $75,000 – $30,000 of it in bonuses – and a 15 percent stake in the Oakland franchise, and was the greatest reason for optimism for the ABA's survival.

The preliminary game, however, was nearly as much an attraction for the fans.

Marvel, who had left the Pacers at the end of the previous season to work full-time for the United States Auto Club, had organized a benefit to raise funds for race driver Bob Hurt, who had been paralyzed from the neck down in a first-turn crash while practicing for the Indianapolis 500 the previous May. It would feature a team of race drivers – the USAC "500" All-Stars – against a team of local media personalities, billed as PERT (Press, Entertainment, Radio and Television). All the proceeds beyond expenses would go to the USAC Benevolent Fund, and were earmarked for Hurt's rehabilitation expenses. Tickets for the doubleheader cost $2 across the board, with no reserved seats.

The 14-member USAC team featured some of the premier drivers of the era, including A.J. Foyt, Mario Andretti, Bobby Unser, Al Unser, Parnelli Jones, Johnny Rutherford, Roger McCluskey and the retired Rodger Ward., along with Bob Harkey, Sam Sessions, Bill Vukovich, Larry Dickson, Art Pollard and Gene Hartley. They, along with the media reps, wore outfits provided at no charge by the J.B. Hinchman Uniform Co., a local designer and manufacturer of racing uniforms. They were precious, consisting of short pants and short-sleeved jerseys with racing stripes down the front and sides. Programs were donated by the Coca-Cola Co, and printed without charge by S-M Offset Printing.

Marvel went all out to add finishing touches. An STP Turbine race car from the previous "500" was placed on display in the Coliseum lobby. A luncheon was held at the Speedway Motel two days before the game, with members of both teams in attendance. Speedway owner Tony Hulman was brought in to throw out the ball for the opening tip. An introverted man by nature, he was nervous and unsure of what to say over the public-address microphone. He went with Netolicky's suggestion: "Gentlemen, start your game!" a takeoff of his traditional "Gentlemen, start your engines" command

Media members converge on one of the drivers in the USAC-PERT preliminary game before the exhibition game at the Coliseum on Oct. 3. That's A.J. Foyt, second from the left in the top photo. The game eventually deteriorated into a pie fight. Parnelli Jones, at left in the bottom photo, got in a good lick on media member Bill Robinson.

for the race. Sid Collins, a local legend as the radio voice of the race, handled public address duties for the game. Speedway starter Pat Vidan and Overpeck served as referees. Cleon Reynolds, coach at Marian College and a longtime official of the "500," theoretically coached the USAC team and Tom Carnegie, a local television sportscaster and the public-address announcer at the Speedway, led the PERT team. Writers for the Society sections at the *Star* and *News*, Mary Ann Butters and Betty Fruits, were recruited as water girls.

The game, which consisted of four five-minute quarters, was an absolute joke, but also an absolute success. It raised nearly $14,000, after expenses, for Hurt, a former high school basketball star in Maryland, who watched from the sideline in a wheelchair. And, in its unique way, it was entertaining.

Bobby Unser, who had won the "500" the previous May, sprained his ankle in pregame warmups, a sign of the folly to come. During the game, the 5-6 Andretti climbed on the shoulders of McCluskey to get a better view of the basket. The drivers tried to kick a field goal at one point. Later, a ball with no air was introduced into the proceedings. Three media members playfully attacked Foyt, who was notoriously uncooperative with them at the Speedway. Finally, with the drivers leading 7-4, members of both teams flooded the court with balls and began throwing up shots. It ended in a tie at 11. Appropriately, a custard pie fight concluded the "game."[3]

It was ridiculously silly and impossible to imagine in future decades, but perfectly representative of the spirit of the time.

What followed would remain the most significant preseason game in Pacers franchise history for decades to come, if not forever. With Barry making his ABA debut and Daniels making his Coliseum debut as a Pacer, 7,889 fans – easily a record for an ABA exhibition game – flocked to the Thursday evening game between the two teams expected to contend for the season's championship. It nearly was as exciting and meaningful as the franchise opener the previous season, although this time no tickets were

---

[3] Afterward, Foyt suggested the game become an annual affair, and it was played through at least 1973. Hurt fought hard to overcome his paralysis, traveling to Russia, Sweden and throughout the United States for experimental treatments. He died of prostate cancer in 2000, age 61.

given away. Then again, at $2 a pop, the potential for a financial windfall for the franchise was limited.

Freddie Lewis scored 44 points to lead the Pacers' 141-131 victory which featured, according to Overpeck's story in the *Star*, "48 minutes of the best basketball Indianapolis has ever seen." Netolicky had 26 points, hitting 12-of-18 shots. A tightly-wound Daniels hit just 9-of-23 shots, but still finished with 25 points and grabbed 10 rebounds. Rayl solidified his grip on a starting backcourt position with the team's most complete performance: 16 points, seven rebounds and a game-high nine assists.

The only individual disappointment was Brown, who was called for three fouls in the first five minutes and scored just two points. Peeples replaced him and played his way into extended minutes with 14 points and 13 rebounds.

Barry didn't disappoint, scoring 51 points while hitting 17-of-36 field goal attempts and all 17 foul shots, and adding a game-high 15 rebounds. He and Peeples squared off early in the fourth quarter, but were separated before serious punches could be thrown.

All in all, it was more than the most enthusiastic Pacers fan could have hoped for.

Storen had given up on scheduling regular season games in high school gyms throughout the state as he had done the first season, but not exhibition games. The two teams headed for New Castle High School the following night, where Barry scored 42 points to lead Oakland's 142-119 victory before 2,138 fans. Lewis led the Pacers again with 30. They then moved on to Shelbyville High School, where they played for the third time in three nights. Barry's 48 points, nine rebounds and seven assists led Oakland to a 147-138 victory. Daniels had his best game so far with 25 points and 16 rebounds, and Rayl had 20, hitting four straight three-pointers in the first quarter, but the Pacers somehow managed to commit 37 turnovers. Barry averaged 47 points over the three-game series and hit 45-of-46 foul shots.

After a break, the Pacers defeated Denver at Lebanon High School and again at their former training camp site at St. Joseph's College in Rensselaer. Daniels, settling in, continued to play well, but the most notable performance at St. Joseph's came from Denver's center, McGill, the player the Pacers had

Freddie Lewis dribbles off Roger Brown's screen of Larry Brown in an exhibition game against Oakland. Lewis scored 44 points to lead the Pacers' 141-131 victory.

so readily and harshly released the previous summer. He scored 18 points, hitting 9-of-12 shots, and grabbed nine rebounds.

The Pacers followed by defeating Kentucky at Orleans High School in southern Indiana. Daniels scored 28 points and grabbed 18 rebounds. Rayl added 17 points and hit four three-pointers. They finally moved on to Colorado to close out their exhibition schedule with two more games against Denver. Rayl had to skip the trip because of National Guard duty, but the Pacers won both games, first in Colorado Springs and then at a high school gym in Greeley.

Mel Daniels (34) tries to prevent Rick Barry's scoring attempt in the exhibition game against Oakland on October 3, 1968. Barry scored 51 points in his Coliseum debut.

Mike Lewis' tip at the buzzer provided the winning margin in the final game before 1,000 fans. Daniels led the scoring with 22 points but left the game in the fourth quarter after injuring his back when Denver guard Jeff Congdon undercut him on a drive to the basket. Peeples left in the second quarter after an elbow shattered his glasses and left a gash over his left eye. Neither injury was regarded as serious, and hardly enough to spoil the positive vibe.

The season was five days away. The Pacers had won their final five pre-season games to finish 6-3. Their roster included four All-Stars from the previous season (Daniels, Brown, Lewis and Netolicky), the Rookie of the Year and a first-team all-league member (Daniels), and a second-team all-league member (Brown). Netolicky was reported in the newspapers to be more mature than the previous season. Lewis was further establishing himself as a leader. As for Rayl, Overpeck wrote the Pacers had tried to trade him over the summer, and expected to cut him during training camp. But he had secured a starting position with his three-point shooting and passing.[4]

In the front office, John DeVoe had taken over as team president, localizing the leadership. The front office and owners had a season under their collective belt, and were enthusiastic about the new season. Their optimistic mood was founded on three primary factors beyond the team's upgraded roster: (1) season ticket sales had collected $82,627, compared to $57,395 the previous year, (2) the radio network had expanded to 16 stations throughout the state and (3) Channel 13 agreed to televise 11 road games, five more than the previous season — five of them in color.

---

[4] The Pacers' payroll in the second season: Daniels, $30,000; Brown, $23,000; Netolicky, $22,250; Freddie Lewis $21,000; Rayl, $17,000; Harkness, $17,000; Mike Lewis, $17,000; Peeples, $15,000; Wagner, $11,500; and Hooper, $11,000. A later addition, Don Dee, also was paid $11,000. The team spent $12,000 on signing bonuses — $5,000 to Mike Lewis, $3,000 to Dee and Thompson and $1,000 to Wagner. Storen was paid $20,000, Staverman $16,000 and Lareau $9,200. Storen enjoyed recalling his negotiation with Brown. The rule at the time was that if an agreement could not be reached after a player completed a one-year contract, the player was guaranteed at least 90 percent of his previous salary. When Brown asked what they would do about the car that had been leased to him, Storen said, "You get to keep the car, and I get to keep the keys." They obviously came to an agreement for a sizable raise.

Oakland rookie Warren Armstrong pulls down a rebound in traffic in the exhibition game at the Coliseum. He would become well-known to Pacers' fans later in the season when the teams met in the playoffs.

Phil Wagner, shown with commissioner George Mikan, wound up playing 12 games for the Pacers and started four.

As part of the build-up to the season, a Tipoff Banquet was held on Tuesday evening at the Elks Lodge, $5 per head, with Mikan returning as the featured speaker. Netolicky got up and predicted a win in the season-opener against the Oaks. Rayl, full of enthusiasm as a member of the starting lineup, praised Brown for having that intangible "it" quality the great players possess, and added, "so does the organization and the coach, and there are 10 ballplayers who've got it." The players also paid a return visit to the Eagledale Shopping Plaza on Thursday, where merchants once again passed out some tickets, but not as many as the previous season.

Mostly, though, the focus was on Daniels. Oh, and money.

"Now that we have Mel we have the potential to go all the way," Netolicky told Denny in the *News*. "Getting last-place money instead of first-place money in the playoffs last season should be incentive enough for anybody to do better."

The roster was upgraded, the front office was settled and fan enthusiasm had never been greater. What could possibly go wrong?

"I'm going to tell you guys something. We're going to lose together and we're going to win together. You go to the hilt for me and I'll go to the hilt for you. And I want to tell you one other thing. I don't want to hear any of this nigger or honky shit."

No More Mr. Nice Guy

The ABA had taken its first wobbly steps in the Summer of 1967, forever known in pop culture as the Summer of Love. It was a colorful and free-spirited time, made for rejecting conformity and expanding consciousness. A complex, inventive Beatles album, "Sgt. Pepper's Lonely Hearts Club Band," kicked off the summer with a June 1 release, and an uncomplicated Beatles single, "All You Need Is Love," was atop the Billboard chart by the end of August. In between, songs such as "Respect," "Groovin'" and "Light My Fire" reached No. 1 – perfect accompaniment for the incubation of the daring new basketball league.

The mood was much darker in 1968, which accumulated anger and unrest with each passing month. The Vietnam War escalated, in turn prompting more frequent and violent student protests on college campuses. Martin Luther King was assassinated in Memphis on April 4, fueling an already burning civil rights movement and setting cities ablaze. Presidential candidate Robert Kennedy, whose calming words had prevented an uprising in Indianapolis the night of King's murder, was assassinated in Los Angeles on June 5. In August, anti-war activists clashed with police officers outside the Democratic National Convention in Chicago.

Just how and why all the tragedy and tumult influenced the attitude of Pacers fans was impossible to measure, but one thing was certain: their well of patience and understanding was far shallower than the previous season. Waves of discontent, in fact, began lapping on the franchise's shore on opening night when the Oaks returned for a Friday game at the Coliseum. Acquiring Daniels had instilled optimism in the fan base, but the positive vibes would be forgotten quickly if the team struggled.

The bands from Butler University and Scecina High School provided the music, the Flip Twisters from Ohio returned yet again for halftime entertainment, and Mayor Lugar handled the ceremonial opening tip. Attendance was 8,889, a few hundred short of a sellout because some of the tickets handed out at Eagledale Shopping Center had gone unused. It didn't help that the game was competing against high school football, but Storen wanted to make as big a splash as possible, and had to agree to a Friday date to get the Barry-good Oakland team as the opposition. The failure to sell out was a bit disturbing given all the promise of the season and the performance in the pre-season, but at least the financial intake was greater than the previous year's opener because fewer tickets were given away.

The result wasn't as good, though. The Pacers lost, 144-133, and it wasn't that close; they trailed by 22 points with four minutes left. Barry led a balanced attack with 36 points. Netolicky continued to sparkle with 31 points and 14 rebounds, but couldn't contain Barry. Daniels, in his official debut as a Pacer, finished with 24 points and 17 rebounds. Rayl scored 21 points and hit a franchise-record five three-pointers.

The Pacers and their hometown media members accused the referees of giving Barry preferential treatment, an argument that would rage throughout the season. Brown aired a complaint to reporters after the game. Overpeck agreed, and reported Barry – whom he dubbed "Golden Boy" – had not been called for charging violations after knocking Pacers to the floor three times. The Pacers, though, couldn't realistically blame the defeat on the refs. Their offense was stagnant and Larry Brown pointed out they "started soloing" after they fell behind, just as they had done the previous year. And, even in their season opener, effort was an issue.

The starting lineup for the opening of the 1968-69 season was, from left to right, Jimmy Rayl, Bob Netolicky, Mel Daniels, Roger Brown and Freddie Lewis.

The backups included, left to right, Bobby Hooper, George Peeples, Mike Lewis, Jerry Harkness and Phil Wagner.

"I can't say we quit, but when things don't go right we just don't hustle," Staverman said. Already he was talking of changes, such as slowing the tempo and moving Netolicky away from the basket to give Daniels more room to operate.

Most disturbing of all, though, was the behavior of the fans. They threw wadded paper and cups at the referees and at Barry throughout the game. "It is disgusting to see a player subjected to physical abuse just because he plays the game so well," Overpeck wrote in a followup column. Oakland coach Alex Hannum also was targeted, nailed in the back with a cup at one point.

One section of fans booed Staverman and Rayl during pregame introductions. Staverman was booed throughout the game as well, and the entire team was booed heading off the court. The previous season's poor finish had begun to turn public opinion against the coach, and his own admission of not being tough enough on his players set him up for criticism. The anger toward Rayl was more perplexing. Less than seven months earlier, fans had voted him the team's most popular player, and he had played well in most of the exhibition games. Neither of the Indianapolis newspapers had written about his clashes with Staverman, so it was difficult to determine what turned them against him.

The Pacers lost their second game as well, to Kentucky at the Coliseum, after leading by 14 points at halftime. Daniels finished with 24 points and 26 rebounds, but according to Conard's count touched the ball only three times in 21 possessions in the third quarter. The Colonels were leading 109-108 in the final minute when someone heaved a cup of ice from the upper level while a Kentucky player was preparing to shoot a free throw. After the game was stopped to dry the court, the free throw was missed, but the Colonels went on to win, 112-108, before just 3,488 fans.

Dampier, the Indianapolis native, scored 26 points. He drew some of his motivation from the abusive fans sitting behind the Colonels bench.

"I always like to do well here, but some remarks a guy made made me mad and I tried that much harder," he said afterward. "You can't help but hear the fans when they're that loud and I was angry at myself anyway when the coach took me out."

Dampier said fans had yelled insults such as "Put Dampier back in for defense!" a sarcastic knock on his primary weakness, and "You ought to get your sideburns cut!" Tame stuff, but enough to irritate and motivate.

The atmosphere at the Coliseum had become so toxic that Overpeck and Conard felt compelled to devote columns to it. Conard detailed the vitriol directed at Staverman and Rayl the previous two games and called out the "hidden boob in the crowd, who probably never pulled on the short pants and sneakers once in his life, to play his role of TI – Town Idiot." Overpeck ended his column by stating, "The first two games indicate that the Coliseum crowd is different than it was a year ago. It is more demanding and when it isn't satisfied, it's going to make its wrath heard."

It was, after all, an era for protests.

The Pacers dropped their third game, too, by three points at Kentucky, prompting Staverman to announce he would shake up the starting lineup by replacing Netolicky, Lewis and Rayl with rookies Mike Lewis, Hooper and Wagner for the fourth game against Denver on Halloween night. He later changed his mind, merely subbing Mike Lewis for Daniels, who had been pressing to live up to expectations.

The Pacers won that one, 122-100. Harkness sparkled off the bench with 10 points, eight rebounds, seven assists and lockdown defense of Bob Verga, who had moved from Dallas to Denver in the off-season. Coming off the bench didn't help Daniels, though, as he hit just 3-of-18 shots, committed five errors and three goaltending violations, and fouled out. A re-energized Netolicky finished with 21 points and 19 rebounds, silencing the boos. Mike Lewis had 15 points and 15 rebounds, providing a glimpse of what he could become.[1]

The crowd of 3,187 saved most of their boos for the referees this time, raining ice and wadded cups onto the court. The game was delayed several minutes at one point to clean up and restore order. Rayl came in for more boos, too, despite not even playing.

Daniels stuck up for him in the *News* the next day.

"... that was unbelievable," he said. "I guess the people pay their money and that gives them some rights. But I never witnessed anything like it anywhere. Here we are representing Indianapolis and Indiana and they boo their own players."

Rather than a step toward improvement, that first victory turned out to be a mere blip on the radar of a fading team. The Pacers lost their next game, at the Coliseum, to Houston, one of the ABA's worst teams. They led by 21 points in the third quarter and by 15 entering the fourth, then dissolved by hitting just 4-of-22 field goal attempts and 2-of-8 foul shots, and committing nine turnovers. Overpeck called it "the worst fourth quarter the American Basketball Association has ever seen."

---

[1] McGill got further revenge on the Pacers for releasing him the previous year and insulting him on the way out the door by scoring 26 points in this game. He scored 20 in the next game between the two teams in Denver, and averaged 16.2 against the Pacers that season.

Staverman kept the locker room closed for 25 minutes. He gave the players "a good chewing-out, and we deserved it," according to Harkness. Brown took the blame for missing six of his nine foul shots, including three in the final period. Daniels, who scored 28 points, talked of bad breaks and promised the team would "get it together." The silver lining was provided by Harkness, who had earned a starting assignment with his performance against Denver and followed up with 17 points, seven rebounds and eight assists.

A players-only meeting was held the day after that game, at which Daniels and Harkness were elected captains. That helped bring about a better performance in the next game, against the Minnesota Pipers,[2] but the result was the same. Minnesota won, 121-120, as Connie Hawkins scored 42 points.[3] Brown, motivated by playing against his high school rival, bounced back with 31 points, nine rebounds and 14 assists. Rayl, taking a pass from Brown with a second left, missed a rushed three-pointer from 26 feet at the final buzzer that could have won the game.

The crowd of 3,203 cheered the players for their effort as they left the court. They were 1-5, but things had gotten to that point. The players were encouraged, too.

"I don't think we had enough dedication before," Peeples said, referring to the team meeting. "Now Mel and Jerry have the right to criticize and we agreed to stamp out any inkling of individualism."

---

[2] It isn't often a team wins a championship and then picks up and moves, but Pittsburgh moved to Minneapolis because Mikan thought it would look bad if the city in which the league headquarters was located did not have a team. Pittsburgh had not drawn well despite winning the championship, so owner Gabe Rubin was agreeable and sold majority interest in the team to Bill Erickson in Minneapolis.

[3] Minnesota Pipers coach Jim Harding used just one reserve in the game, for nine minutes. Hawkins injured his back with five minutes left, but remained in the game. That was Harding's style, and it proved costly. A former college coach, this was his first pro job, and he took a militaristic approach. He held three practices a day in training camp, and rarely substituted. Much to the relief of his players, he wound up getting fired over All-Star break when he got into an argument with Rubin at the banquet the night before the game and initiated a fist fight.

Denny, who liked Staverman a great deal and was sympathetic to his plight, took to pleading for help from the heavens.

"Somebody up there ... anybody up there ... smile on our Pacers," he concluded in his article in the *News*. "They're beginning to do their part. Now they need your help."

Divine intervention couldn't overcome the schedule, however. The Pacers were to play their next 10 games on the road, divided into two segments over three weeks. There would be games in Denver, Oakland and Los Angeles over four days, a six-day break back in Indianapolis, then seven more games over an 11-day stretch.

The ABA had initiated a cost-cutting measure in the off-season, limiting rosters to 11 players, one less than the previous season. Only 10 players were permitted to dress for road games, although teams had the option to travel with 11 in case of an injury on an extended road trip.

The Pacers elected to travel with 10. And to leave Rayl at home.

"Jim hasn't lived up to the standards of the ball club," Staverman told Overpeck in the *Star*. Denny reported it as "a disciplinary problem" in the *News*.

The news surely came as a surprise to the fans, even those who had booed him, because Rayl had just played well against Minnesota. But, again, something had happened.

Rayl was passionate about basketball, and reacted emotionally when basketball didn't love him back. He was high-strung by nature, an attribute no doubt amplified when his father, Durwood, died suddenly of a heart attack when Jimmy was 13 years old. Perhaps his flare-ups with coaches related to that tragic event.

The primary example, a story Rayl often retold in later years, occurred during a Thursday practice in college at I.U., after he threw the ball away a time or two in a half-court scrimmage. The court was elevated, and the ball had to be chased down onto a dirt surface surrounding the court. "Make good passes, boy, make good passes," his coach, McCracken, barked as Rayl retrieved the errant ball.

Rayl already was in a foul mood. He had scored just two points in the previous game against Iowa, in which he took just seven shots and had clashed with his coach, either over his early shot selection or his inability to get open for shots. The friction lingered. Rayl sailed the ball back to his coach with a crisp two-handed chest pass and a suggestion: "Why don't you stick that up your ass?" He turned and began walking off the court.

"You step off that court, boy, and you're off the team!" McCracken shouted.

"That's the best news I've heard all day!" Rayl replied, throwing up his arms as he walked off the court. He calmly paused to get a drink of water and then headed for the locker room. After showering, he drove home in a fit of anger. He drove back that night, however, after a sportswriter who covered the team for the Bloomington *Herald-Telephone*, Gary Galloway, brokered a truce. McCracken agreed to let Rayl return if he apologized to the team, and Rayl did so, sincerely. Before practice on Friday, he addressed his teammates who were sitting in the bleachers at the fieldhouse, some of them stifling snickers over their teammate in trouble. "I know how I'd feel if one of you guys did that, and I don't blame you if you're mad at me," Rayl said. "The only thing I know to do is come out and play my hardest on Saturday."

Saturday brought Michigan State to IU's campus. Rayl played his hardest and scored 56 points, hitting 23-of-48 field goal attempts. He matched the university and Big Ten scoring records he had set the previous season in an overtime win over Minnesota, and he did so without a three-point line and in an era when the clock did not stop during dead balls, thus shortening the game. He was removed from the game with 1:09 remaining, inspiring boos rather than cheers from the fans who wanted McCracken to let Rayl break his record. He had reached 49 points with 7:40 remaining, but hit just three of his last 14 shots before asking to come out.

His performance was of such significance in Bloomington that a story ran on Page 1 of the afternoon *Herald-Telephone* the following Monday. (The paper had no Sunday edition.) The article mentioned no conflict between Rayl and McCracken, but the *Star's* account of the game on Sunday hinted at the drama behind the curtain. "During the week, rumors leaked out that McCracken and Rayl weren't seeing eye-to-eye on some things, but Branch refused to comment on the reported friction prior to last night's game," it read.

Ultimately, though, Rayl valued close relationships with his coaches. He had remained close with his high school coach, Platt and decades later remained proud of the fact McCracken was sitting in the second row of the church in Kokomo, smiling widely, when he and his high school sweetheart, Nancy Ousley, were married.

Rayl was calm and congenial with his teammates away from the action, and made friends easily. Netolicky and Mike Lewis had driven to Kokomo to help panel his basement the previous summer, and Freddie Lewis, in a display of leadership and friendship, had taken a cup of coffee to him on the team bus one morning on a road trip.

During games, however, Rayl's temper flared when things didn't go well. He wasn't entirely apologetic about it, as he often channeled his anger into playing with more energy and focus. But he looked back on some incidents with regret. Such as the time when Freddie Lewis told him he (Rayl) had missed him for an open shot on the previous possession while they were running back on defense. "You've been missing me all year!" Rayl replied.

Rayl had even barked at an underclassman, Steve Redenbaugh, during his senior season at IU. Redenbaugh, a sophomore, had shot an air ball in his first varsity game, prompting Rayl to shout, "What the hell are you doing? The name of the game is to put the ball in the basket!" Rayl immediately felt bad about that one, and the two became good friends.

Rayl was struggling to contain his temper this season, too. It had started with such promise, with him in the starting lineup, averaging 14.3 points in exhibition play, and scoring 21 points while hitting five three-pointers in the season-opener. He followed with 15 points in the second game, but with the losses beginning to accumulate he and Freddie Lewis were benched in favor of rookie guards Wagner and Hooper for the game against Denver. Staverman said he couldn't find much fault with either of them, but felt a change was needed after three losses to open the season.

Rayl barely played the next game against Houston, but his bounce-back game against Minnesota seemed to make things right again. He didn't play until three minutes remained in the third quarter, but he scored 13 points in the final 15 minutes. His missed 26-foot three-pointer at the buzzer that could have won the game wasn't the first option of the play call, and by the time he took Brown's pass, he had to rush the shot to get it off in time. But, frustrated by the loss of that game, the losses in all but one of the season's six games and his loss of playing time, he lashed out in the locker room. He flung a bar of soap against the wall, perhaps punctuating it with a personal gripe of some sort.

"This is a team!" Daniels shouted at him.

"Screw the team!" Rayl shouted back.

It wasn't what Staverman wanted to hear. When the team practiced the next day, a Wednesday, Rayl told Staverman he had to report for weekend National Guard duty again. "That's OK, you're not going on the trip anyhow," Staverman replied, according to Conard's report in the *Kokomo Tribune*.

The Indianapolis and Kokomo newspapers put Rayl's suspension in headlines. The *Star's* story indicated Storen had originally planned to waive Rayl, but had changed his mind. Rayl would rejoin the team in practice the following Monday.

Rayl wound up missing one of the most eventful road trips in franchise history, a game-changer for him and the franchise. It began, appropriately enough, with a bomb threat. The Pacers traveling party had to disembark the intended flight to St. Louis and switch planes after the threat was phoned in.

That night in Denver, Staverman and Denny went for a long walk downtown. Staverman knew the noose around his neck was getting tighter, but insisted he would not resign. He believed in himself, and blamed the current state of misery on his team's inexperience – relative to other ABA teams that had older former NBA players on their rosters – and the lack of support from fans at the Coliseum.

"I don't think the booing of Jimmy Rayl and other players has been warranted," Denny reported him saying.

"We've got young players who need enthusiasm and encouragement, and they're not getting it the way we did early last year. I feel the fans have gone from devotion to being against us. The ball club belongs to the people and it's difficult for the players to do well under the conditions that have existed in the Coliseum this season.

"Many of our problems would be licked if the players knew the fans were totally behind them. We're still not a mature team and we need help from the fans. Other teams are getting it. Why not Indiana?"

Getting away from the angry fans at home didn't help, though. The Pacers lost to the Rockets, 109-107, in overtime, to fall to 1-6. The emphasis on keeping chins up continued, however. Afterward, Staverman thanked the players for their hustle and everyone put their hands together and huddled, Storen included.

"We're just inches away from finding the secret," Harkness told Denny.

"We're going to make it work," Freddie Lewis added.

Their optimism had merit. The five defeats following the opening-night loss to Oakland had come by a total of 12 points. Poise was a greater issue than effort, and some of the issues were outside the coach's control. Daniels, for example, scored 29 points and grabbed 16 rebounds against the Rockets, but missed a close shot that would have won the game in regulation and then fumbled a pass from Mike Lewis while trying to score a game-tying basket in overtime. He also missed seven of his 14 foul shots. Netolicky missed seven of his 12 free throws, but finished with 23 points and 19 rebounds.

Denny asked Storen afterward if he was considering a coaching change.

"No comment," Storen said, before commenting. "We face a paradox. If there was dissension, you might make a change, but there isn't. And if Larry had lost control of the club you might make a change, but he hasn't. You really can't put your finger on anything except the fact we can't seem to break a losing streak."

The fatal collapse came the following night in Oakland, with a 153-128 loss in which the Pacers gave up the most points in the ABA's brief history. The Oaks had already established themselves as the league's best team, but Staverman and Storen laid much of the blame for the one-sided defeat on Moyers, the infamous referee from the previous season. Moyers had been fired over the summer, but had been brought back to fill a vacancy for this game. He surprised the Pacers when he walked onto the court shortly before tip-off.

"Moyers upset our club last season and they were beat before the game began," Staverman told Denny afterward.

"I didn't want Moyers officiating our games last year and I don't want him officiating our games now," Storen said. "He completely upsets our club."

Blaming Moyers for the loss seemed excessive, given the fact the Pacers managed to give up 47 points in the first quarter and went on to trail 69-42 with four minutes left in the half, at which point Barry was ejected by the other referee, Tom Frangella. The Oaks apparently had some complaints, too.

Oakland coach Alex Hannum – who had jumped to the ABA during the off-season after a highly successful NBA coaching career in which he won championships with St. Louis in 1957 and Philadelphia in 1967 – sought out Staverman after the game to tell him the first quarter explosion was the best his team had played all season. Barry offered consolation as well. "Indiana has a lot of talent and is better than most clubs in the league," he told Denny. "I couldn't believe it when I read about all the games the team had lost. Tell them to relax."

That was good advice for Daniels most of all. Although he finished with 20 points and 13 rebounds, he hit just 6-of-17 free throws against the Oaks, making him 13-of-31 from the foul line over the previous two games. The losing was getting to him, affecting his poise and confidence.

The Pacers were now 1-7 and coming off their worst loss of the season. All the losses but the two to Oakland were close and the players were showing no signs of mutiny, but Storen decided he could wait no longer. After an off day on Friday, which gave him time to finalize plans, he met Staverman for breakfast on Saturday at the hotel coffee shop in Los Angeles and fired him. Staverman was deeply wounded, but accepted the decision gracefully. Given the option by Storen of coaching that night's game, Staverman said he wanted to coach it.

Staverman confided only in his wife, Joyce, before the game, with a telephone call back home. She was so angry she got down on her hands and knees and scrubbed the kitchen floor to burn off her adrenaline. And then did it a second time. He said nothing to his players of his impending fate.

He went out with a victory. The Pacers overcame a six-point fourth quarter deficit for a 112-107 victory over the Stars, as Brown and Freddie Lewis hit crucial free throws down the stretch. Los Angeles contributed by playing its worst game of the season according to the *Los Angeles Times* account, committing 30 turnovers and missing 24 of its 54 free throw attempts. After so many bad breaks, with so many losses resulting from missed foul shots and mistakes by uptight players, Staverman had finally caught a wisp of good luck. Too late.

He walked into a locker room of celebrating players. Storen was waiting there, too – in case he decided to blast the organization for firing him, Staverman assumed. Still, Staverman didn't let on to his players. He congratulated them, reminded them of the reasons they had won, and told them they weren't going to become a winning team until they developed the dedication and discipline to do those things all the time.

"Then I walked out and walked around the building and cried my eyes out," he recalled years later.

He had fallen on his sword, coaching as best he could to the very end and bowing out as graciously as possible. His players, who didn't find out about his firing until they arrived back in Indianapolis on Sunday, were sympathetic.

Harkness praised his emotional half-time speech: "He screamed, and I felt something," he told Denny.

An anonymous player took the blame on behalf of the team. "This basketball can be a terrible life," he said. "Ask any of the players and they'd tell you, they liked Larry and had confidence in him. It was our fault. We didn't play well enough for him."

Storen had issued a press release back in Indianapolis an hour before tip-off in Los Angeles to announce a press conference for Monday at 1 p.m. at the Pacers office on 38ᵗʰ St. The speculation in the Sunday newspapers pointed toward the obvious, a coaching change, and reported the likely successor: Bob Leonard.

Leonard, 36, oozed Indiana's basketball tradition. He had been a high school star in Terre Haute and a college star at Indiana University. He had hit the game-winning free throw in IU's NCAA championship victory over Kansas in 1953, and earned second-team All-America honors as a senior the following year. After serving two years in the Army, he went on to play seven seasons in the NBA, and then took over as the Chicago Zephyrs' coach on Dec. 28, 1962, age 30, replacing Jack McMahon. He moved with the team to Baltimore the following season, where it became the Bullets.

His combined record for his season-and-a-half in the NBA was only 44-78, but he had coached young teams with no realistic chance of winning. The Bullets had started 3-12 his only season in Baltimore, but put a couple of winning streaks together and got to 27-34 in mid-February before injuries took their toll and left him with a sorely depleted roster. Just 31 when the season ended, he had been the NBA's youngest coach while directing the league's youngest team. Hardly a formula for success. Trager, the Bullet's owner who remained based in Chicago, understood the circumstances and gave Leonard a vote of confidence at the end of the season despite the team's poor finish.

Leonard appeared on course to return for the following season after participating in the Bullets' draft and a major trade with Detroit, but his resignation was abruptly announced on Aug. 7, 1964. The *Baltimore Sun* and wire services reported it as the result of Trager's rejection of Leonard's request for a three-year contract. Leonard, meanwhile, gave the impression that he was seeking stability and relief from the professional grind to spend more time with his family, which now included three children at home.

"I've been thinking about getting out of pro ball for some time now," he told Baltimore reporters by telephone from South Bend, where his wife Nancy's parents lived. "They can say what they want about pro basketball coaches, but I don't think there is much security in the job. I'm more interested in coaching college or high school ball. I'd like to go back to school and obtain my Master's degree. I feel more coaching opportunities will be available to me then."

The truth was, Leonard had been fired and was playing the role of good soldier. Buddy Jeannette, who had been a player and player-coach with the original Baltimore Bullets in the late 1940s, was hired to replace him by general manager Paul Hoffman – a former Purdue All-American who went on to become a teammate of Jeannette's in Baltimore. Trager praised Leonard for doing "a fantastic job under the circumstances" after the change, and reportedly allowed him to stay on the team's payroll as a consultant after negotiating a downgrade of his $15,000 salary.

Trager was in the process of selling the team at the time, another complicating factor. The sale was negotiated all summer and finally made official on Oct. 24. A three-man group headed by Abe Pollin took it off the hands of the 15-man Chicago syndicate (that often drove Leonard crazy with its myriad and conflicting phone calls and suggestions) for slightly more than $1 million.

Leonard later moved his family to Kokomo, where he began working for Herff Jones on July 1, 1965. He roamed the northern part of the state, putting his good name to use by selling class rings and graduation supplies to high school students. He had a territory of 58 schools and a built-in advantage as most of the school principals were sports-minded and remembered his high school and college playing careers in the state. His wife, Nancy, meanwhile, taught business classes at Taylor High School just outside of Kokomo.

Storen, who also had moved with the Zephyrs to Baltimore, said he had approached Leonard about coaching the Pacers from the start, but was rebuffed, a memory that contradicted Collins' claim the owners were leery of Leonard. Either way, Leonard was naturally reluctant to give up a comfortable job to take on the risk of coaching in a new league with a shaky future. He and Nancy were enjoying a peaceful lifestyle in a smaller city. They had bought a new home a few miles outside of town and were settled.

Leonard had, in fact, reiterated his lack of interest in professional coaching in a speech to the Kokomo Downtown Kiwanis Club on April 21, 1966.

"I wouldn't trade my experience as a pro player and coach, but I wouldn't care to undergo the strain and pressure again," he said. "It's too much."

He had been lurking in the background for the Pacers all along, however, never far from the action. He had recommended Staverman for the coaching job, having coached him with the Zephyrs in the 1962-63 season and briefly the following season in Baltimore. He had helped run the open tryouts in the summer of '67 along with Lovellette at the request of Storen, who recognized the practical and public relations value of tapping into Indiana's basketball tradition by bringing in two former NBA players who had grown up in the state. He also had scouted some games the first season, and stayed in contact with Storen. He was photographed sitting with Storen and Storen's wife, Hannah, on Jan. 10 the first season, when the Pacers defeated Minnesota the night after the All-Star game, looking on with interest from the front row.

Now, having gained more confidence in the future of the ABA and seen the Pacers' potential with Daniels at center, he decided to take the plunge. He had nothing to lose but sleep. Storen agreed to let him keep his day job with Herff Jones,[4] and Leonard figured he could perform both until the ABA folded. He and Nancy had just purchased new furniture for their home, and the salary from the Pacers would pay off their debt.

Years later, he recalled his thought process: "This league isn't going to last with that red, white and blue ball and that three-point line, but I can do both of these jobs and make enough money to pay for this furniture."[5]

The players were excited to have him in their corner. Netolicky and Rayl had met Leonard a few times for beers at the Red Carpet, a lounge

---

[4] Leonard kept his job with Herff Jones through 1974, with administrative help from Nancy and the children, who contributed by packing items to be delivered to the schools in assembly line fashion.

[5] Leonard's initial contract was for two seasons and called for an annual salary of $22,500, with the first season likely pro-rated. He was to be paid a bonus of $3,000 for winning the Eastern Division, $1,000 for winning the first round of the play-offs, $3,000 for winning the second round and $5,000 for winning the league championship. If the franchise was sold, his contract would be binding.

on the west side of Indianapolis, the summer after the first season. Leonard told them he didn't think the team had played up to its potential, and won them over with his bold charisma — not to mention his willingness to bend elbows with them. One time, Netolicky recalled, Leonard ordered three drinks. When the waitress began walking away, he called her back and asked, "Aren't you going to take their order?"

His energy, confidence and communication skills were alluring, particularly juxtaposed with the more composed and conservative Staverman. It didn't take Netolicky long to begin dropping hints to Storen about hiring Leonard, and the team's slow start only revved up the desire for change.

Clearly, Staverman's fate was at least in doubt, and probably determined, before the road trip. Overpeck later reported in the *Star* Leonard had met with Storen for two hours before the team headed West. Years later, Netolicky recalled Leonard had told Rayl and him during another visit to the Red Carpet shortly before the Western trip that he would be coaching the team soon. "We just got super-excited about it," Netolicky said. And, at the end of the season, Leonard would acknowledge he had considered Storen's offer to coach the team for a week before accepting.

Staverman inspired widespread support in the newspapers after his release. He was praised for being a nice guy ("maybe too nice" was sure to follow) and for being a victim of expectations that perhaps were excessive. He also was clearly not to blame for all those missed free throws.

Most of the blame for the disappointing start was placed on the players in the media.

"There aren't enough tigers on this team," Collins wrote in the *Star*. "Not enough players who place winning above personal average or achievement."

Added Overpeck: "The players are not without blame for their lack of fire. They have been something less than great self-starters. And in the end, motivation must to a large extent be self-enforced."

Players offered public support for their former coach in the newspapers, but most were ready for a change. None more than Rayl, though. While his relationship with Staverman had been strained, he and Leonard were friends with much in common. Both had been high school stars in Indiana who earned All-America recognition at IU. Both were passionate about the game, and temperamental about it, too.

They had known one another for years, but became closer after Leonard moved his family to Kokomo in 1965. Rayl had a clear memory of Bob and Nancy visiting him and his Nancy at their new home one evening shortly before or during Staverman's fateful road trip. Sitting at their dining room table, Leonard told Rayl he was about to take over the team, and assured him that for as long as he was the coach, Rayl would have a spot on the roster.

Just days after being left home from the road trip, Rayl was getting a fresh start.

Conard, upon receiving word of the Monday press conference, called Leonard at his home Saturday evening while the Pacers were playing in Los Angeles. Leonard had to remain coy with his on-the-record comments, but dropped a hint.

"I know one thing," Leonard told Conard. "This is the second time Indiana has had a crack at professional basketball, and by golly I'd do anything I could to see that it stays."[6]

The Nov. 11 press conference made it official. The next coach would be Leonard, a class ring salesman who had been let go from his previous coaching job three years earlier after winning just 36 percent of his NBA games. He had no logical reason to be confident about what he could do with an underachieving team in an unproven league. But his nature

---

[6] It wasn't the second time, technically, but Leonard's first memory of professional basketball in Indianapolis was the Olympians. He hitch-hiked from Bloomington to watch them play the Celtics one night, and later became a close friend of Ralph Beard's. After his banishment from the NBA, Beard was drafted into the Army and assigned to Fort Leonard Wood in Missouri for basic training. Leonard was waiting for him there as a drill instructor and immediately gave him a weekend pass. They wound up playing a lot of basketball together during their time there, going at one another in fullcourt one-on-one games or teaming up to humiliate opposing teams.

was to be bold and optimistic, and his introductory remarks reflected that. He declared the Pacers' talent to be as good as that of any team in the league, and predicted a 50-28 final record despite the 2-7 mark he was inheriting. He promised to make every player feel part of the team and drive them beyond what they thought they could achieve. He would make them play faster more physically, with fewer called plays. He would demand more enthusiasm, too.

Leonard had the good fortune of having four practices before the team would play again, a break in the schedule Storen no doubt had targeted for a coaching change. He had the bad fortune of opening with seven road games, however.

The first practice was conducted the evening of the press conference at 8:30 at Brebeuf Preparatory School, and would become legendary among the participants. In a highly unusual and humane gesture, Leonard invited Staverman to attend. The suddenly-former coach accepted, and took his oldest son. "I couldn't turn him down, because I'm too much a part of this organization," Staverman told Denny. He and Leonard were trading positions to some degree, with Staverman moving to an advisory, scouting and administrative role to fulfill his contract.

Staverman's lasting memory of the evening was Rayl shooting smirks at him now and then, as if he had won their personal battle. The players would have other memories of it.

The start of Leonard's indoctrination process lasted two hours and 45 minutes and amounted to a crash course in a different approach to basketball. Conard and Overpeck attended, and Conard provided detailed coverage of it in the next day's *Kokomo Tribune*, offering a rare glimpse into a franchise's turning point.

"We're going to press 'em and make 'em like it!" Leonard told the players after they gathered on the court. "We're not going to have any of this standing around, dribbling and ignoring the open man, either. We're going to use a pattern only when we have to. The name of the game is 'Get the ball and go for the bucket.' It's the little things that make a ball club and we're not ever going to give (opponents) the least opportunity.

"You're going to work and drive yourself. And don't you worry … you're going to put out. The trouble with you guys is that you're afraid to beat somebody physically, make it tough on 'em or put the hammer to 'em. Well, that's going to change from now on."

Without allowing the players a warmup, Leonard immediately began installing his offensive and defensive systems. That would include more emphasis on exploiting the presence of Daniels, the league's leading rebounder to that point of the season but an underused resource on offense. Daniels, however, was going to have to become more disciplined with his shot selection. In later years, he would tell the story of Leonard stopping practice after he missed a mid-range shot and threatening to punch him in the nose if he ever attempted another shot like that. Neither Conard nor Overpeck reported that, but Overpeck did write that Leonard grabbed a piece of chalk and drew a semi-circle 10 feet in front of the basket.

"Daniels, do you want to get paid as a center or do you want to get paid as a guard?!" Leonard shouted.

Daniels confirmed he was a center.

"Then get inside where you belong! I don't want you taking a shot from beyond there!"

Conard reported Leonard went after Daniels after he missed a 12-foot hook shot. "No, no, no, Mel!" he shouted. "You take that ball and drive it down through that hoop, and if your man gets in your way, take him with you!"

The next time down, Conard wrote, Daniels "nearly put Mike Lewis and the ball in the net."

Leonard also let Netolicky know a new era had arrived.

"What are you Netolicky, some kind of sissy?!" Leonard shouted. "Buddy, you better start going for the bucket, and with a little muscle, too!"

Netolicky responded with five consecutive baskets.

Leonard also managed to slip in support of Staverman. "You cost this man his job!" he shouted, pointing toward the former coach. "You're not going to cost me mine!"

The three practices that followed were equally intense. Clearly, the Pacers were under a more demanding brand of leadership. Problem was, the new leader didn't have sufficient time to install his system before it was time to return to playing games. They were going to have to learn on the fly, and on the road at that.

Leonard implemented a double post offense with Daniels and Netolicky setting up on opposite sides of the foul lane and a fullcourt pressing defense, which he planned to utilize all 48 minutes to improve on the one that ranked second-to-last in the ABA in points allowed. He also set a goal of a 5-2 record for the upcoming road trip, which would begin in Minneapolis against the defending champion Pipers, but told reporters he would settle for 4-3. He said he wanted a "professional attitude" from the players, and for them to "treat this like a business."

He also wanted them to form a tighter bond off the court. The previous season's team had divided somewhat along racial lines. There were no major problems, just a lack of communication and camaraderie between the black and white players. Staverman had hardly promoted such an atmosphere, being the coach brave enough to play five blacks together in an era when such a decision inspired protests from the fans, but he hadn't tackled it head-on, either.

Netolicky recalled that Leonard cleared the air on that issue at one of his first meetings with the players.

"I'm going to tell you guys something." Leonard said. "We're going to lose together and we're going to win together. You go to the hilt for me and I'll go to the hilt for you. And I want to tell you one other thing. I don't want to hear any of this nigger or honky shit."

A distinctly new day had dawned. What lay ahead was anybody's guess.

11

"I've been looking closely to see who on this club wants to win, every night, and now I've made up my mind."

Tumult and Tragedy

Bringing in a different coach with a different approach and personality didn't guarantee different results, of course. It would take time to establish a new chemistry and culture that reflected Leonard's personality, and who's to say it was going to work out anyway?

His records with the Zephyrs (13-29) and Bullets (31-49) might have been understandable given the circumstances, but a career record of 44-78 was hardly proof he could provide an upgrade over Staverman. Leonard might not have proved he was a poor coach because of what he had to work with, but he hadn't proved he was a good one, either.

His debut with the Pacers in Minneapolis on Nov. 15 resulted in a 105-95 loss. Brown led with 23 points, but sprained his left knee in the first quarter and played limited minutes after that. Netolicky added 20 and a revived Rayl 18 off the bench. Hawkins led the relocated Pipers with 35 points, 20 rebounds and "at least five blocks," according to the *Star's* article.

As a coaching career was being relaunched, however, a relaunched playing career was ending. Harkness, who had played well to that point of the season – scoring in double figures in four of the previous six games and establishing himself as the team's best backcourt defender – started the game along with Lewis, Brown, Netolicky and Daniels. It quickly became evident, however, he wasn't going to be part of that core's promising future.

He was trying to coax another season out of his 28-year-old body by babying the knees that had been weakened by all those games on asphalt courts around New York City and the miles accumulated in high school distance runs. By doing so, he strained his back. He had missed a couple of exhibition games, but was gradually working his way into shape when Leonard was hired. He scored 11 points in Leonard's debut, but one play in the second half sent an urgent warning. He tried to put a fake on Chico Vaughn and nearly crumbled to the floor. "It felt like a knife was sticking in my back," he said a few weeks later. He stayed in the game, though, anxious to impress the new coach.

He returned to Indianapolis to try to rehabilitate his pains while the team continued along on the remaining six games of the second chapter of the road trip. Already, though, Storen and Leonard were in the process of trying to improve the backcourt. Overpeck reported in the *Star* they were seeking Charlie Williams from the Pipers or Freeman from Miami, and were willing to give up notable players to get them.

"Informed sources say the Pacers are willing to part with Freddie Lewis and/or Roger Brown for the right deal," Overpeck wrote. "But they're not going to give away either." Those "informed sources" could only have been Storen or Leonard, if not both.

Staverman, having swapped roles with Leonard and working as a scout and consultant, urged caution, and was particularly in favor of keeping Brown. Brown's play had been erratic, as was his acceptance of authority – an attitude rooted in his fractured family life in New York and his banishment from college basketball and the NBA. Brown, Staverman recalled years later, had a way of looking at him sideways, with squinting skepticism, whenever he tried to instruct him. Still, Staverman believed the positives of Brown's talent and potential far outweighed his inconsistency and questionable attitude.

With Rayl replacing Harkness in the starting lineup, the Pacers won their second game under Leonard in New York, 114-91, over a weak Nets team that was led by ex-Pacer Darden's 22 points and 13 rebounds. The most memorable moment of that game came when Nets forward Wilbert Frazier punched Daniels in the nose in the second quarter, breaking and bloodying it. "Only half his own team plus the Nets' burly Hank Whitney kept Daniels from returning the favor with interest,"

Overpeck wrote. Daniels played on, scoring 13 of his 21 points in the second half with blood dripping from his nostrils.

The game would have a lasting impact on his career. He said afterward he had been too cautious since joining the Pacers, and would become more aggressive. "It would take more than a punch in the nose to make me a dirty ball player and I'll never go out of my way to hurt a player," Daniels said. "But one of these nights they're going to catch me when I don't want to get hit."

The game also was notable for the condition of the playing court. It sat on top of hockey ice, and had recently been waxed, the combination of which left it so slick players slid on it throughout the game despite an application of rosin.

The Pacers flew to Dallas the next day. By then, Overpeck's published trade rumors had gotten back to the players and created a stir. Brown learned of what Overpeck had written in a telephone conversation with his wife, Carolyn, and called Overpeck – not out of anger, but curiosity and fear. Overpeck invited Brown and Lewis to his hotel room. Daniels arrived with them. He wasn't on the trade block, but the pain of being traded was still fresh in his memory, and his nature was to support his teammates. He knew how good Brown and Lewis could be, and he had quickly bonded with them.

Brown was stunned to know he was being offered in a trade, and the news only made him that much more skeptical of authority figures. Now he knew what all professional athletes learn eventually: he was a commodity.

Lewis was more pragmatic.

"I've known ever since the first of the season they were talking of trading me," he told Overpeck. "The only thing you can do is go out and play your hardest and prove that they are wrong."

The Pacers lost in Dallas, 110-107, but won the following night in Houston despite blowing all but two points of a 26-point third-quarter lead. Leonard sat Daniels, Netolicky, Brown and Rayl at the start of the game – "so I can show them what I've been talking about" – but put them in with four minutes left in the first quarter and had them on the court to close it out. Rayl figured prominently in that one, scoring 19 points and feeding Lewis for two crucial layups late in the game. The Pacers lost the following game in New Orleans, their third game in three nights, and lost their next two as well, both in Miami against the Floridians, to complete their road trip with a 2-5 record – the opposite of the goal Leonard had publicly stated in the *Star*.

They had fallen to 4-12, last in the Eastern Division. Still, there were hints of improvement. The pace was faster, the defense was better, and Daniels was becoming more comfortable close to the basket. Staverman had wanted to play that way, too, but had tried to get his point across in a gentler manner. Wrote Overpeck: "Staverman explained, asked, almost begged the Pacers to do what they had to do to win. Leonard tells, insists and demands what he wants done."

Leonard's nickname was "Slick," given to him by Mikan during Leonard's second season as a Minneapolis Laker, when Mikan was coaching the team. The Lakers were on a late-night bus trip during the exhibition season, and Leonard and Mikan were playing Hollywood Gin while teammates slept. Leonard won the hand as the bus rolled toward a restaurant, at which point Mikan said, "How about buying me a cup of coffee, you're too slick for me." Leonard's teammate and partner in crime, Hot Rod Hundley, was waking up in the seat behind them and overheard Mikan's comment. From that point on, he called Leonard "Slick," and it stuck to varying degrees along Leonard's career path.

It was an appropriate nickname, not only for Leonard's stylish sartorial habits, but his ability to manipulate his players. He knew how to motivate, whether by striking fear into them with physical threats or instilling confidence and optimism with quiet words. He was equally capable of a kick in the backside or a pat on the back, and this he believed was a time for encouragement.

"I'll tell you one thing," he told Overpeck, "we're going to win this thing (the Eastern Division championship) or be right there before it's over. People are going to say I'm crazy ... but I mean it. I know it!"

One of the primary examples of Leonard's methods was Don Dee, who had joined the team on Oct. 29, when the Pacers were 0-3. The 6-8 forward had been a mid-round draft pick out of St. Mary of the Plain in Kansas. (He had begun his career at St. Louis University, but a knee

George Peeples (43) fights for a rebound while Dallas' Spider Bennett (6) smacks him in the face. Cincy Powell (35) also tries to get involved.

Above: Mel Daniels has to be separated from a Dallas player as tempers flare in Bob Leonard's home game as the Pacers' coach on Nov. 27, 1968. Dallas won, 106-100.

Right: Nancy Leonard voices her opinion during her husband's first home game. She is joined by John DeVoe (left), Jane DeVoe and Mike Storen.

injury led him to leave school for a year.) His arrival to the Pacers was delayed because he had been a member of the U.S. Olympic team that won a gold medal in Mexico City. He was 25 years old, married, and father of three children. He had not played much in the Olympics – averaging just 4.3 points – because coach Hank Iba didn't consider him a strong defender, but Staverman had given him playing time right out of the gate. He made a splash in his third game, his first extended opportunity, by scoring 16 points and grabbing 12 rebounds in a homecourt loss to Minnesota, but quickly returned to limited action.

Leonard inherited Dee, and grew to like his attitude and effort. He moved him into the starting lineup in his eighth game as head coach, and his first at the Coliseum, on Nov. 27 – the team's first appearance there in 23 days. Leonard switched Brown to the backcourt with Lewis and started Dee and Peeples at forward, with Daniels at center. Netolicky was coming off a 20-point, 11-rebound performance in the final game of the road trip in Miami, but later admitted to reporters his play had been "indifferent." He went to the bench.

An above-average crowd of 5,265 fans turned out, eager to see the team that had changed so dramatically since the last time it had played at the Coliseum. They saw a familiar result, however, as the Pacers lost again, to Dallas, 106-100, to drop to 4-13 – the worst record in all of pro basketball. Leonard, who had tried to fire up his players with an impassioned pregame speech, told reporters afterward they had been too anxious. They had shot poorly, turned over the ball in the fourth quarter, and suffered from the fatigue of the long road trip as well. [1] He wasn't so understanding in the privacy of the locker room, however. Denny reported Leonard "seared the walls with an angry dressing down" after the game.

The Pacers won their next game, 108-103, over the Los Angeles Stars. Netolicky, back in the starting lineup, finished with 22 points

---

[1] Hawkins set an ABA scoring record with 57 points this same night, against the Nets, surpassing the 54 points Dampier had scored against the Pacers at the end of the previous season. Also, Slater Martin quit as Houston's coach in protest of the front office making three trades without his approval.

Los Angeles guard Steve Chubin defends Freddie Lewis during the Pacers' 108-103 victory over the Stars. Chubin scored 27 points, leaving an impression that helped change the direction of his career.

and 16 rebounds, playing a complete game for the first time in two weeks, according to Overpeck. Stars guard Steve Chubin, meanwhile, left a lasting impression by muscling his way into the lane to draw enough fouls to attempt 19 free throws. He hit 17 of them, on his way to 27 points.

Two days later, on Dec. 1, Overpeck devoted his Sunday column to trade rumors, with an expanded list of targets that included not only Freeman and Williams, but Chubin, Darel Carrier of Kentucky, Larry Jones of Denver and Walt Simon of New York. Overpeck wrote all the Pacers were available for a trade other than Daniels and Dee. Putting Dee in such an elite category would seem odd in later years, but at the time it wasn't so far-fetched. Although Dee's playing time on the Olympic team had been limited because of his lack of defense, Leonard had psyched him into believing he was a great defender, pumping him up at every opportunity. Denny and Overpeck had written stories to that effect on consecutive days, Dec. 7 and 8, in which Leonard called Dee "damned near as good a defensive forward as I've ever seen," and said, "I'd put him up against any forward in this league."

Dee wasn't nearly *that* good, but he bought into Leonard's praise and hustled. Leonard was essentially trying to create a standout defender, and likely was sending a message to Brown by holding up the Olympic gold medalist as an example of what effort and attitude could bring.

"Slick would be in the locker room before the game saying, 'We've got to watch this guy and this guy and this guy, but we don't have to worry about this guy because Donnie's on him,'" Netolicky recalled in later years. "He actually had Dee believing all this. He had Dee believing he was the greatest defensive player on the face of the earth. And he'd go out and play his ass off."

So, Dee and Daniels were safe, and everyone else apparently was up for grabs. Overpeck reported Freddie Lewis had nearly been traded for Freeman the previous summer, only to have Muskies/Floridians coach Pollard step in and cancel the deal at the last minute. That explained why Lewis had known he was on the block from the start of the season. Clearly, something was going to happen soon. Neither Storen nor

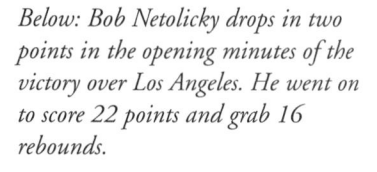

Left: Jimmy Rayl drops off a pass for rookie Mike Lewis during the victory over Los Angeles. Rayl hit two three-pointers and scored eight points, but the clock was ticking on his career.

Below: Bob Netolicky drops in two points in the opening minutes of the victory over Los Angeles. He went on to score 22 points and grab 16 rebounds.

Leonard was the type to be patient amid struggle, and neither was opposed to taking a risk.

Besides, another guard position was about to come open. Harkness had reconnected with the team after an 11-day absence for the home game with Dallas, but by then had been nearly forgotten amid the shuffling lineups. He played briefly at the end of the game, scoring two points and grabbing a rebound, then rode the bench two nights later in the victory over Los Angeles.

Harkness was the odd-man-out for the road trip that began on Dec. 1 with a road game in Miami. Then finally, on Dec. 4, he announced his retirement. He had hoped to stay on the roster and dress for the home games while he continued to rehabilitate, but to his mild dismay he was given no choice. "I guess they don't want to take a chance on my back going out again, but I think I deserved a chance to win my job back," he told the *Star*. [2]

He also wished he hadn't played in the homecourt loss to Dallas. His brief appearance cost him a double-figure scoring average for his final professional season, dropping it from 10 to 9.2 over his 10 games.

The Pacers offered to put Harkness on waivers so another team could claim him, and Pollard wanted to sign him in Miami. Harkness, though, was neither physically nor emotionally inclined to start over somewhere else. He had successfully scratched his itch to play professional basketball again, and made his huge gamble pay off. Eighteen months earlier, he had been pounding the pavement as a salesman for Quaker Oats, a man with a promising corporate career but a dream he couldn't wake up from. Barely more than a year earlier, he had hit the longest shot in the history of professional basketball. He had been named a captain at the start of his second season, and earned a starting position.

---

[2]   Decades later, Harkness would recognize his early retirement as a blessing that prevented further damage to his body. Team physician Dr. F. Robert Brueckmann had gently advised him to give up his career, and it turned out to be the right call as he was able to avoid a knee or hip replacement.

He had accomplished so much in such a short period of time. But now his body was betraying him and it was time to move on.[3]

Storen treated him well, keeping him on the payroll as a scout and broadcaster and sending out resumes on his behalf to other teams. It was a more graceful exit than most players manage. Years later, Daniels would tell Harkness he and Brown had shed a few tears over the forced exit, but everyone moved on. Having lost by five points in Miami two nights earlier, they left for Louisville on the same morning as Harkness' retirement announcement for a game against the Colonels that evening. They lost that one, too, by two points – a margin made that close only by three-pointers from newly acquired forward John Fairchild and Rayl in the final seconds.

Their record had dropped to 5-15. They were 3-8 under Leonard, who in that passing moment had a career record of 47-86, and he had seen enough. Having proclaimed when he took over the team he had sufficient talent to compete with any team in the ABA, he now was convinced he needed two more versatile players – one for the frontcourt and one for the backcourt – to contend.

"We just don't have enough to win with as it is," he told Denny after the loss to Kentucky. "I'm going to Mike tomorrow and tell him we must make some trades … You can expect some changes in the next four or five days."

He added, without elaboration: "I've been looking closely to see who on this club wants to win, every night, and now I've made up my mind."

---

[3] Harkness went on to build a successful career outside of basketball, breaking racial barriers throughout Indianapolis – appropriate for someone who had been inspired by Jackie Robinson. He became the city's first black fundraiser as a fulltime employee of United Way, a co-founder of Black Expo, and the state's first black television sportscaster for Channel 13, the ABC affiliate. He had no background or training in the profession, but the station was under pressure to hire a minority, and selected him. He admittedly was "terrible" at first, but grew to become capable and popular. He also worked early mornings for the city's "black" radio station, WTLC. For a while, he multi-tasked like a mad man, going to the radio station in the morning, working for United Way during the day and working some evenings and most weekends at the television station.

Those comments only added to the anxiety his players were feeling, and it showed in their performance. They barely held on to beat New Orleans by three points the following night after squandering a 22-point lead. Only 2,308 fans turned up at the Coliseum for it, the smallest home crowd in franchise history.[4] Netolicky, "coming off a listless and virtually ineffective performance" against Kentucky, according to Overpeck, led with 32 points and 14 rebounds. Daniels added 27 points and 12 rebounds and Brown perked up a bit with 19 points, five rebounds and six assists.

Daniels, whose collision with Bucs forward Jackie Moreland during the game had required Moreland to get six stitches, blamed the trade rumors for the team's uneven performance. "What we need is two wins in a row and to cut out all this talk about trades," Daniels said. "That really has the club upset. Trade next year, but let us alone now and let us try to get settled down."

Daniels couldn't have been happy, then, if and when he picked up the *News* the next afternoon and saw Fuson's column, headlined "Leonard Has Pacers Trade Flag Waving." Fuson reiterated Overpeck's assertion that everyone on the roster was available except Daniels and Dee. Leonard again was quoted saying he needed both a guard and a big man, but added he and Storen still weren't in panic mode. Nobody said which players Storen and Leonard were most anxious to trade, but Fuson wrote that Brown "may be on the bubble."

In the *Kokomo Tribune*, Conard wrote that Leonard and Storen were talking with several clubs about trades, and added they had brought in a guard from the Eastern League, Jay Neary, for a tryout. Conard also reported offers had been made for Daniels, none of which were taken seriously, and added New York's Levern Tart to the list of guards the Pacers coveted.

---

[4] A game such as this one exemplified the financial challenge of the early seasons. It generated just $4,063.30 in revenue. From that, the Pacers had to pay the standard 15 percent cut to the visiting team, in this case $609.50 and another five percent ($203.16) to the league office. Deducting the season ticket revenue already collected, they gained just $1,095.18 from the game.

The next game after the victory over New Orleans was back in Commack, Long Island against New York. It turned out to be one of the most bizarre games in franchise history, for reasons beyond the 117-102 defeat that dropped them to 6-16. The bus ride from the team hotel to the arena took 90 minutes. The temperature outside was less than 20 degrees. Inside Long Island Arena, it was 15 degrees warmer – maybe, according to Overpeck.

"It was the first basketball game in history where the fans – all 438 of them – started fires in the stands to keep warm," he wrote. "You could see your breath better than you could see the players."

He wasn't exaggerating.

Long Island Arena was intended for hockey, and was meant to be kept cold to prevent the ice from melting. The basketball court placed over it was merely a temporary distraction from its intended purpose. Players could see their breath during pregame warmups, and without enough fans on hand to contribute significant body heat, the arena never came close to approaching room temperature.

Darden, who played 30 games for the Nets that season upon being released by the Pacers, recalled the Nets' locker room having no lockers per se, just nails on which to hang their clothes. Ball boys would rush out and dry off one end of the court with towels when play was at the other end. One night it got so bad, Darden recalled, the Nets essentially threw a game when the floor was so slick neither team could function well. The Nets' let the opponent win to avoid a protest, or perhaps lawsuit, because of the playing conditions. The franchise also didn't want the league office to find out about the dreadful playing conditions.

"It was just terrible," Darden recalled. "You thought you were in a third-world country."

The Pacers – who wore overcoats during pregame warmups – never warmed to the task at hand in this game, failing to hit a field goal until nearly six minutes had passed. They trailed 32-18 after the first quarter, fought back within seven points in the fourth, but then went four minutes without scoring. Tart, a rumored trade target, led the Nets with 32 points. Darden once again thrived against his former teammates with 15 points and 15 rebounds. Fairchild led the Pacers with 23.

Leonard kept the team in the locker room for 65 minutes after the game, but he didn't heat things up nearly as much as people would have assumed. He talked plenty, but also opened the floor to the players to air grievances and ask questions. It was the kind of session that could only take place in an era when teams spent the night in hotels after games and flew out on commercial airlines the following morning, rather than rushing off to catch a charter flight.

"I said some things and I wanted the players to speak out," Leonard told Denny on the bus ride back to the hotel. "We've got to get some communication and some spirit."

Leonard's lecture continued on the bus, as he showed both the fiery and sentimental sides of his nature.

"You're in the first-class section again!" he shouted from the back of the bus toward the front at Netolicky, who had turned in another listless performance. "Come on back here to the tourist class and be one of the team."

Leonard also told his players about meeting a man inside the arena who had traveled with the Minneapolis Lakers when Leonard played for them. The man had lost his first wife in a fire and his second wife to cancer, leaving behind 13 children. He and Leonard had reminisced about the difficult travel conditions in the NBA in the Fifties.

"You guys don't have it so tough after all, and you ought to stop thinking so much about yourselves and more about the team," he said.

That plea for hardy resilience aside, Leonard told Denny he should have walked out of the arena when the team arrived, and promised not to play there again under similar conditions. "A guy could get pneumonia playing in this kind of condition, sweating and then sitting and shivering," he said.

Leonard also announced a lineup change. Hooper, who had been chosen in the Rounds 11-15 segment of the previous draft, had hustled his way to eight points, seven assists and "at least six steals" according to Denny. He would start the next night back at the Coliseum against Miami.

"He's smart and he's got it here," Leonard said, pointing to his heart.

The long evening on Long Island would become a turning point.

The Pacers responded with a 117-100 victory over Miami, which fell to 8-14. They scored 37 points in an error-free first quarter and hit 16-of-27 shots. Only 2,467 unconvinced fans attended the game, but they gave the players a standing ovation when they headed to the locker room at halftime with a 65-47 halftime lead. And, unlike the game against New Orleans, they didn't relinquish much of it in the second half.

Daniels led with 26 points and 11 rebounds against his former teammates. Lewis had 25 and nine assists, playing what Denny wrote might have been his best all-around game as a Pacer. Fairchild, who had played a season with the Lakers in the NBA before the ABA began play, had another strong game with 19. Netolicky had 14 points on just nine field goal attempts and "hustled on both ends of the floor" in Overpeck's estimation. Hooper got the start Leonard had promised, and finished with 11 points and five assists. It was the seventh starting guard combination of the season, but Leonard declared it the last until someone could beat out Hooper.

The Pacers won the next game as well, in Louisville, with a 115-107 victory over Kentucky, the first time all season they managed consecutive victories. Netolicky played another inspired game, "with more nerve and intelligence than ever before" Denny wrote. Denny also reported Colonels forward Randy Mahaffey walked up to Netolicky late in the game and asked, "Who lit you guys' fuse? You're not the same ball club we've been playing."

Leonard was jubilant after the game, declaring he finally had found the ingredients he had been seeking: tough defense, rebounding, a faster pace and confidence. Hooper, who hit 5-of-6 shots and scored 12 points, appeared to be a catalyst, as had all the postgame communication in New York.

The Pacers won a third straight game the following evening, but the outcome was immediately overwhelmed by tragedy.

In the final few minutes of their 112-103 victory over Houston on Dec. 14 at the Coliseum, team president John DeVoe died of a heart attack while seated across from the scorer's table. Just 34, DeVoe was in good spirits before the game, but collapsed with about two minutes remaining and could not be revived by doctors and a fire emergency crew as the game played out. He was pronounced dead on arrival at General Hospital. No autopsy was performed, but he had played tennis that day while suffering from the flu. Perhaps a virus had affected his heart, and was made worse by his physical exertion.

It was more than a blow to the Pacers. It impacted the entire city. DeVoe, the captain of Princeton's basketball team in 1956, had been essential to the franchise's formation and survival to that point. He was an intelligent, ethical and charismatic leader, so respected it was said he didn't have to seek clients in his role with the Gregory and Appel insurance company, they came looking for him.

His motivation regarding the Pacers was altruistic. He simply thought having a professional basketball team would be good for Indianapolis, help it grow in many areas. He had been paid $2,500 for all the hours he put in during the first season, but had spent far more than that to purchase stock in the franchise, as had other members of his family. He wasn't seeking a financial profit. In fact, he was looking forward to the day he could back away from the franchise. He was earning about $40,000 annually from his insurance business, and didn't need the aggravation of a professional basketball franchise while supporting his wife, Jane, and their three children.

"I'm not going to spend my life going to basketball games," he told Jane.

DeVoe was involved with other civic organizations, and was looking forward to being involved in more projects for the city after the Pacers were up and running under someone else's leadership. As a native of Indianapolis, he was frustrated by its stagnation and was in constant search of ways to help it advance. Jane recalled going to dinner at St. Elmo's one evening and seeing a man living in a refrigerator box in an alley near the restaurant.

"That's how downtown was," she said.

That's the downtown DeVoe was trying to change, a traffic-less concrete evening desert, a place to escape from rather than flock to. His efforts did not go unrecognized. His office was near the headquarters of the *Star* and *News*, and he often met with Fuson and Collins to pitch ideas and promote causes, so they were well-positioned to pay tribute.

"He was one of the new breed of young men here who didn't believe that things had to remain as they were, just because that was the way they had always been," Fuson wrote.

Collins wrote that DeVoe "already had become a force in our community. He was a leader, a fact that he accepted naturally, without pretense. His future, in business and in public life, appeared to be unlimited. John was the epitome of the All-American boy – handsome, clean living, talented and possessing an appealing combination of modesty and self-confidence."

Denny's reaction was telling. He had flown to Chicago on assignment rather than cover the Pacers game on Saturday because the *News* didn't publish on Sunday. He called his wife from the airport before catching his flight home. When told DeVoe had died, he was so stunned he left his typewriter by the pay phone and flew home without it.

"I can't imagine what he might have done, for the Pacers and the city," Denny said years later.

The next game, on Monday in Minneapolis, was postponed out of respect for DeVoe's sudden passing. Another game against the Pipers the following night in Duluth, Minn. also was announced as postponed, but was reinstated the next day.

That game would become legendary.

The Pipers were playing eight "home" games in Duluth (and even one in St. Louis) to take their show to masses outside of Minneapolis. This one was their sixth of the eight in Duluth, and drew a crowd listed at 2,800, but no doubt less than that rounded-off number. They saw Minnesota hold on for a 111-109 victory that ended the Pacers' three-game win streak, but didn't get to see what happened in the Pacers' locker room at halftime.

The facility in Duluth was built for hockey, and was hardly suited for a professional basketball game. Just as in Commack, it was freezing outside and cold inside – so cold Leonard would claim in later years Netolicky was wearing an overcoat and gloves during pregame warmups, although he might have confused the game with those in Commack. Duluth sat at the edge of Lake Superior, 150 miles north of Minneapolis, and was so cold and desolate it appeared to most players as if it belonged on another planet.

The Pacers trailed 64-51 at halftime, and Netolicky had been one of the primary contributors to the deficit. Leonard by then realized he would have to constantly prod the rich-kid-son-of-a-surgeon to get the most out of him, and *could* do it to send a message to the rest of the team, so he began screaming at Netolicky in the locker room, threatening bodily harm. To emphasize his point, he grabbed a hockey stick and headed toward Netolicky, who jumped up and headed for a stall in the adjoining bathroom.

In Netolicky's version of the story, he sat on a toilet and began laughing, fully aware Leonard was using him to motivate the rest of the players. In Leonard's version, Netolicky was "scared to death." Either way, Leonard slammed the stick over the top of the stall door over and over until finally breaking it.

As the years passed, the story evolved the way stories tend to do. In Leonard's retelling at banquets or in interviews, Netolicky led a come-from-behind victory with a brilliant second half in which he scored more than 20 points. Daniels was more specific in *Loose Balls*, saying Netolicky finished with 26 points and 19 rebounds, with nearly all the production coming in the second half, and led a victory. Daniels added the detail that Netolicky hung his head and mumbled to himself while Leonard raged in the locker room.

The truth is less dramatic and less fun. The Pacers lost the game, 111-109. And while they did rally from a 13-point halftime deficit, no mention was made of an inspired second-half performance from Netolicky in the wire service articles – neither the *Star* nor *News* had a reporter at the game – or in the *Minneapolis Tribune*. He finished with 19 points on 6-of-18 shooting and 11 rebounds. Brown – still playing off the bench – led the surge by scoring 21 of his 25 points in the second half.

Daniels wasn't even there, having stayed back in Indianapolis and missing a second straight game with the flu. That forced Netolicky to play center, a task made much easier by the fact Hawkins didn't play for Minnesota because of a ruptured blood vessel in his right arm.

Leonard did indeed light a fire under Netolicky, but the impact came the following night back at the Coliseum when the Pacers defeated Miami in overtime, 122-118. Hooper hit a three-pointer with three seconds left in regulation to force overtime, then Freddie Lewis scored eight of his 29 points in overtime. Netolicky, though, was the catalyst, playing what Overpeck wrote was his best game as a pro. He finished with a career-high 39 points – hitting 13-of-19 field goal attempts and 13-of-17 foul shots – and 16 rebounds.[5]

Overpeck, having heard word-of-mouth accounts of what happened the previous night, wrote Leonard "was so mad at Netolicky at halftime of Tuesday night's game in Duluth he could have hit him," but didn't elaborate.

The victory lifted the Pacers out of last place. Their record was now 10-17 – 8-10 under Leonard – and they had won five of their previous seven games. Something was starting to happen.

---

[5] This was the Pacers' first home game since DeVoe's death. A eulogy was offered before tip-off by the senior minister of Second Presbyterian Church, Dr. William Hudnut – who was destined to become Indianapolis' four-term mayor.

"Hey, I'd better watch out or I'll really bawl."

A Heartless Profession

The persistent and publicized effort to make a trade was finally realized on Dec. 19, when the Pacers dealt Mike Lewis to Minnesota for Chubin. It was notable at the time because the Pacers traded their promising rookie for an established guard, but it would become increasingly notable for another reason in later years.

Namely, that they didn't trade Brown instead. Not for lack of trying, though. As it stood, the trade set in motion a series of events that eventually altered lives and broke hearts, including those of some fans, although it could have been much worse than they realized.

Lewis, the prized draft pick from the previous Spring when he was penciled in as the starting center, was averaging 8.2 points and 7.5 rebounds in 19 minutes per game. He was a solid player, but undersized for his natural position, center, and hadn't fit as well into Leonard's up-tempo style as in Staverman's system. Chubin, meanwhile, was a playmaking guard capable of strengthening the Pacers' depleted backcourt, and perhaps becoming a starter. He had averaged 18.2 points for Anaheim the previous season, then moved with the franchise to Los Angeles. He was averaging 16.6 for the Stars, but was traded after 17 games to Minnesota, where he – like most of the players – clashed with coach Jim Harding.

The Pacers had good reason to want Chubin, given what they had seen of him in person. He had scored 38 points against them the previous season, hitting all 18 foul shots, and had hit 17-of-19 free throws in their victory over Los Angeles on Nov. 29, Leonard's second win.

Those games in which he wore a path to the free throw line reflected his reckless style of play, which reflected his lifestyle. He was not a perimeter shooter, having hit just two three-pointers his rookie season, but he made up for that by drawing fouls, which he accomplished by constantly attacking the basket. In one five-game stretch in February during his rookie season, he had averaged 16.8 free throw attempts – an incredible stat, especially for a guard. He averaged 18.2 points as a rookie, placed third in the ABA in assists and set the league's single-game assist record with 22.

Apart from the numbers, he was colorful and charismatic. He played with a smile and a bounce in his step, and lived that way off the court as well. He was a man's man, with a rugged demeanor and down-to-earth sense of humor, but he was a ladies' man, too, with chiseled features and natural charm.

At 6-foot-2 and 200 pounds, he was so hard-nosed that although he had not played football in high school or college, he received tryout offers from the NFL Baltimore Colts and Dallas Cowboys after his senior year of college at Rhode Island. He wasn't interested. He got his fill of contact on the basketball court, where he played like a running back on offense and a linebacker on defense. After having been limited to five fouls before expulsion in college basketball, getting six in the pros seemed too good to be true. He made it a point to deliver a hard fist or elbow to the chest of the opponent he was guarding early on, just to send a message, even if it meant an early foul call.

"God gave you an extra foul," he recalled. "It was a gift. I made sure I got a good one in in the first quarter of every game. I loved to hit people and I loved to get hit, so I had an advantage."

The quality of Chubin's play, however, directly coincided with his mood, which directly coincided with his playing time. If he liked his coach and teammates and was playing a heavy load of minutes, he was in love with life. If he was riding the bench or didn't feel connected to his coach, he was miserable, his play suffered and he wanted out. It wasn't his nature to be patient and weather storms.

His ABA career had sprinted out of the gate in Anaheim because he had bonded immediately with his coach, "Colorful" Al Brightman, a kindred free spirit famous for off-court indiscretions. Four games into the ABA's first season, after scoring 14 points in a loss to the Pacers, Chubin had begged Brightman for a starting role. Brightman told him he would have to either wrestle or arm wrestle him to get it, but Chubin eventually prevailed with old-fashioned pleading. In the next game, six days later at Kentucky, he scored 42 points on just 16 field goal attempts without hitting a three-pointer. The starting job was his for the rest of the season.[1]

Chubin continued to have big games the second season after the franchise moved to Los Angeles and became the Stars, including a 40-point outing at Oakland in the second game, 34 points against Minnesota in Duluth and 27 against the Pacers. But he didn't connect with the Stars genteel, straight-laced coach, Bill Sharman, and was traded to Minnesota for Jim Jarvis and a draft pick. There, however, he quickly clashed with Harding and was relegated to a reserve role. He never scored more than four points and totaled just 54 minutes in eight appearances with the Pipers before the Pacers rescued him.

Chubin wasn't alone in his feelings toward Harding, whose coaching style careened beyond a militaristic approach to irrationality. He was new to professional coaching, having built a 200-51 record at the high school and collegiate levels, but had left behind a trail of turmoil and hard feelings, not to mention NCAA violations.

ABA guard Roland "Fatty" Taylor, one of Harding's players at his most recent stop, LaSalle, remembered Harding less than warmly in an interview years later:

"He was one crazy guy. Forty years later, if I saw him today sitting in a wheelchair, I'd walk over and smack him. ... Priests (at LaSalle) would wander into the gym every now and then and say hello to the players. Harding would storm over, get right in the priest's face, and

---

[1] "Colorful" Al Brightman – yes, that was his nickname, at least among the Anaheim players — was fired after the Amigos started 13-24. Well, not exactly fired. He had a contract and was going to have to be paid, so he became the team's public relations director, a natural position for his personality. It's not clear how long he stayed in that position.

seethe like a drill sergeant, 'Don't you ever come in here and interrupt my practice.' In a matter of weeks, the man had completely destroyed my confidence."

Chubin was wasting away on the bench in Minnesota behind Williams and Vaughn, and eventually lost playing time to another backup guard, Steve Vacendak. In fact, Vacendak might have expedited Chubin's exit in the "hockey stick game" in Duluth, when he started in place of the injured Vaughn and scored 21 points and hustled his way to 17 rebounds. Vacendak and Chubin were similar in their playing styles – quick, aggressive playmakers, but poor perimeter shooters – although Chubin was much stronger and more aggressive. The Pipers didn't need both, and needed more depth on their front line.[2]

Chubin, meanwhile, was miserable over his lack of playing time.

"When I was with Los Angeles my goal was to make the All-Star team," Chubin told a *Minneapolis Star* reporter. "Now my goal is to play."

Sitting on the bench was bad enough. Sitting for a coach like Harding made it even worse. Harding's demeanor was so repellent the Minnesota players nicknamed him "Ack" – short for maniac.

Chubin recalled Harding once screaming at Minnesota's center, Tom Hoover, after a loss, berating his character and cussing him fiercely. After Harding left the room, Chubin couldn't resist poking the bear, telling Hoover with mock seriousness: "You're one of the toughest guys I know, but if you don't go in there tomorrow and beat the shit out of him, I don't want to talk to you again."

Hoover didn't follow up on that request, but it didn't matter. He was soon traded to New York, and Harding soon took a leave of absence because of a heart condition exacerbated by his manic style of coaching.

Chubin's frustration was further enhanced by the neuroses of his travel roommate, Art Heyman. The No. 1 overall pick of the 1963 NBA

---

2   Vacendak's playing career in the ABA was brief, but he later laid claim to a notable achievement in basketball. As Duke's associate athletic director in 1980, he was the person most responsible for convincing athletic director Tom Butters to hire Mike Krzyzewski to fill the head coaching vacancy.

draft, Heyman had been an All-American at Duke, the national Player of the Year by some media outlets and the Most Valuable Player of the East-West College All-Star game after his senior season, and then went on to average 15.4 points as a rookie for New York. His NBA career gradually came apart, however, and after playing the 1966-67 season in the minor leagues, he was among the players to get a second chance in the ABA. He was talented but difficult, not just for coaches but for teammates, as Chubin found out. Heyman kept him up late at night seeking endless feedback — on his jump shot, his overall play, what he could be doing better, anything and everything.

"Art, you're driving me crazy!" Chubin would finally shout. "Leave me alone!"

Chubin and the Pacers seemed made for one another. Chubin was yearning for a winning team with teammates who played hard and together, and in front of a devoted fan base. The Pacers, meanwhile, needed another guard, preferably one who would bring a more physical, aggressive demeanor.

What wasn't acknowledged publicly was that Storen and/or Leonard had offered Brown for Chubin — a deal that if made would have drastically altered the future of the franchise beyond what anyone could have imagined at the time. Along with the articles in the Indianapolis newspapers that mentioned Brown as a prime trade candidate, a story in the *Minneapolis Tribune* on Dec. 18, one day after the hockey stick game in Duluth, left no doubt. It was headlined "Indiana Offers Brown to Pipers for Chubin," and the lead paragraph of the story by the Pipers' beat writer was clear:

"Coach Bob Leonard of Indiana is seeking guard strength and is interested in combative Steve Chubin of the Pipers and has offered forward Roger Brown to the Pipers for Chubin."

A year later, the *Pittsburgh Post-Gazette* would report a three-team deal had been attempted when Chubin was playing for Los Angeles that would have sent Chubin to the Pacers and Brown to the Pipers, with an unnamed player going from Minnesota to Los Angeles.

Indiana Offers Brown to Pipers for Chubin

By TOM BRIERE
Minneapolis Tribune Staff Writer

Coach Bob Leonard of Indiana is seeking guard strength and is interested in combative Steve Chubin of the Pipers and has offered forward Roger Brown to the Pipers for Chubin.

Vern Mikkelsen, Piper general manager, said Wednesday, "Sure, I'd trade again if I thought I was really helping the ballclub, but not just for changing faces. We've got manpower at the guards and every club in the ABA is seeking to deal with us."

Leonard benched B r o w n from regular duty and the Pacers went to winning . . . Brown came off the bench in Duluth Tuesday night, however, to almost catch the Pipers with 21 of his 25 points in the second half, but Minnesota prevailed 111-109

Commissioner George Mikan of the ABA returned

Chubin

Leonard

Brown

from Miami meetings to report that Nick Mileti, Cleveland promoter, has not talked to him about an ABA franchise . . . Mileti told Gopher coach Bill Fitch that he bought Cleveland Arena with the idea of bringing pro basketball in, perhaps the Houston franchise. . .

"We haven't decided to move the Houston franchise yet," said Mikan . . .

The commissioner indicated that Olympic rules will not be used this season, unless they are sampled in the All-Star game Jan. 28 in

Louisville. . . "We've set up a study committee on the Olympic rules and we'd like to use them on a trial basis in exhibitions next fall, then decide for the 1969-70 season," said Mikan. . .

The ABA is considering fan voting to make All-Star player selections. . . A year ago first - place coaches handled East - West Stars. . . Miami has a l r e a d y entered a bid for the 1970 All-Star game. . . Televising of the 1969 All-Star game is pending. . .

A supervisor of officials is

being sought by the ABA as a replacement for Ed Mikan.

PIPER POINTS. Pipers coach Jim Harding reversed his field yesterday and announced practice sessions are open. . . Guard Charlie Williams may have to undergo impacted wisdom tooth surgery. . . Flu-ridden Chico Vaughn and sore-elbowed Connie Hawkins are expected to play for the Pipers Friday night at Houston. . .

The Pacers, according to various media reports, offered Roger Brown for Steve Chubin, but were turned down. Much to their future relief.

The failed attempt to trade Brown for Chubin was further detailed in Hawkins' biography, *Foul!* Hawkins, a member of the Pipers at the time of the trade, said Harding prevented the exchange:

> *"Harding brushed off an opportunity to get Roger Brown from the Indiana Pacers. Roger was feuding with coach Bob Leonard, and Indiana was willing to part with him for Steve Chubin. But ... Brown, despite great skills, had a justified reputation for arrogance and occasional lackluster play. 'Brown isn't my kind of guy' Harding told (trainer Alex) Medich. 'Mikkelsen may want this deal but I don't want Brown on my team. And my word is law.'"*

Leonard also had tried to land guard Ron Perry from Miami, but the Floridians wouldn't accept what the Pacers were offering – Brown, possibly – and later traded Perry to New York.

Chubin's arrival, along with the recent purchases of guard Jack Thompson and forward Jay Miller, left the Pacers with 12 players, two over the league travel limit. Following a dominant homecourt win over Kentucky two days after the trade, in which a still-motivated Netolicky finished with 34 points and 16 rebounds, Leonard had to decide who to leave behind for road games in New York and Miami. One was Thompson, which came as no surprise. The other was Brown, which was a major surprise – to outsiders, at least.

Brown had been an All-Star and second-team all-league selection the previous season, not to mention the Pacers' Most Valuable Player, but he was declining under Leonard. He was moved from forward to guard shortly after the coaching change, back to forward, back to guard and then to the bench after the frozen game in New York on Dec. 10, when he failed to register a stat other than one assist. That was the game in which Hooper came off the bench to contribute eight points, seven assists and "at least six steals," thereby supplanting Brown in the starting lineup.

Brown hadn't played in the next game against Miami. There was no mention of an injury or illness in the newspapers, so he likely had been benched. He followed with four points in the next game, then six, then had his 25-point effort off the bench in Duluth when he – not Netolicky – sparked a second-half comeback after Leonard waved the hockey stick at halftime. But he followed with two points against Miami and three against Kentucky, prompting Leonard's bold decision to leave him home.

Brown's considerable pride no doubt was hurt by coming off the bench behind Dee at forward and Hooper at guard, and that surely affected his attitude and performance. The publicized reports of the Pacers' attempts to trade him couldn't have helped, either. Leonard, however, was trying to establish a new culture, and Brown was going to have to find a way to fit in and accept this new authority figure in his life or risk being traded.

Whether it was his life experience or simply his personality, Brown's approach was to take the easy way out whenever possible. Although he was popular with his teammates for his cool demeanor and sense of humor, they agreed he needed prodding from time to time. They talked of a player who still had an impressive vertical jump, but only jumped as high as absolutely necessary, and was motivated by money most of all.

"Roger needed a kick in the butt more than anybody," Netolicky said years later, although Brown might have nominated Netolicky for that distinction. "Roger did just enough to get by. He was still better than most players, but he needed motivation. Slick gave it to him."

Leonard also didn't appreciate Brown's style of play, which was rooted in the playgrounds of New York. He had great one-on-one moves, but often dribbled too much to set them up, grinding the offense to a halt. Leonard wanted quicker decisions and more passing.

The Pacers got along fine without Brown in New York. The arena was cold once again and Leonard threatened not to send his team onto the court, but relented at the last minute. The Pacers won, 125-110. Darden had another strong game against his former team with 24 points and 15 rebounds, further evidence they had released exactly the kind of player they now were looking for.

The story of any team includes a variety of subplots, a dozen or so individuals with rising, descending or stagnant careers. With this group, Brown was slipping from favor and up for trade, but Chubin was overjoyed to be in a better circumstance with a fiery and freewheeling coach who valued relationships with his players. He scored 20 points off the bench in his second outing with the Pacers, hitting 8-of-12 shots, and passed out six assists. "I want to grow with the team and help win the championship," he told Denny afterward.

Playing their third game in three nights, the Pacers then lost in Miami, 118-109,[3] but they had plenty of reasons to be in good cheer as they headed home for Christmas on the morning of Dec. 24. They had won six of their previous eight games and would play the next six at home. But another subplot was thickening.

---

[3] The *News* account of the game in Miami mentioned that Jerry Kissel, who had replaced Bill Marvel as publicity director, had been fired. What went unreported was that Kissel, angered by Storen's decision, threw all his files into the trash, leaving a gap in the team's collection of archival material.

They regathered for practice on the morning of Dec. 26, to work off Christmas dinner and prepare for that evening's game against Minnesota. As Rayl recalled, he and Chubin were playing H-O-R-S-E before practice began when Peeples – who also had fallen out of the playing rotation – was called into the locker room to meet with Leonard and Storen. When he came out, he told some of his teammates at the other end of the court he had been released. Brown then walked into the locker room to talk with Storen and Leonard. When he emerged, he told Rayl they wanted to see him.

"Due to the size of your contract, we're going to have to let you go," Storen said after Rayl entered the room. Shocked, Rayl looked at Leonard, who had promised him a secure roster spot during that conversation in Rayl's dining room before Leonard's hiring became official. Leonard stared at the floor, refusing to make eye contact. As Rayl recalled, he quietly took off his shoes, left them on the floor, gathered his belongings, and drove home to Kokomo.

Rayl would forever remain convinced Brown had talked Storen into cutting him instead of Peeples on racial grounds. Years later, Storen would acknowledge Rayl's account could be valid, and Netolicky would agree. Peeples and Chubin would say they had no memory of the occasion. Other players maintained varying degrees of uncertainty.

Without question, the skin tone of the roster had become lighter since the first season, when Storen and Staverman dared to defy NBA norms. Of the 14 players the Pacers selected in the 1968 draft, 11 were white. The new additions to the team, other than Daniels, also were white, as were the recent additions to the starting lineup, Dee and Hooper.

Few teams dared to start five black players in that era, and to even play five at any point during a game was rare and bold, especially at home. Staverman had done so on occasion the first season, particularly when Netolicky sat out with the mumps, and recalled hearing shouts of "Nigger lover!" from fans for doing so. Had Peeples been released, the Pacers would have had just three black players on the roster, after having as many as eight the first season. Given that, along with Brown's demotion from the starting lineup and dismissal from the two-game road trip, it wouldn't have been surprising for the black players to be concerned with the recent trends.

Were Leonard and/or Storen trying to "whiten" the roster? Their personal histories did not indicate racial hang-ups. As Netolicky recalled, Leonard had delivered that stern lecture in his first team meeting after taking over as coach, warning the players against allowing racial divisions to infiltrate the team. Or, as he put it, "none of this nigger or honky shit."

Regardless, it was a sensitive time for racial issues throughout the country, and Indianapolis was hardly an exception. A conservative city within a conservative state, its black and white populations were heavily segregated, as some of the black Pacers had learned when they tried to find housing in apartment complexes. Although the team members generally got along well and Leonard had succeeded in building camaraderie, the black players were pioneers in a sense, and suffered slings and arrows in the community — particularly those who dared step out with a white woman.

Aitch and his wife had found that to be true because of their mixed marriage, which became known to the general public when Karen was included in a photo with other players' wives for a story on what meals the wives liked to cook for their husbands in the *Star's* Women's Section, on Oct. 8, six days before the season began. She once complained to Storen about the reaction they received from the public, but societal norms were beyond the general manager's control. Peeples also received blowback for dating the Jewish daughter of a local judge, although the two wound up having a long-term relationship.

Brown, apparently, had succeeded in rescuing Peeples from the scrap heap. But if management and/or ownership truly was trying to adjust the tint of its roster, it might have been understandable at least on financial grounds. The franchise was in survival mode and looking to sell every ticket possible. Its leaders no doubt felt pressure to cater to a fan base that by far was mostly white.

Regardless of the motivation for releasing Rayl, another once-glorious basketball career had ended quietly and unhappily. He had gone scoreless in his final token appearances in New York and Miami, a deflating and ironic ending for the sharpshooting former high school Mr. Basketball, college All-American and Most Popular Pacer.[4]

Leonard's arrival had revitalized his spirit and provided a fresh start. He had considered Leonard a friend. They played golf together in Kokomo, and as the city's two most noted celebrities made a few appearances together, such as before the Russiaville Lion's Club on Dec. 4 during the first season, long before Leonard became coach. After Leonard took over the team, they rode to practice together occasionally.

Rayl averaged 16.2 points in their first six games together, but his role faded quickly. Leonard always leaned toward street-tough defenders such as Hooper over shooters such as Rayl in the backcourt. Rayl's three-point percentage in late November had led the league and still ranked third (.370) at the time of his release.

Surprisingly, the removal of one of the state's biggest basketball names elicited little coverage in the Indianapolis newspapers. The *News* devoted one paragraph to it, and the *Star* three. The *Kokomo Tribune*, meanwhile, offered a five-paragraph story on its hometown star, and dropped a hint that supported Rayl's version of his release.

Conard, close enough to Leonard that he could have an off-the-record conversation, wrote that Leonard "wasn't entirely pleased by the decision to trim Rayl."

"Jim did some great things for us, but sometimes things don't work out like you want 'em to," Leonard was quoted. "I hate to see him go."

Rayl returned to Kokomo and floundered for a while before settling into a new career. He had some money saved, and needed time to adjust to a life without basketball. He tried his hand at a couple of sales jobs, but quit in frustration. Eventually a friend from Marion, Tito Guerrero, called and told him about an opening that had just come up with Xerox, the copy machine company. Unaware even what business Xerox was in, Rayl was hired on the spot by a manager who had once lived in Kokomo

---

[4] Rayl had been so popular the previous season that he was paid $50 to film a commercial for Chesty potato chips. Sitting on a sofa at home with his wife, Nancy, and son, Jimbo, Rayl espoused the virtues of the chips while Nancy tried to control the wiggly infant. At one point, he hit his head on the coffee table while she wrestled with him. They didn't bother to reshoot the spot.

and knew all about Rayl's popularity there. Rayl wound up staying with the company for 30 years before retiring.

"I had more luck than sense," he said of that career. "My name helped me when I made sales calls. All I knew was basketball. Getting up every day and putting on a suit and tie was a new experience."

Rayl remained mildly bitter for the rest of his life, but didn't let it consume him. He participated in golf outings hosted by the Pacers and attended occasional games for as long as his health permitted. But he always told the story of his release the exact same way to confidants. Regardless of the circumstances behind it, he had the respect of teammates, even if they were frustrated by his occasional emotional outbursts. It wasn't long before Harkness called and set up a Sunday lunch in Kokomo that included the wives. And years later, Freddie Lewis remained in his corner.

"I thought Jimmy should have been with us," Lewis said. "He brought a lot to the team. He was a down-to-earth guy. He told it like it was and he played hard.

"You can't figure some things."

Deposed players are quickly forgotten amid the ever-changing tides of professional basketball. Faces come and go, the games march on relentlessly and the public's focus is constantly shifting. Besides, the Pacers were moving into a new era, which was obvious in the game played the night of Rayl's release. They defeated Minnesota in overtime, 134-133, on a 15-footer by Lewis at the buzzer, an appropriate ending to what would forever stand as one of the franchise's most dramatic regular season victories.

Story lines abounded in that one. Hawkins, for one, came off the bench to play with a 103-degree temperature and finish with 39 points, 15 rebounds, 10 assists and display "moves no other human can make, including Oscar Robertson," according to Denny's article in the *News*. But it wasn't enough.

Netolicky scored 33 points and grabbed 18 rebounds, both team-highs, and hit a 12-foot baseline jumper at the buzzer to force overtime.

He was now averaging 30.4 points in the five games following his halftime encounter with the hockey stick in Duluth. Daniels added 29 points and 14 rebounds. Chubin further endeared himself to the home fans by scoring 20 points while hitting all 12 foul shots and playing with reckless abandon against his former team. Denny wrote that he "fought himself into the heart of every Pacer fan with his tenacity."

Leonard got into the act as well. As soon as the buzzer sounded, he ran onto the court, grabbed the ball from a stunned Minnesota player, dribbled a couple of times and fired a shot at the basket – and swished it.[5]

A crowd of 7,116, the best turnout in the Coliseum since the season-opener, left delirious over what they had just seen from this reborn team.

Denny led his story the next day with a declaration: "Major league basketball … has arrived in Indianapolis."

Overpeck referred to it as "about the best game Indianapolis has ever seen."

Fuson wrote a column to capture some of the color: "People were standing on their chairs, they were yelling, they were laughing, they were crying. The old Fairgrounds Coliseum really rocked."

It was a drastic departure from opening night, when the fans had booed during the loss to Oakland, or those other games when only a

---

[5] Mike Lewis, meanwhile, scored eight points off the bench for the Pipers. He would go on to play four solid seasons in the ABA, peaking the following year when he averaged 16.2 points for the Pipers back in Pittsburgh and made the All-Star team. An Achilles tendon injury cut short his career, however, "just as I was figuring out how to play," after playing in 15 games for Carolina in the 1972-73 season. He tried to rehab himself and return the following season, but had to retire after three games. The only game he was ejected from in his career was against the Pacers, when he got tired of the physical play around the basket and blurted out a profane protest to the referee.

He played more with his future teams, but remained disappointed by the trade from the Pacers because of the potential he saw blooming. "I shouldn't be leaving here, these people are going somewhere," he recalled feeling. After he was forced into retirement, he worked out of Pittsburgh for Converse for seven years, selling sporting goods to retail outlets, then moved to North Carolina and worked as a salesman for a paper company for 30 years.

few thousand bothered to show. Daniels, who called it "the best basketball game I've ever played in," had nothing but praise for the fans this time.

"That was a beautiful crowd," he said. "That's the way a home crowd should be. It was the first time I've felt the crowd in a long time."

The game seemed the perfect prelude for the one two nights later with Oakland. An even bigger crowd, 8,397, turned out on a Saturday to see the Pacers take on the league's best team. They appeared to get a break when it was learned Barry would sit out because of an injury to his left leg in his previous game, but that wasn't enough. They played poorly, and Barry's teammates seemed inspired by his absence. Oakland's 129-121 victory was led by its 6-3 rookie sensation, Armstrong, who finished with 25 points, 12 rebounds and nine assists. Larry Brown added 22 points and six assists.

Daniels, by now comfortable in Leonard's system, led the Pacers with 27 points and 27 rebounds. Netolicky scored 19, but admitted to being flat. The most encouraging sign, however, was that Brown, still playing off the bench, had his best game since shortly after Leonard's arrival, with 24 points, 13 rebounds and five assists.

That loss, however, was a mere interruption for a team on the rise. The Pacers proceeded to go on a six-game winning streak, with four of the victories by double-figure margins. All kinds of good things were percolating now.

Daniels, for one, was dominating. He had 25 points and 17 rebounds against Kentucky, then 28 points and 18 rebounds against New York, then 33 points and 18 rebounds against New Orleans. He had what amounted to an off night with 19 points and 10 rebounds in a rematch with Minnesota at the Coliseum, but the Pacers won again, 103-102, before 8,397 fans – the exact same number who had watched the loss to Oakland, amounting to either an amazing coincidence or lazy doctoring of the attendance figures. Chubin had 19 in the game – 11 from the foul line – further meshing with the team's fabric.

"Bob Leonard is a championship coach," he told Denny after the game. "He won't settle for anything else and I know I won't, either."

The Pacers won again the following afternoon – yes, afternoon – in Houston, their third game in less than three days. Lewis, who was becoming

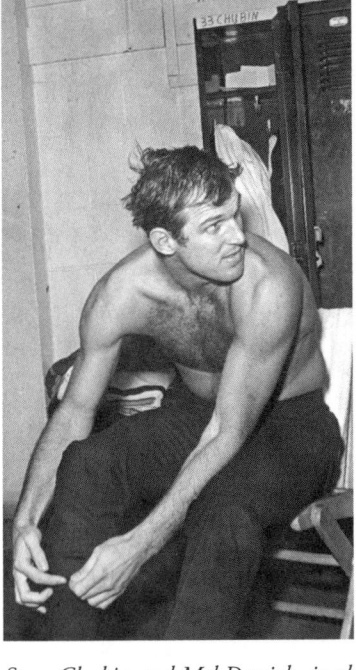

Steve Chubin and Mel Daniels, in the Pacers' locker room at the Coliseum following the one-point victory over Minnesota on Jan. 4. It was luxurious, compared to the visitors' quarters.

Leonard's kind of point guard, carried them through that one with 27 points, eight rebounds and eight assists. After a day off, they picked up a franchise record sixth consecutive victory in New Orleans, 120-106, lifting their record to 19-19. Leonard had promised to have the team at .500 by Jan. 15 when he took over, and he was eight days ahead of schedule despite the team's 5-15 record after losing to Kentucky on Dec. 4.

The most important long-term impact from the win streak was the revival of Brown, who worked his way back into the starting lineup and Leonard's heart during the run. He had scored 24 off the bench in the loss to Oakland, then eight and 11 off the bench in the next two games at the start of the streak. Leonard put him in the starting lineup for the home game with New Orleans on Jan. 3, claiming he wanted to go with a taller lineup to match up with the Bucs.

He told Denny that Brown had not been left behind on the road trip because of a bad attitude, but because he hadn't adapted to Leonard's style of play and wasn't showing enough "zip." The truthfulness of that statement would depend on one's definition of "attitude." Brown wasn't an emotional player who talked back to coaches, and his raw talent usually masked his occasional lack of intensity, but he was a challenge to reach on a personal level. Teammates confirmed he rebelled against Leonard at first, and the friction between them was uncomfortable, if not ugly. He also took pride in conserving energy, particularly in practice. With a body already wearing down by all those hours spent on playground asphalt before he even began his professional career, he was always in energy-preservation mode.

Denny, more than any media member throughout Brown's life, established a rapport with him. They had met in the Pacers' office before the first season began, but Brown, still insecure about his professional future, wasn't yet ready to reveal his story. He had recovered his spirit with his early success in the ABA, but now Leonard was challenging him in a new way. No coach had ever dared treat him so harshly.

Denny's story before the game with New Orleans introduced a side of the enigmatic star rarely seen by the public – a chastened player who offered unprecedented self-examination. It would stand forever as unique insight into a man who prized cool above candor and shielded himself from a world of which he had grown wary. Being left behind on the road trip had been a blow to his pride. So had being publicly offered up for a trade. Worst of all, no other team had been willing to give up a player good enough to get him.

"It hurt very much not to go on that last road trip," Brown said. "You make every game in two years and then suddenly you don't go. It's a helluva thing to feel that nobody wants you."

Brown went on to say he realized he didn't show his emotions as much as Daniels, who "kicks chairs and gets it out of him," but claimed the losses still hurt him. He said the unsuccessful trade attempts had been a "jolt," adding he didn't want to leave Indiana and would "try my darndest to give 'em a championship." He acknowledged the validity of the criticism that he dribbled too much, but said he would adjust his style of play if needed. He also admitted to shying away from contact, but revealed he had a damaged disc in his back.

"I want to stay alive in the game so I can provide for my family," he said. "I don't have a college education, so what would I do if I got hurt badly?"

Finally, he promised to conform.

"Now I'm going to try to prove to everybody that I can do what Bob wants," he said. "I respect him and his coaching techniques."

Brown started at guard against the Bucs and scored 11 points. Then he started at forward – in place of Dee – against Minnesota and scored 22, with nine rebounds and no turnovers. He followed with 15 points at Houston, then 23 points, 11 rebounds and six assists when the team won its sixth straight game at New Orleans.

The win streak ended with road losses at Kentucky and Minnesota, but Brown continued to play well. Although alternating between guard and forward, he had re-established himself in the starting lineup. He had one of his finest games in Minneapolis, scoring 32 points by hitting 11-of-17 shots and 10-of-13 free throw attempts. The Pacers rallied from a 16-point deficit entering the fourth quarter, but couldn't overcome Hawkins' 47-point effort and Arvesta Kelly's four-point play with 22 seconds left and lost, 122-119.

They almost overcame Leonard's absence, though. He was hit with a technical foul early in the second quarter, and then, with 90 seconds remaining in the half, protested referee Charlie Marino's lack of foul calls on the Pipers by shouting "One more call like that and I'll be out to hit you!" Hit with a second technical, he stormed out to Marino at the foul line and grabbed him before his players could restrain him. Lewis took over the team from that point and led a late rally that tied the game, but then fouled Kelly's backbreaking three-point shot.

The penalty for Leonard's harsh reaction remains uncertain. The standard fine for an ejection at the time was $250. The *Minneapolis Tribune*, however, reported that commissioner Mikan, who had briefly coached Leonard on the Lakers, had let him off with a $100 fine and a warning that the next infraction of that magnitude would warrant a suspension. The *News*, however, reported a few weeks later that Mikan hit Leonard with a $500 fine and stated, "We just don't care for that. We're not going to let anyone do that. I still run the league."

Just as the newspaper accounts reported different fines, they didn't agree on the referee's name. Denny reported it as Moreno, rather than Marino. Regardless, Leonard probably considered whatever fine he paid a good investment. Such dramatics, even in the losses, were instilling a fighting spirit in his players that translated to more aggressive play on the court. Lewis later told Overpeck a story from the game in Houston, where they trailed the lowly Mavericks by three points with just over two minutes left. Playing their third game in less than three days, the players were fatigued and morose when they headed to the bench for a timeout.

"What are you guys worried about?" Leonard shouted. "You can still win this thing by 10 points."

They settled for a six-point victory.

Leonard also was building camaraderie. He had promised to throw a party for the players when they won five consecutive games. They achieved that with the victory in Houston, but he delayed the party a day until they reached New Orleans, where the liquor laws were more favorable for festivities. He picked up the tab for a steak dinner and drinks, and they responded the following night with a 14-point victory to complete that six-game win streak.

Leonard was devoting special attention to Netolicky, whether with a hockey stick or encouraging words.

"I'm going to keep after him until he's a ballplayer," he had said shortly after taking over, and he was doing just that.

Netolicky had one of the best games of his career the night after the loss in Minneapolis with 36 points and 21 rebounds against New Orleans back in Indianapolis on Jan. 11. The Pacers were playing their seventh game in nine days, but Netolicky's energy carried them to a 128-114 victory. Overpeck called him a "potential superstar" and said he "bears little resemblance to the Bob Netolicky who moped through games earlier this year."

Brown was emerging as well. He followed his 32-point effort in Minnesota with 21 points, 13 rebounds and seven assists against New Orleans. He gradually was settling in as a forward, rather than switching back and forth to guard. Lewis, meanwhile was establishing himself as the team leader, and gaining confidence as its point guard.

The other guard spot remained uncertain, with Hooper, Chubin and Brown filling in, but it didn't seem to matter who started. A four-player nucleus of Daniels, Netolicky, Brown and Lewis was solidifying. All the team needed at the other starting position was a solid guard who could do at least one thing well – shoot, defend, pass or some combination of the three. An All-Star caliber player hardly seemed necessary with four other All-Stars in the lineup.

The following game in Houston on Jan. 14 was notable mostly for the attendance, or lack thereof: it was listed at 200, no doubt a rounded-up number, which left 8,800 empty seats and an eerily quiet backdrop.[6]

Denny and Overpeck were among the non-attendees. The *Star* and *News* both sent backup reporters – Cy McBride and Lyle Mannweiler, respectively – and they failed to agree on the game's most important basket. McBride had Brown hitting a 20-footer with two seconds left that gave the Pacers a 114-113 lead. Mannweiler called it a 14-footer with four seconds left. Either way, it preceded a technical foul on Houston for calling a timeout it didn't have, a two-minute delay to determine where the ball should be inbounded (the baseline won out thanks to Netolicky's determined argument), an inbound pass that went awry and two more Pacer foul shots that finished off a 116-113 victory.

Lewis led the scoring with 29 points. Brown had 23 and hit all five field goal attempts in the fourth quarter. Hooper missed the game with an injured right thumb after slamming his car's trunk lid on it at the airport the previous day, so Chubin got his first start with his new team and scored 14 points.

The Pacers lost the following night in Dallas, 127-120 in overtime. Cliff Hagan, a 36-year-old player-coach (just seven months older than Leonard), put himself in the game for the final three minutes of overtime and picked up three

---

[6] Not surprisingly, the Mavericks were playing their last season in Houston. They already were in the process of moving to Charlotte, N.C. to become the Carolina Cougars. They had been sold for $650,000 at the beginning of the year and the league had taken over operation of the franchise, utilizing the performance bond the owners had funded.

assists to help clinch the victory. Chubin scored 19 in that one on just 11 field goal attempts, thanks to his knack for getting to the foul line.

The Pacers played again the following night in Indianapolis, their third game in three nights, and came out with a 96-94 victory over New York after Chubin hit a 10-foot jumper off a broken play over Perry for the game-winning shot. He finished with 19 in that one as well, cementing his place in the starting lineup.[7]

Hooper continued to make his presence felt, too, with his supreme aggression. He was applying his customary fullcourt, hand-checking defense to Nets guard Bobby Lloyd in the third quarter as Lloyd brought the ball upcourt. After crossing the midcourt line, the frustrated Lloyd threw a hard elbow to move Hooper away. Hooper responded with a left cross to Lloyd's cheek that cleared the benches and provided a jolt of adrenaline for the Pacers, who had trailed by five points at halftime. Hooper's penalty: a foul, nothing else.

Brown had tied the game at 94 with 36 seconds left with a five-foot hook shot. "That was the first time I've shot a hook shot since 1956 when I was a freshman in high school," he said afterward, laughing.

Then he turned to Hooper. "How's everything, Cassius?" he asked, referring to the boxing champion formerly known as Cassius Clay.

It was another unifying victory, one that returned them to a .500 record. They had a fourth chance to achieve a winning record in the next game, against Los Angeles, but failed once again with a 129-128 overtime loss, their fourth defeat in the previous seven games. Chubin once again scored 19 points. He also had eight rebounds and 10 assists and hit a driving layup with eight seconds left that gave the Pacers a two-point lead. Leonard called out "yellow," the signal to commit an intentional foul when the Stars crossed the halfcourt line, but the players were too busy celebrating Chubin's shot while running back on defense to take notice and Larry Miller hit a three-pointer from the right wing with three seconds left.

---

[7]   The Nets were struggling, to say the least. A week later, their coach, Max Zaslofsky, was ordered to take a few days off after fainting in the locker room during halftime of a game at Denver, where the Nets lost their eighth straight game.

Daniels led with 33 points and 14 rebounds, but was rewarded with another broken nose for his trouble. With Leonard in full bloom, however, even the losses were bringing the team closer together. Talking with Denny in the locker room after the game while downing cans of beer, he defended his players, defended himself, vented his frustration with the fans and issued a warning to the next opponent.

He acknowledged he had wanted someone to foul Miller, but understood the difficulty of getting to him in time after the Stars' long inbound pass.

"I'm sure not down on anybody on this club," Leonard said. "We might win this whole thing before it's over."

Fans had complained loudly about the lack of defense on Miller's shot, but Leonard complained about the complaints.

"I think it's time we quit knocking everything the Pacers do and try to build them up a little," he said.

"I think the fans have a coach who's as good as anybody in basketball. If they start booing me like they did Larry Staverman, I'll know it's all over. I don't need this."

He wasn't in a resigning mood, though.

"Kentucky had better watch out, because we're going after 'em from the gun and whip 'em good," he declared.

They did just that two nights later at the Coliseum, 141-129. Brown hit 16-of-24 shots on his way to 36 points, and added 12 rebounds and five assists. Daniels, broken nose and all, added 26 points and 22 rebounds. Hooper returned to the starting lineup to try to contain Dampier, but gave up 33 points, while Carrier scored 31.

Chubin played off the bench this time and finished with 15 points and nine assists. He hit just 3-of-14 shots, but earned praise from Leonard for knocking Dampier down. That came naturally to Chubin. Peeples also got credit for dumping Carrier and opening a cut on Carrier's forehead. That didn't come naturally for Peeples, an intellectual college graduate (and future dental surgeon) from a strict, religious home. More than anyone, he represented the change Leonard was instilling in the team, and even decades later expressed surprise over his transformation.

"I purposely went for him," Peeples told Denny in the *News*. "The next time it will make him think.

"I didn't mean it as a dirty move. If you don't go out and pound somebody, they're going to pound you. It's like in football. You have to learn to take punishment. I've been slapped in the face before and they didn't say, 'I'm sorry.' My conscience is free. I think this is what the team needs – the killer instinct."[8]

Peeples was surprising himself with such words and deeds. He was slender – 196 pounds spread over his 6-foot-8 frame – and admittedly "too soft," a player who relied on his exceptional jumping ability rather than his limited physicality. Leonard's personality was seeping into his play, however, just as with most of his teammates.

"He taught me how to be tough," Peeples said decades later. "Because *he* was tough. I respected my intelligence and ability, but there's another component to the game. He had this unique ability to criticize what you were doing, and threaten to kick your ass, but at the same time give you compliments. It was a nice mix. Some coaches are men. Others live in ivory towers and treat men as kids. He treated men as men.

"He shared a brew with you and he'd share a nasty joke with you, too. He'd call you names, whatever. In practice he'd say, 'What the — are you doing out there? This is simple. Let's go, let's get this done.' If it wasn't done in the amount of time he wanted it done, there were penalties."

Hooper reflected the change Leonard was bringing to the Pacers as well as anyone. The late-round draft pick out of Dayton (he was an eighth-round pick of the Knicks in the NBA, too), would not have made many teams in either league, but found a niche with the Pacers because he fit the mold of what Leonard wanted to see in a player. He had made the team under Staverman, and hustled for him, too, but connected with Leonard because of their street-fighting natures.

---

[8] Dee rejoined the team for this game after returning from President Richard Nixon's inauguration ceremony, an invitation earned as a member of the U.S. Olympic basketball team. His warmup jacket, however, contained an embarrassing typographical error, as "Indiana" was spelled I-N-D-A-I-N-A.

Hooper marveled at Leonard's ability to bring out the fire in players. He would sit Netolicky down at a hotel bar and have a heart-to-heart talk. He knew what to say to Brown and Daniels. He knew what to say to Hooper, too.

"He'd walk by me and say, '(Larry) Brown's going to eat you up tonight. He's going to destroy you,'" Hooper recalled.

"He knew that would have me churning the whole day. He knew the hot button of everybody on that ballclub."[9]

The city was taking notice. The Pacers had averaged 5,779 fans over their previous 10 home games, best in the ABA and better than three-fourths of the NBA teams, according to Denny. A smaller crowd turned out for the next one against Miami (4,277) but the Pacers put on another show in a 140-117 victory that finally achieved the season's first winning record. They scored 45 points in the second quarter to take a 26-point halftime lead. Leonard told the players during the break he would give them the next day off if they led by 28 after three quarters, and warned them during timeouts if they were falling off the pace. The period ended with Daniels going all out for what seemed a meaningless tip-in a few seconds before the buzzer to achieve that 28-point lead.

Most likely, Leonard would have given them a break anyway. They had just played 13 games in 18 days, and wouldn't play again for three days. A day off was practically a certainty, but Leonard got what he

---

[9] Hooper applied his intensity in the business world after his one-season professional basketball career, but it came back to haunt him. He started an insurance business, and within six months had hired 22 people. At his peak in the mid-Seventies, he was earning about $200,000 per year, a phenomenal sum in those days. But money wasn't bringing fulfillment. He became addicted to drugs and alcohol, and lost everything. He attempted suicide twice, first with a knife and then with pills, and came close to succeeding the second time. A date with a schoolteacher led him to a new life, in which he became a born-again Christian. He sought out a blue-collar job on an asphalt crew and kept it for three years to regain a consistent lifestyle and work off his anxieties. He then returned to school at Dayton and completed work for his degree in 1981, 17 years after he enrolled in college. He told friends he graduated in five terms – Johnson, Nixon, Ford, Carter and Reagan. He went on to teach and coach basketball in high school, and become a pastor.

Steve Chubin dribbles off the screen set by Mel Daniels during a 23-point victory over Miami. Chubin scored 15 points. Daniels had 24, and helped earn his teammates a day off with a tip-in at the third-quarter buzzer.

wanted: a serious and complete effort, with six players scoring between 15 and 24 points. The third quarter was a reflection to the degree in which the players were sold on the coach.

Brown scored 19 and happened to hit his final three field goal attempts, which became relevant in the next game against Denver. With a day off and one day of practice, the refreshed Pacers delivered a 131-122 victory to 7,888 fans at the Coliseum. Brown hit all 14 shots on his way to 29 points, for a streak of 17 consecutive field goals, a league record.

"What'd you expect?" he told Overpeck. "They were all layups. You're not supposed to miss them."

Actually, Brown hit three mid-range jumpers amid his streak, and the layups came on defended, acrobatic drives to the basket. Over the three previous games, he had hit 39-of-53 field goal attempts, 74 percent.

That game led into the All-Star break in Louisville. Daniels and Netolicky started for the East while Brown and Lewis, who had made the team the previous season, were left off the roster. Netolicky had 11 points and 11 rebounds in the first quarter, but rarely saw the ball after that. Daniels took a nasty fall with 5:05 left in the game after a foul from Moe and injured his head and back. At first it appeared he might have to be carried off the court on a stretcher, according to newspaper accounts, but he managed to get up and hit both free throws before leaving the game. He was reported to be in extreme pain afterward, but X-rays were negative.[10]

---

[10] Ligon, who had been released by the Pacers in training camp before their first season, played in the All-Star game for the East and scored three points. He went on to play seven seasons in the ABA and had double-figure scoring and rebounding averages in each of his first four seasons. He stayed in Louisville after his playing career ended but battled alcoholism and died homeless. Several people tried to help him financially, including the VanArsdale twins, Tom and Dick, who played against him in the 1961 Indiana state high school championship game, which was won by Ligon's Kokomo High School team in overtime. The story around the league was that at least one team's game program listed his college as Penn State – because he had been in the "State Pen" in Indiana.

Things were getting rough all over the ABA. Harding, the East coach in the All-Star game because Minnesota led in the standings, was fired in the wee morning hours the day of the game after he punched his boss with the Pipers, Gabe Rubin, at the banquet. Nobody was sure what started the confrontation in front of about 50 people at 1:30 a.m., but heated words broke out after Harding sat down at a table with Rubin. Harding threw the first punch and Rubin connected with one that scratched the coach's face.

The Pacers' first game after the break was in Denver, the beginning of a run of five games in five nights, the first three on the road. Bad weather in Indianapolis forced them to bus to Louisville and fly out the morning of the game, setting up a journey that lasted 7 ½ hours in all. It no doubt was a factor in the 131-128 loss that ended their three-game winning streak.

Brown hit his first four shots to run his streak of consecutive field goals to 21, but was called for a traveling violation while spinning to the basket for the potential game-winning points in the final seconds. He drew a foul on the play, but the violation came first. The Pacers protested loudly, and Denny took up their cause in the next afternoon's newspaper.

"Perhaps Brown did travel but it was so far from being a flagrant violation it should have never been called in such a pressure situation," Denny wrote. "Roger used his immense talent to its best advantage and got penalized. Indiana had every right to be angry."

That anger was but a polite warmup for the next night's game in Oakland, where the league-leading Oaks took a 146-143 overtime victory that Denny described as "one of the most disgraceful American Basketball Association games ever played." It featured three fights, two of them major, and what might have been a first in professional basketball: a player allowed to continue in the game after fouling out.

Brown and Gary Bradds started things off with a bench-clearing melee late in the first quarter. Brown's version of it was that Bradds threw an elbow, so Brown slapped his arm down, then Bradds threw another elbow, and Brown turned on him and began swinging. "When he hit me again I went after him," Brown told Denny, "and I was trying for a knockout." The two went down to the floor as they tussled, and teammates tried to separate them. An Associated Press wirephoto sent an image of it to the rest of the country, where it ran in many newspapers. The *Fresno Bee's* caption referred to it as a "Pier Sixer."

If nothing else, the fight displayed Leonard's ability to connect with Brown. The player who had been left home from a road trip for playing too casually was now literally fighting for his teammates.

Lewis and Larry Brown went at it briefly later in the first quarter, then another major confrontation stopped play midway through the second period. It began when Dee and Oaks guard Henry Logan squared off after chasing down a loose ball. Barry tried to pull Dee off Logan, so Dee turned on Barry. The two wrestled one another onto, and then over, the scorer's table and into the stands. Barry was merely trying to be a peacemaker. Dee, however, took advantage of the opportunity to go after the league's most prominent and wealthy player, who was regarded by some in the league as arrogant.

"Everybody wanted a piece of Barry," Chubin said years later.

One could have argued the league's players should have mailed thank-you notes to Barry for all the tickets he sold throughout a league fighting for survival, but competitive spirits ruled the day.

The fights inspired referees Bill Kunkel and Denoy to call the game more closely to maintain order, which resulted in five Pacers – Lewis, Daniels, Dee, Miller and Brown – fouling out, setting a league record. Peeples suffered a badly bruised heel and arch in his right foot in the third quarter and was unable to play, so Brown had to stay in the game after picking up his sixth foul to enable the Pacers to keep five players on the court. A technical foul was assessed for that, and another would have been added for each subsequent foul, had he committed any.

"We flat got hosed tonight," Leonard said afterward. "Every time they went to the basket, those two (referees) put them on the line."

The Pacers were called for 43 fouls in all, a league record, which led to Oakland shooting a league-record 69 free throws and hitting a record 54. The two teams combined for a record 289 points, and an unofficial record 81 fouls.

Oakland's coach, Hannum, complained, too: "Normally, I'm yelling about them not calling enough, but tonight ..."

Adding to the bizarre spectacle of the game, Oakland center Jim Eakins played with his head wrapped in gauze. He had been in an automobile accident two days earlier and received 66 stitches in his forehead, but Hannum received permission from the team's trainers to play him. The bandage was knocked off his head during a scramble for a rebound in the third quarter, but he was re-wrapped and he continued to play.

Moe led Oakland with a career-high 41 points, while Lewis led the Pacers with 26. Daniels and Netolicky each finished with 24 points, although Denny reported Netolicky was "listless" until the fourth quarter. Chubin was "exuberant as always," but committed four turnovers in the final seconds of regulation and in the overtime.

The Pacers had to forget fast, though. Later that night they boarded an overnight flight to Minneapolis for a game the following evening. Brown and Lewis were looking forward to giving payback to Harding for leaving them off the East team in the All-Star game (the coaches were allowed to select the reserves). Brown claimed he and Lewis had sent a message to Harding in Louisville that they would "repay him for his kindness when we get to Minnesota." To their disappointment, however, he wasn't waiting for them, having been fired over the All-Star break.

The Pacers won anyway, 117-110, to move within 2 ½ games of the Pipers' lead in the Eastern Division. The Pipers were without the injured Hawkins and Heyman, but were jubilant over also being without their "Coach Ack." Playing their first game since the All-Star break, they were coached by Verl (Gus) Young, who took over on an interim basis. Williams scored a career-high 45 points, but Young wasn't up to the task. He played all nine of his available players in the first quarter and made 15 substitutions in the first half.

When only 1,719 fans attend a game, it's easy to hear the catcalls. The *Minneapolis Tribune's* story reported one fan shouted, "Suit up, Gus, you're going in next!" Another was heard to say, "He must be getting paid by the substitution." Young took responsibility for the loss afterward, admitting he had gotten a bit carried away when he continued making substitutions after his team built a seven-point lead in the fourth quarter.

Daniels finished with 35 points and 17 rebounds, while Netolicky added 27 points and 17 rebounds. Brown and Lewis, perhaps deflated by Harding's absence, scored 15 and 12, respectively. Brown hit just 4-of-19 shots, due in no small part to a swollen right thumb caused by punching Bradds the previous night in Oakland.

The game was most memorable for Chubin, who started again and scored 17 points against his former teammates. Returning a second time to Minneapolis since the trade to the Pacers, he had time to pause and reflect on his considerable good fortune. The Pacers had gone 16-8 since his arrival, improving from a 10-17 record to 26-25. Of the eight losses, six had come on the road and one of the home court losses was to Oakland, the league's best team. He had scored in double figures in 13 consecutive games and was averaging 13.8 points and 5.2 assists with the Pacers.

Although he wasn't scoring as much as in previous stops because of the talent surrounding him, he believed he was playing the best basketball of his career. He was developing chemistry with Lewis in the backcourt, and felt that playing with the Pacers' All-Star frontline made his job easy. All he had to do was get into the lane, try to draw contact and either dish off for an easy basket or go to the foul line. And that was just in the halfcourt offense. Leonard had them running at every opportunity, which made it all that much more fun.

Years later, the memories remained clear in his mind.

"All of a sudden, every time I got the ball it was like magic," he said. "The ball would never hit the ground, and it was fabulous. I never even looked at the floor, I just passed ahead."

He also loved living in Indianapolis, where fans flocked to him whenever he went out in public. Older fans rushed up and hugged him, and plenty of young females also recognized the team's new matinee idol. "Girls would come up to you left and right," he said. "Pretty girls. It was like walking on velvet. Like walking on a cloud. I was slapping myself. It was too good."

Even better: when he went out with some of those girls on dates, they wanted to talk basketball.

He loved his teammates, too, none more than Brown, with whom he roomed on the road trips and joined in late night escapades.

"We were chasing everybody," he recalled, laughing.

Chubin also had found the perfect coach in Leonard – a fiery mentor who didn't care what the players did off the court as long as they played hard and won. He loved Leonard's pregame and halftime locker room talks, the ones where he'd take off his jacket, roll up his sleeves, and fire up the players. Sometimes he'd even throw his jacket against the wall to make a point.

He also loved the fact Leonard had targeted him as a trade acquisition for so long, had even been willing to trade Brown to get him. It made him feel wanted, and brought out his best. He and the coach had seemed to form a special bond on his first road trip with the Pacers to New York, when they went out after the game and got "drunk as skunks" before going to get hamburgers. Years later, he recalled that evening as "phenomenal." After playing for the prim, proper and polite Sharman and the harsh drill sergeant Harding, he was thrilled to have a coach he could connect with, even more than "Colorful" Al Brightman.

He also loved Leonard for the confidence he instilled in the team. During afternoon conversations in hotels on road trips, Leonard would tell his players they were the best team in basketball, NBA included. The standings didn't objectively support that argument, but Leonard was a motivator, not an analyst. They were making a climb, becoming more and more competitive with Oakland, and Leonard was predicting great things for them.

He had fallen in love away from basketball, too. He had been invited to attend a Miss Indianapolis pageant as a celebrity guest, with the winner getting a date with him. They had hit it off and were in the beginning stages of a relationship.

He simply couldn't believe his good fortune. He was a professional basketball player on a winning team that seemed destined for a championship, if not championships, with a coach and teammates he loved, in a city that loved basketball, and with an active social life. He woke up every morning in a state of anticipation, excited to see what adventures the day would bring and expecting to win the next game. He was loving everything about his life.

Which is why he was stunned and devastated when, in the locker room after the game, Leonard told him he had been traded.

The deal sent him to the last-place New York Nets, for Ron Perry. Overpeck was told of it during the game, while Chubin was helping lead a comeback from a seven-point fourth quarter deficit, and managed to get a four-paragraph announcement in the following morning's *Star*.

Denny had time to cover it more thoroughly for the *News*. The postgame locker room, he wrote, was like a morgue. Daniels, naturally, offered the most passionate defense of Chubin.

"Perry will help us, but he's going to have a big pair of shoes to fill," Daniels said.

Another anonymous Pacer mused that the deal could "hurt team morale."

The Pacers were flying back to Indianapolis that night, but apparently had a few hours to kill. Chubin's memory was that he visited Hawkins at his apartment after the game and literally cried in Hawkins' arms. If so, he caught up to his suddenly former teammates at the airport for the overnight flight back to Indianapolis. They toasted him in the lounge, where Chubin, according to Denny's article, was misty-eyed but accepting of his cruel fate.

"Someday I'd like to coach and I'd like to be like you, Bob," Chubin said, looking directly at Leonard. "You're the greatest, and I'd like to be like you. You're tough, but you treat players like men and you're fair. I hope you go all the way, and if you do I'll be there to watch.

"Hey, I'd better watch out or I'll really bawl," he added, forcing a laugh. "I'm getting too serious."

Leonard was emotional as well.

"I want to stress that Steve did a helluva job for us," he told Overpeck and Denny. "He played with all his heart, all the time. If the time ever comes I can get him back, I'll do it in a flash."

As was usually the case, it was difficult to know whether Leonard or Storen was the driving force behind the deal, if not both. It was certain, however, that no deal could be made without Storen's final approval, and that Leonard wasn't going to publicly question his general manager's decisions. Leonard said he valued Perry's outside shooting, an asset missing from the Pacers' offense since Rayl had been released. Perry had hit 38 percent of his three-pointers in the 23 games he had played for the Nets to that date, and averaged 19.3 points. Leonard had tried to land Perry early in the season, believing a three-point threat was crucial to the team's title hopes, and never lost interest. He only had one player hitting better than 30 percent of his three-point attempts at the time, and that was the seldom-used Fairchild.

Rumors and theories would forever linger about other possible reasons for the trade, some of them scandalous. Chubin, without question, was more than a bit rambunctious off the court. While some players were fun/crazy, one of the Pacers later claimed, Chubin veered toward crazy/crazy. He was the star of legendary stories on road trips, to the degree Mike Lewis would recall always asking for a "Chub story" when he ran into Netolicky over the course of the season.

Chubin's teammates loved him for his adventures, but Storen might have feared he would cause embarrassment to the franchise. Then again, Perry was no wallflower. In fact, Daniels and Netolicky would later nickname him "Alfie," after the womanizing lead character in the movie of the same name. Besides, if Chubin was that much of a risk, why was Leonard immediately hoping to get him back?

Chubin forever believed Perry had lobbied behind the scenes to bring about the deal, having befriended Leonard and Netolicky. Perry steadfastly claimed he had no idea why the trade was made. He had heard Storen's wife, Hannah, had attended Radford University near Perry's alma mater, Virginia Tech, and perhaps she had lobbied her husband to trade for him.

Regardless, New York wanted Chubin badly. He was from the Queens borough in New York City. He also was identified as Jewish, so the Nets front office – led by Zaslofsky, their Jewish coach and general manager – thought he would attract new fans.

In retrospect, he wondered if that had worked against him in Indianapolis. Not long before the trade, he had received a call from someone representing the Indianapolis B'nai B'rith chapter, a Jewish service organization. It wanted to make a presentation to him before a game at the Coliseum, for no other reason than to recognize his Jewishness and promote the organization.

Chubin played along, but it held no special meaning for him. His father was Jewish, his mother was Catholic, and he didn't affiliate with either religion. Jewish players were so rare in professional basketball, however, that Jewish organizations pointed with pride to any who could be linked to the faith. Grasping for an explanation decades later, Chubin later wondered if that had been a factor in his trade to the Nets. Perhaps someone in the Pacers' front office wasn't comfortable with it. He could only wonder. It seemed unlikely, given the franchise's close affiliation with the Jewish Community Center in Indianapolis.

There's two sides to every trade, however, and if a player from one side of it is heartbroken, a player on the other side is probably ecstatic. That was Perry. He had scored 15 points in a victory over Houston the same night the Pacers won in Minneapolis. Afterward, Zaslofsky called him into his office. Perry had scored 22 and 27 points in the two games prior to that, so was expecting a pat on the back. Instead, Zaslofsky told him he had been traded to Indiana.

"I nearly jumped up on the table, I was so excited," Perry recalled years later. "I was like, You've got to be kidding me!"

News of the trade spread quickly, even before the morning newspaper came out. Radio play-by-play announcer Jerry Baker announced it before he signed off that night, and it spread by word of mouth in Indianapolis. To say the least, it was not well-received.

The phone rang at the home of Chuck DeVoe, the newly minted team president in place of his brother, John, about 2 a.m. the following morning, three or four hours after the game ended. "What the hell are you doing?!" the voice at the other end of the line screamed, followed by some garbled rant that DeVoe struggled to understand as he tried to clear the cobwebs from his brain.

"What's going on?" DeVoe's wife sleepily asked.

"I don't know, but I think we just traded Chubin," he said.

Storen took a more direct hit. Someone dumped trash in his front yard the next day. "Thank God you're the general manager and not me," DeVoe told him later.

Leonard, who had a listed phone number, also heard from irate fans, and more than 100 people called the Pacers office to voice their vitriol in the days following the deal. Several letters were sent to the newspapers as well in support of Chubin, a couple of which were published. One man took a swipe at what he perceived to be Leonard's itchy trading finger, calling the Pacers "the Hoosier version of Let's Make a Deal," a reference to the popular television game show. Another was written as an open letter to Chubin, telling him, "You must have wondered, Steve, what was wrong, and so do thousands of fans."

Chubin had just learned the same harsh lesson Rayl had learned a month earlier, and that Brown nearly did as well. It didn't matter how popular you were, or had once been, or even how well you had played. You were at risk to be released or traded at any time if management thought it necessary.

Just as with Harkness and Rayl, the schedule didn't permit time for reflection or sympathy from Chubin's former teammates. The Pacers had a game the following night at the Coliseum against Los Angeles, the team that had defeated them in overtime two weeks earlier on Miller's three-point basket. A few fans held up hastily-made hand-lettered signs of the "We Want Chubin!" variety, but if the players were upset over losing him it didn't show in their performance. Playing their fourth game in four nights, they scored 172 points. As in one-hundred-seventy-two. The Stars settled for 141.

The Pacers' point total obliterated the league scoring record of 153 Oakland had set against them in November – the game some thought cost Staverman his job, although the decision likely had already been made. It fell one point short of the NBA scoring record, set by Boston in 1959. The combined score fell just three points short of the NBA record for two teams in one game.

The Pacers scored 90 points in the second half, 51 in the fourth quarter, and hit 60 of 70 foul shots. Los Angeles fouled them 15 times in the third quarter, when they hit 25 of 28 free throws. Sharman, who was a member of the record-setting '59 Celtics team, was so incensed he levied fines throughout his roster and added more practice time to his schedule.

All but two of the Pacers scored in double figures. Brown led with 34, followed by Netolicky with 30. Daniels had the most efficient game, with 25 points on 8-of-12 shooting and 13 rebounds.

The Pacers had drawn motivation from their recent overtime loss to the Stars, and Leonard had primed them for the possibility of negative fan reaction to the trade. "The only way to stop criticism," he told his players before the game, "is to go out there and beat hell out of Los Angeles."

The record-setting victory didn't completely squelch fan distress, though. One woman, Storen later told reporters, called the Pacers office the next day and shouted, "You idiot! If you hadn't traded Chubin you would have scored 200 points!"

Perry made an appearance late in the game despite having played in New York the previous evening. He flew to Indianapolis Saturday afternoon, suited up with his new teammates and scored seven points. Despite their anger over losing Chubin, many of the fans gave Perry a standing ovation when he entered the game, and a dozen or so greeted him as he came off the floor afterward. It was confirmation of why he wanted to join the team so badly, and why Chubin was so upset over having to leave: the fan support was unmatched in the ABA – when the team was winning, at least.[11]

Chubin, with nothing else to do that night, solemnly watched the game from a seat high up in the Coliseum. He flew to New York the next day to resume his career with the Nets. His life would never be the same again.

---

[11] Perry also broke his nose in the game, courtesy of George Stone's elbow, although it wasn't discovered for nearly two weeks after headaches and breathing difficulty led to X-rays and a reset.

"We're coming to play basketball.
But if they want to fight, we'll be ready for that, too."

A Team is Born

Following Chubin's trade and the record-setting victory over Los Angeles, the Pacers had one more game to complete their five-in-five stretch, which would forever stand as the longest in franchise history. It was in Miami, a favorite destination, but by then the fatigue of their travels and the aftershocks of the outrageous game against the Stars caught up with them. They lost, 130-113, but Leonard took it in stride given the schedule.

Netolicky and Daniels actually were playing their sixth game in six nights because of their participation in the All-Star game in Louisville before the start of the road trip, and it showed. Netolicky scored 12 points in a listless performance, but at least he showed up at the airport on time. Daniels overslept and missed the team's commercial flight to Miami. He caught a later flight on his own and arrived just 2 ½ hours after the team. He hit 3-of-16 shots in the first half, but finished with 26 points. Brown scored 33 points and grabbed 13 rebounds in a second consecutive strong effort. Lewis had 22 and got knocked down twice, hard enough for Lareau to rush onto the court to tend to him and for Leonard to jump off the bench screaming at the referees.

With a day off before the next game in New Orleans, Leonard called a meeting at the hotel in Miami before the afternoon flight. The team was tired and needed a lift, so he came up with a prank to pull on Daniels. Before the All-Star center arrived for the meeting, Leonard told the other players he was going to ask them how much Daniels should be fined for missing the previous day's flight. He told them to agree on $1,000.

"Oh, my, he's gonna put his fist right through that wall," Brown said.

Daniels didn't, either because he got wind of the ruse or because he could read the expression on his teammates' faces. But, it was pointed out in the *News*, he was first in line for the flight to New Orleans later that day.

Leonard had less of a sense of humor with Netolicky, and pulled him out of the starting lineup because of his lack of defense and rebounding in Miami. He spared no verbal rod, either.

"When he comes to play, he's great. When he doesn't, he hurts us," he told Corky Lamm, who covered the game for the *News*.

By now Netolicky's mode was obvious, whether he was playing for Staverman or Leonard. He had superior athleticism, finesse and IQ, but inferior self-motivation. He was more fun-loving than blue-collar, the yang to Daniels' yin, seemingly equally capable of dominating a game or disappearing from it.

"That guy had more God-given ability than two people," one of his teammates said in later years. "But some nights it was like he was in another world. His athleticism was ridiculous, for a guy his size to be able to run and jump like that. But if he didn't want to play, Jesus Christ could have come back and said, 'Give me a good effort,' and he would have said, 'Screw you.'"

The team responded to the day off and Leonard's motivational methods in their 138-117 victory at New Orleans. Brown had a third straight standout game with 32 points, nine rebounds and eight assists. Daniels, forgiven and driven, had 30 points and 23 rebounds. Netolicky, chastened and reinvigorated, came off the bench with 27 points and 10 rebounds. Perry, already in the starting lineup, scored 13 points.

The Pacers played again the next night back at the Coliseum, their seventh game in eight days. They were fatigued, but still defeated Denver, 125-109, before what Overpeck described as a "grumpy gathering" of

Mel Daniels looks to hand off to a cutting Ron Perry during a loss to Oakland on Feb. 8. Oaks center Jim Eakins defends while wearing a bandage to protect the stitches he had received to repair cuts suffered in an automobile accident.

4,421 fans. Daniels had 36 points and 21 rebounds. Lewis scored 27 points, and Netolicky 18.

Brown, though, quietly had the best game of all, with 26 points on 6-of-10 shooting and 14-of-15 free throws, along with 10 rebounds and eight assists. It was his fourth consecutive standout effort since the game in Minneapolis when he had played with a swollen thumb. He was back now, more confident than ever, and sold on his coach. But he had recovered his considerable pride, too. The chastened, introspective player of a few weeks ago had reverted to his foundation of quiet arrogance. Forget any personal shortcomings, he told Overpeck, he was only playing better because he was playing more.

And, he had been pacing himself for the playoffs.

"I didn't want to burn out early," he said. "I want to be at my peak when it really counts."

Brown was indeed the master of conserving energy. It was part of his nature, something he had practiced even in high school, when he questioned Harkness for running grueling distance races to win a medal rather than just jumping over a bar as he did.

The only struggling starter now was Perry, who hit just 1-of-8 shots and scored two points against Denver in his first start at the Coliseum. He admitted to nerves, knowing he was replacing a popular player in Chubin, but Leonard remained in his corner — and was plotting something on his behalf.

"This guy's going to do the job for us," Leonard said. "just wait 'til we play New York. Then we'll see."

Next up, though, was Oakland – the mighty Oaks, by far the ABA's elite team. The game sold out in advance, and 1,228 standing room tickets were purchased despite a heavy snowfall and a rare telecast of a home game. The Pacers were rising fast, having moved into a tie with Kentucky for second place in the East. The memory of the overtime loss in Oakland nine days earlier, which featured two major fights and the undercard bout between Lewis and Larry Brown, remained fresh in the Pacers' memory.

"We're coming to play basketball," Leonard told Denny the day before the game. "But if they want to fight, we'll be ready for that, too."

There were no fights this time. In fact, the Pacers didn't put up much of a fight. Oakland, playing once again without Barry, who had reinjured his left knee the previous night in Louisville after scoring 41 points, walked out of the Coliseum unscathed and with a 118-103 victory. The Pacers hit just 40-of-123 shots (.325), missed their first 15 shots of the third quarter and hit just 25 percent over the second and third periods, combined. The only starter to play particularly well was Perry, who hit 7-of-17 shots for 19 points, passed out six assists and "played bang-up defense" on Logan, according to Overpeck's story.

Larry Brown, who always seemed to play his best in Barry's absence, did the most damage for Oakland with 19 points, nine rebounds and 13 assists.

Hooper had the worst night of all. Playing off the bench behind Perry, he hit just 1-of-10 shots, and broke his thumb.

The Pacers and Oaks were developing the kind of rivalry that almost guaranteed controversy. This time it featured Daniels and Oakland center Ira Harge. They were longtime friends, having known one another in Detroit and Daniels having followed Harge to Burlington Junior College and New Mexico. Harge, three years ahead of Daniels, was sitting with Daniels when Daniels signed his scholarship to New Mexico, a moment revealed by a photograph in the *Albuquerque Journal*. Harge finished the game with 10 points and 13 rebounds. Daniels had 20 points and 24 rebounds, but hit just 7-of-22 shots. Afterward, Denny paid a visit to Oakland's locker room where Barry, who watched the game in street clothes, proclaimed that Harge "ate Mel up."

Hannum overheard the comment and asked Barry to stop, but he continued.

"I don't care what they say, he (Harge) ate his (Daniels') lunch."

Daniels wasn't pleased when Denny passed along Barry's comments.

"This is what I've got to say," he said. "If we play Oakland for the championship, we may not win if Oakland plays without Barry. But if he does play, we'll win."

The Pacers won their next game, in Minneapolis on Feb. 9, by a point, a game made closer by Vaughn's meaningless three-pointer at the buzzer. They were scheduled to play two nights later in New York, where they would reunite with Chubin, but an 18-inch snowstorm forced postponement of the game. Eventually. The Pacers' traveling party gathered at the airport at 3:30 a.m., only to learn Kennedy Airport was closed. A call to New York to inform the Nets of the need for postponement was met with insistence the game could be played, so reservations were made on a flight at 1 p.m. The Pacers' traveling party went to a nearby hotel to pass time, but Lareau was told by an official from the bus company that was to provide transportation from the airport they couldn't get to them. Meanwhile, the 1 p.m. flight was canceled, as was a 3 p.m. flight. Finally, the Nets conceded the game could not be played.

Suddenly, the Pacers had a five-day break. The next game, in Denver, wouldn't be played until the 14th. Leonard took advantage of the practice time to put in a new offense. Never mind that his team had set the league scoring record on Feb. 1 with 172 points, had scored 140 or more on three other recent occasions and had scored 100 or more in 13 straight games.

Also during the break, on Feb. 13, the Pacers did what seemed impossible early in the season: they became a first-place team. For about a day, anyway. Minnesota lost a home game played in St. Louis, giving the Pacers a lead of two percentage points. But, new offense and all, the Pacers lost in Denver the following night, 112-103, to drop back into third place behind Miami and Minnesota.

The altered offense, which spread the court to create more room for the guards to cut to the basket, wasn't the primary issue. They hit just 20-of-42 foul shots, played poor defense and had a troubled guard situation. Lewis was in foul trouble, and with Hooper out with his broken thumb, Perry had to play heavy minutes with cotton stuffed up his broken nose because he refused to wear the protective mask Lareau provided for him. He scored 13 points, but the Pacers had nobody who could deal with Rockets guard Larry Jones, who scored 39.

They lost again the following night at the Coliseum, to Dallas, and then lost the next night in New York, 112-96, before 1,012 fans who braved the snow drifts from the storm that had postponed the game the previous week. Chubin got the better of his matchup with Perry, finishing with 14 points, nine rebounds and nine assists while Perry had 13 points on 5-of-16 shooting, three rebounds and two assists. Brown, moved to the backcourt to aid the depleted guard corps, scored 27, many of them against Chubin, but fouled out with six minutes left.

The biggest issue, however, was Daniels. For the second time in two weeks, he missed the flight out of Indianapolis. This time, he didn't arrive at the game until halftime. And this time he didn't contribute much, scoring a career-low four points on 2-of-6 shooting.

His flight mishaps were posing a delicate problem for Leonard. What should be done about a great player with a great attitude who oversleeps a couple of times and puts his team in jeopardy of losing?

"It's difficult to know what to do," Leonard told Denny. "If it was a guy who was always giving you trouble, there'd be no question. But Mel isn't like that. He's no trouble. He has difficulty relaxing after a game and it probably was 3-4 a.m. Sunday before he could go to sleep."

It was 5:30 a.m., according to Daniels. Flying out of Indianapolis the morning after a home game was always a challenge for him, given

Roger Brown's shooting form was picture-perfect, as shown in the Feb. 18 victory over Minnesota. This game, however, featured Mel Daniels, who made amends for missing another flight.

how long it took him to wind down. And it was no coincidence his two missed flights came after homecourt losses. He said he wouldn't have even caught the later plane to New York if Lewis hadn't called him at home from the airport when the players were gathering for their flight.

Leonard never revealed if he fined Daniels, but he and Storen came up with a way to discipline him while taking the edge off the frustration of the three-game losing streak. Before the next game against Minnesota back at the Coliseum, Daniels was presented with a $3.98 alarm clock

as a gift and told to stand on a chair in the locker room and read a poem
Storen had written.

"There once was a center named Mel
Whose habits of sleeping were hell.
He stayed in the rack
Failed to go with the pack
And his team from the top really fell."

The mood lightened, the wide-awake Pacers defeated the Pipers,
140-133. Daniels, who said he had "hit rock bottom" because of his
guilt over two missed flights, vented his frustration by scoring 40 points
and grabbing 22 rebounds. With a 31-30 record, the Pacers were back
in the race for the Division title.

"Now we're going again," Daniels said.

Something else happened that day of more lasting significance.
Hooper was out and Perry and Lewis were playing with injuries, so the
Pacers signed veteran guard Tom Thacker to fill the void. For a franchise
chock-full of good fortune in its formative years, this was yet another
fortuitous moment.

Thacker had been a member of the University of Cincinnati's NCAA
championship teams as a sophomore and junior in 1961 and '62, and
was a senior on the '63 team that lost to Harkness and Loyola. Thacker,
in fact, was standing next to Loyola's Vic Rouse as Rouse scored the
game-winning basket off a rebound at the final buzzer, but wasn't tall
enough to prevent it.

Thacker played three NBA seasons for the Cincinnati Royals, then
was claimed by the Bulls in the same expansion draft that sent Bonham
from Boston to Chicago. He played in one exhibition game before an
injury led to his release. He played for the Muskegon, Mich. team in
the North American Basketball League as he recovered, helping it to a
championship in 1967, and then caught on with Boston the following
season, 1967-68.

He won another championship with the Celtics as a backup guard, taking the spot left by K. C. Jones' retirement, but became a victim of the expansion draft again when Milwaukee selected him after the season. He declined to report to the newly-formed Bucks, opting instead for Dallas in the ABA. He lasted but a few days before being released. He then returned to Cincinnati and was alternating between teaching high school and serving his National Guard duty when the Pacers called. Again, connections had paid off. Storen knew Thacker from the two seasons (1964-65 and 1965-66) they both were employed by the Royals, and Brown knew him from playing summer pickup games in Cincinnati.

Thacker was a poor shooter, but an outstanding defender, a decent playmaker and a wise head who brought needed maturity to the Pacers. He fit in immediately, even arriving with a classy sobriquet. In college, his teammates had assigned nicknames to one another based on popular television cartoon characters. Thacker's was "Augie Doggie," later shortened to "Dogg." With two Gs.

He played 21 minutes against the Pipers, contributing four points and five assists in his hastily-arranged debut, but Daniels' declaration that the Pacers were "going again" turned out to be premature. They lost three nights later in Dallas, a defeat they put on the officials for allowing the home team 10 more free throw attempts. "If we ever got a break from the officials, we'd be tough," Leonard said. "I'll tell you this; we're going to the hoop against Kentucky right from the start and see if they put us on the line."

That didn't work, either, as they lost to the Colonels the following night at the Coliseum, 118-108, before a capacity crowd of 10,472. They were now 5-7 since trading Chubin, a point some of the frustrated fans reminded them of late in the game. Leonard only used eight players, and three of them only sparingly. He kept all of them in the locker room for 45 minutes after the game, however, for another thunderous lecture.

Peeples questioned the team's "heart, pride and spirit."

"Everybody is at fault," he told Denny in the *News*. "Instead of saying to hell with the injuries and the officiating and sticking with it, we're quitting. There was a time when things were pretty bad and Bobby stuck with us. Now things are bad again and it's time we stuck with him."

The Pacers had another three-day break before their next game, which had its pros and cons. It was good for Leonard, who had more practice time to work out kinks. It was bad for the players, who had to endure the demands of their angry coach. They conducted what Denny called a "Vince Lombardi-like scrimmage," one in which Dee and Butch Joyner, a former Indiana University player who had been added to the roster to fill out the backcourt, both suffered ankle injuries.

Coincidentally or not, something began to click from that point. They won their next game at home against a Miami team that had won 12 of its previous 13 games, 128-123, before another sellout crowd of 10,687. Brown finished with 32 points, nine rebounds and seven assists and gave "another all-around brilliant show of moves and passes" according to Denny's story. Peeples came off the bench to contribute 18 points and 16 rebounds.

The schedule turned downhill from there, fueling their momentum.

Brown followed with 41 points the next night in New York, a season-high for a Pacer, scoring 16 of them in the fourth quarter of a 113-104 victory. He followed that with 34 points, 12 rebounds and 11 assists in a routine 133-128 homecourt win over Houston back at the Coliseum. Daniels had 39 points despite sitting out six minutes of the first half in foul trouble, and 17 rebounds. Peeples continued to excel off the bench with 17 points and 14 rebounds. Netolicky, though, continued to struggle, finishing with six points and five fouls. The fans booed him late in the game.

Leonard, who had blistered his erratic forward behind closed doors, stuck up for him in the newspaper.

"That should make a guy play that much harder and most do. But some of these fellows are young and it could bother them. This is the only town in the league that boos its own players. That's their right and I hope they keep coming out. One of these nights, though, Neto is going to bust loose for about 40 points."

The winning streak was three, with more winnable games ahead.

Next up was a doubleheader at the Coliseum, featuring the best and worst the ABA had to offer. Houston's franchise, already announced as headed to Carolina for the following season, was drawing fans by the dozens rather than thousands. It was losing money by playing at home, so it took its game with Oakland to the Coliseum to be played as a preliminary to the Pacers' game.[1] The Pacers followed with a 131-96 win over Dallas that broke an eight-game losing streak against the Chaps, their first victory since Harkness hit the 88-foot game-winner early the previous season.

Lewis, shedding a protective pad on his left arm, matched his franchise record point total with 43 points, and added nine rebounds and seven assists. Brown pitched in a routine 31, but the most noticeable performance came from Peeples, who started in place of Netolicky and followed through on the Leonard-inspired bravado he had blared in the newspapers.

Peeples scored 14 points and grabbed a game-high 18 rebounds. His primary purpose for starting, though, was to defend Dallas forward Cincy Powell, who had averaged more than 30 points against the Pacers that season. He held Powell to 19 points on 7-of-22 shooting. He also made a point of taunting him. After committing an intentional foul late in the game, he rubbed Powell's head and walked away. Powell responded by throwing the ball and grazing Peeples' head.

"Yeah, we rubbed it in," Peeples told Denny.

That victory, the Pacers' fourth in a row, set up one of the most anticipated home games in the franchise's early history: Chubin was returning to town with New York, five weeks since the trade that devastated so much of the fan base. Denny referred to him in his advance story as "possibly the most popular player the Pacers ever had and

---

[1] The Pacers also had taken in a nearly homeless team the previous season. New Orleans had committed to playing some of its home games in Memphis, but they drew so poorly there early on they rescheduled the remaining ones in other cities. The Pacers let them play Anaheim in what amounted to a JV game before they played New Jersey. Attendance was listed at 5,999, although most of them arrived toward the end of the first game.

Steve Chubin poses with a home-made banner made by adoring and discontented fans before his first game at the Coliseum since his trade from the Pacers.

certainly the most popular player the Pacers ever let go," adding Chubin "probably could be elected mayor of Indianapolis if he were ever to become an Indiana Pacer again."

Storen conducted a press conference the day before the game to announce the franchise's effort to lobby Butler for use of its fieldhouse again for the playoffs because of a scheduling conflict with the Coliseum. He opened by saying, "We are not beginning this meeting by saying we have reacquired Steve Chubin. But if everybody who has called me about Chubin were to call Butler about the playoffs, we might get some action."

The Friday night game drew 6,065 fans, most of whom were still carrying their crush for the guard done wrong. Homemade signs were scattered throughout the building, the likes of "Super Chubin," "We Love Steve" and "Welcome Home Steve." A few other more determined fans – Mr. and Mrs. John Meyer and Mrs. James Warner – made a neatly printed banner about a foot wide and six feet long that read, "TRADE STOREN FOR CHUBIN." They paraded it onto the court before the game, and Chubin posed with it for a photo.

It was a sign of the times, indicative of a unique era. In another decade, the professional game would become too corporate for a team to permit such a public protest, and for an opposing player to take time out from warmups to pose for such a picture. But fans were afforded wide leeway at the time. Smoking inside arenas was permitted, throwing trash on the court to protest a call was tolerated and hurling insults at referees and opposing players was expected, so making a sign to protest their team's trade was hardly unanticipated.

Chubin had been playing well for the Nets. He had averaged 21.6 points in his 14 games since the trade, and scored 27 or more eight times. He was still drawing fouls, too, averaging 8.3 free throw attempts. Perry, meanwhile, was averaging 11 points in his 16 games with the Pacers. He had brought the desired perimeter shooting, though, hitting 13 three-pointers while Chubin had yet to hit one with the Nets.

There was this stat, too: The Pacers had gone 16-8 with Chubin, but were 9-7 since Perry's arrival.

With so much buildup to the game, Leonard wasn't going to let Perry – or Storen or himself – be embarrassed. As he had hinted earlier — *"... just wait 'til we play New York. Then we'll see,"* — he ran the offense through Perry, sending him off endless screens to get open. Perry responded, scoring 35 points – one short of his career-high and more than he would ever score again professionally – by hitting 12-of-24 shots, including three three-pointers and all eight free throws. He started quickly, scoring nine in the first quarter and six more early in the second, and never looked back. When he left the game with a couple of minutes remaining, the Pacers' 143-124 victory nearly complete, he received a standing ovation.

The headline in the next day's *News* read, "Perry Shoots Chubin 'Monkey' Off His Back."

Lewis nearly finished it off with fireworks. As the final buzzer sounded, he flung a hook shot from a foot inside the baseline that swished through the net at the other end. It was thought to be longer than Harkness' shot in Dallas, but was let go a second too late. Lewis finished with 33 points, though, giving the Pacers' starting backcourt a combined 68-point effort.

Ron Perry drives off Roger Brown, while Chubin tries to defend. Just five weeks earlier, he would have been receiving such a screen. Now he was being jostled by his former teammates, and the emotional pain was tremendous.

Leonard felt as if he had been pardoned.

"This was the showdown," he told Denny. "Either come up with it or you don't. It's time we give Ron credit. The fans have been putting him down long enough. He was what I was looking for when we traded Steve. I thought our club needed more outside shooting.

"But Steve is still one of my boys. I'd like to have both of them. I promised him that if I could, I'd get him back, and I'll try to do it."

Perry, who had been booed and heckled with calls of "We want Chubin!" by some fans during his poor shooting games at the Coliseum, said he felt nauseous when he arrived for the game. He also said he took no personal satisfaction in his performance, but was relieved he had taken pressure off Leonard and Storen for making the deal.

Chubin had a solid game with 21 points, but lived through a nightmare. Being back in the Coliseum, seeing his former teammates, hearing the fans and seeing the signs they held up only rekindled his memories of the dream he had lived with the Pacers. Then to go out and have former teammates such as Daniels and Brown – guys he loved – setting screens and bumping him to get Perry free for shots brought both physical and emotional pain. It felt as if they had turned on him. And then to see Perry receive a standing ovation from the same fans who had cheered him so lustily just a couple of months before … it all combined for a horrible memory that never went away.

"I was a nervous wreck," he recalled. "Even my teammates were nervous for me. Then they got mad at me, telling me to relax. It was awful. It was sad. It was a tough situation for me. I was shaking the whole game. I didn't want any part of the deal."

Chubin was greeted by a swarm of autograph seekers outside the Nets' upstairs locker room – a crowd "bigger even than for Rick Barry," Denny wrote. Among them were two high school students who said they planned to start an official fan club for him.

"When I left Indianapolis, I must have got 25 letters the first week," Chubin told Denny. "It was really neat. Nothing like that ever happened to me.

"It's not the same playing for New York. It's not any fun with no chance of making the playoffs. I don't play half as well as I did for the Pacers. The fast break is my game, but we don't go, go at New York like we did with Leonard."

While Chubin trudged off on the rest of his dreary existence with the last-place Nets, the Pacers continued their run. They defeated Miami two nights later, 128-123, duplicating the score from when the two teams played nine days earlier. Playing before their biggest crowd ever, 10,687, the fourth sellout of the season, they won their sixth straight game. The victory knocked the Floridians from the Eastern Division lead, setting up a race to the finish line between them, Kentucky and the Pacers.

Freeman scored 39 points for the Floridians, but the Pacers had too many weapons. Brown scored 38 points. Lewis had 34 and outscored Freeman in the final quarter, 15-8. Netolicky, still coming off the bench but recovering his game, had 21. Daniels settled for 19 points and 21 rebounds.

The victory exacted a physical toll, though. Perry got a bloody nose when Les Hunter threw an elbow after Perry intentionally fouled him, Lewis suffered bruises to his jaw and neck when he collided with Freeman and Daniels had a headache after falling hard off the end of the court while chasing a rebound. Brown, on the other hand, was gliding through the season, averaging 33.5 points on 51 percent shooting, 8.8 rebounds and 5.5 assists in the win streak. He was forging a relationship with Leonard, trusting him like he had never trusted an adult, but money remained a primary motivation. Each player on the league championship team was to get a $5,000 bonus – more than a quarter of the annual salary of most of the players.

"We can smell those George Washingtons," Brown said.

Netolicky, meanwhile, saw Brown as a role model for his recent struggles.

"I had a little slump and I was down on myself," he said. "I was to this point where I wasn't hustling. I think I was right where Roger was early in the season. Maybe it will work out the same way for me."

Brown set a franchise scoring record with 46 points and added eight rebounds and six assists in the next game, a 122-112 victory back in New York. A private audience of 517 witnessed. It would be the Pacers' last trip to the Long Island Arena in Commack, a place Denny described as "the most desolate, depressing spot a pro team in any sport has to play in today." Nobody who played there, whether on the home or visiting team, would have argued.

Leonard called just one timeout to help keep his players warm. The game plan was to get it over with as quickly as possible, and get out of town without catching cold. Brown, for one, wasn't impressed with himself, his team or the facility.

"I thought I was terrible and I thought the team played badly," he said. "It was just too cold for basketball."

Brown's version of "terrible" differed from most. His 46-point effort raised his average over the previous seven games to 35.3 points. He shot better than 50 percent from the field in that span, drew enough fouls to average 11 free throw attempts and hit 89 percent of them.

Denny compared him to Gale Sayers, the Chicago Bears' running back, for his spontaneous agility.

"Call it improvisation, inventiveness, body control, self-preservation, determination, anything," Denny wrote. "Brown and Sayers have it and the hard-to-describe quality someday should earn Roger his due in fame and fortune."

Brown's streak of standout performances provided Denny an opportunity to delve a bit deeper into the private man's personal life. Brown recalled growing up "in the heart of the ghetto" in the Bedford-Stuyvesant section of Brooklyn, one of five children with a single mother and living in a three-story house with two other families.

"I imagine I'd probably be a thug or a junkie or dead somewhere now if it hadn't been for basketball," he said. "The game almost took my life away when I was suspended by Dayton and barred from the NBA. But the ABA has returned my life."

The games were becoming easy now, thanks to the Pacers' burgeoning chemistry and gentler schedule. They beat the Nets again back at the Coliseum in the next game, although Leonard had to "raise some hell" at halftime when the game was tied. His players responded with an 83-point second half and a 125-87 victory. The Pacers outscored New York 15-0 in one 2-minute, 17-second stretch in the third quarter during which, Denny wrote, they "literally tore apart the Nets" — which would have been gruesome to watch if literally true.

A 144-113 victory over Minnesota in a Sunday afternoon game followed. That one got an assist from American Airlines, which was on strike. The Pipers, who had lost in Oakland on both Friday and Saturday night, had to fly to Indianapolis on National Airlines instead. They

Ten-year-old Pat O'Brien gets a lift from Nets center Tom Hoover and referee Ron Rakel to fix a tangled net during the Pacers' 125-87 victory over New York.

made stops in Houston, Shreveport and Memphis before reaching Indianapolis at 12:30 p.m. on the day of the game, completing a nine-hour journey. No wonder, then, they weren't up to playing at 4 p.m. Hawkins had reinjured his knee the previous night and played just 21 minutes off the bench, making it that much easier for the Pacers.

Those factors dulled the significance of the Pacers' individual performances, but they still counted in the box score. Lewis scored 36 points, 19 in the third quarter. It was RCA Family Day, so he received a portable stereo as the game's MVP. Daniels had 26 points. Thacker, increasingly comfortable with his new team and new league, had 10 points and 13 rebounds. Perry scored 15 points in the first quarter, hitting seven consecutive field goals through one stretch, and finished with 21 points in 23 minutes.

That provided Leonard another opportunity to defend Perry, and, indirectly, the trade.

"Ron proved he was a winner to me a long time ago," he said. "When he had that broken nose – and it wasn't a simple break – he stayed out there and played and took a lot of heat from the fans."

New York came back to town two nights later for the fourth game between the two teams in 12 days. The furor over Chubin's trade was fading by then. The Pacers' win streak had reached nine games, which contributed to the fans' acceptance of Perry. And, this time, Daniels provided a memorable distraction in a 143-114 victory.

Only 4,796 fans showed up for the Tuesday night game, but they saw something special. Daniels scored 56 points, 10 more than the franchise record Brown had set a week earlier over the forgiving Nets' defense, and just one short of Hawkins' ABA record, set against the Nets the previous December. Clearly, these Nets were meant for shredding, the perfect accomplice for a hot shooter. Still, Daniels became just the 13th ABA or NBA player since the NBA began play in the 1949-50 season to score that many points. He was two days too late to receive a portable stereo for his trouble, so he settled for a franchise scoring record.

Daniels hit 25-of-38 shots, league records for both attempts and made field goals. He also feasted on the Nets' 65 missed shots, helping himself to a franchise-record 31 rebounds, one short of Harge's league record. It was such an outstanding performance that it inspired both hyperbole and simile from the beat writers.

Overpeck wrote that Daniels "broke more records than a clumsy disc jockey would in two years." Denny, pointing out the willingness of the other Pacers to get the ball to Daniels, wrote that he "got more help from his teammates than a pretty girl with a flat tire on an expressway."

Daniels compiled 23 points and 14 rebounds in the fourth quarter alone, but the Nets did put up some fight the last couple of minutes by double- and triple-teaming him to keep him from breaking Hawkins' record. Leonard called timeout with eight seconds left to set up a play to give Daniels one last shot at the mark, but his attempt from 22 feet rimmed out.

Denny's story in the *News* was revealing, both for Daniels' disappointment at being traded to the Pacers and his early season frustrations with the team, and his appreciation for being a part of a blossoming team.

"No, I wasn't too happy when I first got here," he said. "But I am now. There is a togetherness on this club the same as we had at Minnesota last year. There's no color distinction. We're men and we pull together. Every last one of the guys helped me tonight."

Daniels wasn't just the recipient of the team's togetherness, he was the primary instigator of it among the players. The diversity of his bloodlines and upbringing in Detroit helped him feel comfortable around anyone, and the combination of his warrior's mentality and poet's sensitivity drew teammates to him.

"Mel brought the team together as far as everybody palling around together," Netolicky said years later. "We had hung around a little bit, but when the game was over we didn't go out together, especially the black and white guys. That changed when Mel got there."

Daniels even had the power to attract fans who might not otherwise have crossed the color barrier. He said he once received a letter from someone in northern Indiana who wrote something along the lines of,

"We don't think black ballplayers are as good as white ballplayers, but we like you. Can we have your autograph?"

He mailed back a signature.

The Pacers had one more home game, against Minnesota again, before finishing the season with four road games. Daniels was honored beforehand as the team's Most Valuable Player and received gifts from sponsors: a watch, a vacuum cleaner and a color television.[2]

The previous season's team MVP, Brown, then went out and scored 35 points and passed out nine assists in a 132-113 victory that extended the win streak to 11. Lewis added 32 points and 10 assists. Daniels, two days after his 56-point explosion, settled for 21, but grabbed 26 rebounds. It was another gimme for the Pacers, as Minnesota was without four key players, including three starters.

Dee returned from a three-week absence due to the sprained ankle suffered in Leonard's Lombardi-like practice, but Peeples missed the game because of a sprained ankle suffered in the previous practice. That opened the door for Netolicky to return to the starting lineup, something Leonard probably was hoping to do anyway with the playoffs approaching. Netolicky responded with 18 points and reclaimed his spot.

Attendance was 8,963, raising the homecourt season total to 237,789, an average of 6,097.[3] Denny dusted off his hyperbole machine and called it "one of the most amazing pro sports attendance stories in history." If not that, it was at least impressive. The Pacers drew more fans than all but six NBA teams despite (1) playing in a market smaller than all the NBA teams, (2) playing in an arena smaller than all but one

---

[2] Some fans also got together and presented a gift certificate to a local hair salon to Heyman, who sported a combover that he often fussed with during games.

[3] Overpeck reported different numbers in the *Star*: an average attendance of 6,006, which ranked sixth in all of pro basketball. Take your pick. The NBA teams that drew more than the Pacers that season were New York (15,404), Los Angeles, Philadelphia, Boston and Baltimore. Denver had the ABA's second-best attendance, at 4,294. Houston ranked last, with an average attendance of 828, and that number probably was exaggerated.

in the NBA and (3) playing against less established opponents who didn't boost the gate as, say, the Lakers or Celtics would as a visiting team.

The ABA's league-wide attendance average was barely more than 3,000, just a couple hundred more than the first season. For talent and fan support, the Pacers were becoming the envy of 10 other ABA teams, not to mention about half the NBA teams.

Among the fans on hand for the victory over Minnesota was O.J. Simpson, the reigning Heisman Trophy winner and one of the greatest running backs in the history of college football. Simpson sat in the front row with Barnes of Sports Headliners, who represented Simpson's business dealings, and a photograph of them ran in the *Star* the next morning. Simpson had been the No. 1 pick in the NFL draft but was having a difficult negotiation with the Buffalo Bills. Barnes arranged a press conference the next day at the Speedway Motel, at which Simpson claimed he was considering a four-year, $1 million offer to play for the Indianapolis Capitols of the Continental Football League.

"It could happen," Simpson said. "The CFL is playing fine ball and is on the way up. And Indianapolis is a good area. The crowd at the Pacer basketball game Sunday indicates that."

It didn't happen, of course. The Bills improved their offer, Simpson entered the NFL and moved on to a career of fame, fortune and infamy.

The Pacers led the Eastern Division by 1½ games after defeating Minnesota. They flew out the next morning for Los Angeles, where they were to play the Stars on consecutive days and then Oakland on the third day. Then, they would have a six-day break before ending the season at Kentucky. It was nearly a repeat of the previous season, when they had a seven-day break before finishing the season at Kentucky, the gap that swallowed Harding.

Leonard wanted to wrap up the division title before the game at Kentucky. That would require his players to maintain their momentum against the Stars, a weak but well-coached team that had allowed them 172 points on Feb. 1 and was on the brink of elimination from the playoff race with a 32-39 record. So, he threw out a challenge in the newspaper.

"There might even be some fisticuffs," Leonard told Denny. "I'll be damned if I'm going to let (Sharman) fire up his club and beat us out of it. There's too much at stake."

Without fisticuffs, the Pacers dominated the Stars, 140-124. L.A. played hard and well, hitting 57 percent of its field goal attempts and committing just 13 turnovers, but the Pacers had more weapons – mainly Brown, who finished with 45 points (20 in the fourth quarter), 11 rebounds and 10 assists. Denny wrote that he was "literally a man with a million moves" in the second half.

The Pacers beat the Stars again the following night, 134-123. Netolicky, revived and relieved over his return to the starting lineup, led with not 40 points as Leonard had predicted for him, but 31 — on 14-of-19 shooting — and 15 rebounds. He gave exactly what Leonard wanted to see from his unpredictable forward heading into the playoffs: hustle and humility.

"Yes, what Leonard did helped me," Netolicky confessed to Denny. "I sat back and took a look at myself. I wasn't putting out and I was pacing myself too much, maybe. I realize now what I had to do. I'm pushing myself harder and I'm rebounding better. I'm also taking better care of myself. I'm peaking in my condition."

Daniels added 29 points while hitting 14-of-20 shots and grabbed 21 rebounds. Brown followed the previous night's triple-double with 24 points and 10 assists, but only five rebounds before fouling out.

The Pacers' winning streak was at 13 games, but there were some qualifications.[4] Ten of the victories had come over losing teams. Nine had come at home, where the fans were in full roar. Five had come over hapless New York, which was coasting to the finish line, a broken team. Two had come over a good team, Minnesota, that was depleted by injuries

---

4 Fifty seasons later, it would still stand as the longest win streak in franchise history. Second-longest was a 12-game streak in the 1993-94 season that included the first four playoff games.

and a travel mishap. Then again, nine of the wins were by double-figure margins, six by 19 points or more and three by more than 30.

The Pacers then headed up the coast to Oakland. They had lost five consecutive games to the Oaks, beginning with the season-opener when Staverman was their coach, so one of the streaks was going to end. It turned out to be the wrong one for the Pacers, as the Oaks took a 122-110 victory before all of 1,904 fans. The Pacers had champagne on ice in the locker room to celebrate an Eastern Division title in case they won, but were outmatched throughout the game – the result of fatigue from playing their third game in three nights, the anticipation of clinching the title or the fact they were playing a better team.

"We're lucky we didn't get beat any worse than 12 points," Leonard said.

They drank the champagne anyway. No point letting good alcohol go to waste.

The game was a typically rugged ABA game, supporting the gist of a column written just a few days earlier by Jim Murray of the *Los Angeles Times*.

"In the ABA, basketball is not so much a game as a dock fight with backboards," Murray wrote. "They recruit their teams in Central Park after dark. If they did on a street corner what they do under the basket, someone would call the cops."

In this one, Peeples blasted Larry Brown on a screen in the first quarter, knocking him out of the game with a badly bruised shoulder, then teammates Logan and Bradds collided in the second, sending Logan to the hospital with a possible concussion. There wasn't a fight, though, a victory in itself. Armstrong, the 6-3 forward on his way to succeeding Daniels as the league's Rookie of the Year, was about all the Oaks needed amid his team's depleted roster. He finished with 26 points, 19 rebounds and six assists.

Leonard wasn't discouraged. His team had won two-of-three on the road trip, and still had a chance to win the division title. And more.

"We can win this whole thing with another 13-game winning streak," he said.

The Pacers clinched their division title three nights later back in Indianapolis while resting and preparing for their final game, as Oakland did them the favor of beating Kentucky, 119-112. That rendered their final regular season game in Louisville meaningless. Leonard approached it with his usual sideline intensity, but his team shot poorly and lost again, 132-127, despite the loud presence of 1,027 Pacers fans who made the trip from Indianapolis in eight busloads. Daniels led the scoring with 32 points but contributed 14 points to the Colonels' offense by committing seven goaltending violations.

"He got one of those psychological things and kept going after all of them," Leonard explained.

The Pacers finished the season 44-34, one game ahead of Miami and two games ahead of the Colonels for the Eastern Division title. The title already in hand, they knew they would have something to celebrate after this game, so they packed champagne again, doused one another in the locker room and threw Leonard, new suit and all, into the shower.[5]

The team that had started the season 1-7, weathered a coaching change, bottomed out at 5-15 and made a couple of bold personnel moves, had come a long way from getting booed on its home court.

For Chubin, life couldn't have been more different than what his former Pacer teammates were experiencing. Something had happened the night of his first return to the Coliseum, when Perry went off and the Pacers dominated the Nets.

He didn't play the next night in Los Angeles, when the Nets ended their 10-game losing streak with a 120-110 victory. He got in at the end of the game the following night in Oakland, scoring one point in a loss. He played seven minutes and went scoreless against the Pacers two nights

---

[5]   The Pacers offered a bus trip for fans to the game in Louisville. The $10 package included a $3 seat, round-trip transportation and a box lunch. It proved to be a smashing success, as 1,027 fans purchased the package. One left-out fan ran a classified ad in the *Star*, hoping to buy a ticket from someone looking to back out. Eight buses carried the group to the game, half of whom spent the better part of the evening blowing long plastic horns.

later back in New York, and then was scoreless again in a brief appearance the next game.

Overpeck reported in the *Star* he had been suspended, but gave no reason. Apparently, Chubin had vented his frustration toward Zaslofsky in the locker room after his emotional return to the Coliseum. "He said some things in the dressing room (in Indianapolis) that pissed Max off," Hoover remembered years later.

Chubin's comments to Denny, about it being "not the same playing for New York" and "not any fun with no chance of making the playoffs" couldn't have helped, if they got back to Zaslofsky.

Zaslofsky was a New York native who had starred at St. John's for one season before turning pro, and had played in the NBA for the New York Knicks and other teams. When he retired in 1956, he was the league's third all-time leading scorer. He had no coaching experience before taking over the ABA's New York team in 1967, though. Hired for his name recognition by a franchise desperately trying to compete for attention with the Knicks, he was not taken seriously as a coach by most of his players – Chubin included. Fainting in the locker room after the loss in Denver earlier in the season hadn't exactly enhanced his reputation among the players.

Chubin gradually regained his playing time, scoring 22 points at Oakland in a game in which the Nets' burst dam of a defense gave up 169 points, and then 21 at Houston as they gave up 149 to the Western Division's last-place team. They finished the season with a 14-game losing streak and a 17-61 record.

He could only sit back and wonder what it must be like to be part of the surging Pacers team that had discarded him. But his chance would come again.

# 14

*"We found out what Slick has been preaching about all season.
We found out what playing as a team really means."*

Turning Point

The Pacers called an afternoon press conference on Saturday, April 5 for
a major announcement that surprised practically nobody: Daniels had
been voted the ABA's Most Valuable Player by the United States
Basketball Writers Association.

The player who had been practically stolen from the desperate
Muskies had come a long way since his Rookie of the Year season.
Leonard had helped transform him into a legitimate center, starting
with that first practice at Brebeuf when he supposedly threatened to
punch him in the nose if he kept taking jump shots and drew a boundary
line to mark his territory for him.

Daniels still took mid-range shots now and then, but operating closer
to the basket proved beneficial. He had little choice, given the fact he
was playing center instead of forward, but refined the turnaround jump
shot over his right shoulder and drove to the basket more frequently. As
a result, he raised his field goal accuracy from 41 percent as a rookie to
48 while averaging 24 points and a league-best 16.5 rebounds. Hawkins,
the previous season's MVP, averaged 30.2 points on 51 percent shooting
and 11.2 rebounds, but missed 31 games with knee injuries.

Hawkins was regarded as a good teammate, but Daniels went beyond
that. He had established himself as the team's inspirational leader, by word
and deed, helping instill a far greater degree of physical toughness without
sacrificing his humanity. According to Denny's story in the *News*, he had
suffered "three broken noses, a dislocated toe, two bouts with the flu and
hundreds of bruises" while playing in 76 of the 78 games. His physical

presence was that much more impressive considering his relatively slight frame. He was listed at 6-foot-9 and 220 pounds, and his appropriate nickname among his teammates was "Slim." His legs were so skinny that in later years the trainer would wrap them in white gauze to fill them out.

All things considered, he could be forgiven a couple of missed flights.

His ingrained respect for authority also helped establish a culture. Daniels was accustomed to bold, tough-minded coaches, so he had less trouble adapting to Leonard than most of his teammates. That helped quell rebellion and maintain a cohesive unit. He was the perfect liaison between Leonard and the rest of the team. Leonard's style was to develop his team to the point it was a self-policing organization, and Daniels was at the head of that flow chart.

Not that he was always a company man. He wasn't afraid to speak his mind, even at the press conference announcing his award when asked his thoughts on pro basketball. "I love it, but not the tactics," he said. "The players are nothing more than cattle to be traded to get money. I guess that's part of life, but I never will get used to it."

Clearly, the trade that had sent him to the Pacers still stung.

Brown had nearly been traded as well, although unlike Daniels the previous year, his close call was performance-related. The effort to trade him and the embarrassment of being left behind on a two-game road trip helped serve as a wake-up call. He averaged 27 points over the season's final 33 games, and 21 points, 6.8 rebounds and 4.5 assists for the season. Lewis, whom Leonard made captain shortly after taking over the team, averaged 20.4 points and established himself as the undisputed quarterback. Netolicky, object of coach-swinging hockey sticks and mud-slinging fans, averaged 18.9 points on 51 percent shooting and 10.2 rebounds. Perry, booed for not being Chubin, came through with 36 percent three-point shooting and a 13.5-point average.

They had won 13 consecutive games before losing the last two, the last of which was meaningless in the standings. They had captured the Eastern Division championship, as Leonard had predicted almost as soon as he took over. A league championship seemed a realistic goal despite Oakland's dominance during the regular season, if for no reason other than the belief Leonard had instilled.

As the playoffs approached, the issue of the Coliseum's availability lingered in the background. It was booked early in April for the annual appearances of both the Boat, Sport and Travel Show and the Shrine Circus, limiting the number of dates available to the Pacers. Hinkle Fieldhouse on the Butler campus was the obvious Plan B. It was the only facility within the city limits large enough to satisfy public demand, and had been provided (reluctantly) for the All-Star game the previous season.

The Pacers' brain trust asked politely, but was turned down quickly and brusquely. It then resorted to applying pressure through the media. Overpeck, with backing from Collins, who remained a de-facto member of the Pacers' front office – an unpaid advisor, basically – brought the issue to the public's attention with a column in the March 2 *Star*, in which he suggested Hinkle as an alternative site for home playoff games when the Coliseum was not available. He mentioned the fact many non-university events had been conducted there over the years, particularly the high school tournaments that rented the facility at a "dirt cheap" rate.

"So why are the pros left out?" Overpeck asked. "You tell me."

The next-best local alternative appeared to be Indiana Central's gymnasium, which held only 4,500 fans – an undesirable choice, obviously. So Storen, Chuck DeVoe and Dick Tinkham conducted a press conference on March 6 to apply more heat to Butler's stubborn university officials. They hinted that the ABA home office might force them to play all their playoff games on the road rather than allow them to play in a small college gym. They said they had already met with Butler's Board Chairman Harry T. Ice and Mayor Lugar on the issue, but wanted a full hearing with Butler's Board of Trustees.

Butler officials, Storen said, had stated NCAA rules prohibited the use of college facilities for professional teams. He claimed it was a recommendation, not a rule, and indeed the NCAA's latest guidelines, passed in January, had left open the possibility of "a professional team's isolated use of college facilities in emergency cases." The Pacers considered this to be an emergency. Ice did not, because Indiana Central was available on those dates the Coliseum was not.

Fans put their appeal to Butler University in writing, hoping to convince them to make Hinkle Fieldhouse available to the Pacers for playoff games.

Fuson speculated in his column in the *News* that some Butler officials were jealous of the media attention and crowds the Pacers were generating, sometimes at the university's expense. Ice denied that. The university's board was outnumbered, though, by fans who got into the act by writing letters and making phone calls to Butler officials and bringing signs to Pacers games at the Coliseum. Two of them, Larry Moon and Charles Bryant, painted a bed sheet to read "BUTLER HAVE A HEART OUR PACERS NEED HINKLE."

Even Butler's student newspaper, *The Collegian*, supported the Pacers' cause. Sports editor Allen Smith wrote, "Butler University was founded on Christian principles and beliefs. One of the basic mores of Christianity is humanitarianism, but when it comes to the case of the Indiana Pacers pro basketball team, Butler turns stone cold.

"Where is the Christian ethic? It seems Butler is more than a little hypocritical in its actions."

A columnist for the *News*, Fremont Power, joined in the media onslaught. He pointed out that Butler's arts center, Clowes Hall, was often used by professional entertainers, and that the Cincinnati Bengals of the AFL had used the University of Cincinnati's stadium. "What we have here is the difference between bush league and big league," Power concluded.

On the same day Power's column ran, Chuck DeVoe read an article in the *Saturday Evening Post* that detailed some of the problems with the Coliseum. Relating life on the road for the comedy team of Rowan and Martin, it mentioned the discomfort of their appearance in the Fairgrounds Coliseum. Their dressing room was a "stark, barren little cubicle that also served as the apartment for the building custodian," and the building's humidity and odor of cow manure was pervasive.

"The worst thing," Dick Martin told the article's author, "is that we have to come back and do the second show."

Overpeck listed four concerns of Butler officials: (1) The Olympians scandal, (2) unspecified issues involving Olympians players and Butler female students, (3) concerns that Pacers games would bring undesirable fans to the campus, and (4) renting to the Pacers would lead to requests from other sports promoters, such as for roller derby.

Overpeck tried to shoot down each of those arguments in a column on March 16, and stressed that Butler had an obligation to serve the community that supported so many of its campus events.

The consistent pressure applied by the newspapers eventually touched nerves. Robert Early, the *Star's* managing editor, angrily called the sports department one night and said, "I want to talk to that damn Overmeyer!" He had friends on Butler's Board of Trustees, and ordered the staff to back off.

Butler's final and absolute response – a resounding no – came on March 26. Collins wrote a story detailing part of Ice's statement that ran for 17 paragraphs. It referred to the Pacers' effort to secure use of the fieldhouse as "a pressure campaign," and claimed "abusive, profane and obscene calls have been made to the secretaries and female members of the families of the president and chairman by some men who purported to be Pacer fans."

Ice reiterated his stance that the university was merely following the guidelines of the NCAA, and that there were sufficient open dates at the Coliseum or Indiana Central to conduct playoff games. His statement ran: "The Pacers have a fine team and many fine, loyal fans. It is regretted that tactics of the Pacers' management have left no alternative except to make this statement. The use of the university property will be determined by the proper authorities in light of the facts, past experience and reason, and not by clamor. The question has been so resolved."

Yes, it had. But one lingering element of all the fallout gave hope to Pacers management and their fans, if they happened to notice one of Ice's comments amid Fuson's column:

"Someday, pro sports will thank us for not letting them use our facilities, because this will force the city fathers into action on a civic auditorium and professional sports center."

Clearly, the Coliseum was increasingly inadequate for a growing professional basketball franchise. It had not been improved in any substantial way since the first season. For a fee of $800 on weeknights and $1,000 on weekends, the Pacers still had to hire their own personnel to staff the game, including parking attendants and ushers, and they got none of the revenue from parking or concessions. Their only source of income beyond ticket sales was the profit from the T-shirts and souvenirs they sold at the games.

The visiting locker room remained decrepit, with its one shower head (or perhaps two or three) and inconvenient location on the second level and the Pacers' quarters weren't much better, with the concrete floor and ancient metal lockers. The building was poorly maintained, too. Nobody bothered to clean it out between the back-to-back home games against New Orleans and Minnesota on Jan. 3 and 4, leaving a mess for the fans who showed up the second night.

Storen had an ongoing feud with the Fair Board, and had fired off numerous letters expressing his disgust. One of them was written after the Oct. 3 exhibition game with Oakland. He listed 10 points of contention. They included the front doors not being staffed at the time the Pacers wanted them opened; new chairs not being used as agreed upon, and the chairs that were used being "totally incorrect" in their setup; no advertising billboards; no information on the date of the opening night game; courtside seats and baskets not being set up until 7 p.m.; tables not set up at the end of the court as requested; and a typewriter being stolen.

"In closing, I can only say that I am once again reiterating a request for the same things which we have been asking for for one year and a half," he wrote.

The Fair Board also hadn't authorized painting a Pacers logo on the court's center circle, so a radio host new to town, Gary Todd of WIBC, took up the cause. He led a movement on the air to rally community support, and then convinced station management to pay the cost of hiring someone to do the job.

"We just ended up doing it," Todd said years later. "The Fairgrounds wasn't going to do it."

The logo was painted inside the jump circle, framed by "Pacers" above and "Eastern Division Champions" below. It was unveiled shortly before tipoff for Game 1 of the playoff series with Kentucky, but, just like the three-point lines the previous season, it wasn't done properly.

"I'm not sure what paint they used to paint it, but when the players started to sweat it started to fade," Todd said. "I'm sitting there scared to death the whole thing was going to go away. After that it was painted again and (didn't fade)."

The league office aided the Pacers' cause by delaying the start of the first-round series with Kentucky so the Coliseum would be available. The series opened on April 8, six days after the Pacers had completed their regular season in Louisville, and five days after the Colonels finished their season against Minnesota.[1]

Game 1 at the Coliseum, on a Tuesday, drew a disappointing crowd of 6,319. The result was a letdown, too, a 128-118 loss. The fact the Pacers had played just one game over the previous 12 days was likely a factor. So were Carrier's 40 points for the Colonels. The Pacers placed most of the blame on the officiating, however, after being outscored 40-

---

[1] That game had been a classic only-in-the-ABA kind of experience. The Colonels and Pipers needed to make up a game that had been snowed out in Minneapolis earlier in the season, but it couldn't be played there because of a conflict with the arena. So, the two teams met in Louisville in what was technically a home game for the Pipers. The Colonels were paid the standard 15 percent visiting team's share of the gate, and therefore had no reason to care if anyone came. Not many did – just 873 – but they won, 109-101. The franchise probably grossed no more than $400 for its trouble, but the Pipers probably didn't cover their travel expenses with their larger share.

The Coliseum court received a newly-painted center circle for the playoffs, thanks to the dedication of local radio host Gary Todd of WIBC.

18 at the foul line – specifically Sid Borgia, who happened to be the working director of league officials.

The Pacers, who opened the game in a fullcourt press, were called for five fouls in the first two minutes. Perry, who had scored 27 points in the final regular season game for a needed confidence boost, picked up two of the early fouls, was thrown out of sync and hit just 2-of-13 shots. Brown and Netolicky eventually fouled out, although Brown still scored 38 points while hitting 17-of-26 field goal attempts, grabbed 12 rebounds and unofficially blocked about six shots, according to Denny's story in the *News*.

The mood was ugly in the locker room afterward. One player, not wanting to risk the league's mandatory $500 fine for publicly criticizing the officials, offered an anonymous and detailed summary of what he considered Borgia's biggest mistakes, and concluded with this summary to Overpeck in the *Star*: "I'll tell you what I think of Borgia. He's a senile old (expletive) who shouldn't be out there. And you can print that!"

Brown said the officials "cost us the game," and Daniels agreed.

"The officiating stunk," Daniels said. "If Borgia wants to showboat, that's fine. But don't do it at our expense. We're playing for a lot of money. The officials haven't given us a break all season. All I ask is for a halfway decent break and we'll do the rest.

"We're not going to lose the second one," he added. "They might as well go back to Kentucky right now."

The two teams met again the following night. Denny, writing both a cover of Game 1 and advance of Game 2 in his story, chose a fight analogy, stating the Pacers were "decked with a hard right to the chin thrown by the Kentucky Colonels," in his lead paragraph, then adding "they vow they'll get off the canvas and land a haymaker on the Colonels tonight." The story's headline reflected the theme: "Pacers Must Land 'Haymaker' Tonight."

It was ominous.

The Pacers won Game 2, 120-115, and the haymakers were literal. A fight broke out in the fourth quarter that was the worst (yet) seen at the Coliseum, equaling the widespread nature of the one in Oakland during the regular season. Conard, writing in the *Kokomo Tribune*, reported it to be "the greatest melee since the Japs sneaked into the Harbor in '41."

It started with 4:17 left in the game, when Kentucky's backup center, Jim Caldwell, threw an elbow into Daniels' back on a drive to the basket. Daniels, claiming later to be fed up with Caldwell's season-long physical play, responded with a hard elbow, and they squared off. The no-longer-soft Peeples then ran off the bench and hit Caldwell in the back of the head, setting off a bench-clearing brawl that spread into the stands and involved fans in the south stands. Referee Ed Middleton took a hard punch from one of the players during the commotion, which required "all of 10 minutes" to control, according to Conard.

Once order was restored, Caldwell and Peeples were charged with technical fouls but not ejected. Daniels escaped without punishment, although both the *Star* and the *News* the next day ran photographs of him exchanging punches with Caldwell as they fought near the baseline, where some lucky photographers had ringside seats. Caldwell also was given a personal foul.

The Pacers held on despite Kentucky scoring 39 points in the fourth quarter on 71 percent shooting. Lewis, who scored 28 points, hit four crucial free throws in the final 49 seconds as the Colonels fouled to stop the clock.

Brown followed his 38-point Game 1 effort with 35 more, and 11 rebounds. Afterward, he declared a personal victory.

"(Bobby) Rascoe is a good defensive man, but I've got his number now," Brown said. "Yeah, and we're playing for the big stuff (money) now, too."

Netolicky had 24 points and 12 rebounds. Daniels was ineffective following the brawl but had 20 points and nine rebounds.

Leonard contributed a couple of strategic ploys. Perry's early foul trouble led him to move Brown to the backcourt to defend Carrier and moved Peeples into the starting frontline. He then started Hooper in the second half on Dampier and moved Lewis over to defend Carrier. Although Dampier finished with 31 points, 20 in the second half, the move was deemed successful because of how hard he had to work and how well he had to play to do it.

"Tonight, the guys really stuck together," said Hooper, who reinjured the left hand he had broken during the season in the brawl. "Maybe the fight was what we needed."

Added Peeples: "This is what it's going to take to win ... I wanted to win so bad I had to help Slim. They don't like us and we don't like them."

Daniels was still furious after the game – at the Pacers' fans. Some of them had thrown objects onto the court in the first game, and the fourth-quarter ruckus inspired a rainshower of trash from the stands, some of which hit him.

"It's awful," Daniels told Denny. "And they're hitting their own players. I got hit in the eye with a penny. Supposing I had got hit with something that had a sharp point. I could have been blinded."

He wasn't, but he did suffer a sprained pinky finger and sprained ankle in the fight – the right ankle according to the *News* and the left ankle according to the *Courier-Journal*.

Colonels' business owner Charlie Mastin, meanwhile, filed a protest with the league office over inadequate security. Only one police officer was assigned to Kentucky's bench, and Storen refused to provide more after fans began pelting them with litter. "You can't argue with Mastin," Overpeck wrote a few days later in his Sunday column. "Through the concerted effort of a minority, Indianapolis fans have earned the dubious honor of being the worst-behaved in the league. And considering the conduct in such cities as Dallas, Denver – and Louisville – this took some doing."

Mastin's protest went nowhere. If nothing else, there wasn't time for the skeletal league office to review and react. The two teams were back at it the following night in Louisville, their third playoff game in three nights.

Kentucky dominated in Game 3, 130-111. No fights broke out, although the *Courier-Journal* ran a photo of Carrier sprawled on his back after taking a hard elbow in the stomach from Brown. He still scored a game-high 34 points, while Dampier added 26. Darden, cut by the Pacers in preseason and then traded from New York to the Colonels late in the season, added 18 points off the bench.

Daniels was just 75 percent of full strength because of the injuries suffered in the fight, according to Leonard, but still led the Pacers with 23 points and 12 rebounds. He had been outplayed by Kentucky's rookie center, Gene Moore, in the first two games, but, responding to taunts from Colonels fans, came to life in the second half despite the injury.

The teams got a two-day break before Game 4, in which the Colonels put the Pacers on the brink of elimination with a 105-104 overtime victory. Carrier drew a foul from Perry and hit two foul shots with 10 seconds left to give Kentucky a 105-104 lead, then Dee missed a jumper and Daniels' rebound putback was blocked by Ligon just before the final buzzer. Brown was called for three fouls in the first four minutes and had to sit out the rest of the half, and therefore was limited to 19 points – by lack of playing time, not defense. Daniels hit just 1-of-13 shots in the second half, although Overpeck's game story claimed he was fouled on many of them.

Regardless, Kentucky had just delivered the Pacers a crushing defeat, taking a 3-1 series lead. It had won nine of the 13 games between the two teams over the course of the season, so it had every reason to be confident about closing out the series – either back in Indianapolis the next night, or in Louisville the following night.

In the jubilant locker room following the Game 4 victory, Colonels rookie Wayne Chapman told his coach, Gene Rhodes, to take two suits to the Coliseum for the next one, because one of them was sure to get wet when he was thrown in the shower during their postgame victory celebration.

"We've got everything going for us," Chapman told the *Courier-Journal*. "We'll end it up there."

Rhodes didn't feed into his rookie's naïve assumption. He acknowledged in the newspaper the Pacers were capable of winning three in a row. It was never reported whether he took an extra suit to Indianapolis for Game 5. Years later, he couldn't remember if he had or not.

The Pacers, meanwhile, were in a desperate situation, just one loss from soiling the glistening finish to their regular season with a first-round playoff elimination. Such a desperate time might have called for a desperate measure. Some players, including Lewis, Netolicky and Peeples, remembered Leonard and Storen promised each of the players a $1,500 bonus if they came back and won the series, although Storen denied it in later years.

It would require three consecutive victories against a team that had dominated it to that point of the season.

The headline in the *News* summed it up: "38th Street Miracle Is Pacer Need."

The Pacers won Game 5, 116-97. They led by just two points after three quarters, but outscored Kentucky 36-19 in the fourth. Leonard made another lineup change by starting Thacker alongside Lewis in the backcourt, and the veteran defensive specialist limited Carrier to 4-of-18 shooting. Carrier still got to the foul line enough to score 21 points, but he and Dampier struggled to come up with 34 points between them as they combined to hit just 2-of-14 three-point shots.

The frontline took care of the other details. Netolicky hit seven consecutive shots on his way to 15 first-quarter points and finished with 35 on 15-of-24 shooting. Brown had 34, including 16 from the foul line. Daniels hit just 2-of-18 shots, but grabbed 24 rebounds – nine in the fourth quarter when Kentucky hit just 2-of-19 shots. He

*Bob Netolicky stuffs two points through the rim in the Game 5 victory over Kentucky –
the first stride in a long climb back.*

also managed to avoid getting into a fight, although he and Rascoe squared off and nearly came to blows midway through the third quarter. Brown said afterward he took motivation from comments in the newspapers, perhaps referring to Chapman's comments in the *Courier-Journal*.

"They talk too much," Brown said of the Colonels. "I like to make them eat their words."

Daniels had acknowledged the Pacers were too uptight earlier in the series, but one victory had changed that.

"They're a tired ball club," he said of the Colonels. "Neither team was fresh. The teams would play for the third consecutive night in Game 6, but Daniels didn't think it would affect the Pacers as much as Kentucky because of the demanding practices they had endured throughout the season.

"The man runs you," he said.

The man, Leonard, offered a prediction: "If we win No. 6, they will not beat us in the seventh game," he declared.

The Pacers won Game 6, 107-89. Thacker smothered Carrier again, limiting him to 11 points on 3-of-12 shooting. He also wound up with a golf ball-sized knot on his forehead after taking a hard hit on a drive to the basket. The all-stars, meanwhile, came out in force. Brown (25), Lewis (22) and Daniels (20) led the scoring, and Netolicky grabbed a team-high 15 rebounds. Dampier scored 27 for Kentucky, but committed seven turnovers. The Pacers also got spirited contributions from Peeples, Hooper, Perry and Dee off the bench, as well as on it. The camaraderie was in full bloom now, extending all the way to the last reserves. Perry and Dee sat together on the bench and cheered their teammates, and even managed to collect some of the coins thrown at the Pacers by the Kentucky fans.

"I can truly say I enjoyed sitting on the bench tonight," Perry told Denny, "Don Dee is a humorist and I made six cents. I missed the quarter someone threw from the crowd.

"I felt like I was really part of the team. I've never cheered more in my life. Don and I were calling the shots and fouls and I don't think I missed more than one."

Like the Pacers' fans earlier in the series, Kentucky's fans lodged their complaints with the officiating by lofting cups, coins and ice onto the court – "enough junk to make Freedom Hall look like the municipal dump," according to Overpeck.

Daniels, like Brown after the previous game, claimed to have drawn motivation from published quotes – this time attributed to Rhodes. "He really got us oiled up with things he said in the paper," Daniels told Denny. "He said Bobby (Netolicky) was lucky against Jim Ligon Monday night and that Rascoe could do a job on Roger Brown. That really got us fired up."

Neither of the Indianapolis papers or the *Courier-Journal* included any such quotes from Rhodes. They came instead via Thacker, the 27-year-old elder statesman who, decades later, confessed to partaking in such psychological ploys. From his experience in the NBA, he had learned the value of dropping casual but inciteful comments to teammates, like a kid trying to start trouble on the playground. *You should have heard what he said about you!*

While playing in Cincinnati, he and his Royals teammates had done it to arouse the unemotional Robertson on occasion. *This guy said he's going to kick your ass!* He also had seen it during his one season with the Celtics, John Havlicek firing up the professorial Tom Sanders with supposed comments from opposing players when energy lagged during the season.

"Some guys don't play until they get mad," Thacker said years later.

Thacker's season with the Celtics in a championship season taught him that joining a team with a winning culture elevated a player's performance. "It makes you believe you're the best," he said. "You automatically elevate your game because of the whole psyche." The Pacers team he joined in mid-season was beginning to win, but still lacked confidence and professionalism. Some of the players, he believed, cared more about fun than winning, because they had never been part of a championship program. Of the 18 Pacers who dressed for a game that season, Harkness was the only other one who had won a collegiate national championship or professional title, and he was long gone. The rest of them just didn't know any better.

Mel Daniels tries to block Kokomo native Jim Ligon's hook shot in the Game 5 victory over Kentucky. Ligon scored 17 points in the Pacers' victory.

Thacker did, from winning titles in the NCAA tournament, the semi-pro league in Michigan and the NBA. He knew that winning was a habit that could be formed if the talent was right. He also knew the pleasure of receiving bonus money from advancing in the playoffs.

"Once you get that spirit of winning, you want to always win," he recalled. "Once you know how, it's easy to win. You put all that knowledge and experience into winning. I was on a serious mission to make some (playoff) money."

If it took messing with his teammates' heads to get that money, he was willing and able. Brown, Daniels and Netolicky were his primary targets. Brown was laid-back by nature and sometimes needed a jolt. Daniels was virtually the opposite and sometimes needed to be calmed, but his emotional nature made him an easy target for gimmickry when Thacker thought it necessary. And this was one of those times.

"I got in the locker room and told Mel how those guys were talking about him," Thacker recalled. "I exaggerated a little bit."

Thacker sometimes worked on boosting confidence, too. He balanced Leonard's occasional verbal harangues of Netolicky with ego-boosting praise. "You really had to pump Neto up," he said. "You had to tell him how good he was. I'd say, 'You've got the best hook shot in the world, man. They must have taught you something at Drake. You had to be the best player in the Missouri Valley Conference.'"

He told Brown he was the best small forward in either league. It wasn't much of an exaggeration, if at all, but Brown surely loved hearing it from an older player who had the credibility of Thacker. Brown, Thacker said, was "slow, but quick," a player who could lull defenders to sleep with his pauses and graceful movements and then strike like a snake with a quick burst to the basket. "He had his own rhythm," Thacker said. "Every move was calculated."

Just like Thacker's words.

Nearly lost amid the excitement on the afternoon of Game 6 was the league draft that had been conducted in Charlotte – future home of the Houston Mavericks. As in the first two drafts, the round-by-round

Mike Storen shares a lighter moment with draft picks Bill DeHeer of Indiana and Billy Keller of Purdue.

selections after the first round were not announced, "so that no boy knows if he is second, third or fifth," Storen said.

Storen claimed the priority of finding a tall guard, and took Drake's Willie McCarter, a 6-3 guard out of Gary, Ind., with the Pacers' first pick. Later selections included two 6-4 guards, Dick Grubar from North Carolina and Tony Masiello from Canisius. Storen also traded a pick for Notre Dame's Bob Arnzen, a 6-5 forward who had been drafted by the Nets. Almost as an afterthought, Storen settled on taking one short guard: 5-10 Billy Keller, a member of the Purdue team that had reached the final game of the NCAA tournament and was voted the inaugural winner of the Francis Pomeroy Naismith Award for the nation's best player under 6-foot tall. He later was listed as a seventh- or eighth-round pick.

Collins took credit for it in later years, claiming he called Storen and said, "Did you know you're going to draft Billy Keller?" When Storen offered an objection, Collins gave him the reasons to do it. Keller was a winning player, a better shooter than people realized, and was hugely popular in Indianapolis.

If true, Storen knew what to say after the draft.

Fans line up at the Pacers' 38ᵗʰ St. office for tickets for Game 7 of the first-round series with Kentucky. They would get their money's worth.

"We like Keller," he said. "He has tremendous desire. I put him in a class with our Bob Hooper for ability and desire."[2]

The Pacers' Game 6 victory set up what would be by far the biggest game in the franchise's brief history. With one day off to prepare, the

---

[2] The Pacers had no more success signing McCarter than they had Walker the previous year. Harkness, who moonlighted as a scout to fulfill his contract, scouted him and tried to wine and dine him after games, but learned Chamberlain was doing the same thing in Los Angeles for the Lakers, who made him their first-round draft pick. McCarter, who was voted the MVP of Senior All-American game after the draft, wound up playing in 155 NBA games over three seasons and averaged seven points.

Pacers held a light workout. The *Star* sent a photographer to snap some posed pictures. One showed Brown and Lewis standing next to a crouched Leonard, having a "strategy conference" according to the caption. Another showed Daniels defending Netolicky's running hook shot. They were the kind of orchestrated, trivial photos normally taken on Media Day before the season began, and in a way the Pacers were beginning a new season. A new era, perhaps.

"I just want one helluva effort from everybody," Leonard told Overpeck in the accompanying story. "And I'll get it."

Tickets for the Thursday night game went on sale at 10 a.m. Wednesday. A line snaked from the front door of the team's office on 38th St. around the side of the building and into the parking lot. The city clearly had fallen for the team now, hooked on the fumes of talent, effort and emotion wafting from its games. If it was possible to designate the day on which the franchise and its fan base truly melded, this was it.

Tom Thacker hounds Kentucky guard Darel Carrier, providing the defense that was a major factor in the Game 7 victory.

The largest crowd in franchise history, 11,005, jammed into the Coliseum for the ultimate game of the series, the seventh game in 10 days. Nearly 2,000 of them stood for the privilege of attending. The game had sold out by 3 p.m. that afternoon, and scalpers reportedly were getting $25 for the premium $5 tickets. No need to paper this house. Fans gave the team a standing ovation during pregame introductions that lasted at least a minute, according to the newspaper reports, and "cheered throughout the contest like you've never seen a crowd cheer."

The cheering continued to the final buzzer and beyond, and the echoes reverberated for weeks. During the final minute, the outcome assured, the Pacers' players on the bench stood and cheered, hopping up and down and hugging one another in joyful anticipation. And when it was finally over, the 120-111 victory completing the improbable comeback from the 3-1 deficit, some of the fans ran onto the court and celebrated with the players as if they had won the championship. A few of them helped carry Leonard off the court.

Netolicky was part of that scrum, and never forgot the bedlam.

"I was so tired I could barely get to the locker room," he recalled. "We were trying to carry Slick, and everybody was beating me. They almost killed me."

Leonard hadn't taken any chances in the game. He used his bench sparingly, leaving the starters on the court as long as possible. Peeples was the only reserve to score, hitting six foul shots.

Netolicky, cited by Overpeck as "often booed for lackadaisical play," played his most meaningful game as a Pacer, leading all scorers with 32 points and all rebounders with 16 despite feeling ill most of the day. Brown added 29 points, equaling his average for the series.

The most crucial contribution, however, came from Thacker. He not only stifled Carrier, who hit just 5-of-18 shots on his way to 16 points, nine below his average for the first six games, he also scored a professional career-high 19 points, two more than his best with the Celtics.

For Thacker, the game was an excused absence from National Guard duty at Fort Knox in Kentucky. He had missed some meetings the previous season while the Celtics were in Los Angeles facing the Lakers in the NBA Finals, and had to make them up now. He had barely slept the previous night — 90 minutes according to the story that ran in the *Star*, and an hour according to the *News*. "There were 40 guys in the barracks, all snoring," he told Overpeck. He had been awakened for breakfast at 5:30 a.m. on Thursday, drove his 1968 Corvette convertible to Indianapolis, arrived at 3:30 p.m., and played that night.[3]

Thacker was a standout defender because he never backed off from the man he was guarding, and always tried to make him go away from his strong hand. He also used his left hand well enough to block the shots of right-handed shooters. One year earlier, with Boston, he had blocked one of Jerry West's shots in the NBA Finals. That Celtics team

---

[3] All in all, Thacker's military obligation was a breeze. He had been able to watch the Colonels training camp at Ft. Knox the previous fall, before he knew he would become a Pacer, and he played a lot of basketball, as well as flag football and baseball. A friend made a cast to put on his arm to get him out of washing dishes, which he took off to play at night with officers. He'd have it back on for roll call the next morning. "I literally did nothing when I was in the Army," he said.

The buzzer sounds, and the Pacers begin celebrating their Game 7 victory over Kentucky, a landmark moment in franchise history.

Bob Netolicky and fans carry Bob Leonard off the court amid the bedlam of the series-clinching victory over the Colonels.

overcame a 3-1 deficit to beat Philadelphia in the second round of the playoffs, so this game didn't intimidate him in the least.

He got into Carrier's head by blocking his shot early in the game. "He didn't know I was too tired to block another," Thacker said after the game. The fatigue also might have helped Thacker offensively. Having hit just 34 percent of his field goal attempts in his 18 regular season games with the Pacers, he was relaxed enough to hit 7-of-14 shots.

The Pacers had another advantage, one invisible to the fans. They were coming together, their chemistry with one another and their coach improving every week, while the Colonels were fractured. Rhodes' coaching experience before he was hired by the Colonels consisted of a high school job in Kentucky and an assistant's position with Western Kentucky University. His style reflected that. He was a screamer who sometimes berated his players, conducted long, harsh practices and maintained early curfews on the road. He probably could have gotten away with his approach, even thrived on it, if he had Leonard's ability to connect with his players and bring them together, but apparently did not. Kentucky's players, with Darden as their spokesman, had called a meeting and presented him with a petition signed by all of them but Dampier and Bud Olsen to air their complaints. Owner Wendell Cherry later met with the players, but didn't institute any changes.

The victory was a landmark moment in the Pacers' fledgling history, but also more than that.

Denny, still caught up in the frenzy, led off his follow-up story two days after the game by referring to the Pacers' season as "one of the most amazing success stories in sports history" – quite an embellishment for a team that had merely and barely won a first-round playoff series. Fuson, in his column in the *News*, more accurately called it "one of the great moments in Indianapolis sports history," adding, "seldom, if ever, has this town got as excited about anything as it has about the Pacers." As evidence of the passion of the moment, the *News* ran a photo of ball boy Jim Smulyan pouring a beverage over Netolicky's head in the locker room.

Leonard, via his indomitable will, had forged a hard-nosed and tightly-knit unit. The private harangues behind the locker room's closed doors, the public praise in the newspapers, his ability to run his players hard in practice and then drink hard with them in bars, had molded a team in every sense of the word. Brown had been won over by an authority figure like never before. Daniels had taken his game inside and played like a center, from where his passion radiated through his teammates. Lewis was becoming a leader, a quarterbacking point guard. Netolicky had become more motivated, and the perfect complement to Daniels and Brown on the frontline. Everyone else was just happy to be on the team.

Asked after the Game 7 win how the Pacers had pulled off such a comeback, Daniels smiled, pounded his chest and proclaimed, "Thirteen hearts!" And they were, by all accounts, a wonderfully unified team – the kind of unity, Denny wrote, "that wins wars, conquers diseases, makes blacks and whites brothers and earns pro basketball playoff titles."

Added Netolicky: "We found out what Slick has been preaching about all season. We found out what playing as a team really means."

The reserves were all in, too. Miller, just two years out of Notre Dame but already playing for his fourth professional team, said he felt like he had played 48 minutes despite not playing at all. He had run eight laps the night before the game to stay in shape, he said, just in case he was called upon.

"Even though I'm not playing as much as I'd like, I want to be ready and I'll be ready whenever Slick calls on me," he told Denny.

Perry, having fallen from the peak of his 35-point game against the Nets, played just one minute, but lavished praise on Thacker. So did Hooper, the former starter who played 10 minutes off the bench. "I sat there and admired everything that guy did," Hooper said. "I hardly wanted to go in the game."[4]

---

[4] The next day, Saturday April 19, was O.J. Simpson Day in Indianapolis – at least according to Sports Headliners, the agency founded by Barnes that represented the Heisman Trophy-winning running back from USC. Simpson made four appearances at local shopping centers between 10:45 a.m. and 5 p.m.: Eagledale, Greenwood, North Eastwood and Washington Park.

One postscript to the victory: the $1,500 bonus supposedly offered to the players when they were down 3-1 to the Colonels? If it was offered, they never got it. Decades later, it remained a popular topic of conversation when players from the team were together.

"That's money we'll never get," Lewis said.

Delaying the start of the first-round series had enabled the Pacers to play their home games at the Coliseum, but nothing could be done to secure it for the next series with Miami. The front office got a break, though, when the mayor of Anderson called and made what Storen considered an "encouraging offer" to use their high school gymnasium.

It wasn't your typical high school gym. Anderson High School's facility, affectionately known to locals as the Wigwam because the school's nickname was "Indians," was one of the largest of its kind in the world, holding nearly 9,000 people. It was about an hour's drive north of the Coliseum, but not overly inconvenient for Pacers fans who lived on the north side of Indianapolis.

Anderson officials offered a brand of cooperation the Pacers had not experienced with the Fair Board that ran the Coliseum. They painted new boundary lines to change the high school court to the professional length and refinished the surface. They also provided security, parking attendants and ticket sellers, and gave the Pacers a percentage of concession sales. The Pacers, meanwhile, offered fans the service of charter buses, which would leave from the Downtown terminal, at a cost of $3 for round-trip fare, game ticket excluded.

Storen conducted a press conference in Anderson two days before the first game against Miami, during which he thanked city officials and took questions from media members. One asked about the likelihood the franchise would be able to draft Rick Mount after he finished his career at Purdue the following year. "We intend to get the draft rights to Mount, one way or the other," Storen said.

With the heated memory of the first-round playoff series with Kentucky still fresh in his mind, Storen also made clear his feelings

Roger Brown grabs a rebound in traffic while members of the media and Anderson High School's pep band look on in the Game 2 victory over Miami at the Wigwam.

about the Colonels. "We really hate them," he said. "There's nothing about them that we like."

The opening game of the second-round series with Miami was trouble-free on all counts. The Pacers rewarded the fans who made the trip to Anderson with a 126-110 victory. Small wonder, though. Miami had clinched its first-round series with Minnesota the previous night, and then traveled all day from Miami. The Pacers, who had been off for two days after eliminating Kentucky, led by 32 points early in the fourth quarter and coasted from there.

Daniels dominated with 32 points and 14 rebounds against his former team, and Netolicky had another strong performance with 26 points on 12-of-16 shooting and 13 rebounds. A crowd just a couple of hundred fans short of capacity watched, and was "orderly and enthusiastic" according to Denny's account, a sharp contrast to the fans in the Coliseum during the series with Kentucky.

The tickets for Game 2, two days later, incorrectly listed the starting time as 2:30 p.m., rather than the scheduled 8:10. The newspapers and other media outlets in Anderson tried to get out the word, but those who arrived 5 ½ hours early at least were on hand for the entirety of the preliminary game between the Anderson Launderers and Marion Plymouth Club. They also saw the Pacers arrive late, falling behind 15-3 before rallying for a 131-116 victory. Brown led with 33 points, 12 rebounds and five assists. Netolicky missed his first four shots but hit his last 14 on his way to 31 points, and added 19 rebounds.

The Pacers won Game 3 in Miami as well, but failed to sweep the series when they lost Game 4, 114-110. The four-game playoff win streak and the day off between games in sunny southern Florida caused them to lose their edge – except for Brown, who scored 44 points while hitting 15-of-24 shots. Leonard kept the team in the locker room afterward for another wakeup call.

Peeples admitted to lack of mental preparation on the part of most of the players.

"I played shuffleboard too long and I just wasn't right," he told Denny.

Thacker recalled players swimming in the ocean that day.

"Sometimes we did everything contrary to what we were supposed to do," he said.

The loss returned the series to Indianapolis the following night. The Pacers could have gone back to Anderson, but Storen felt obligated to give a game to Indiana Central because officials there had made its facility available all along. It also was a way of reaching out to fans on the south side of Indianapolis, who had a longer drive to get to the Coliseum and to Anderson.

The walk-up crowd of 3,528, short of capacity, got to see another example of the team's all-for-one mentality. Late in the third quarter, when Miami pulled within 13 points, and with Brown and Netolicky each carrying five fouls, and with Peeples, Dee and Miller having been part of a group that just gave up a 10-0 run, Leonard studied his options during a timeout. He decided to call on Fairchild, who had only played four scoreless minutes in the previous 11 playoff games, and had in fact worked the previous night's game as an analyst on the television broadcast because of the rule permitting only 10 players to dress for road games.

After a Pacers turnover following the timeout, the 6-8 forward stole Don Sidle's inbound pass near midcourt and drove in for a dunk, igniting the boutique audience. He went on to score eight more points in the fourth quarter while fouling out two of Miami's starters, Thoren and Hunter. He finished with 10 points and six rebounds over the final 14 minutes of a 127-105 victory that sent the Pacers to the ABA finals against Oakland.

Fairchild could have taken advantage of his sudden star turn to argue for more playing time. He didn't.

"I understand coach Leonard's position," he told Denny. "I don't think I could ever be a coach. I was just happy to do my part."

Lewis led the scoring with 35 points, hitting eight consecutive field goals from late in the second quarter to late in the fourth. Daniels added 25. Thacker passed out eight assists and held Miami guard Freeman to five points in the second half after Freeman had scored 21 in the first.

Thacker's defense and playmaking – he led the Pacers in assists with just over eight per game in the series with Miami – would be vital in the finals against Oakland. The Oaks had won all six games during the regular season, from the opener to the second-to-last game, four of them by double-figure margins. It hadn't mattered if Staverman was coaching the Pacers or Leonard. It hadn't mattered if Barry played or not. It hadn't mattered if a fight had broken out or not. The Oaks simply had more depth, balance and experience.

They also had the league's best rookie in Armstrong, the wondrous 6-2 guard/forward out of Wichita State. Armstrong was strong and stubborn, bold and aggressive and a startling athlete who might as well have been 6-9 given his jumping ability. He also was intimidating, largely because of an incident during the second quarter of a game in Los Angeles against the Stars on Jan. 22.

The short story was that Jarvis – who had been traded to the Stars for Chubin early in the season – had deflected the rebound of Armstrong's missed layup and chased after the ball. Armstrong, feeling he had been fouled, gave a karate chop to Jarvis's back, knocked him down, and stepped on the right side of his face. Jarvis suffered a broken tooth, a gash that required six stitches to close and a badly bruised face, but was able to return in the fourth quarter.

Armstrong, who was ejected from the game, apologized afterward and said it had all happened so quickly he wasn't sure what came over him. "I feel terrible about it," he said.

The more likely in-depth story was that, in Armstrong's mind, the play served as a metaphor for the societal ills he so adamantly opposed. Armstrong's white teammate in Oakland, Barry, seemed to get a foul call every time he drove the lane, and had plumped his league-leading 34-point scoring average with 13 free throw attempts per game, of which he hit 89 percent. Armstrong – either a prideful black man or militant, depending on one's point of view – believed he was equally aggressive in driving to the basket, but averaged only 7.6 free throw attempts.

Barry was an established star and crucial to the survival of the ABA, and no doubt was protected by the referees – a charge the Pacers made after the season-opener — while Armstrong was a rookie. Armstrong, however, saw discrimination as a factor in the different treatment they received from officials. So, when Armstrong drove to the basket in the second quarter and drew contact from Jarvis, also white, but received no whistle, he was incensed. And when he looked at the referee, also white, and the referee ignored him, it was a tidy summary of what Armstrong saw as a much larger issue. White people received preferential treatment, white people got away with more, and white people with status ignored injustices. Armstrong's temper flashed at that moment, and he took out all of his anger on Jarvis.

Mikan took nearly a week to levy his punishment, which enabled Armstrong to play in one game after the incident. Armstrong was fined $250 and suspended for 15 days, missing seven games as a result — two of them against the Pacers. He returned to finish the season well and so did the Oaks, whose 60-18 record was 14 games ahead of second-place New Orleans in the Western Division, and 16 games better than the Pacers' East-leading record.

Oakland's season-opening 11-point victory at the Coliseum seemed a decade ago for the Pacers, given all the changes they had experienced since then. They hadn't defeated the Oaks since that opening exhibition game, which didn't count, but they were drawing confidence from their late-season 13-game winning streak, their dramatic comeback from the 3-1 deficit against Kentucky, their dominance of Miami in the second round, and Leonard's aura. They also could draw hope from the absence of Barry, who had been lost for the season after injuring his left knee at Kentucky on Feb. 7, and undergone surgery on March 3.

Oakland had defeated the Pacers the night after Barry's injury, after which an angry Daniels made his prediction the Pacers would beat the Oaks in the playoffs if Barry played, but might not if he didn't play. But contrary to the impression left that night in Indianapolis, the Oaks were not better without him. They had gone 30-5 when he played, and 30-13 when he didn't. They had, however, won their last six games of the regular season without him, and after surviving a seven-game series with Denver in the first round had swept New Orleans in the second.

Armstrong's emergence had partially off-set Barry's absence. He had averaged 21.5 points and 9.7 rebounds in the regular season to easily win the Rookie of the Year vote. He had filled in for Barry at forward on occasion, and operated effectively around the basket because of his strength and jumping ability. His only weakness was perimeter shooting; he had hit just 25 percent of his three-pointers.

Thacker's late-season emergence offered hope in containing him.

"I'm looking forward to guarding Warren Armstrong," Thacker said after the series with Miami was clinched. "I'm pretty sure I can limit him to a minimum of points."

He didn't. Nobody on the Pacers roster could have at that point. Armstrong scored 29 points and grabbed 16 rebounds in Game 1 in Oakland, but still played a supporting role to Bradds, who finished with 40 points and 17 rebounds in the Oaks' 123-114 victory. Bradds – who had set several Big Ten scoring records at Ohio State, some of which were later broken by Mount – had been Baltimore's first-round draft pick in 1964 when Leonard coached the Bullets. Leonard's replacement, Jeannette, didn't hold Bradds in the same regard, however. The slender 6-8 forward played 41 games with Baltimore as a rookie and three the following season before he was released. He played the rest of that season and the next in the North American League while teaching ninth grade science, then signed a two-year guaranteed contract with Oakland to join the ABA.

He became a starter after Barry went down, and was flourishing under Hannum's leadership. Brown, three inches shorter than Bradds, was called for four fouls in the first quarter of Game 1 (after scoring 11 quick points) and only played 20 minutes. Brown complained afterward of "lousy officiating," while Leonard promised his team wouldn't back down despite its winless season record against the Oaks.

"We aren't conceding anything," he said. "We're going to run it right at 'em and it could get to be a physical series."

The Pacers broke loose from Oakland's grip two nights later with a 150-122 victory, setting ABA playoff records for scoring and margin of victory. It was just one win, but it confirmed their new-found bravado. They rebounded aggressively, ran for several easy baskets and sagged on defense to cut off the Oaks' penetration.

Brown, unburdened by fouls this time, scored 39 points, showing "an amazing variety of moves," according to Denny, although apparently not a million as Denny had claimed in the earlier game. Daniels picked up his fourth foul in the first quarter and didn't return until midway through the fourth, but Netolicky stepped into the center position and scored 36 points. Hannum declared his performance "utterly fantastic." Lewis, outplaying Larry Brown, added 35. Hooper contributed 15 off the bench.

Leonard made a lineup change, starting Peeples at forward to defend Bradds and moving Brown to guard to contend with Armstrong, so Thacker came off the bench. Bradds scored just 14, but Armstrong – who played both guard and forward – remained unstoppable with 31 points and 16 rebounds. Brown, at least, was able to outscore him.

Denny's story in the *News* claimed Storen had shouted at the players before the game. He and Leonard declined comment on it, but Hannum seemed to be aware of it. "Indiana had the advantage of their manager coming in and screaming at them behind closed doors," he said. "They came out like tigers." Years later, Storen would have no memory of it, nor did a few of the players.

Game 3 was played the following night in Indianapolis, another bizarre playoff home/road back-to-back necessitated by the Coliseum's limited availability. But if the teams were fatigued from the 2,500-mile journey, they put on a spirited overtime game that essentially decided the series, and would remain one of the most memorable and significant games in franchise history.

Brown drew a foul with five seconds left in regulation with the Pacers leading 117-115. He had been a 78.5 percent free throw shooter during the regular season, and was establishing himself as a clutch player. All he had to do to clinch the victory was hit two free throws, and he had three chances to do it. But he failed, missing the first attempt, bouncing the second one in off the rim and missing the third. Bradds grabbed the rebound and called timeout.

Hannum, coaching his first season in the ABA, began to draw up a play for someone to drive to the basket, but his players, in unison, reminded him of the three-point shot. Moe asked to take it, but Hannum set it up for Armstrong – "because he has the power to shoot from that range," he said afterward.

Larry Brown inbounded from in front of the scorer's table near midcourt. Armstrong caught it about 35 feet from the basket, at a 45-degree angle to the left of it. He had hit just 2-of-17 shots in the first half. He had hit just 2-of-16 three-pointers in the postseason. He had hit just one-fourth of his three-point attempts in the regular season. But, catching Brown's pass with his back to the basket, he took one dribble, turned and sent a multi-colored comet across the hazy Coliseum sky that fell cleanly through the net. Overtime! It was one of those shots, observers said, that looked good from the moment it left his hand. Armstrong said he felt the same way.

With the oxygen drained from the building, the Pacers succumbed in overtime. They were within a point after Thacker's layup off a jump ball with 1:58 left, and had a chance to take the lead after Thacker stole a pass at midcourt. He was driving for the basket with Hooper at his side, but when they reached the foul line, according to Overpeck's account, both somehow wound up on the floor and Oakland's Logan somehow wound up with the ball. No foul was called. Moe followed with two free throws and then Armstrong hit a 22-footer to clinch a 134-126 victory and a 2-1 lead for the Oaks.

"Now let somebody dispute the value of the three-point basket!" declared the injured Barry, who watched the game in street clothes.

Armstrong, who had scored Oakland's last nine points in regulation, finished with 37 points and 13 rebounds. Brown and Daniels had 29 each. Lewis had 22, including six in a 10-0 run midway through the fourth quarter that gave the Pacers the lead, but fouled out with 1:37 left in regulation.

Some incensed Pacers fans attacked referees Ron Rakel and Andy Hershock as they left the court, and this time use of the word "literally" would have been appropriate. The *Oakland Tribune's* story said the fans "beat them to the floor." Rakel suffered a cut lip and Hershock was punched in the head. Hannum also said he had been "maliciously" tripped by a fan as he left the court at halftime.[5]

The agony of the defeat was made worse by the fact Leonard had called "yellow," his signal for an intentional foul, before Armstrong's three-pointer. That would have only allowed Oakland two foul shots, not enough to overcome a three-point deficit without the unlikely sequence of missing the second free throw intentionally, grabbing the rebound and scoring. But Thacker, thinking Armstrong was too far from the basket to score, either made no effort or hesitated a moment and didn't get to him in time.

Years later, Hooper recalled their brief conversation as the huddle broke and the players returned to the court.

"I'm not going to foul him," Thacker said.

"Tom, you've got to do it," Hooper said.

"I'm not going to do it," Thacker said.

Years later, Thacker said he had good intentions.

---

[5] The city presumably was more hospitable to Hannum two days later, on the afternoon of Game 4, when he and three of his players – Barry, Moe and Brown – visited the Indianapolis Motor Speedway to experience a practice day at the track. The *News* ran a photo of him talking with a member of the Goodyear tire company's racing staff.

"I was going to foul him, but by the time I got there he was in the air already," he recalled. "I just couldn't get to him in time. I played too far off him."

The players shared the blame for the loss. Brown accepted responsibility for not hitting one more free throw with five seconds left that would have clinched a victory in regulation. Hooper, who helped spark the late comeback in regulation, blamed himself for taking a bad shot with nine seconds left.

Leonard didn't single out anyone, but said he had told his players to foul before the ball even reached an Oakland player's hands on the inbound pass.

"I hate to see 'em play so hard and make one silly mistake that costs the ball game," Leonard said. "Hell, yes, we should have won. You can't make mistakes and win championships. Now we've got the hard way to go."

Too hard, it turned out. Oakland won Game 4 at the Coliseum, 144-117. The deflated Pacers hit just 7-of-29 shots in the first quarter, fell behind by 11, got within four a few times in the second period, and trailed by 10 at halftime. Oakland began the third quarter with an 8-0 run and Leonard cleared his bench midway through the period to rest his starters. Fairchild wound up their leading scorer with 18 points, hitting four three-pointers.

Overpeck singled out "Middleton's Disease" as a factor as well, a reference to referee Middleton's job performance. Middleton and partner Tom Frangella at least had no problem with fans, as a squadron of police officers escorted them off the court at halftime and after the game in response to the attack on Rakel and Hershock following Game 3.[6]

Once again, the Pacers trailed 3-1 in a playoff series. They had recent experience with that sort of dilemma, but this was a different set of circumstances than in the first-round series. Oakland was loaded with veteran players who had graduated from college a few years before the

---

[6]   Rakel didn't have it easy as a referee. Dallas player-coach Cliff Hagan had shoved him after picking up two technical fouls early in the third period in the second game of the Chaps' first season in a win over Houston.

Referees Ed Middleton, front, and Tom Frangella are escorted by police officers to the court for Game 4 of the series with Oakland.

Bob Leonard voices his opinion to Ed Middleton during the Pacers' Game 4 loss to Oakland. He was not called for a three-second violation for being in the lane too long.

ABA was formed, and a brilliant rookie in Armstrong. It was so talented, Leonard said, "you don't even have to have a coach." Just in case, though, it had an outstanding one in Hannum, who had coached two teams to NBA championships, including Philadelphia just two years earlier.[7]

Overpeck declared the series over, leading his game story in the next day's *Star* with the following paragraph: "The Indiana Pacers died last night. Funeral services are planned tomorrow evening in the Oakland Coliseum." He ended the article by writing, "Miracle workers should report to dressing room E, Coliseum Arena, Oakland, Calif. tomorrow night." The following day, advancing Game 5 in Oakland, he wrote, "the 95th game (of the season) figures to be the last." He ended that story by pointing out the obvious: "The odds are long."

The Pacers, however, didn't cave, fighting back from a 12-point deficit in the third quarter to take a 119-115 lead with 2:33 remaining. Oakland scored the next six points, the final two on Brown's lay-in. Daniels blocked the shot, but Rakel – who reunited with Hershock to work the game – ruled goaltending and counted the basket.[8]

After Lewis and Armstrong each hit one free throw, leaving Oakland with a two-point lead, Leonard called timeout and set up a play to get a three-pointer for either Perry or Fairchild. Perry took one that missed, but drew a foul from Ira Harge with five seconds left. With the three-to-hit-two penalty in play, he hit the final two attempts to tie the game and force overtime.

---

[7] Hannum was on his way to a Hall of Fame coaching career, but he had a coach on the floor in his point guard, Brown, who was planning to retire following the season. Brown, in fact, already had landed the head coaching job at Davidson College, where he would replace Lefty Driesell. "I've always wanted to coach intelligent kids who are interested in something other than basketball," he told Denny during the playoff series. Brown, however, wound up only staying about a month at Davidson before changing his mind and returning to play in the ABA. He later claimed some promises had not been kept by the university. It was the first time he left a coaching job, but hardly the last.

[8] Leonard declared Rakel's call "unbelievably terrible." Storen later protested the fact Rakel and Hershock, the two referees who had been assaulted by Pacers fans after Game 3, were allowed to work this game. "One of them (Rakel) has threatened to sue us," Storen told Overpeck. "Now what's he doing refereeing our game?"

The Pacers were within a point late in the overtime period, but Moe and Brown each hit two free throws to clinch their championship.

Armstrong finished with 39 points on 15-of-24 shooting and 12 rebounds, an appropriate finish to his dominating season. He averaged 33.2 points in the series despite hitting just one three-pointer – the one that forced overtime in Game 3. He had failed to score in double figures in just one game all season – the one in which he was ejected for stepping on Jarvis' head.

Barry dressed for the game, although he was ineligible to play because of his status on the injured list. He declared Armstrong's three-pointer in Game 3 the shot that won the series, and predicted Armstrong would become "one of the game's great players."

"I think if everybody on our team was healthy," Barry added, "we could play against most NBA teams."

He probably was correct. Oakland at the time had the ABA's best collection of talent and experience, even without Barry. It had dominated the Pacers throughout the regular season, and while Armstrong's three-pointer in Game 3 had been a turning point, it was going to be difficult to beat regardless.

Leonard wasn't depressed by the outcome. His players, who had begun the season 1-7 and under the direction of another coach, had proved something – to others and to themselves.

"Our guys don't feel inferior anymore," he said.

Meanwhile in Cincinnati, the mood was less hopeful.

Two days after the Pacers' season ended with great optimism for the future, the Royals fired Jucker, who had turned down the Pacers' coaching offer two years earlier. Jucker's teams finished 39-43 and 41-41, and he was criticized by some – Robertson included – for implementing a deliberate, collegiate style of play contrary to the nature of the NBA.

The Royals were fading fast. They had no television contract and only sporadic radio coverage during Jucker's second season, and played several home games out of the city in hopes of drawing more fans — 11 in Cleveland and two in Omaha. Jucker retreated to Division II Rollins

College in Florida, where he coached for five seasons before becoming the school's athletic director — far from the "big leagues," to where the Pacers seemed headed.[9]

As for Staverman, he moved on after the Pacers' second season. He got another brief shot at coaching a decade later as an interim coach with the Kansas City Kings in the 1977-78 season, going 17-27, but spent most of his career as the general manager of the Cleveland Municipal Stadium and a consultant on the construction of the Tennessee Titans' stadium.

The players had liked Staverman, but sometimes took advantage of his good nature. They liked Leonard, too, but from another perspective. Their sentiment was tinged by a degree of fear, because they never knew when he might bolt the locker room door to clear the air, or grab a hockey stick to make a point. At the same time, he was equally capable of a heart-to-heart conversation that reached deep inside a player's psyche and helped bring out his best.

"Staverman was the kind of coach you wished you played better for," Harkness said years later. "Slick was the kind of coach you *did* play better for."

For some players, he became a father figure, or at least a respected authority figure. Over time, the players grew into wanting to please him.

"When you get right down to it, you wanted to make him proud of you," Netolicky said. "When we did well, he'd compliment us. It's something everybody needs, more than you know. I was the type of kid who really didn't have a father who would do that. We're all young kids

---

[9] Jucker's replacement, Hall of Fame guard Bob Cousy, was introduced the same day Jucker was let go. It didn't go any better for Cousy, whose only season in Cincinnati produced a 36-46 record. Although he was 41 years old and had been retired as a player for six seasons, he activated himself for seven games early in the season, without success. He also clashed with Robertson, and tried to trade him to Baltimore for Gus Johnson, a deal that was vetoed by Royals management. Robertson, fed up after a decade with the franchise, demanded a trade following the season and was sent to Milwaukee, where he later won his only NBA championship. The Royals moved to Kansas City in 1972.

away from home for the first time. You're three or four years away from mommy and daddy. That coach takes the place of daddy."

Despite being fired, Staverman never regretted his coaching fling with the Pacers. He wished in hindsight he had become a player-coach, as Hagan had been in Dallas, to lead by example. He was only 30 when hired, and felt like he could have worked himself back into shape and given the players the benefit of his experience. He wished he had been consulted more on personnel matters. He wished Storen and the owners had been more patient with him, or at least emphasized the need to win right away rather than build a program, as he was attempting to do. He also wished he had been less patient with the players when they became too selfish.

He thought the coaching experience helped him mature, though, and helped him become a better father to his five kids. And, the standings didn't lie. He couldn't ignore the results after Leonard took over.

"There's no way I can sit here and tell you I could have done with that ballclub what Leonard did, because of his intimidation factor," he said years later. "I more or less babied them, while he used shock treatment."

Still, he looked back with pride on his job performance, believing he had contributed to the franchise's early success. And he felt like he had helped some players. One of his proudest moments, in fact, came late in the season or after the season, before he moved his family out of Indianapolis.

Out riding bikes with his kids one day, he returned home to find a strange car sitting in his driveway. Rayl and Brown had stopped by – after having a few drinks, Staverman thought. As Staverman recalled years later, Rayl said he had been thinking about Staverman and wanted to tell him something. "You were one of the most honest coaches I ever played for," he said. "I just wanted to thank you for the type of person you are."

Staverman later walked into the house and told his wife, "You know, that's one of the nicest things anybody has ever said to me."

Moments such as that took the edge off being fired, and made him want to coach again. He felt that way for the rest of his life

"The hardest thing to come to grips with was being a failure," he said years later. "But when Jimmy Rayl comes by your house, then you realize you aren't a failure. If you reach one person in your life, it wasn't wasted.

"I was part of it, whether they admit it or I admit it."

15

"It looks like it's leaning toward my not coming back right now.
But I wouldn't want the guys ever to feel I'd walk out on them."

Commitment

The previous year, the lingering postseason question was Reggie
Harding's future. This time, it was Leonard's.

When he took over as head coach nine games into the season, he
saw it as a trial run. He already had a steady, lucrative sales job with
Herff Jones. Most of the school principals he called on were former
coaches or athletes who were fans of his basketball career, so he had an
immediate advantage over the competition from the rival company,
Jostens. His wife, Nancy, was the head of the Business department at
Taylor High School, just outside of Kokomo, and was taking graduate
school classes at the Indiana University extension in the city.

They were enjoying life in the $55,000 home they had purchased
on the outskirts of town after a decade of renting apartments and houses
throughout his transient existence as an NBA player and coach in
Minneapolis, Los Angeles, Chicago and Baltimore, and were expecting
to live out the rest of their working careers in Kokomo with their
children.[1] He was a people person, not suited to sitting behind a desk,
so the job was perfect for him. He cashed in on his popularity and
people skills while roaming his territory of 58 schools in central and
northern Indiana while Nancy administered the operation from their
home. When material was ready to be delivered, the children spread out

---

[1]   They had four at the time and would later have a fifth child. The oldest was a
    daughter, Terry. The boys were named Tommy, Timmy, Bobby and Billy.

on the living room floor to package the orders, forming a miniature assembly line.

Leonard had agreed to coach the Pacers as a practical matter. He figured the crazy new league with the red, white and blue ball and three-point line wasn't going to last, so he had nothing to lose by coaching the rest of the season. His $22,500 salary would pay off the furniture in his new home, and more. It would have been foolish to give up his steady day job for such a risky endeavor, so he made his calls during the day and coached games and most of the practices in the evenings. The road trips made it more difficult to keep up, but he utilized the synergy between his two jobs to his advantage. Coaching the Pacers made his sales job that much easier, and he met with clients at a restaurant near the Coliseum before games. It didn't hurt that he could give them tickets to the games.

Following the final loss to Oakland, it was time to make a decision. The drive from Kokomo to the Coliseum was about 50 miles each way, and took about an hour. The drive to and from the Indianapolis airport was even longer. To continue coaching, he would have to move his family closer to Indianapolis and hire someone to help with his day job. Even then it would be exhausting, carrying on two full-time jobs, each of which demanded extensive travel.

Having coffee with Denny in Oakland after the season-ending loss, he said he would wrap up his Herff Jones duties for the school year before the Indianapolis 500 at the end of the month, take his family on a vacation and then decide.

"It looks like it's leaning toward my not coming back right now," he said. "But I wouldn't want the guys ever to feel I'd walk out on them."

Nobody close to him really believed that. Despite what he had said after his supposed resignation in Baltimore in August of '64 about not wanting the lifestyle of a professional coach any longer, and despite what he had told the Kokomo Downtown Kiwanis Club in April of '66 about not wanting to "undergo the strain and pressure again," the job stoked his competitive fire. And this particular group of players had inspired an inferno within him. They won for him often, fought for him occasionally and challenged him always.

The headline on Overpeck's column two days after the loss in Oakland read, "Leonard Likely To Coach Again," and the article quoted Leonard as saying, "I've never settled for No. 2. I've always gone for the top – and we didn't make it this year." Storen also had predicted Leonard would return during his press conference in Anderson to announce the playoff games against Miami.

Coming so close to a championship with a team that only figured to get better excited him. He had played on a national championship team as a junior in college, but otherwise had fallen short of championships in high school and in the NBA. The teams he coached in Chicago and Baltimore had lacked the experience to win big, but this squad gave him a genuine opportunity to prove himself as a coach. If Brown had hit one more foul shot or Thacker committed one more foul in that Game 3 loss to Oakland at the Coliseum, when a victory would have given the Pacers team a 2-1 lead and series momentum, he might have won a championship right out of the box.[2]

He had been lucky, too. What if the efforts to trade Brown and Freddie Lewis had succeeded? The cliché about the best trades sometimes being those that aren't made had never been more accurate than for the Pacers that season. They were franchising-shifting "failures."

The primary issue for Leonard, seemingly, was control of personnel. "If he gets the authority he wants, he no doubt will return," Denny wrote. "If not, he won't. It's just about that simple."

That might have been a reference to the release of Rayl and the trade of Chubin. Leonard had given the impression he was against both of those moves, and the argument could be made they were mistakes. Rayl shot a better three-point percentage than Perry that season for the Pacers, and the irony wasn't lost on Rayl that the Pacers later traded a popular player in Chubin for a perimeter shooter barely more than a

---

[2] Leonard finished third in the Coach of the Year balloting by the league coaches that season, behind Oakland's Alex Hannum and Babe McCarthy of New Orleans. The voting was taken before the playoffs – sort of the equivalent of collecting MVP votes for an All-Star game with five minutes remaining. Leonard was voted Coach of the Year by media members, but the coaches' vote counted as the official award. Leonard never would win an official ABA Coach of the Year honor.

month after they released him. They could have kept him and Chubin and saved everyone a lot of trouble, although intangibles also factored into those moves.

Regardless of any issues, Leonard returned. He had been pictured with Storen and just-signed draft pick Dick Grubar in a wire service photo on June 8 and then a press conference was conducted on June 25 at the Pacers' office to formally announce his return. "There was no real doubt in my mind about coming back, it just took time to work things out," he said.

He said in later years he won more control of personnel matters. Storen, however, said Leonard had a say in personnel all along, aside from the late-night, beer-fueled phone calls after tough losses when Leonard called and wanted to trade someone who had just played poorly. "Let's talk about it in the morning," Storen would say, and then more often than not it was forgotten.

Either way, there was no doubt about Leonard's reason for coming back.

"The only thing we're interested in is the ABA championship," he said at the news conference. "I'll be taking the club into camp and have more time to work on different phases of the game. The big thing is we are going to be together from the start."

The Pacers' future was promising. They had a nucleus of four All-Stars, including a league MVP. They had a coach who had won the Coach of the Year voting by the ABA media, although the official award, voted upon by the coaches, went to Hannum. Together, they had contended for a championship despite coming together nine games into the season and establishing their chemistry as they went along.

They had a galvanized fan base, too, along with a proven front office and a dedicated, although hardly wealthy, group of owners.

Anything seemed possible.

Epilogue

The problem with most historical events is that you don't realize they were historical until it's too late. What seems ordinary today might seem extraordinary decades later, but you can't tell the difference between fine wine and sour grapes when the vines are growing.

I certainly didn't as a 12-year-old kid, when the Pacers began playing. It's not like I knew they would still be playing 50 years later, and I would be writing about them. If so, I would have found a way to get a ticket, then found a way to get to the Fairgrounds Coliseum for that first game on Oct. 14, 1967. I would have taken a camera, taken notes and tried to record every detail for future reference – especially who scored the first basket in the first game, which appears lost to history.

Nobody has that kind of peripheral vision, though. I once asked the team's original radio voice, Jerry Baker, if he had recorded the first game for posterity's sake. He said no, at the time everybody around the Pacers was focused on mere survival. Nobody was even considering the possibility the franchise would still be playing in 2017.

I did get to a few games that first season. The first was against the Oakland Oaks, when Rick Barry was sitting out after jumping over from the NBA and working as an analyst for the team's radio broadcasts. Looking at that season's schedule, it likely was on Nov. 15. A couple of friends and I ran down to get Barry's autograph before the game, and on the way back to our seats stopped to get Baker's autograph. I still have them, on the same slip of paper.

I also have the Reggie Harding autograph I mentioned in the Acknowledgements. I got it on March 14, 1968. I know, because my mother recorded the moment among the day's events in her journal. My father, older brother and I were at the airport that evening to meet her incoming flight. We saw Harding sitting by himself in a coffee shop, so my brother and I scrambled to locate a piece of paper and pen and dashed back to ask for his signature. He was calm and polite, and neatly signed my small slip of paper.

See?

The weird thing about it is that this day was sandwiched between home games. The previous day, Harding had played his best game as a Pacer, perhaps the best game of his life, by scoring 30 points, grabbing 22 rebounds and blocking "at least 10 shots," as the local newspaper accounts reported, against Mel Daniels and the Minnesota Muskies. The next day, against Kentucky, he would score 23 points, grab 25 rebounds and pass out five assists.

That fleeting flicker of time was a peak moment in Harding's troubled life. He had a fresh start, was entrenched with a promising team, was dominating the competition, and was so popular in his new city that kids were hunting him down for autographs in the airport. But why was he there? Was he going to fly to Detroit that night and return the next day before the game? Was he there to meet someone? He didn't have a car, so why would he take a cab to the airport if not for a good reason? We probably don't want to know.

My memory of my encounter with Harding is instructive. I would have sworn it happened on a Sunday afternoon, but Mom's journal proves it was a Thursday evening. (Her flight was scheduled to arrive at 6:56 p.m., in case you were wondering.) That's why I understand when memories of events from 50 years ago turn out to be inaccurate. That's why I'm not a fan of oral histories that aren't supplemented by extensive research. That's why in this book I have done my best to research as many details as possible, and present both versions of a story when accounts conflicted.

Sometimes you have to throw out someone's recollection entirely. One former Pacer provided me with a specific and dramatic account of the incident in Duluth, when coach Bob Leonard went after Bob Netolicky with the hockey stick. This player confidently asserted Leonard had broken the stick over a chair and jabbed the jagged end of it in Netolicky's chest, threatening bodily harm if he didn't pick it up in the second half. It was a colorful anecdote, the kind an author wants to be true. Only problem was, this player wasn't even at the game. Wasn't even on the team at the time, in fact.

As memories fade and photos and records get tossed, history is lost. I hope I've revived as much of it as possible. The Pacers' first two difficult seasons set the stage for all the drama that was to follow – three ABA championships, entrance into the NBA, a franchise-saving telethon, a move to an arena that helped ignite the revival of Indianapolis' downtown, another move to an even better facility, and countless triumphs and calamities.

I hope to produce a book on the remaining ABA seasons someday, and another on the Kautskys and Olympians. *Reborn* ideally will become the middle volume of a trilogy. There's plenty more to tell about some of the players covered in this volume, not to mention players yet to arrive. Steve Chubin is going to return to the Pacers — for awhile, anyway. Daniels, Leonard and Roger Brown are going to have Hall of Fame careers. Freddie Lewis is going to set himself up to become the most underrated player in franchise history. Some players will be traded, some will want to be traded, some will file lawsuits and some will be sued. But all of them, eventually, will be forced into the real world. Some will struggle when they get there, some will have tremendous success.

You know, life. And death, too. Eight of the players from the first two teams are no longer with us: Reggie Harding (1972); Jay Miller (1991); Bobby Joe Edmonds (1991); Roger Brown (1997); Matthew Aitch (2007); Don Dee (2014); Mel Daniels (2015); and Ron Bonham (2016). Coach Larry Staverman passed away in 2007.

One way or another, they all contributed to a franchise that's still making history.

Index

Abdul-Jabbar, Kareem, 214

Ackerman, James, 38

Aitch, Karen, 63

Aitch, Matthew, vi, 51-52, 62-63, 85-86, 88-89, 103-105, 114-115, 121, 124, 147, 167-168, 194, 203, 298, 397

Albuquerque Journal, 328

Alexander, John, 46

All-Star game (ABA), 148, 151, 153, 156, 160-61, 163, 165, 220, 233, 263, 313-314, 316, 324, 352, 393

All-Star game (East-West college), 89, 139, 161, 293

All-Star game (NBA) 3-5, 114, 148, 153, 163

American Basketball League (ABL), 21, 34, 38, 56, 64, 67-68, 71-72, 74-75, 76, 91, 148, 172, 331

American Bowling Congress, 11

American Football League (AFL), 19-21, 148, 163

American Hockey League, 19

Andretti, Mario, 238, 240

Angelopolous, Angelo, 9-12

Angelopolous, Jimmy, 85

Armstrong, Warren, 237, 245, 302, 347, 378-383, 386-387

Arnzen, Bob, 367

Auerbach, Red, 43, 148

Autry, Gene, 25

Bailey, Pete, 1

Baker, Jerry, vi, 150, 208, 321, 395

Ball State University, 53

Ballard, Florence, 175

Baltimore Bullets, 41, 261-262, 269, 280

Bannon, Joe, vi, 26-30, 39, 42, 52, 68, 124, 220, 222

Barker, Cliff, 4

Barnes, Chuck, vi, 23, 27, 46, 77, 156, 345, 374

Barnes, Jim, 32

Barton, John, 18, 124

Basketball Association of America, 3, 36

Baylor, Elgin, 16, 21

Beard, Ralph, 4-7, 67, 126, 265

Beasley, Charles, 50-52, 63

Beasley, John, 130, 132, 135, 157, 160

The Beatles, 247

Beck, Byron, 190

Bee, Clair, 9-10

Bellamy, Walt, 14-15, 40, 173

Belmont, Joe, 131-132, 200

Benedict, Dave, 234-235

Benjaminson, Peter, 175

Bernath, Bob, vi, 122

Big Ten Conference, 52, 62, 114

Binstein, Mark, 32, 93

Bonham, Ron, vi, 96-101, 104, 106, 109, 113-114, 119-121, 138-139, 143, 167, 203, 223, 331, 397

Borgia, Sid, 357

Boston Celtics, 71, 172, 174, 265, 322, 332, 345, 364

Bowes, Robert, 29

Bradds, Gary, 314, 317, 347, 380-382

Brady, Denny, 74

Branson, Jesse, 199

Brian, Frankie, 12

Brown, Larry, vi, 136, 143-144, 159-160, 237, 242, 248, 302, 315, 327, 347, 381-382

Brown, Mel, 79, 123

Brown, Roger, vi, 66-67, 69, 85, 87, 89, 94, 104, 106-107, 111, 113, 115, 119-121, 125-126, 132, 136, 142, 147, 153, 165, 167-168, 185-186, 188-189, 190-192, 196, 198-199, 201, 205-206, 222-225, 237, 241-242, 244, 246, 248-249, 253, 257, 260, 269-271, 275, 277, 280-281, 288-289, 293-298, 302-309, 311, 313-318, 322-326, 329-330, 332-326, 329-330, 332-334, 337-340, 342, 344, 346, 351, 357, 359-361, 363-364, 366, 369, 371, 374, 376-377, 381-384, 386-87, 389, 393, 397

Brueckmann, Dr. F. Robert, 79, 279

Bryant, Charles, 353

Buntin, Bill, 83-86

Butler Fieldhouse, 4, 7-8, 18

Butler University, 2, 39, 148, 248, 353

Butters, Mary Ann, 240

Butters, Tom, 292

Cadou, Jep, 15

Caldwell, Jim, 358

Caldwell, Joe, 173

Carnegie, Tom, 240

Carrier, Darel, 147, 277, 309, 356, 359-361, 363, 370-371, 373

Cazzetta, Vince, 187

Central Washington State, 234

Cervi, Al, 11

Chamberlain, Wilt, 21, 29-30, 32, 47, 84, 91, 173-174, 368

Chapman, Wayne, 361, 363

Cherry, Wendell, 175, 373

Chicago Bulls, 53-54, 77, 86, 118, 174, 180, 181

Chicago Coliseum, 15

Chicago Herald-American, 3

Chicago International Amphitheater, 15

Chicago Packers, 14

Chicago Stadium, 3, 15

Chicago Tribune, 40, 89, 140, 180

Chicago Zephyrs, 261

Chmielewski, Bill, 169-170

Chubin, Steve, vi, 128-129, 276-277, 289-294, 296-297, 301-303, 307-309, 312, 315-324, 327-329, 332, 334-338, 342, 348-349, 351, 378, 393-394

Cincinnati Bengals, 353

Cincinnati Enquirer, 64, 73, 98, 161

Cincinnati Royals, 13-16, 19-20, 30-32, 39, 41-43, 45-46, 64-66, 71, 73, 75-77, 101, 116-117, 124, 148, 161, 231, 331-332, 364, 387-388

Clark, Richard, 51

Clowes Hall, 353

Coffin, James, 178

Collins, Bob, vi, 19-20, 23-26, 28-29, 31, 39, 43, 46, 52, 66, 74, 90, 92-94, 99-100, 102, 109, 117-119, 121, 123-124, 126, 132, 140, 193, 221, 262, 264, 286, 352, 354, 367

Collins, Sid, 240

Colvard, Dean, 137

Conard, Gene, v, 94, 106-107, 126, 190, 251, 257, 265-267, 281, 299, 358

Congdon, Jeff, 244

Continental Football League, 345

Counts, Mel, 180-181

Courier-Journal (Louisville), 120, 123, 125, 159, 203-204, 221, 359-360, 364

Cousy, Bob, 6, 388

Crispus Attucks High School, 9, 82, 84

Crowe, Ray, 31, 43, 117

Dampier, Louie, vi, 51, 56, 77, 146, 159, 195, 203, 251, 275, 309, 359-361, 363, 373

Daniels, Bernice, 226

Daniels, Maceo, 227-228

Daniels, Mel, vi , 49, 58, 75-77, 107, 153, 159-161, 165-166, 183, 185, 189, 201, 219-223, 225-233, 237, 240-244, 246, 248-253, 257-259, 263, 267-272, 274-275, 277, 280-282, 284, 287-288, 297, 301-304, 307, 309, 311-313, 315-317, 319-320, 323-333, 338-339, 342-344, 346-348, 350-351, 357-361, 363-366, 369, 374, 376, 378, 380-381, 383, 386, 396-397

Darden, Oliver, vi, 95-96, 103-107, 113-116, 120-121, 125-126, 130-131, 133, 143, 165, 184-186, 189, 196-198, 200-201, 206, 214, 235, 270, 282-283, 296, 360, 373

Davidson, Gary, 27-28, 148, 386

Davidson, Ken, 27-28, 148, 386

Davis, Baron, 83, 129

Dawson, Jim, vi, 50, 62, 88-89, 104, 106, 109, 113, 120-121, 125-126, 153, 220, 223, 225

Daytona 500, 46

Debusschere, Dave, 176-177, 180, 214

Dee, Don, 217, 244, 272, 275, 277, 281, 295, 310, 315, 333, 344, 360, 363, 377, 397

Dee, Johnny, 72, 75

Denny, Dick, 47-48, 74, 87, 105, 107-108, 119, 123, 140, 143-144, 185-187, 190, 192-195, 201, 208, 224, 235, 246, 254, 257-260, 266, 275, 277, 280, 283-284, 286, 296, 300-302, 304, 306-307, 309-311, 314-316, 319, 327-329, 332-334, 337-340, 343-344, 346, 349-350, 357-359, 363-364, 373-374, 376-378, 381, 386, 392-393

Denoy, Pat, 128, 145-146, 315

Des Moines Register, 59-60, 209, 295

Detroit Free Press, 47, 114, 175, 179, 209

Detroit News, vi, 172, 176-177, 214

Detroit Pistons, 16, 51, 63, 67, 83, 86, 95, 172, 180, 210-211, 213-214, 225

DeVoe Jane, 274

DeVoe, Chuck, v-vi, 29, 121-122, 220-221, 236, 321, 352, 354

DeVoe, John, 20, 33, 35, 47, 49, 129, 233, 244, 274, 285

Dickson, Larry, 238

Dill, Craig, vi, 50, 55-56, 89, 103-104, 107, 110, 153, 189

Dischinger, Terry, vi, 14-16, 40, 44-46, 118, 214

Dove, Sonny, 214

Downey Jr., Morton, 50

Drake University, 50, 58-61, 155, 366-367

Driesell, Lefty, 386

Dukes, Walter, 176

Eagledale Shopping Plaza, 122, 246

Eakins, Jim, 316, 326

Early, Penny Ann, 237

Eastern League, 144, 181, 281

Ebershoff, Dick, vi, 26, 29

Eddy, Ray, 97

Edmonds, Bobby Joe, vi, 84-87, 89, 100, 104, 106, 109-110, 113-115, 121, 128, 133, 143, 188, 196-197, 215, 397

Eli Lilly Company, 6, 103

Elk's Club, 120

Ellis, LeRoy, 32

Ellis, Richard "Boo," 88

Erickson, Bill , 253

Erickson, Keith, 181

Ervin, Bill, 211, 214

Fairchild, John, 280, 283-284, 320, 377-378, 384, 386

Fairgrounds Coliseum, 8, 28, 71, 191, 195-196, 201-202, 204, 206, 231, 237-240, 243, 245, 248, 251-252, 257-258, 275, 281, 284, 285, 288, 301-303, 309, 313, 321-323, 325, 327, 330, 332-336, 338, 340, 348-349, 352-358, 361, 370, 375-377, 382, 384, 386, 392-393, 390, 395

Falls, Joe, 71, 114, 179, 210

Forbes, Dick, 97

Fort Wayne Zollner Pistons, 6-9, 11-12

Foyt, A.J. , 238-240

Francis Pomeroy Naismith Award, 367

Frangella, Tom, 259, 384-385

Franklin Daily Journal, v, 125

Frazier, Wilbert, 270

Freeman, Donnie, 153, 165, 225, 270, 277, 339, 378

Frenzel, Otto, 152

Fresno Bee, 315

Fruits, Betty, 240

Fuson, Wayne, vi, 19-20, 193, 281, 286, 301, 353, 355, 373

Gaidjunes, Frank, 50

Gardner, Jack, 9

Gardner, Willie, 83

Gates, Hilliard, vi, 12

Gills, Joseph A. , 209

Givens, John, 75, 126, 195

Gold, Joe Dan, 4, 22, 44, 71, 119, 128, 137, 154-155, 231, 275, 277

Golden State Warriors, 237

Grace, Tom, 19-20, 175

Greater Indianapolis Progress Committee, 18, 25

Gregory, Mamie, 124

Gregory, Joe, 48, 124, 221, 237

Groza, Alex, 4-7, 67

Grubar, Dick, 367, 394

Guerrero, Tito, 299

Hadnot, Jim, 110, 195

Hagan, Cliff, 131, 158, 164, 307, 384, 389

Hampton, Bill, vi, 82

Hannum, Alex, 250, 259, 316, 328, 381-383, 386, 393-394

Harding, Jim, 253, 289, 291-292

Harding, Nadine, 177, 180, 210

Harding, Reggie, vi, 169-192, 194-203, 205-216, 223, 225-226, 228-229, 391, 396-397

Harding, Reggie Jr., 177, 214

Harge, Ira, 189, 327-328, 343, 386

Harkey, Bob, 238

Harkness, Jerry, vi, 89-90, 98, 103-105, 109-116, 121, 129-140, 143, 146, 168, 188, 191, 194, 203, 244, 250, 252-253, 258, 260, 269-270, 279-280, 300, 322, 326, 331, 334, 336, 364, 368, 388

Harlem Globetrotters, 2, 8-9, 11, 21, 54, 67, 92, 128, 176

Harrison, Les, 3

Hartley, Gene, 238

Hartman, Sid, 41, 221

Harvey, Doug, 145-146

Havlicek, John, 364

Hawkins, Connie, 66-68, 110, 112-113, 153, 158, 168, 189, 205-206, 253, 269, 275, 288, 294, 300, 305, 316, 319, 342-343, 350

Hayes, Elvin, 216

Herff Jones, 166, 262-263, 391-392

Hershock, Andy, 383-384, 386

Heyman, Art, 144, 292-293, 316, 344

Hightower, Wayne, 32

Hinchman, J.B., 238

Hinkle Fieldhouse, 148, 150, 152-153, 161, 166, 352-353

Hinkle, Tony, 151

Hoffman, Paul, 262

Holland, Joe, 4

Holstein, Jim, vi, 73-74, 79

Hooper, Bob, 283-284, 288, 295, 297, 299, 307-311, 327, 329, 331, 359, 363, 368, 374, 381-384

Hoover, Tom , vii, 190, 292, 341, 349

Hornback, Ted, 13

Hudnut, Dr. William, 288

Hudson, Lou, 32

Hulman, Tony, 238

Humes, Larry, vii, 53-55, 86-87, 89, 98, 100-101, 104, 106, 108-112, 194

Hundley, Hot Rod, 272

Hunter, Les, 29, 89-90, 138, 339, 378

Hurt, Bob, 238, 240

Iba, Hank, 275

Ice, Harry T., 151-152, 352-355

Indiana Central College, 1, 82, 112, 237

Indiana Professional Sports, Inc., 29

Indiana University, 6, 10, 14, 16, 40, 55, 100, 158, 261, 333, 391

Indianapolis 500, 18, 55, 70, 222, 238, 392

Indianapolis Capitols, 345

Indianapolis Jets, 3-4, 28

Indianapolis Motor Speedway, 103, 222, 383

Indianapolis Olympians, 4-10, 12, 20, 22, 28, 94, 114, 119, 151, 265, 354, 397

Indianapolis Times, 14

Iowa University, 67

Ireland, George, 136

Jamoco Saints, 54

Jarrett, Richard, 179

Jarvis, Jim, 291, 378-379, 387

Jeannette, Buddy, 262, 380

Jewish Community Center, 89, 103-104, 141-142, 166, 203, 224, 321

Johns, Maury, 58-59

Johnson, Gus, 388

Johnson, McKinley, 176

Jones, Gerry, 50

Jones, James, 49

Jones, K.C., 49

Jones, Larry, 203, 277, 329

Jones, Parnelli, 238-239

Jones, Wallace, 4

Joyner, Butch, 333

Jucker, Ed, 72-73, 75, 77, 97, 161, 387-388

Kallay, Ed, 237

Kaufman, Nate, 11

Kautsky, Don, 94

Kautsky, Frank, 1-3, 94

Kautskys basketball team, 1, 3, 9-10, 28, 397

Keller, Bill, 74, 367-368

Kelly, Arvesta, 157, 305

Kennedy, J. Walter, 20

Kennedy, Robert, 247

Kerner, Ben, 10

Kerr, Johnny, 54, 180-181

Kim, Art, 34, 145-146

Kimbrough, Babe, 4

King, Bob, 58, 230

King, George, 12, 74

King, Martin Luther, 171, 247

Kissel, Jerry, 296

Klein, Dick, 54

Kohl, Herb, 49

Kokomo Morning Times, 124

Kokomo Tribune, v, 88, 106, 122, 124, 126, 163, 190, 257, 266, 281, 299, 358

Korshak, Marshall, 15

Kozlicki, Renee, 224-225

Kozlicki, Ron, vii, 50, 56, 87, 89, 104, 113-114, 121, 133, 167, 220, 223-225

Kuhn, Bill, 154

Kunkel, Bill, 315

Lafayette Country Club, 26

Lamm, Corky, 13-14, 100, 325

Lane, Frank, 14

Lareau, Bernie, 79, 104-105, 121, 153, 167, 205, 244, 324, 328-329

Lee, Clyde, 32

Leonard, Bob, viii, 6, 10, 14-15, 41, 72, 74-75, 80-81, 84-85, 88, 90, 101, 140, 166, 222, 261-272, 274-275, 277, 279-281, 283-284, 287-289, 293-299, 301-311, 313, 315, 317-320, 322-325, 327-330, 332-334, 336-340, 342-348, 350-351, 359-361, 363, 366, 369-373, 377-378, 380-381, 383-389, 391-394, 397

Leonard, Joe, 222

Leonard, Nancy, vii, 261-263, 265, 274

Lewis, Freddie, vii, 64-66, 69, 104-107, 109, 111, 113, 115, 120-121, 125, 128, 133, 142-146, 153, 165-166, 168, 185-189, 193, 196, 199, 201, 203-204, 206, 222-223, 232, 242, 244, 249, 256, 258, 260, 270, 276-277, 288, 300, 393, 397

Lewis, Mike, vii, 217-218, 223, 234-235, 244, 250, 252, 256, 258, 267, 278, 289, 301, 320

Ligon, Jim "Goose" , 87-88, 124, 313, 360, 364-365

Lindhorst, Ambrose, 31, 76

Lloyd, Bobby, 308

Logan, Bob, 180

Logan, Henry, 180, 315, 327, 347, 382

Lombardi, Vince, 333, 344

Long Island Arena, 282, 339

Los Angeles Lakers, 16, 56, 64, 83, 114, 173-174, 180-181, 210

Louden, Hubert, 204

Loughery, Kevin, 72

Love, Bob, 77

Lovellette, Clyde, vii, 9, 80-81, 84, 88, 140, 263

Lowery, Lana, 97

Lucas, Jerry, 32, 64, 76

Lugar, Richard, 154, 233, 248, 352

Madison Courier, v, 112

Mahaffey, Randy, 204, 284

Major League Baseball, 19, 135, 228

Mannweiler, Lyle, vii, 307

Manual High School, 45, 88

Marian College, 156, 240

Marott Hotel, 70, 92, 154, 196, 223

Marshall, Hubie, 15, 50, 55, 81, 89, 104, 106, 108, 110

Martin, Dick, 354

Martin, Slater, 148, 275

Marvel, Bill, vii, 77, 79, 82, 91-92, 113, 127, 134, 150, 152-153, 155-156, 160, 190, 238, 296

Masiello, Tony, 367

Mastin, Charlie, 359-360

May, Don, 217-218

McBride, Cy, 307

McCarter, Willie, 367-368

McCarthy, Babe, 85, 137, 159-160, 393

McCloskey, Jack, 14

McCluskey, Roger, 238, 240

McCracken, Branch, 45, 202, 254-256

McDermott, Barry, 161

McGill, Billy "The Hill," 55, 81, 83-86, 241, 252

McGlocklin, Jon, vii, 45-46, 101, 118

McGowan, Bill, vii, 115-116

McGrady, Thurlo, 163

McKee, Ed, 50, 52-53

McMahon, Jack, 15, 60, 64, 101, 261

McShane, John, 22, 37

Merriweather, Willie, 88

Meyer, Ray, 36

Michigan Chronicle, 210

Mikan Drill, 36

Mikan, George, vii, 9-10, 23, 27-28, 33-34, 36-38, 49, 91-93, 102-103, 120-121, 124, 126, 151, 153-155, 159-162, 164, 216, 246, 253, 272, 305, 379

Miller, Dick, 8

Miller, Jay, 294, 315, 374, 377, 397

Miller, Larry, 308-309, 322

Milwaukee Hawks, 10

Minneapolis Lakers, 6, 10-11, 36, 73, 272, 283

Minneapolis Star, 153, 292

Minneapolis Tribune, 201, 221, 288, 293, 305, 316

Missouri Valley Conference, 59, 366

Mitchell, Leland, 198

Mittman, Dick, vii, 14, 86, 229

Modell, Art, 25

Moe, Doug, 160, 237, 313, 316, 382-383, 387

Molinas, Jack, 66-68

Moon, Larry, 353

Moore School for Boys, 169

Moore, Gene, 360

Moreland, Jackie, 281

Mount, Rick, 74, 161, 375, 380

Moyers, Gene, 131, 204, 259

Mr. Basketball, 13, 45, 53, 74, 96, 100-101, 299

Mueller, Erwin, 32

Murff, Barry, 24

Murphy, Dennis, 22-23, 29

Murphy, Johnny, 29

Musial, Stan, 24

Naismith Basketball Hall of Fame, 36, 134

Nashville Christian High School, 172

National Basketball Association (NBA), 3, 5-16, 19-24, 28-34, 36, 38, 40, 43-49, 51, 54-57, 60, 63-65, 67, 69, 71-72, 74-77, 80, 83-84, 91-92, 101-103, 107, 114, 116-118, 126, 139, 144, 148, 153, 155, 159, 161, 163-164, 172-174, 176-177, 179-180, 183, 210, 213, 216-217, 226, 231, 237, 257, 259, 261, 263, 265, 270, 283-284, 292-293, 297, 310-311, 318, 322, 331, 340, 342, 344-345, 349, 364, 366, 368, 371, 386-388, 391, 393, 395, 397

National Basketball League, 3-5, 36

National Invitation Tournament, 22

NBA Players Association, 43

Neary, Jay, 281

Netolicky, Bob, vii, 50-51, 56-58, 60-62, 81, 89-90, 103-104, 106-107, 113, 120-121, 126, 130-131, 133, 143-144, 147, 153, 155, 165, 167-168, 181, 185-186, 188-189, 194-196, 198, 200-201, 203, 206, 216, 222-224, 230, 234-235, 237-238, 241, 244, 246, 248-250, 252, 256, 258, 263-264, 267-269, 271, 275, 277-278, 281, 283-284, 287-288, 295-298, 300, 302, 306-307, 311, 313, 316-317, 320, 323-326, 333-334, 339, 343-344, 346, 351, 357, 359, 361-364, 366, 369-371, 373-374, 376-377, 381, 388, 397

New Castle High School, 100, 108, 241

New York Knicks, 66, 89, 114, 310, 349

New York Rens, 2

New York World Journal Tribune, 33

North American Basketball League (NABL), 65, 84, 89, 111

Olsen, Bud, 373

Overpeck, Dave, 106, 127, 132, 146, 150, 155-156, 168, 184, 186-187, 191, 194, 201, 206, 222-223, 235, 240-241, 244, 248, 250-252, 254, 264, 266-267, 270-272, 277, 281-282, 284, 288, 301, 306-307, 313, 319, 325-327, 343-344, 349, 352, 354, 357, 360, 364, 369, 371, 382, 384, 386, 393

Park Tudor, 234

Pavy, Ray, 100

Peeples, George, vii, 86, 89, 104, 107, 113-114, 121, 168, 181, 201, 206, 241, 244, 250, 253, 275, 297-298, 309-310, 315, 332-334, 344, 347, 358-359, 361, 363, 371, 377, 381

Perry, Ron, vii, 294, 308, 319-321, 323, 325-327, 329, 331, 336-339, 342, 348, 351, 357, 359-360, 363, 374, 386, 393

Philadelphia 76ers, 32

Piontek, Dave, 71

Pittsburgh Post-Gazette, 110, 293

Pittsburgh Press, 174, 187

Pittsburgh Rens, 67

Platt, Joe, 102, 256

Podoloff, Maurice, 6-7, 10, 12, 172

Pollard, Art, 238

Pollin, Abe, 262

Powell, Cincy, 273, 334

Power, Bill, 30

Power, Fremont, 353

Professional Sports Management Company, Inc. , 22

Purdue University, 2, 12, 14, 26, 30, 44, 52, 54, 62, 74, 86, 96-98, 158, 161, 181, 205, 262, 367, 375

Purkhiser, Bob, 62, 89, 104

Quick, Bob, 217

Quinn, Michael, 118

Rakel, Ron, 145, 341, 383-384, 386

Rascoe, Bobby, 232, 237, 359, 363-364

Rayl, Jimmy, vii, 98-106, 109-114, 121, 124, 131-132, 146-148, 166-168, 188-192, 194-204, 206, 224, 237, 241-242, 244, 246, 248-257, 263-266, 269-271, 278, 280, 297-300, 320, 322, 389-390, 393

Rayl, Nancy, vii, 256, 265, 299

Redenbaugh, Steve, 256

Reed, Willis, 173

Reynolds, Cleon, 240

Rhine, Kendall, 232

Rhodes, Gene, vii, 6-7, 195, 361, 364, 373

Richards, Bob, 155

Richardson, Mike, 125

Ricke, Tom, 209, 211, 214

Riley, Pat, 56, 79

Ripley's Believe It Or Not, 134

Risen, Arnie, 2-3, 7, 9, 36

Robertson, Bailey, 82

Robertson, Oscar 6, 13, 14-16, 19-21, 25, 28-33, 42-46, 51, 64, 66, 72-73, 76, 82, 96, 100, 106, 113, 116-118, 233, 300, 364, 387-388

Robinson, Jackie, 135-136, 280

Robinson, Will, vii, 213, 226

Robson, Boynton, 166

Rochester Royals, 3, 9, 36

Rosen, Charlie, 12

Rouse Vic, 139, 331

Rowan and Martin, 354

Rubin, Gabe, 187, 253, 314

Rudolph, Mendy, 11

Rupp, Adolph, 56

Russell, Bill (ABA), 50

Russell, Bill (NBA), 3, 21, 30, 47, 82-83, 85-87, 89, 104, 107-108, 173-174

Russell, Dick, vii, 82-83, 85-87, 89, 104, 107-108

Rutherford, Johnny, 238

Sahm, Walt, 89, 225

Samaras, Bob, 170-171, 212

San Diego (Rockets), 22, 24, 46, 55-57, 60-61, 65-66

Sanders, Tom, 364

Saperstein, Abe, 21

Savoy Big Five, 2

Sayers, Gale, 340

Schaeffer, Herm, 7

Schaeffer, Norb (Bud), 7

Schellhase, Dave, vii, 54, 86, 98, 118, 181

Schottelkotte, Jim, 76

Scott, Carl, 211-212

Seagren, Bob, 50

Seattle (SuperSonics), 22, 24, 65, 106

Seattle University, 67

Seredin, Connie, 22-24, 37-38

Sessions, Sam, v, 36, 80, 89, 105, 233, 238

Sharman, Bill, 291, 318, 322, 346

Shelbyville High School, 186, 241

Shields, Larry, 34, 219-222

Sidle, Don, 378

Simmons, Connie, 9

Simon, Walt, 277

Simpson, O.J. , 345, 374

Sizemore, Ted, v, 228

Sloan, Jerry, 53

Smith, Adrian, 148

Smith, Allen, 353

Smith, Fran, 176

Smith, Jim, 166

Smith, Sam, 75, 219

Smulyan, Jim, 373

Sommer, James, vii, 33-34, 38

Sports Headliners, 23, 52, 77, 156, 345, 374

St. Joseph's College, 73, 79, 104-105, 107, 141, 166, 241

St. Louis Bombers, 3

St. Louis Hawks, 164

Starczyk, Dick, 204

State Fair Board, 121, 149

Staverman, Joyce, vii, 260

Staverman, Larry, vii, 41, 71-72, 75, 80-81, 84, 86, 88, 90, 103, 105-106, 108, 110-111, 120-121, 127, 130-132, 140, 145-148, 165-168, 184, 187-190, 195, 200, 202-204, 206-208, 218, 223-224, 234-235, 244, 250-254, 256-260, 263-270, 272, 275, 289, 297, 309-310, 322, 325, 347, 378, 388-389

Steinbrenner, George, 21

Stone, George, 323, 353

Stone, Keith, vii, 30

Storen, Mike, vii, 39-43, 46-56, 60-61, 63, 65, 68-75, 77, 79-80, 85, 87-88, 90-91, 95-96, 101-103, 105-106, 108-110, 113, 116-118, 122-124, 126-128, 134, 140, 142, 147-149, 151-154, 156-158, 163, 166, 169, 181-185, 187, 191-193, 195, 200, 203, 205-208, 213, 217, 219-224, 233, 241, 244, 248, 257-260, 262-264, 266, 270, 274, 279-281, 293, 296-298, 319-321, 323, 330-332, 335-336, 338, 352, 355, 360-361, 367, 375, 377, 381, 386, 389, 393-394

Strack, Dave, 96

Stultz, Max, 128

Syracuse Nationals, 11

Tart, Levern, 282-283

Tatum, Goose, 176

Taylor, Graham, 112-113

Taylor, Roland "Fatty" , 291

Tennessee State, 85, 172

Thacker, Tom, vii, 138-139, 331-332, 342, 361, 363-364, 366, 370-371, 373-374, 377-378, 380-383, 393

The Lively League, 24

The Masters, 52

Thomas, Lillie, 211

Thompson, Jack, 244, 294-295

Thoren, Skip, 185, 378

Thurmond, Nate, 180

Tinkham, Richard, vii, 24, 30, 33, 39-40, 42, 49, 56, 60, 68, 80, 118, 121, 125, 151-152, 154, 181-182, 191, 205, 207, 219, 352

Todd, Gary, vii, 356-357

Toledo Jeeps, 3

Tosheff, Bill, 10

Trager, Dave, 15, 40-41, 261-262

Treece, Lyn, vi-vii, 26, 29-30, 118, 220-221

Trester Award, 45, 100

Tuchman Cleaners, 122

Tuchman, Sid, 122, 134, 206

Tucker, Bud, 20

University of Cincinnati, 13, 72-73, 331, 354

University of Dayton, 67, 170

University of Evansville, 53, 86

University of New Mexico, 49, 75, 230

University of Notre Dame, 10, 39, 53, 63, 71-72, 75, 89, 115, 225, 367, 374

Unseld, Wes, 216

Unser, Al, 238

Unser, Bobby, 238, 240

Vacendak, Steve, 292

Van Arsdale, Dick, 45-47, 85, 87-88, 100-101, 105, 118

Van Arsdale, Tom, vii, 45-47, 85, 87-88, 100-101, 105, 118

Vaughn, Chico, 187, 214, 270, 292, 328

Verga, Bob, 159, 252

Vidan, Pat, 240

Vukovich, Bill, 238

Wagner, Phil, 217, 235, 244, 246, 250, 252, 256

Waldmeir, Pete, 46, 177, 179

Walk, Paul, 3

Walker, Jimmy, 50-51, 118, 368

Walsh, Donnie, 136, 144

Ward, Rodger, 238

Washington, Gene, 50

Washington, Stan, 56
Washington, Tom, 75
Welch, Robert, 19, 116
West, Jerry, 16, 21, 174, 371
Wheatley, Sandra, vii, 77-78, 119
Wheeler, Ted, vii, 228-230
Wiese, J. Fred, vii, 30, 220-221, 236
Wigwam (gymnasium) , 375-376
Williams, Charlie, 270, 277, 292, 316
Williams, Marvin, 209
William, Ted 99
Wilson, Pepper, 20, 65, 75-76, 101

Wolf, David, 68
Woodard, Ron, 29
Wooden, Johnny, 1-2, 7, 139
Woodstock Country Club, 120
World Professional Basketball Tournament, 2
Wulk, Ned, 64
Yardley, George, 12
York, Bill, vii, 79-80
Young, Bob, 39
Young, Verl (Gus), 316
Zaslofsky, Max, 32, 308, 320-321, 349
Zollner, Fred, 12, 176